DODGE & PLYMOUTH
Omni·024·Charger·Rampage
Horizon·TC3·Turismo·Scamp
1978-1987
SHOP MANUAL

ALAN AHLSTRAND
Editor

JEFF ROBINSON
Publisher

629.2872
D664
1987

CLYMER PUBLICATIONS

World's largest publisher of books
devoted exclusively to automobiles and motorcycles

12860 MUSCATINE STREET • P.O. BOX 4520 • ARLETA, CALIFORNIA 91333-4520

FIRST EDITION
First Printing January, 1979

SECOND EDITION
First Printing July, 1980

THIRD EDITION
Revised by Ron Wright to include 1979-1981 models
First Printing December, 1981

FOURTH EDITION
Revised by Kalton C. Lahue to include 1982 models
First Printing April, 1982

FIFTH EDITION
Revised by Kalton C. Lahue to include 1983 models
First Printing February, 1984

SIXTH EDITION
Revised by Kalton C. Lahue to include 1984 models
First Printing November, 1984
Second Printing May, 1985

SEVENTH EDITION
Revised by Kalton C. Lahue to include 1985 models
First Printing February, 1986

EIGHTH EDITION
Revised by Kalton C. Lahue to include 1986 models
First Printing November, 1986

NINTH EDITION
Revised by Kalton C. Lahue to include 1987 models
First Printing April, 1987

Printed in U.S.A.

ISBN: 0-89287-297-7

MOTORCYCLE INDUSTRY COUNCIL

Production Coordinator, Linda I. Glover

COVER: Photographed by Michael Brown Photographic Productions, Los Angeles, California. Assisted by Ray Wittbrod and Dennis Gilmore. Automobile courtesy of Chrysler Corporation.

CONTENTS

DODGE & PLYMOUTH

Omni · 024 · Charger · Rampage
Horizon · TC3 · Turismo · Scamp
1978-1987
SHOP MANUAL

QUICK REFERENCE DATA

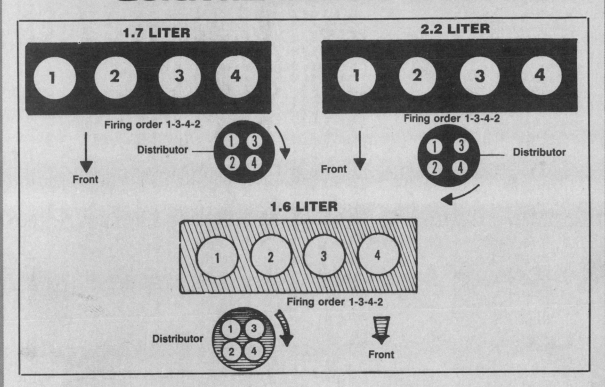

1.7 LITER

| 1 | 2 | 3 | 4 |

Firing order 1-3-4-2

Distributor

| 1 | 3 |
| 2 | 4 |

Front

2.2 LITER

| 1 | 2 | 3 | 4 |

Firing order 1-3-4-2

| 1 | 3 |
| 2 | 4 |

Distributor

Front

1.6 LITER

| 1 | 2 | 3 | 4 |

Firing order 1-3-4-2

Distributor

| 1 | 3 |
| 2 | 4 |

Front

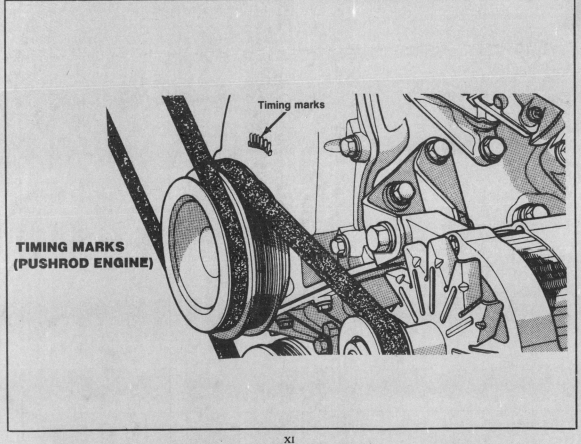

Timing marks

TIMING MARKS (PUSHROD ENGINE)

TUNE-UP SPECIFICATIONS

Valve clearance	
1.6 liter[1]	
Intake	0.010 in. (0.25 mm)
Exhaust	0.012 in. (0.30 mm)
1.7 liter[2]	
Intake	0.012 in. (0.30 mm)
Exhaust	0.020 in. (0.50 mm)
Ignition timing	
1978-1979	15° BTDC
1980	
1.7 liter	
49-state	12° BTDC
California	10° BTDC
1981	
1.7 liter	
Manual	12° BTDC
Automatic	10° BTDC
2.2 liter	10° BTDC
1982-1984	
1.7 liter	
Manual	20° BTDC
Automatic	12° BTDC
1.6/2.2 liter	12° BTDC
1985	
1.7 liter	
Manual	20° BTDC
Automatic	12° BTDC
1.6 liter	12° BTDC
2.2 liter	
Standard engine	10° ±2° BTDC
High performance engine	15° ±2° BTDC
Turbo engine	12° ±2° BTDC
Spark plugs	
Type	Champion RN12Y or Mopar 65PR (3)
Gap	0.035 in. (0.9 mm) (4)
Firing order	1-3-4-2 (No. 1 @ pulley end of 1.7 and 2.2L; @ flywheel end of 1.6L)
Idle speed	See Vehicle Emission Control Information label

1. Clearance must be set on a cold engine.
2. These specifications are for a warm engine. Subtract 0.002 in. (0.05 mm) for a cold engine.
3. 1981 1.7L; Mopar 65PR4.
4. 1981 1.7L; 0.048 in. (1.22 mm).

APPROXIMATE REFILL CAPACITIES*

Engine oil	
1.6 liter	3.5 qt. (3.3 liters)
1.7 liter	4.0 qt. (3.8 liters)
2.2 liter	
Normally aspirated	4.0 qt. (3.8 liters)
Turbocharged	5.0 qt. (4.8 liters)
Manual transaxle	
A-412	1.5 qt. (1.4 liters)
A-460	2.0 qt. (1.8 liters)
A-465, A-525	2.3 qt. (2.1 liters)
Automatic transaxle	
1.6 liter	4.0 qt. (3.8 liters)
1.7 and 2.2 liter	2.5 qt. (2.4 liters)
Automatic differential	1.2 qt. (1.1 liters)
Cooling system	
1.6 liter	6.8 qt. (6.5 liters)
1.7 liter	6.0 qt. (5.7 liters)
2.2 liter	
1981-1982	7.0 qt. (6.6 liters)
1983-on	9.0 qt. (8.5 liters)

* When refilling to approximate capacities, always make final check by observing dipstick or fluid level measurements.

RECOMMENDED LUBRICANTS AND FUEL

Application	Temperature range (degrees F)	Recommended type
Engine oil	+32° to above +100° F	20W-40 SF, 20W-50 SF, 30W SF
	−10° to above +100° F	10W-30 SF, 10W-40 SF, 10W-50 SF
	−10° to +32 ° F	10W SF
	Consistently below −10° F	5W-20 SF *
A412 transaxle	Consistently above −10° F	SAE 90W, SAE 80W-90, SAE85W-90
	As low as -30° F	SAE 00W, SAE 80W-90, SAE 85W-90
A-460, A-465 and A-525 manual transaxles		
Through 1986	All temperatures	DEXRON II ATF
1987	All temperatures	5W-30 engine oil
Automatic transaxle	All temperatures	DEXRON II ATF
Automatic differential	All temperatures	DEXRON II ATF
Power steering	All temperatures	Mopar power steering fluid
Fuel	All temperatures	91 octane regular unleaded

* 5W-20 is not recommended for sustained high-speed operation.

DRIVE BELT TENSION SPECIFICATIONS (1978-1980)

	New (ft.-lb)	Used (ft.-lb.)
Tension method (all belts)	120	70
Torque method		
Air conditioning	55	40
Air pump	65	45
Alternator*	70	50
Power steering pump	40	25

*See text on 1980 models.

DRIVE BELT TENSION SPECIFICATIONS (1981-ON)

	Tension Method	
	New (ft.-lb)	Used (ft.-lb.)
Air conditioning		
1.7 liter	90	45
2.2 liter	40	35
Air pump		
2.2 liter	45	35
Air pump/water pump		
1.7 liter	70	40
Alternator/water pump		
1.6 liter	37	28
1.7 liter	65	40
2.2 liter	110	80
Power steering pump		
1.7 liter	80	50
2.2 liter	75	55

	Belt Deflection	
	New	Used
Air conditioning	5/16 in.	3/8 in.
Air pump		
1.6 liter	7/32 in.	5/16 in.
2.2 liter	13/64 in.	1/4 in.
Air pump/water pump		
1.7 liter	3/16 in.	13/64 in.
Alternator/water pump		
1.6 liter	3/16 in.	1/4 in.
2.2 liter	1/8 in.	1/4 in.
Power steering pump		
1.6 liter	3/8 in.	7/16 in.
1.7 and 2.2 liter	1/4 in.	5/16 in.

INTRODUCTION

This detailed, comprehensive manual covers the 1978-1987 Plymouth Horizon/TC3/Turismo/Scamp and Dodge Omni/024/Charger/Rampage models including the Charger 2.2 and Shelby Charger. The expert text gives complete information on maintenance, repair and overhaul. Hundreds of photos and drawings guide you through every step. The book includes all you need to know to keep your vehicle running right.

General information on all models and specific information on 1978-1983 models is contained Chapters One through Twelve. Specific information on 1984 and later models is contained in the supplement at the end of the book.

Where repairs are practical for the owner/mechanic, complete procedures are given. Equally important, difficult jobs are pointed out. Such operations are usually more economically performed by a dealer or independent garage.

Where special tools are required or recommended, the tool numbers are provided. These tools can sometimes be rented from rental dealers, but they are available for purchase from Miller Special Tools, 32615 Park Lane, Garden City, Michigan 48135.

A shop manual is a reference. You want to be able to find information fast. As in all Clymer books, this one is designed with you in mind. All chapters are thumb tabbed. Important items are indexed at the rear of the book. All the most frequently used specifications and capacities are summarized on the *Quick Reference* pages at the front of the book.

Keep the book handy. Carry it in your glove box. It will help you to better understand your car, lower repair and maintenance costs and generally improve your satisfaction with your vehicle.

CHAPTER ONE

GENERAL INFORMATION

The Plymouth Horizon and Dodge Omni were the first U.S.-built metric cars from Chrysler Corporation. All drive train components, fasteners, body panels and tires are designed to metric standards. Metric tools are required to work on the vehicle.

The base engine on all 1978-1980 models and those 1981-1983 models first sold outside California is a 1.7 liter displacement, water-cooled overhead cam 4-cylinder. This engine was replaced in mid-1983 models by a 1.6 liter displacement 4-cylinder pushrod engine. A 2.2 liter displacement water-cooled overhead cam 4-cylinder engine is standard on 1981-on passenger cars first sold in California, all Rampage/Scamp pickup trucks, the Charger 2.2/Turismo 2.2 and the Shelby Charger and is optional on all other 1981-on cars.

All engines are mounted transversely (sideways) in the engine compartment. The spark plugs, distributor and oil filter are mounted on the front side, providing easy serviceability.

All 1978-1980 engines are equipped with a 2-barrel Holley Model 5220 carburetor. Those 1981-on engines using an electronic feedback carburetion system are equipped with a 2-barrel Holley Model 6520 carburetor; all other 1981-on engines use the Model 5220 carburetor.

A 4-speed manual transaxle is standard on all models except the 1983 Charger 2.2, Turismo 2.2 and Shelby Charger, which are equipped with a 5-speed manual transaxle. The 5-speed manual is optional on other 1983 models. A 3-speed automatic transaxle is optional on all models.

The design features independent suspension at all 4 wheels, with MacPherson struts (integral springs and shock absorbers) on the front wheels. The rear suspension uses independent trailing arms connected by an anti-roll bar type crossmember (stabilizer) and integrated coil springs and shock absorbers.

The rack-and-pinion steering system is controlled through an energy-absorbing steering column. Power-assisted rack-and-pinion steering is optional.

Disc brakes are provided on the front wheels, with drum brakes used on the rear wheels. The brake system is diagonally balanced, with the left front and right rear brakes on one circuit and the right front and left rear brakes on the other. There is no proportioning valve.

MANUAL ORGANIZATION

This book provides complete service information and procedures. Most dimensions

Table 1   CONVERSION CHART — MILLIMETERS TO INCHES

mm	in.	mm	in.	mm	in.
0.01	0.0004	0.51	0.0201	1	0.0394
0.02	0.0008	0.52	0.0205	2	0.0787
0.03	0.0012	0.53	0.0209	3	0.1181
0.04	0.0016	0.54	0.0213	4	0.1575
0.05	0.0020	0.55	0.0217	5	0.1969
0.06	0.0024	0.56	0.0221	6	0.2362
0.07	0.0028	0.57	0.0224	7	0.2756
0.08	0.0032	0.58	0.0228	8	0.3150
0.09	0.0035	0.59	0.0232	9	0.3543
0.10	0.0039	0.60	0.0236	10	0.3937
0.11	0.0043	0.61	0.0240	11	0.4331
0.12	0.0047	0.62	0.0244	12	0.4724
0.13	0.0051	0.63	0.0246	13	0.5118
0.14	0.0055	0.64	0.0252	14	0.5512
0.15	0.0059	0.65	0.0256	15	0.5906
0.16	0.0063	0.66	0.0260	16	0.6299
0.17	0.0067	0.67	0.0264	17	0.6693
0.18	0.0071	0.68	0.0268	18	0.7087
0.19	0.0075	0.69	0.0272	19	0.7480
0.20	0.0079	0.70	0.0276	20	0.7874
0.21	0.0083	0.71	0.0280	21	0.8268
0.22	0.0087	0.72	0.0284	22	0.8661
0.23	0.0091	0.73	0.0287	23	0.9055
0.24	0.0095	0.74	0.0291	24	0.9449
0.25	0.0098	0.75	0.0295	25	0.9843
0.26	0.0102	0.76	0.0299	26	1.0236
0.27	0.0106	0.77	0.0303	27	1.0630
0.28	0.0110	0.78	0.0307	28	1.1024
0.29	0.0114	0.79	0.0311	29	1.1417
0.30	0.0118	0.80	0.0315	30	1.1811
0.31	0.0122			31	1.2205
0.32	0.0126	0.81	0.0320	32	1.2598
0.33	0.0130	0.82	0.0323	33	1.2992
0.34	0.0134	0.83	0.0327	34	1.3386
0.35	0.0138	0.84	0.0331	35	1.3779
0.36	0.0142	0.85	0.0335	36	1.4173
0.37	0.0146	0.86	0.0339	37	1.4567
0.38	0.0150	0.87	0.0343	38	1.4961
0.39	0.0154	0.88	0.0347	39	1.5354
0.40	0.0158	0.89	0.0350	40	1.5748
		0.90	0.0354		
0.41	0.0161			41	1.6142
0.42	0.0165	0.91	0.0358	42	1.6535
0.43	0.0169	0.92	0.0362	43	1.6929
0.44	0.0173	0.93	0.0366	44	1.7323
0.45	0.0177	0.94	0.0370	45	1.7716
0.46	0.0181	0.95	0.0374	46	1.8110
0.47	0.0185	0.96	0.0378	47	1.8504
0.48	0.0186	0.97	0.0382	48	1.8898
0.49	0.0193	0.98	0.0386	49	1.9291
0.50	0.0197	0.99	0.0390	50	1.9685

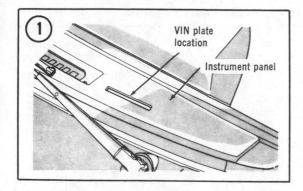

VIN plate location

Instrument panel

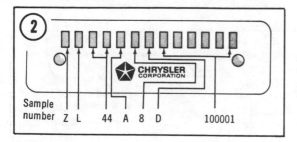

Sample number   Z L   44   A   8   D   100001

CHRYSLER CORPORATION

1

economically done by a dealer or other competent repair shop. Specifications concerning a particular system are provided in the applicable chapter.

The terms NOTE, CAUTION, and WARNING have specific meaning in this book. A NOTE provides additional information to make a step or procedure easier or clearer. Disregarding a NOTE could cause inconvenience, but would not cause damage or personal injury.

A CAUTION emphasizes areas where equipment damage could result. Disregarding a CAUTION could cause permanent mechanical damage; however, personal injury is unlikely.

A WARNING emphasizes areas where personal injury or even death could result from negligence. Mechanical damage may also occur. WARNINGS are to be taken seriously. In some cases serious injury or death has been caused by mechanics disregarding similar warnings.

and capacities are expressed in English units familiar to U.S. mechanics, as well as in metric units. Where conversion to English measure could introduce errors in critical dimensions, only metric measure is specified. In any case, metric tools *are required*. See **Table 1**.

This chapter provides general information.

Chapter Two provides methods and suggestions for finding and fixing troubles fast. Troubleshooting procedures discuss typical symptoms and logical methods to pinpoint the trouble. The chapter also covers some test equipment useful for both preventive maintenance and troubleshooting.

Chapter Three explains all periodic lubrication and routine maintenance required to keep your car in top running condition. Chapter Three also includes recommended engine tune-up procedures, eliminating the need to constantly consult chapters covering various subassemblies.

Subsequent chapters describe specific systems such as the engine, transmission, and electrical system. Each provides complete disassembly, repair, and assembly procedures in easy-to-follow step-by-step form. If a repair is impractical for the owner/mechanic, it is so indicated. Such repairs are usually quicker and more

VEHICLE IDENTIFICATION

A 13-digit vehicle identification number (VIN) is used on 1978-1980 vehicles; 1981-on models have a 17-digit VIN. This number is stamped on a plate attached to the upper left corner of the instrument panel and is visible through the windshield (**Figure 1**).

Figure 2 shows a typical 13-digit VIN plate. Digit identification is as follows:
1. Car line.
2. Series.
3, 4. Body style.
5. Engine code.
6. Model year.
7. Assembly plant.
8-13. Serial number.

The 17-digit VIN is slightly different:
1. Country of origin.
2. Make.
3. Vehicle type.
4. Passenger safety system.
5. Car line.
6. Series.
7. Body style.
8. Engine code.
9. Verification digit.
10. Model year.
11. Assembly plant.
12-17. Sequence number.

An abbreviated version of the VIN is also stamped on the engine block (**Figure 3**) and the transaxle (**Figure 4**). In addition to the VIN number, all engines carry an engine identification number (EIN) to be used when ordering replacement engine parts. The EIN is stamped on the 1.6 and 1.7 liter engine block above the fuel pump (**Figure 5**, typical) and in place of the VIN number (**Figure 3**) on 2.2 liter engines.

A transaxle identification number (TIN) is stamped on a housing boss (**Figure 6**). In addition, an assembly part number to be used when ordering replacement parts is stamped on a pad at the rear of automatic transaxles above the oil pan (**Figure 6**) or on a metal tag attached to the front of manual transaxles (**Figure 7**).

TOWING

It is permissible to tow manual transaxle models on all 4 wheels for any distance, at legal highway speeds. Automatic transaxle models, however, should not be towed on all 4 wheels. Towing is permissible with either the front or rear wheels lifted on manual transaxle models, if transaxle shift lever is in the NEUTRAL position. On automatic transaxle models, towing is permitted with the front wheels lifted for any distance, at legal

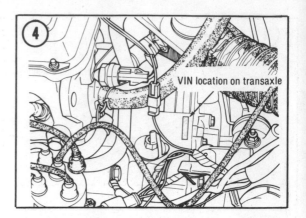

VIN location on transaxle

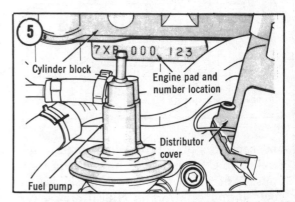

Cylinder block

Engine pad and number location

Distributor cover

Fuel pump

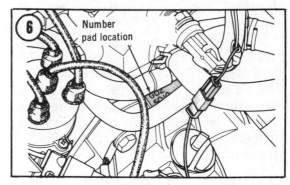

Number pad location

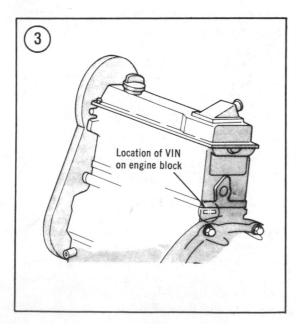

Location of VIN on engine block

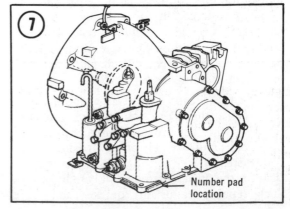

Number pad location

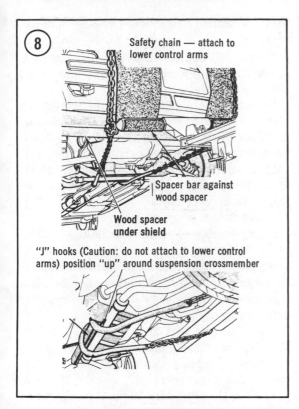

⑧ Safety chain — attach to lower control arms

Spacer bar against wood spacer

Wood spacer under shield

"J" hooks (Caution: do not attach to lower control arms) position "up" around suspension crossmember

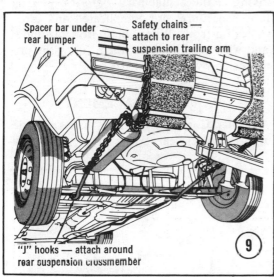

Spacer bar under rear bumper

Safety chains — attach to rear suspension trailing arm

"J" hooks — attach around rear suspension crossmember ⑨

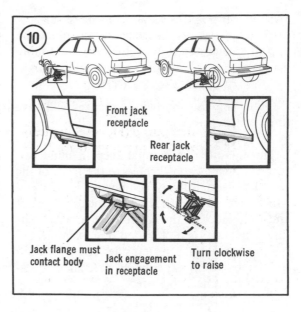

⑩ Front jack receptacle

Rear jack receptacle

Jack flange must contact body

Jack engagement in receptacle

Turn clockwise to raise

1

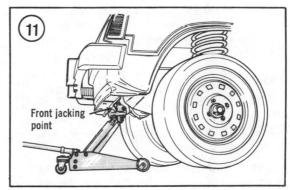

⑪ Front jacking point

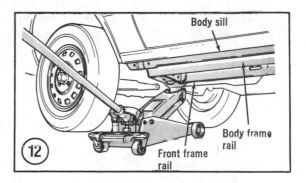

Body sill

Body frame rail

Front frame rail

⑫

highway speeds. When the rear end pickup is used, however, the automatic transaxle shift lever must be placed in NEUTRAL and the vehicle must not be towed more than 15 miles, with a maximum speed of 30 mph. See **Figure 8** and **Figure 9** for attachment points. Do not use bumpers or other points for towing.

JACKING

The scissors jack provided with the vehicle should be used at the jack receptacles located at the body sills (**Figure 10**). DO NOT use a floor jack at these points. If a floor jack is available, it may be used for lifting the front of the car as shown in **Figure 11 or 12** and for lifting the rear as shown in **Figures 13 and 14**. Make sure the car is on a level surface, and always block the opposite wheels to prevent the car from rolling off the jack.

SERVICE HINTS

Observing the following practices will save time, effort, and frustration, as well as prevent possible injury.

Throughout this manual keep in mind two conventions. "Front" refers to the front of the car. The front of any component is that end which faces toward the front of the car. The left and right sides of the car refer to a person sitting in the car facing forward. For example, the steering wheel is on the left side. These rules are simple, but even experienced mechanics occasionally become disoriented.

WARNING
When working under a car, do not trust a hydraulic or mechanical jack to hold the car up by itself. Always use jack-stands.

Disconnect battery ground cable before working near electrical connections and before disconnecting wires. Never run the engine with the battery disconnected; the alternator could be seriously damaged.

Tag all similar internal parts for location and mark all mating parts for position. Record the number and thickness of any shims as they are removed. Small parts, such as bolts, can be identified by placing them in plastic sandwich bags and sealing and labeling bags with masking tape.

Protect finished surfaces from physical damage or corrosion. Keep gasoline and brake fluid off painted surfaces.

Frozen or very tight bolts and screws can often be loosened by soaking with penetrating oil, then sharply striking the bolt head a few times with a hammer and punch (or screwdriver for screws). Avoid heat unless absolutely necessary, since it may melt, warp, or remove the temper from many parts.

Avoid flames or sparks when working near a charging battery or flammable liquids such as brake fluid or gasoline.

No parts, except those assembled with a press fit, require unusual force during assembly. If a part is hard to remove or install, find out why before proceeding.

Cover all openings after removing parts to keep dirt, small tools, etc., from falling in.

When assembling two parts, start all fasteners, then tighten evenly.

Read each procedure in its entirety while looking at the actual parts *before* beginning. Many procedures are complicated and errors can be disastrous. When you thoroughly understand what is to be done, then follow the procedure step-by-step.

PARTS REPLACEMENT

Chrysler Corporation often makes changes during a model year; some minor, some rela-

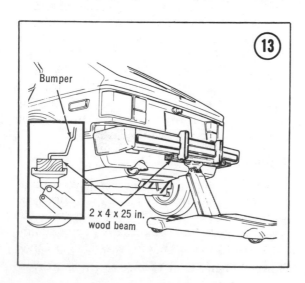

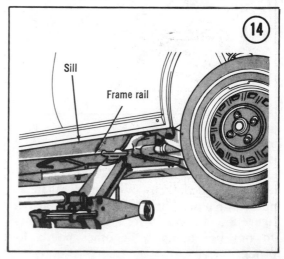

tively major. When you order parts from the dealer or other parts distributor, *always order by engine and chassis number*. Write the numbers down and carry them with you. Compare new parts to old before purchasing them. If they are not alike, get a satisfactory explanation of the difference.

TOOLS

Shop Tools

For proper servicing, you will need an assortment of ordinary hand tools. As a minimum, these include:

- a. Metric combination wrenches
- b. Metric sockets
- c. Plastic mallet
- d. Small hammer
- e. Snap ring pliers
- f. Gas pliers
- g. Phillips screwdrivers
- h. Slot (common) screwdrivers
- i. Metric feeler gauge
- j. Spark plug gauge
- k. Spark plug wrench

Special Tools

Special tools necessary are shown in the chapter covering the particular repair in which they are used. A well-equipped mechanic may

be able to substitute other similar tools that are on hand or possibly fabricate new ones.

> NOTE: *The special tools referred to in this book may be available at your local Chrysler dealer or at a well-equipped auto parts store or tool store. If not, try ordering them from Miller Special Tools, Division of Utica Tool Company, Inc., 32615 Park Lane, Garden City, Michigan, 48135. In Canada, try C & D Riley Enterprises, P.O. Box 2483, Walkersville, Ontario, M8Y-4Y2.*

TEST INSTRUMENTS

Engine tune-up and troubleshooting procedures require other special tools and equipment. These are described in detail in the following sections.

Voltmeter, Ammeter, and Ohmmeter

For testing the ignition or electrical system, a good voltmeter is required. For automotive use, an instrument covering 0-20 volts is satisfactory. One which also has a 0-2 volt scale is necessary for testing relays, points, or individual contacts where voltage drops are much smaller. Accuracy should be ± ½ volt.

An ohmmeter measures electrical resistance. This instrument is useful for checking continuity (open- and short-circuits), and testing fuses and lights.

The ammeter measures electrical current. Ammeters for automotive use should cover 0-50 amperes and 0-250 amperes. These are useful for checking battery charging and starting current. The starter and generator procedures in this manual use one to check for defective windings.

Several inexpensive VOM's (volt-ohm-milliammeter) combine all three instruments into one which fits easily in any tool box. See **Figure 15**. The ammeter ranges are usually too small for automotive work, though.

Hydrometer

The hydrometer gives a useful indication of battery condition and charge by measuring the specific gravity of the electrolyte in each cell. See **Figure 16**. Complete details on use and interpretation of readings are provided in Chapter Eight.

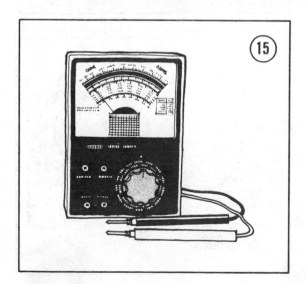

Compression Tester

The compression tester measures the compression pressure built up in each cylinder. The results, when properly interpreted, can indicate general cylinder and valve condition.

Most compression testers have long flexible extensions as accessories. See **Figure 17**. Such an extension is not necessary since the spark plug holes are easily accessible.

Many automotive books describe a "dry" compression test and a "wet" compression test. Usually these tests must be interpreted together to isolate the trouble in cylinders or valves.

Dry Test

1. Warm the engine to normal operating temperature. Ensure that the choke valve and throttle valve are completely open.

2. Remove the spark plugs.

3. Connect the compression tester to one cylinder following the manufacturer's instructions.

4. Have an assistant crank the engine over until there is no further rise in pressure.

5. Remove the tester and record the reading.

6. Repeat Steps 3-5 for each cylinder.

Refer to *Compression Test* in Chapter Three for specifications and interpretation of results.

Wet Test

Add one tablespoon of heavy oil (at least SAE 30) to any cylinder which checks low. Repeat the procedure above. If compression increases noticeably, the rings are probably worn. If adding oil produces no change, the low reading may be caused by a broken ring or valve trouble.

Vacuum Gauge

The vacuum gauge (see **Figure 18**) is one of the easiest instruments to use, but one of the most difficult for the inexperienced mechanic to interpret. The results, when interpreted with other findings, can provide valuable clues to possible trouble.

Disconnect vacuum line from choke diaphragm and connect the vacuum gauge to the line. Start engine; let it warm up thoroughly Vacuum reading should be 18-20 in. at idle.

NOTE: *Subtract one inch from reading for every 1,000 feet (300m) of altitude.*

Figure 19 shows numerous typical readings with interpretations. Results are not conclusive without comparing to other tests such as compression.

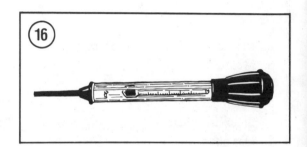

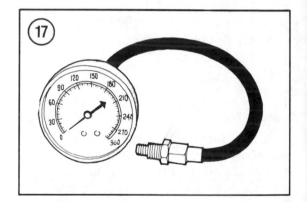

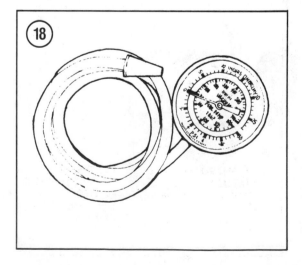

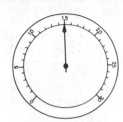

1. NORMAL READING
Reads 15 in. at idle.

2. LATE IGNITION TIMING
About 2 inches too low at idle.

3. LATE VALVE TIMING
About 4 to 8 inches low at idle.

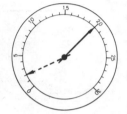

4. INTAKE LEAK
Low steady reading.

5. NORMAL READING
Drops to 2, then rises to 25 when accelerator is rapidly depressed and released.

6. WORN RINGS, DILUTED OIL
Drops to 0, then rises to 18 when accelerator is rapidly depressed and released.

7. STICKING VALVE(S)
Normally steady. Intermittently flicks downward about 4 in.

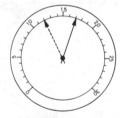

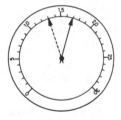

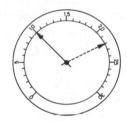

8. LEAKY VALVE
Regular drop about 2 inches.

9. BURNED OR WARPED VALVE
Regular, evenly spaced down-scale flick about 4 in.

10. WORN VALVE GUIDES
Oscillates about 4 in.

11. WEAK VALVE SPRINGS
Violent oscillation (about 10 in.) as rpm increases. Often steady at idle.

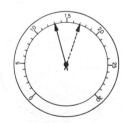

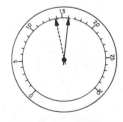

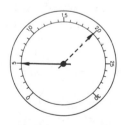

12. IMPROPER IDLE MIXTURE
Floats slowly between 13-17 in.

13. SMALL SPARK GAP or DEFECTIVE POINTS
Slight float between 14-16 in.

14. HEAD GASKET LEAK
Gauge floats between 5-19 in.

15. RESTRICTED EXHAUST SYSTEM
Normal when first started. Drops to 0 as rpm increases. May eventually rise to about 16.

Fuel Pressure Gauge

This instrument is invaluable for evaluating fuel pump performance. Fuel system troubleshooting procedures in this manual use a fuel pressure gauge. Usually a vacuum gauge and fuel pressure gauge are combined.

Dwell Meter

A dwell meter measures the distance in degrees of cam rotation that the breaker points remain closed while the engine is running. Since this angle is determined by breaker point gap, dwell angle is an accurate indication of breaker point gap.

Many tachometers intended for tuning and testing incorporate a dwell meter as well. See **Figure 20**. Follow the manufacturer's instructions to measure dwell.

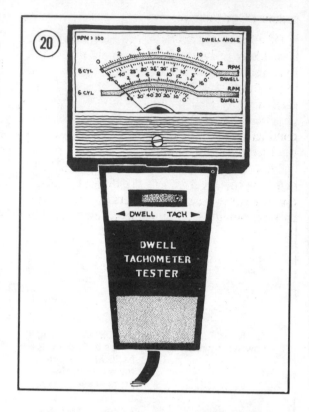

Tachometer

A tachometer is necessary for tuning. See **Figure 20**. Ignition timing and carburetor adjustments must be performed at the specified idle speed. The best instrument for this purpose is one with a low range of 0-1,000 or 0-2,000 rpm for setting idle, and a high range of 0-4,000 or more for setting ignition timing at 3,000 rpm. Extended range (0-6,000 or 0-8,000) instruments lack accuracy at lower speeds. The instrument should be capable of detecting changes of 25 rpm on the low range.

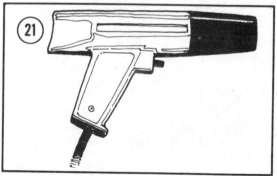

Strobe Timing Light

This instrument is necessary for tuning. It permits very accurate ignition timing. By flashing a light at the precise instant cylinder No. 1 fires, the position of the flywheel at that instant can be seen. Marks on the flywheel are lined up with the transmissions case mark while the engine is running.

Suitable lights range from inexpensive neon bulb types to powerful xenon strobe lights. See **Figure 21**. Neon timing lights are difficult to see and must be used in dimly lit areas. Xenon strobe timing lights can be used outside in bright sunlight. Both types work on this automobile; use according to the manufacturer's instructions.

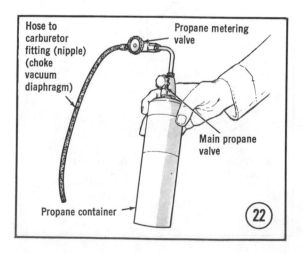

Hose to carburetor fitting (nipple) (choke vacuum diaphragm)

Propane metering valve

Main propane valve

Propane container

Exhaust Gas Analyzer

Of all instruments described here, this is the least likely to be owned by a home mechanic. One instrument samples the exhaust gases from the tailpipe and measures the thermal conductivity of the exhaust gas. Since different gases conduct heat at varying rates, thermal conductivity of the exhaust is a good indication of gases present.

This instrument is vital for accurately checking the effectiveness of exhaust emission control adjustments. Analyzers are expensive to buy, but must be considered essential for the owner/mechanic to comply with today's emission laws.

Propane Metering System

This special tool is required for properly adjusting the curb idle speed and air/fuel mixture. See **Figure 22**. It consists of a propane tank, shut-off valve, adjustable metering valve, and a hose (nipple). The system is used to inject propane into the carburetor to artificially enrich the air/fuel mixture to obtain optimum adjustment of idle speed and mixture to meet performance and exhaust emission standards.

CHAPTER TWO

TROUBLESHOOTING

Troubleshooting can be a relatively simple matter if it is done logically. The first step in any troubleshooting procedure must be defining the symptoms as closely as possible. Subsequent steps involve testing and analyzing areas which could cause the symptoms. A haphazard approach may eventually find the trouble, but in terms of wasted time and unnecessary parts replacement, it can be very costly.

The troubleshooting procedures in this chapter analyze typical symptoms and show logical methods of isolation. These are not the only methods. There may be several ways of solving a problem, but all methods must have one thing in common — a logical, systematic approach.

TROUBLESHOOTING INSTRUMENTS

The following equipment is necessary to properly troubleshoot any engine:

a. Voltmeter, ammeter, and ohmmeter
b. Hydrometer
c. Compression tester
d. Vacuum gauge
e. Fuel pressure gauge
f. Tachometer
g. Strobe timing light
h. Propane metering system or exhaust gas analyzer

Items a-f are basic for any car. Items g-h are necessary for exhaust emission control compliance. Chapter One contains a brief description of each instrument. Consult a basic repair manual for more detailed information.

STARTER

Starter system troubles are relatively easy to isolate. The following are common symptoms and cures.

1. *Engine cranks very slowly or not at all* — Turn on the headlights; if the lights are very dim, most likely the battery or the connecting wires are at fault. Check the battery using the procedures described in Chapter Seven. Check the wiring for breaks, shorts, and dirty connections.

If the battery and connecting wires check good, the trouble may be in the starter, solenoid, or wiring. To isolate the trouble, short the 2 large solenoid terminals together (*not* to ground); if the starter cranks normally, check the solenoid wiring up to the ignition switch and the seat belt interlock relay. If the starter still fails to crank properly, remove the starter and test it.

2. *Starter turns, but does not engage with engine* — This trouble is usually a defective pinion or solenoid shifting fork. It may also be

that the teeth on the pinion, flywheel ring gear, or both, are worn down too far to engage properly.

3. *Starter engages, but will not disengage when ignition switch is released* — This trouble is usually caused by a sticking solenoid, but occasionally the pinion can jam on the flywheel. With manual transmissions, the pinion can be temporarily freed by rocking the car in high gear. Naturally, this is not possible in automatics; the starter must be removed.

4. *Loud grinding noises when starter runs* — This trouble may mean the teeth on the pinion and/or flywheel are not meshing properly or it may mean the overrunning clutch is broken. In the first case, remove the starter and examine the gear teeth. In the latter, remove the starter and replace the pinion drive assembly.

CHARGING SYSTEM

Troubleshooting an alternator system is somewhat different from troubleshooting a generator. For example, *never* short any terminals to ground on the alternator or the voltage regulator. The following symptoms are typical of alternator charging system troubles.

1. *The alternator warning lamp is on constantly* — Before suspecting the alternator, check the drive belt tension as described in Chapter Three. Check the condition of the battery with a hydrometer. Check and clean all electrical connections in the charging system. If the trouble still persists, have the alternator and voltage regulator checked.

2. *Battery requires frequent additions of water or lamps require frequent replacement* — The alternator is probably overcharging the battery. Have voltage regulator checked or replace it.

3. *Noisy alternator* — Check for loose alternator mounting. Check for faulty alternator bearings.

ENGINE

These procedures assume that the starter cranks the engine over normally. If not, refer to *Starter* section in this chapter.

1. *Engine will not start* — This trouble could be caused by the ignition system or the fuel system. First determine if high voltage to spark plugs occurs. To do this, disconnect one of the spark plug wires. Hold the exposed wire terminal about ¼-½ in. from ground (any metal in engine compartment) with an insulated screwdriver. Crank the engine over. If sparks do not jump to ground or the sparks are very weak, the problem may be in the ignition system. See the *Ignition System* section of this chapter for further details. If good sparks occur, the trouble may be in the fuel system. See *Fuel System* troubleshooting.

2. *Engine misses steadily* — Remove one spark plug wire at a time and ground the wire. If engine miss increases, that cylinder was working properly. Reconnect the wire and check the others. When a wire is disconnected and engine miss remains the same, that cylinder is not firing. Check spark as described in Step 1. If no spark occurs for one cylinder only, check distributor cap, wire, and spark plug. If spark occurs properly, check compression and intake manifold vacuum to isolate the trouble.

3. *Engine misses erratically at all speeds* — Intermittent trouble like this can be difficult to find. The fault could be in the ignition system, exhaust system (exhaust restrictions), or fuel system. Follow troubleshooting procedures for these systems carefully to isolate the trouble.

4. *Engine misses at idle only* — Trouble could exist anywhere in ignition system. Follow *Ignition System* troubleshooting procedure carefully. Trouble could exist in the carburetor idle circuit. Check idle mixture adjustment and check for restrictions in the idle circuit.

5. *Engine misses at high speed only* — Troubles could exist in the fuel system or ignition system. Check accelerator pump operation, fuel pump delivery, fuel lines, etc., as described under *Fuel System*. Also check spark plugs and wires. See *Ignition System*.

6. *Poor performance at all speeds, lack of acceleration* — Trouble usually exists in ignition or fuel system. Check each with the appropriate troubleshooting procedure.

7. *Excessive fuel consumption* — This can be caused by a wide variety of seemingly unrelated factors. Check for clutch slippage, brake drag,

defective wheel bearings, and poor wheel alignment. Check the ignition and fuel systems as described later.

8. *Oil pressure lamp does not light when ignition switch is on* — Check the alternator warning lamp. If it is not on either, go to Step 1, *Charging System*. If only the oil pressure lamp is off, open the engine compartment lid and locate the oil pressure sender on engine block. Ensure that the wire is connected to the sender and making good contact. Pull off wire and ground it. If the lamp lights, replace the sender. If the lamp does not light, replace the lamp.

9. *Oil pressure lamp lights or flickers when engine is running* — This indicates low or complete loss of oil pressure. *Stop the engine immediately;* coast to a stop with the clutch disengaged. This may simply be caused by a low oil level, or an overheating engine. Check the oil level and coolant temperature. Check for a shorted oil pressure sender with an ohmmeter or other continuity tester. Listen for unusual noises indicating bad bearings, etc. Do not restart the engine until you know why the light went on and the problem has been corrected.

IGNITION SYSTEM

These procedures assume the battery is in good enough condition to crank the engine at a normal rate.

1. *No spark to one plug* — The only possible causes are a defective cap or spark plug wire. Examine distributor cap for moisture, dirt, carbon tracking caused by flashover, cracks, etc.

2. *No spark to any plugs* — This could be caused by trouble in either the primary or secondary circuits. First remove the coil wire from the center post of the distributor. Hold the wire end about ¼ in. from ground with an insulated screwdriver. Crank the engine. If sparks are produced, the trouble probably is in the rotor or distributor cap. Remove the cap and check for burns, moisture, dirt, carbon tracking, cracks, etc. Check the rotor for excessive burning, pitting, or cracks. Replace both rotor and distributor cap if necessary.

If the coil does not produce any spark, check the secondary wire for opens. If the wire is good, move the wire away from ground and check for arcing at the coil tower while cranking the engine. If arcing occurs, replace the coil.

3. *Weak spark* — If the spark is so small it cannot jump from the wire ¼-½ in. to ground, check the battery condition as described in Chapter Seven. Other causes are dirty or loose connections in the primary circuit, or dirty or burned rotor or distributor cap.

4. *Missing* — This is usually caused by fouled or damaged plugs, plugs of the wrong heat range, or incorrect plug gap. Clean and regap spark plugs. This trouble can also be caused by weak spark (see symptom 3) or incorrect ignition timing.

5. *Failure to start* — Disconnect the wire from the negative coil terminal and remove the secondary wire from the distributor cap center tower. Turn key on and momentarily touch the coil negative terminal with a jumper wire connected to ground while holding secondary wire about ¼ in. from a good ground on the engine. A spark should result. If there was no spark, check for voltage at the coil positive terminal (with ignition key on). Voltage should be at least 9 volts. If proper voltage is present, coil is defective and should be replaced. If not, check ballast resistor, wiring, and connections. If car still does not start, and spark was obtained in the test above, turn key off, connect wire to coil negative terminal, and disconnect 3-wire terminal from distributor (**Figure 1**). Turn key on and measure voltage between connector terminal B (**Figure 1**) and ground. Voltage should be the same as that measured at the battery. If voltage is different, or not present, turn key off and disconnect 10-wire harness at spark control computer (**Figure 2**).

CAUTION

If grease is present on the connector or in the connector cavity on the spark control computer, do not remove it as it is there to keep out moisture. If less than ¼ in. of grease is present in the cavity, apply a liberal amount of multipurpose grease to the end of the connector plug before reinstalling it.

Check continuity between pin B of the 3-wire connector and pin 3 of the 10-wire connector. If there is no continuity, repair the

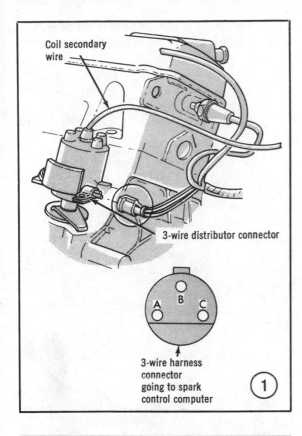

Coil secondary wire

3-wire distributor connector

3-wire harness connector going to spark control computer

①

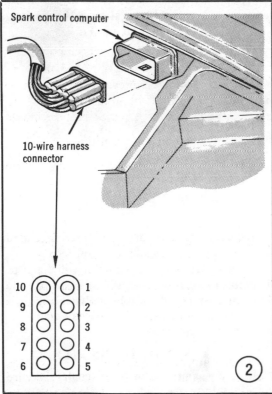

Spark control computer

10-wire harness connector

10
9
8
7
6

1
2
3
4
5

②

wire. If there is continuity, turn key on and measure voltage between pins 2 and 10 (ground 10 of the 10-wire connector). Voltage should be the same as that at the battery. If not, check wiring and connections and repair or replace as required. If voltage is correct, spark control computer is defective and must be replaced.

If proper voltage was present at pin B of the 3-wire connector, turn key on (with 10-wire connector connected) and hold the coil secondary wire ¼ in. from a ground on the engine. Use a jumper wire to momentarily connect pin A to pin C. If a spark was obtained, the Hall Effect pickup assembly is defective and must be replaced. If no spark was obtained, turn key off and disconnect 10-wire connector from spark control computer. Check continuity between pin C of 3-wire connector and pin 9 of the 10-wire connector. Also check continuity between pin A of the 3-wire connector and pin 5 of the 10-wire connector. If no continuity is present, repair the wires and repeat the check. If continuity was present, spark control computer is faulty and should be replaced.

FUEL SYSTEM

Fuel system troubles must be isolated to the carburetor, fuel pump, or fuel lines. These procedures assume the ignition system has been checked and properly adjusted.

1. *Engine will not start*—First, determine that fuel is being delivered to carburetor. Remove the air cleaner, look into the carburetor throat and depress the accelerator several times. There should be a stream of fuel from the accelerator pump each time the accelerator is depressed. If fuel is being delivered, check choke for freedom of action. If choke is not sticking, problem probably is not in fuel system. Check ignition system. If fuel is not being delivered, check fuel and pump delivery (described later), float valve and float adjustment (see Chapter Six). If engine still will not start, check automatic choke parts for sticking or damage. If necessary, rebuild or replace the carburetor. See Chapter Six.
2. *Rough idle or engine miss with frequent stalling*—Check carburetor adjustments. See Chapter Three.

3. *Engine "diesels" when ignition is switched off*—Check carburetor adjustments. See Chapter Three.

4. *Stumbling when accelerating from idle*—Check the accelerator pump diaphragm (see Chapter Six) and the idle speed adjustment (see Chapter Three). Also check fuel filter and replace if necessary.

5. *Engine misses at high speed or lacks power*—This indicates possible fuel starvation. Check fuel pump pressure and capacity. Clean main jet and float needle valve. Check fuel filter.

6. *Black exhaust smoke*—Black exhaust smoke means a badly overrich mixture. Check that automatic choke operates. Check idle mixture and idle speed. Check for excessive fuel pump pressure, leaky float or worn float needle valve. Also check that jets are proper size.

Fuel Pump Pressure Testing

1. Install a T-fitting in the fuel line close to the carburetor.

2. Connect a fuel pressure gauge to the fitting with a short tube.

3. Run the engine at idle speed; fuel pressure should be about 4-6 lb. and remain constant. If pressures vary appreciably, replace pump.

4. Stop the engine. Pressure should drop off very slowly. If pressure drops rapidly, the outlet valve is leaky.

Fuel Pump Capacity Testing

1. Disconnect the fuel line near the carburetor.

2. Fit a rubber hose over the fuel line so fuel can be directed into a graduated container with about one quart capacity.

3. Start engine and run for 30 seconds. There is sufficient fuel in the float chamber for this.

4. Stop the engine. The fuel pump should have delivered about one pint (500cc) or more fuel in 30 seconds.

CLUTCH

All clutch troubles except adjustments require transmission removal to identify and cure the problem.

1. *Slippage* — This is most noticeable when accelerating in high gear at relatively low speed. To check slippage, park the car on a level surface with the handbrake set. Shift to 2nd gear and release the clutch as if driving off. If the clutch is good, the engine will slow and stall. If the clutch slips, continued engine speed will give it away.

Slippage results from insufficient clutch pedal free play, oil or grease on the clutch disc, worn pressure plate, or weak springs.

2. *Drag or failure to release* — This trouble usually causes difficult shifting and gear clash, especially when downshifting. The cause may be excessive clutch pedal free play, warped or bent pressure plate or clutch disc, broken or loose linings, or lack of lubrication in pilot bearing. Also check the condition of transmission main shaft splines.

3. *Chatter or grabbing* — A number of things can cause this trouble. Check tightness of engine mounts and engine-to-transmission mounting bolts. Check for worn or misaligned pressure plate and misaligned release plate.

4. *Other noises* — Noise usually indicates a dry or defective release or pilot bearing. Check the bearings and replace if necessary. Also check all parts for misalignment and uneven wear.

MANUAL TRANSAXLE

Transaxle troubles are evidenced by one or more of the following symptoms:

    a. Difficulty changing gears

    b. Gear clash when downshifting

    c. Slipping out of gear

    d. Excessive noise in NEUTRAL

    e. Excessive noise in gear

    f. Oil leaks

Transaxle repairs are not recommended without the many special tools required.

Transaxle troubles are sometimes difficult to distinguish from clutch troubles. Eliminate the clutch as a source of trouble before installing a new or rebuilt transaxle.

AUTOMATIC TRANSAXLE

Most automatic transaxle repairs require considerable specialized knowledge and tools.

It is impractical for the home mechanic to invest in the tools, since they cost more than a properly rebuilt transaxle.

The following symptoms and test will help you find and verify transaxle trouble. Adjustments and repairs must be handled by your dealer or other competent, well-equipped shop.

1. *No drive in any gear* — Fluid level is low; check. Defective fluid pump or broken gears may be the cause.

2. *No drive in forward gears* — May be caused by defective forward clutch.

3. *No drive when 1 or R is selected* — 1st/reverse band or servo may be defective.

4. *No drive in 1st with D selected* — One-way clutch is probably defective.

5. *No drive in 2nd with 2 or D selected* — 2nd gear band or servo is defective.

6. *No drive in D or R* — Direct/reverse clutch is defective or selector lever cable is incorrectly adjusted.

7. *Poor power transfer in reverse* — Direct/reverse clutch is slipping. Check fluid level. Check selector cable adjustment.

8. *Shift speeds too high* — Defective governor valve or incorrect fluid pressure may be the cause.

9. *Shift speeds too low* — Defective governor valve or incorrect fluid pressure may be the cause.

10. *No upshift to 3rd when D is selected* — Governor valve is defective. Could also be caused by a defective direct/reverse clutch if reverse does not work either.

11. *Harsh engagement when shifting from N to any gear* — Idle speed is too high or vacuum hose is leaking or disconnected.

12. *Poor acceleration (engine output good)* — Normally caused by defective torque converter or one-way clutch. Check stall speed. Could also be caused by low fluid level or slipping bands or clutches.

13. *Transmission fluid discolored or smells burnt* — A burnt band or clutch friction linings may cause this.

14. *Unusual scraping, grinding, or screeching noises* — Defective converter, one-way clutch, or planetary gear set cause these noises.

15. *Excessive fluid consumption* — If accompanied by smoky exhaust, vacuum unit is probably leaking and engine is drawing fluid out. Otherwise, oil seal between transmission and final drive is leaking.

16. *Kickdown does not operate* — Check kickdown adjustment. Adjust or replace kickdown switch. A dirty valve body can also cause this.

17. *Vehicle "creeps" excessively at idle* — Idle speed is too high.

18. *Engine races excessively during upshifts* — Check for improper fluid level. Burnt or worn band clutch friction linings or improper fluid pressure can also cause this.

Stall Speed Test

This test permits rapid torque converter evaluation.

1. Connect an accurate tachometer to the engine. Start the engine, set the handbrake, and warm up the engine.

2. Press the footbrake down firmly. Shift the lever to D.

3. Depress accelerator briefly to full throttle while holding the car at a complete stop with hand and footbrakes. Quickly read the engine speed reached on the tachometer.

CAUTION
This is a severe test and ATF in the torque converter heats very rapidly. Do not run under full load any longer than necessary to read the tachometer (5-10 seconds).

4. If the stall speed is more than 250-350 rpm below the specifications (2,000-2,400 rpm), the torque converter is defective and must be replaced. A stall speed only a few hundred rpm's below specification indicates the engine is not delivering full power and probably needs a

tune-up. A stall speed higher than specified indicates internal slippage.

NOTE: *Stall speed will drop about 125 rpm for every 3,000 feet above sea level.*

EXHAUST EMISSION CONTROL

The following symptoms assume you have adjusted the ignition and fuel systems as described in Chapter Three.

1. *CO content too low* — Ensure that idle speed is not too low. Check idle mixture adjustment (too lean). Check carburetor jets and channels. Clean and/or replace as necessary. Check engine condition with a compression test and a vacuum test.

2. *CO content too high* — Check idle mixture adjustment (too rich). Check for sticking air cleaner, warm air flap, and sticking or defective automatic choke. Check carburetor jets and channels. Clean and/or replace as necessary. Check engine condition with a compression and vacuum test.

3. *Hydrocarbon level too high* — Make sure the throttle valve closes completely. Check spark plug condition and gap. Check breaker points. Check ignition timing (too early). Check intake manifold for leaks. Check valve clearance (too small). Check condition of valves with compression test.

BRAKES

1. *Brake pedal goes to floor* — There are numerous causes for this, including excessively worn pads, air in the hydraulic system, leaky brake lines, leaky calipers, or leaky or worn master cylinder. Check for leaks and thin brake pads. Bleed the brakes. If this does not cure the trouble, rebuild the calipers, wheel cylinders, and/or master cylinder.

2. *Spongy pedal* — Normally caused by air in the system; bleed the brakes.

3. *Brakes pull* — Check brake adjustment. Also check for contaminated brake pads (from leaks), leaky or loose calipers, frozen or seized

pistons, and restricted brake lines or hoses. In addition, check front end alignment and suspension damage. Tires also affect braking; check tire pressure and condition. Replace or repair defective parts.

4. *Dragging brakes* — Check handbrake adjustment. Check for swollen rubber parts due to improper brake fluid or contamination, and obstructed master cylinder bypass port. Clean or replace defective parts.

5. *Hard pedal* — Check brake pads for contamination. Also check for restricted brake lines and hoses.

6. *High speed fade* — Check for contaminated brake pads. Ensure that recommended brake fluid is installed. Drain entire system and refill if in doubt.

7. *Pulsating pedal* — Check for excessive brake disc wear or runout. Undetected accident damage is also a frequent cause of this.

STEERING AND SUSPENSION

Trouble in the suspension or steering is evident when the following occur:

   a. Steering is hard

   b. Car pulls to one side

   c. Car wanders or front wheels wobble

   d. Steering has excessive play

   e. Tire wear is abnormal

Unusual steering, pulling, or wandering is usually caused by bent or otherwise misaligned suspension parts. This is difficult to check without proper alignment equipment. Such checks should be referred to your dealer.

TIRE WEAR ANALYSIS

Abnormal tire wear should be analyzed to determine its causes. The most common causes are the following:

   a. Incorrect tire pressure

   b. Improper driving

   c. Overloading

   d. Bad road surfaces

   e. Incorrect wheel alignment

Figure 3 identifies wear patterns and indicates the most probable causes.

Underinflation—Worn more on sides than in center.

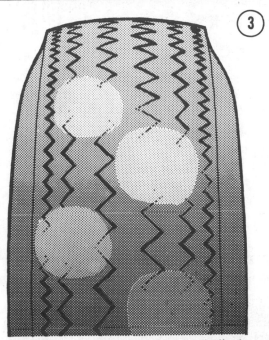

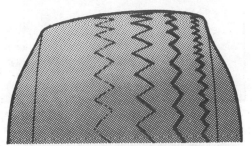

Wheel Alignment—Worn more on one side than the other. Edges of tread feathered.

Wheel Balance — Scalloped edges indicate wheel wobble or tramp due to wheel unbalance.

Road Abrasion—Rough wear on entire tire or in patches.

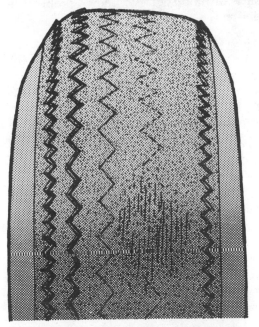

Overinflation—Worn more in center than on sides.

Combination—Most tires exhibit a combination of the above. This tire was overinflated (center worn) and the toe-in was incorrect (feathering). The driver cornered hard at high speed (feathering, rounded shoulders) and braked rapidly (worn spots). The scaly roughness indicates a rough road surface.

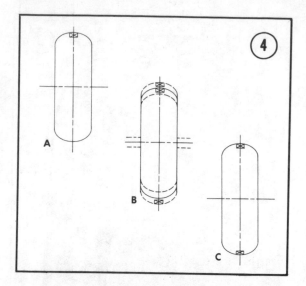

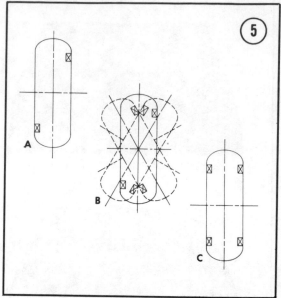

WHEEL BALANCING

All 4 wheels and tires must be in balance along 2 axes. To be in static balance, **Figure 4**, weight must be evenly distributed around the axis of rotation. (A) shows a statically unbalanced wheel; (B) shows the result — wheel tramp or hopping; (C) shows proper static balance.

To be in dynamic balance, **Figure 5**, the centerline of the weight must coincide with the centerline of the wheel. (A) shows a dynamically unbalanced wheel; (B) shows the result — wheel wobble or shimmy; (C) shows proper dynamic balance.

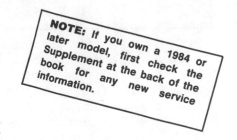

NOTE: If you own a 1984 or later model, first check the Supplement at the back of the book for any new service information.

CHAPTER THREE

LUBRICATION, MAINTENANCE, AND TUNE-UP

Regular preventive maintenance is necessary to ensure good performance, dependability and safety. This chapter outlines periodic lubrication and maintenance for a car driven by an average owner. A car driven more than average may require more frequent attention. Periodic maintenance is also important to a car that is seldom or never driven. Rust, dirt and corrosion can cause unnecessary damage to an idle car. Whether performed by the owner or a dealer, regular attention helps avoid expensive repairs.

The maintenance recommended by Chrysler Corporation falls into different requirements, depending upon year.

Maintenance requirements for 1978 models fall into 2 categories: "required" and "recommended." Required maintenance, which is necessary for proper emission control and vehicle performance, should be performed at the mileage intervals designated for your car on the emission control information label located on the radiator yoke in the engine compartment. This label will indicate either "Maintenance Schedule F" or "Maintenance Schedule G." **Table 1** shows all

scheduled maintenance for 1978 models and specifies whether it applies to Schedule F or G. (**Tables 1-10** are at the end of the chapter.) If unspecified, the item applies to both schedules.

Lubrication and maintenance requirements for 1979 and later models fall into 3 categories: "scheduled," "general" and "severe service." Severe service maintenance is required for vehicles operating under one or more of the following conditions:

a. Extremely dusty conditions
b. Idling for prolonged periods
c. Operating vehicle in heavy city traffic 50% of the time in temperatures of 90° or more
d. Regular short mileage driving
e. Commercial operation such as a delivery service

Table 2 (1979), **Table 3** (1980-1982) and **Table 4** (1983) contain scheduled maintenance tasks for models covered by this manual.

Many of the tasks listed in **Tables 1-4** are part of what has been considered for years the engine tune-up. For this reason the appropriate procedures for performing these tasks are grouped together in this chapter under the heading of *Engine Tune-up*. Also described are checks to be made at each fuel stop. Recommended lubricants and fuels are found in **Table 5**. Approximate fluid refill capacities can be found in **Table 6**.

FUEL STOP CHECKS

The following simple checks should be performed at each fuel stop.

1. *Check engine oil*—Oil should be checked with the engine warm and on level ground. Level should be between the 2 marks on the dipstick; never above and never below. See **Figure 1**. Top up if necessary with oil recommended in **Table 5**.

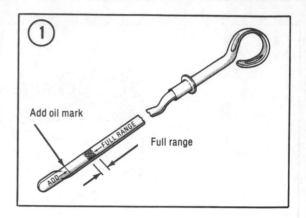

NOTE
The 1.6L dipstick is similar to that shown in Figure 1 but the ADD and FULL lines are not identified as such. Be sure to keep the oil level between the 2 marks.

2. *Check battery electrolyte level*—If it is below the indicator, fill the battery with distilled water only up to the indicator (**Figure 2**). On maintenance-free batteries, observe the condition of the indicator on top of the battery (**Figure 3**). If the indicator is dark with a green dot showing, the battery is fully charged. If the indicator is dark, but no green dot is showing, the battery needs charging. If the indicator is light colored or clear, the battery should be replaced. See Chapter Eight for further battery information.

3. *Check brake fluid level*—The brake reservoir used on all models is shown in **Figure 4**. On 1978-1979 reservoirs, brake fluid level should measure 1/4 in. (6.35 mm) from the top of the reservoir. On 1980 and later models, the brake fluid level should be maintained to the bottom of the split rings. Top up if necessary with brake fluid clearly marked DOT 3.

CAUTION
The use of any other type of brake fluid could lead to early brake failure.

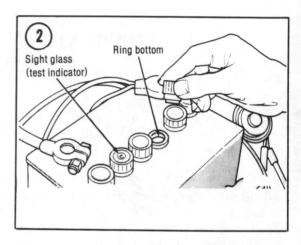

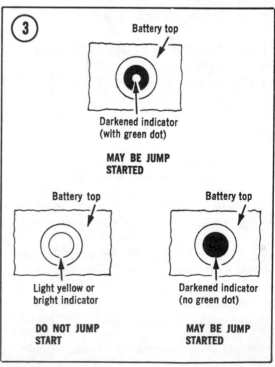

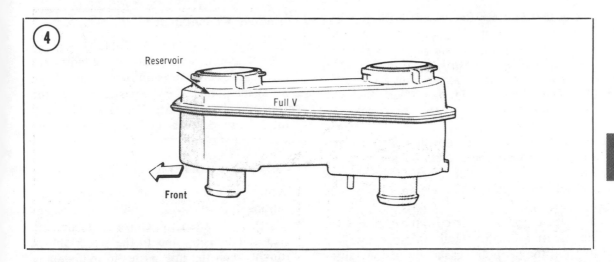

Reservoir

Full V

Front

3

6. *Check windshield washer fluid level*—It should be kept full.

7. *Check coolant level*—This check should be made when the engine is cold. Level should be above the MINIMUM mark on the expansion tank.

PERIODIC CHECKS AND MAINTENANCE

On 1978 models, check the emission control information label in the engine compartment to determine whether Schedule F or Schedule G applies to your car, then refer to **Table 1** for the required maintenance tasks. On 1979 and later models, refer to **Tables 2-4** for maintenance tasks.

Engine Oil and Filter Change

The oil and filter change interval varies depending on the type of driving that you do.

For normal driving including some city traffic, change oil and filter every 7,500 miles or 6 months, whichever comes first. If driving is primarily under those conditions described as severe service maintenance in the introduction to this chapter, change the oil and filter every 3,000 miles or 3 months. Change the oil and filter at least twice a year if the car is driven only a few hundred miles a month.

Any oil used must be rated "SF." See **Figure 5**. Non-detergent oils are not recommended. See **Table 5** for recommended oil grades. Approximate oil capacity is found in **Table 6**.

To drain the oil and change the filter, you will need:
   a. Drain pan
   b. Funnel
   c. Can opener or pour spout
   d. Filter wrench
   e. Adjustable wrench
   f. Specified quantity of oil (see **Table 5**).
   g. Oil filter (when specified)

There are a number of ways of discarding the old oil safely. The easiest way is to pour it from the drain pan into a gallon bleach bottle. The oil can be recycled at many service stations. Check local regulations before discarding oil in household trash.

1. Warm engine to operating temperature, then shut it off.
2. Put drain pan under the oil drain plug and remove the plug.

3. Let the oil drain for at least 10 minutes.

CAUTION
Be sure to use a replacement filter capable of withstanding 300 psi pressure or engine damage may result. The Mopar L-335 filter (part No. 4105409) is recommended for use with all engines.

4. Remove the oil filter with a filter wrench from underneath the car. On 1.7 liter engines, the use of a socket-operated band-type wrench such as that shown in **Figure 6** is recommended.

5. Wipe the gasket surface of the engine block clean with a lint-free cloth or paper towel.

6. Coat the neoprene gasket on the new filter with clean oil.

7. Screw the filter onto the engine *by hand* until you begin to feel resistance as the filter gasket touches the base. Then tighten the filter another 3/4 to one full turn on 1.6 and 1.7 liter engines or 2/3 turn on 2.2 liter engines. Use a filter wrench if necessary.

CAUTION
Proper tightening is particularly important with the 1.7 liter oil filter, as it is possible that the engine may develop high oil pressure for a short time during cold weather. An improperly tightened filter will leak oil under these conditions.

8. Install the oil drain plug and tighten securely.

9. Remove the oil filler cap.

10. Pour in the specified quantity of the recommended oil. See **Table 5** and **Table 6**.

11. Start engine and let it idle. The oil pressure light on the instrument panel will remain on for a short time (15-30 seconds), then it will go out.

CAUTION
Do not rev the engine to make the oil light go out. It takes time for the oil to reach all areas of the engine and excessive engine speed could damage dry parts.

12. While the engine is running, make sure that the drain plug and oil filter are not leaking.

13. Turn the engine off and check the oil level with the dipstick. See **Figure 1**. Add oil if necessary to bring oil up to FULL mark, but *do not overfill.*

Carburetor Choke Shaft

At the intervals stated in **Tables 1-4** apply MOPAR combustion chamber conditioner (part No. 2933500) or equivalent to the choke shaft at the points where it passes through the carburetor air horn. See **Figure 7**. This will remove gum deposits and help prevent the choke from sticking.

Fast Idle Cam and Pivot Pin

Apply MOPAR combustion chamber conditioner (part No. 2933500) or equivalent to the link between the choke shaft and the thermostat housing and to the sealing block through which the link passes to remove any oil or water. See **Figure 8**. Also apply the solvent to the fast idle cam and pivot pin to remove dirt, oil and other deposits. Work the choke plate back and forth to distribute the solvent. Make sure the choke moves freely and that no sticking or erratic motion are present.

Cooling System

The cooling system should be checked at the intervals given in **Tables 1-4**. Inspect hose surfaces for damage from heat and wear. If the hoses are hard, brittle, cracked, checked, torn or abraded or if they have swollen spots, they should be replaced. At the same time, check the water pump belt for wear and proper tension and replace or adjust as required. See *Drive Belt Tension* in this chapter for adjustment instructions.

The radiator cap should be checked for proper sealing and operation. See Chapter Seven.

The face of the radiator should be cleared of accumulated bugs and debris. Apply compressed air from the reverse side to clean. Do not use an ice pick or other tool, as this could damage the radiator.

The cooling system should be drained, flushed and refilled with a 50/50 solution of water and ethylene glycol type antifreeze (MOPAR part No. 4106784, Prestone II or equivalent) at the intervals specified in **Tables 1-4** or whenever the coolant appears dirty, rusty or full of sediment. See Chapter Seven. If the system appears to be contaminated, use any reputable radiator cleaner, following the manufacturer's instructions, before refilling the system.

Coolant level should always be maintained above the MINIMUM mark in the plastic coolant reserve bottle. If the level is low, add coolant to the reserve bottle. It is not necessary to remove the radiator cap.

Carburetor Air Filter

The carburetor air cleaner filter should be replaced at the intervals stated in **Tables 1-4** or more often if the car is operated frequently under dusty conditions. To replace the air cleaner filter on 1.7 liter engines, remove the air cleaner cover, remove the filter and replace with a new filter. On 1.6 and 2.2 liter engines, the following replacement procedure must be followed to prevent air leaks.

1. Unsnap the air cleaner cover hold-down clips. Remove the wing nuts. **Figure 9** shows the 2.2L air cleaner; the 1.6L is similar.

2. Lift the filter out of the housing.

3. Install a new filter with the filter element screen facing upwards (**Figure 10**). Make sure the filter element fits into the plastic bottom section of the air cleaner housing.

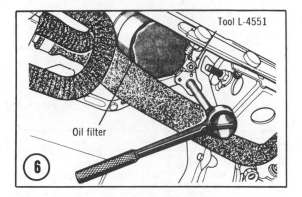

Tool L-4551

Oil filter

6

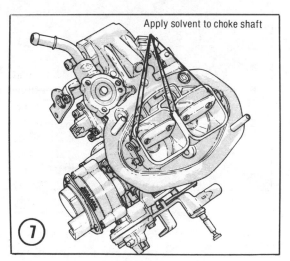

Apply solvent to choke shaft

7

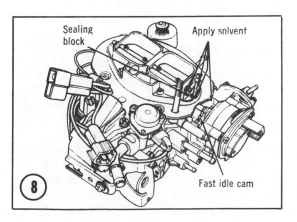

Sealing block

Apply solvent

Fast idle cam

8

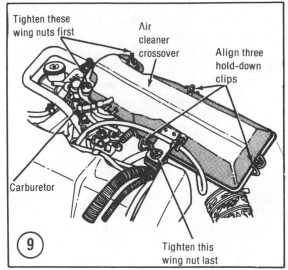

Tighten these wing nuts first

Air cleaner crossover

Align three hold-down clips

Carburetor

Tighten this wing nut last

9

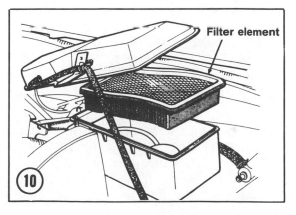

Filter element

10

4. Place the air cleaner cover onto the plastic bottom section, making sure to align the 3 hold-down clips while allowing the carburetor and support bracket studs to stick out through their respective stud holes in the cover.

5. Install the plastic wing nuts on both of the carburetor studs and tighten securely. See **Figure 9**.

6. Install the air cleaner top-to-support bracket wing nut and tighten securely (**Figure 9**).

7. Snap each of the hold-down clips into position.

Positive Crankcase Ventilation (PCV) Valve

The PCV valve should be checked at the intervals stated in **Tables 1-4** and replaced if not functioning properly.

1. To check the PCV valve, start the engine and remove the valve from its seat. If the valve is not plugged, a hissing noise should be heard and a strong suction should be felt when a finger is placed over the end of the valve (**Figure 11**).

2. Stop the engine and shake the valve as shown in **Figure 12**. A clicking noise indicates that the valve is free. If the valve fails either test, it should be replaced. Do not attempt to clean the valve.

3. After a new valve has been installed, repeat the first test with the engine running. If the system still fails to pass the test, clean the hose with a solvent, such as MOPAR combustion chamber cleaner and dry it with compressed air. Remove the carburetor and clear the passage in the PCV hose nipple with a 1/4 in. or slightly smaller drill. Take care not to remove any metal. Reinstall the carburetor and hose and repeat the test. If necessary, replace the hose.

Crankcase Inlet Air Cleaner (2.2 Liter Engine)

The crankcase inlet air cleaner houses the PCV valve and is located beside the air cleaner housing (**Figure 13**). The filter should be removed and cleaned every 52,500 miles. To service the filter, tag and remove the hoses attached to the filter housing. Remove the

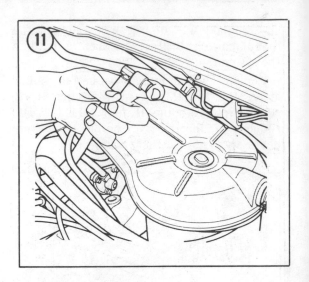

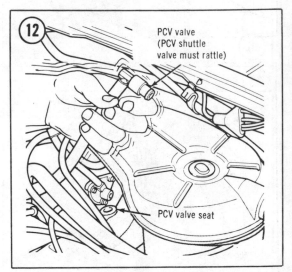

PCV valve
(PCV shuttle
valve must rattle)

PCV valve seat

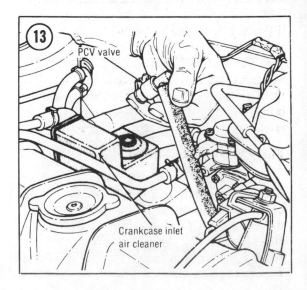

PCV valve

Crankcase inlet
air cleaner

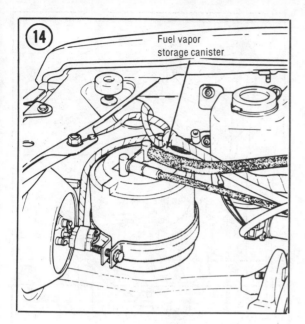

Fuel vapor storage canister

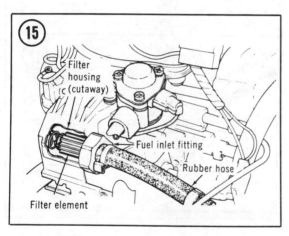

Filter housing (cutaway)

Fuel inlet fitting

Rubber hose

Filter element

filter and wash thoroughly with kerosene and let dry. Invert the air cleaner assembly and wet the filter with SAE 30 engine oil. Position the assembly so that any excess oil can drain through the vent nipple on top of the cleaner housing. Reinstall housing and reconnect attaching hoses.

Fuel Evaporative Canister

The evaporative canister does not require periodic maintenance under normal driving conditions. However, if the car is frequently driven under dusty conditions, the canister filter element should be inspected and replaced, if required, every 7,500 miles. See **Figure 14**.

Fuel Filter (1978-1979)

The fuel filter is located in the carburetor fuel inlet (**Figure 15**). It should be changed after the first 7,500 miles of operation and every 15,000 miles thereafter. To change the filter:
1. Unscrew the fuel inlet fitting.
2. Remove and discard the filter element.
3. Install a new element.
4. Install and tighten the fuel inlet fitting.
5. Start the engine and check for leaks.

Fuel Filter (1980-on)

A disposable inline filter canister is installed in the fuel line just above the fuel pump on all 1980 and later 1.6, 1.7 and 2.2 liter engines. No mileage or interval recommendations are given by Chrysler Corporation for filter replacement but it is a good idea to install a new filter every 15,000 miles.
1. Install a short length of hose and new clamp (provided with the filter) on each end of a new filter.

NOTE
The 1.6 and 2.2 liter filters incorporate a vapor separator and have an extra fuel line fitting on the side for connection to the vapor return line.

2. Slide another new clamp over each filter hose.
3. Cut and remove the clamps holding the short length of hose at each end of the old filter to the fuel line.
4. Pull each hose from the fuel line and remove the old filter.
5. Position the new filter with the stamped arrow indicating fuel flow direction facing the carburetor and slip the new filter hoses over each fuel line. Tighten the clamps snugly.
6. Connect the vapor return line to the proper fitting on the 1.6 and 2.2 liter filter. Tighten the clamp snugly.
7. Start the engine and check for leaks.

Engine Leak Inspection

The engine should be checked visually for leaks. Check the oil pan drain plug, oil pan gasket, oil filter and front cover. Greasy looking dirt at these points may indicate an oil leak. Check the radiator and hose connections for coolant residue or rust. Check the fuel connections (fuel filter, fuel pump, carburetor) for wetness that may indicate gasoline leakage.

Power Steering

The power steering fluid level should be checked monthly. The power steering pump is located on the right side of the vehicle behind the engine. To check the fluid level, first wipe off the pump cap and reservoir to prevent dirt from falling into the reservoir. Remove the pump cap. Fluid level should be maintained at the level indicated on the dipstick (**Figure 16**). Add fluid to bring the level within specifications, if required. Fill with MOPAR Power Steering Fluid (part No. 2084329) or equivalent. *Do not* use automatic transmission fluid.

Steering and Suspension

Every 6 months, check the entire steering and suspension systems. Check ball-joint and tie rod end dust seals. Check tie rods for tightness and damage. Check tire wear which may indicate damaged or worn suspension parts. Check shock absorbers for oil streaks indicating leaks; replace if necessary.

Jack up the front wheels. Move front wheels by hand. The steering wheel should turn as soon as the wheels turn; there should be no free play.

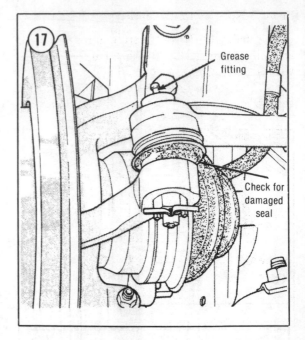

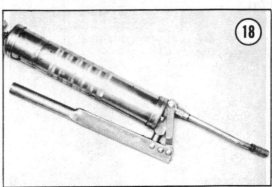

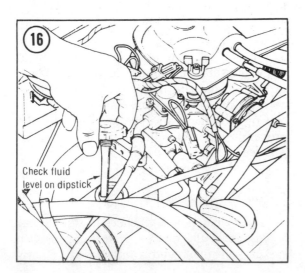

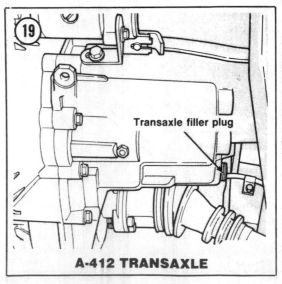

A-412 TRANSAXLE

Front Suspension Lubrication

The ball-joints and steering linkage units are semi-permanently lubricated at the factory with special grease. Every 30,000 miles or 3 years, the grease fitting on each wheel should be lubricated with a special long life chassis

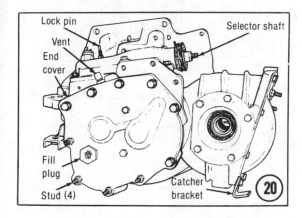

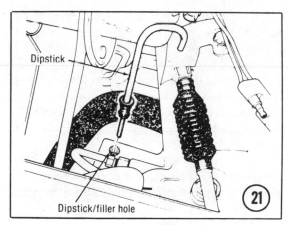

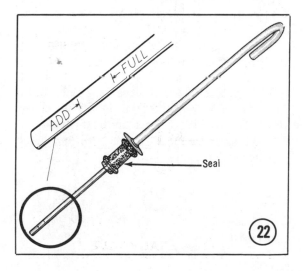

grease such as Multi-Mileage Lubricant (part No. 2525035 or equivalent). See **Figure 17**.

1. Clean the grease fitting and seal area of all accumulated dirt and road grime.

2. Fill the joint with a grease gun (**Figure 18**) until the grease begins to flow from the bleed areas at the base of the seal.

3. Wipe off any grease left on the fitting or at the bleed area.

Manual Transaxle Check

Every 6 months, check oil level in transaxle. To do this, remove the filler plug and make sure that the oil level reaches to the bottom of the hole. See **Figure 19** or **Figure 20**. If the level is low, top up with gear oil recommended in **Table 5**.

Automatic Transaxle Check

> *NOTE*
> *A 14-inch dipstick is fitted to 1981 automatic transaxles. This dipstick is hollow and may act as a vent. A venturi effect from the cooling fan can suck fluid from the transmission through the hollow dipstick. To overcome this venturi effect, a 22-inch dipstick is used with 1982-on models. This longer dipstick is available from your dealer to replace the shorter 1981 dipstick.*

Every 6 months, check the automatic transaxle fluid level. The transaxle must be thoroughly warmed up with the selector lever in PARK and the parking brake applied. With 1983 models, let the engine idle for at least 6 minutes to make sure the oil level is stabilized between the transmission and differential before checking fluid level. Pull out the dipstick (**Figure 21**), wipe it with a clean cloth and reinsert the dipstick. Pull the dipstick out again and check that the level is between the 2 marks. See **Figure 22**. If necessary, add sufficient DEXRON II automatic transmission fluid to bring the level to the correct point on the dipstick but *do not overfill*. If the level is above the top mark, fluid must be drained to restore the proper level or seals may be damaged.

Automatic Transaxle Fluid Change

Under normal driving conditions, no automatic fluid change is required. If the vehicle is used under any of the following conditions, change fluid every 15,000 miles:

a. Extended periods with outside temperature regularly at 90° F (32° C) or more.

b. Very hilly or mountainous areas.

c. Frequent trailer pulling.

d. Commercial use, e.g., delivery.

To change the fluid, you will need the following:

a. 3 quarts of DEXRON or DEXRON II automatic transmission fluid

b. Funnel

c. Pour spout

d. New filter

e. Silicone Rubber Sealer (RTV) part No. 4026070

NOTE
There is no drain plug on the transaxle. The oil pan must be removed to drain the oil.

CAUTION
Do not remove the drain pan if you must work outdoors. Cleanliness is very important when working with an automatic transaxle. Blowing dust can settle on internal transaxle parts and cause serious damage. Let your dealer or local repair shop change the oil if you do not have access to a clean garage.

1. Raise the vehicle front end and secure with jackstands.

2. Place a wide mouth container under the transaxle oil pan.

3. Loosen the oil pan bolts at the front of the oil pan (**Figure 23**) and allow fluid to start pouring out of the transaxle into the container.

4. Carefully remove the remaining oil pan bolts while at the same time allowing the remaining fluid to drain into the container. Then remove the oil pan completely.

5. Remove the oil filter retaining screws and remove the filter.

NOTE
A new filter design which requires a gasket is used with 1983 transaxles. It

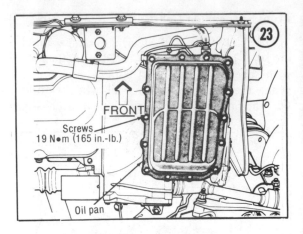

is not interchangeable with earlier filters. Be sure to install the correct filter type in Step 6.

6. Install a new filter at the valve body. Tighten the filter retaining screws to 40 in.-lb. (0.5 mkg).

7. Clean the oil pan and transaxle mating surfaces thoroughly of all old sealer.

8. Apply a bead of RTV sealer around the oil pan mating surface.

9. Install the oil pan and tighten the retaining bolts to 165 in.-lb. (1.9 mkg).

10. Pour 3 quarts of DEXRON II automatic transmission fluid down the dipstick/filler tube (**Figure 21**).

11. Start engine and let idle. Place the gear selector in NEUTRAL. It may be necessary to block the front wheels to prevent the car from creeping forward.

12. Add fluid to bring the fluid level to 1/8 in. below the ADD ONE PINT mark on the dipstick.

13. Idle engine 2 more minutes, then slowly shift transmission through all gears, pausing momentarily at each gear position. Recheck the fluid level and, if necessary, add more fluid to bring the fluid level to 1/8 in. below the ADD ONE PINT mark on the dipstick.

14. When proper level is reached, install the dipstick into the dipstick/filler hole.

NOTE
When the transmission fluid level is established at the ADD mark when the approximate transmission temperature is 70° F (21° C), the fluid level will

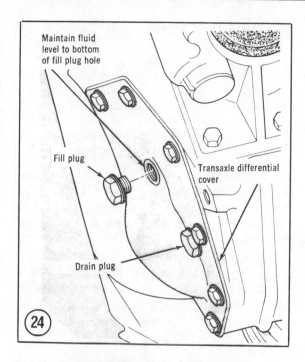

Maintain fluid level to bottom of fill plug hole

Fill plug

Transaxle differential cover

Drain plug

㉔

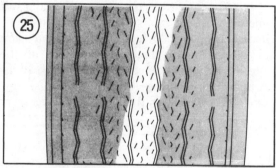

㉕

eventually level at the FULL mark when the transmission reaches normal operating temperature.

Automatic Transaxle Differential Unit

Automatic transaxles used through 1982 models have separate transmission and differential reservoirs. During normal operating service, no fluid changes are required with the differential reservoir. However, the differential fluid level should be checked monthly. To do so, remove the fill plug (**Figure 24**). If the fluid level is not even with the bottom of the fill plug hole, add sufficient DEXRON II automatic transmission fluid through the hole to obtain the correct level. If operating service requires

that the differential fluid be changed (see *Automatic Transaxle Fluid Change*), a drain plug is located on some differential covers. On those units in which a drain plug is not used, it will be necessary to remove the differential cover. When the fluid has drained completely, install the drain plug or apply a bead of RTV sealant to the differential cover and install the cover. Add new fluid through the fill plug hole.

All 1983 automatic transaxles have a common transmission/differential sump. This simplifies checking/changing fluid and prevents a transaxle failure caused by lack of lubrication in the differential.

Hinges and Latches

At regular intervals (oil change time will do) all hinges and latches should be lubricated. Use engine oil on the door, hood and liftgate hinges and pivots. The hood latch should be lubricated with multipurpose lubricant, while Lubriplate or equivalent should be used on the door check straps, the lock cylinders and the liftgate and door latches. Lubriplate also may be used on the window regulators and the window lift systems.

Brake Hoses

All brake hoses should be inspected regularly for tight connections and physical condition. Replace any hose that leaks or is damaged. Hardness, brittleness, cracking, checking, tears, cuts, abrasions and swelling are all signs of deterioration. If any of these conditions are present, replace the hose. The brakes must be bled anytime a hose is disconnected and/or replaced. See *Brake Bleeding*, Chapter Ten.

Tire and Wheel Inspection

Every 7,500 miles, check the condition of all tires. Check local traffic regulations concerning minimum tread depth. Most recommend replacing tires when tread depth is less than 1/32 in. Original equipment tires have tread wear indicators molded into the bottom of the tread grooves. Tread wear indicators appear as 1/2 in. bands (**Figure 25**)

3

when tread depth becomes 1/16 in. Tires should be replaced at this point.

Chrysler recommends that tires be rotated every 7,500 miles. See **Figure 26** for the suggested rotation pattern.

Check all lug bolts and nuts for proper torque of 80 ft.-lb. (11 mkg).

Disc Brakes

When specified in **Tables 1-4**, check brake pad thickness. Brake pads should be replaced if the thickness is less then 0.30 in. (7.62 mm). If necessary, replace all 4 pads to keep pads balanced. Never replace pads on one wheel only. See Chapter Ten.

Drum Brakes

When specified in **Tables 1-4**, remove the wheels and brake drums as described in Chapter Ten and check the brake shoes. Replace the linings if worn to less than 1/16 in. (1.5 mm) thick or if soaked with oil or brake fluid. It is necessary to replace all 4 shoes at the same time to keep shoes balanced. Never replace shoes on one wheel only.

Wheel Bearings

At the intervals listed in **Tables 1-4** check the rear wheel bearing lubrication as described in Chapter Ten. Permanently sealed bearings are used on the front wheels and do not require adjustment. Relubricate the rear bearings, if required, as described under *Rear Brake Drums,* Chapter Ten.

Drive Belt Tension

Since 1978, Chrysler has used several methods of obtaining proper drive belt tension. Depending upon year, the following methods have been used:
  a. Belt tension gauge
  b. Torque equivalent
  c. Belt deflection

Because of engine compartment space limitations with the transverse engine, a belt gauge tool is difficult to use accurately. Therefore the torque equivalent and belt deflection methods are discussed below. Drive belt specifications are found in **Table 7**

for 1978-1980 models and **Table 8** for 1981-on models.

> *NOTE*
> *A belt is considered used after it has run on an engine for approximately 15 minutes. If a new belt is installed, it should be adjusted to new belt specifications and run for 15 minutes. Then stop the engine and adjust belt to used belt specifications.*

Depending upon year, many of the drive accessory brackets are provided with 1/2 in. (12.7 mm) square holes that allow belt adjustment to be completed with a torque wrench. To tension the belt, loosen the accessory drive bracket and place a torque wrench in the 1/2 in. hole. Tension the belt to specifications (**Table 7** or **Table 8**) while tightening the bracket bolts. Variances from this method are discussed below.

Belt Tension 1978-1979

Tension of the power steering and air injection pump belts can be adjusted by installing a 1/2 in. drive ratchet and extension in the mounting brackets. Tension of the alternator and air conditioning belts can be adjusted by using a pry bar or large screwdriver between the body of the accessory

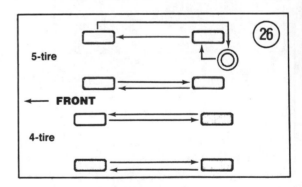

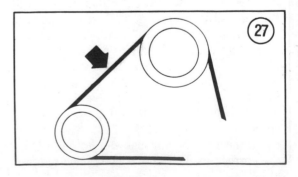

and the engine. When adjusting the alternator belt tension, make sure the lever is applied at the center of the alternator to avoid damage.

To adjust belt tension, loosen all mounting bolts and apply tension with the lever or ratchet until the belt deflects 1/4-5/16 in. when a pressure of approximately 10 lb. is applied at a point midway between the pulleys. See **Figure 27**. Then tighten all mounting bolts and recheck. Readjust if required.

CAUTION
*When adjusting the air conditioning belt, the tightening sequence shown in **Figure 28** must be followed and the nuts and bolts*

torqued to 25-40 ft.-lb. (3.5-5.5 mkg) to prevent early failure of the air conditioning compressor.

Belt Tension 1980-on

Each accessory bracket (except the alternator bracket) is provided with a 1/2 in. (12.7 mm) square hole for torque wrench use. See **Figure 29** (typical).

Alternator Belt Tension Adjustment (1980)

To properly adjust the alternator/water pump belt, adjustment tool C-4586 must be used together with a 1/2 inch drive torque

CAUTION:
WHEN ADJUSTING A/C
BELT AVOID
MISALIGNMENT BY
TORQUING BOLTS IN
THIS SEQUENCE: 1, 2 & 3

Part No. 5214133

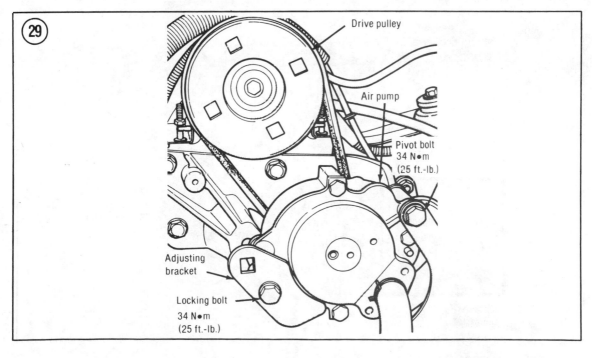

Drive pulley

Air pump

Pivot bolt
34 N•m
(25 ft.-lb.)

Adjusting bracket

Locking bolt
34 N•m
(25 ft.-lb.)

wrench. The adjustment tool C-4586 can be purchased from a Chrysler dealer or fabricated from the dimensions in **Figure 30**.

1. Raise the vehicle on a hoist and secure with jackstands. Remove the splash shield. On vehicles equipped with an air pump, remove the horn for access to the alternator adjustment bolt.

2. Place tool C-4586 onto a 1/2 inch drive torque wrench and position as shown in **Figure 31**.

3. Adjust the belt tension to specifications in **Table 7**.

4. While holding the alternator at the required torque, tighten the adjusting bolt.

5. Remove torque wrench and tool C-4586. Install horn if removed. Install splash shield.

6. Lower vehicle and tighten the alternator pivot bolt to 30 ft.-lb. (4.1 mkg).

Alternator Belt
Tension Adjustment
(1981-on, 1.7 Liter)

Refer to **Figure 32** for this procedure.

1. Loosen the alternator pivot nut.

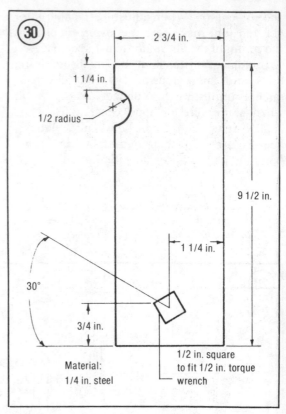

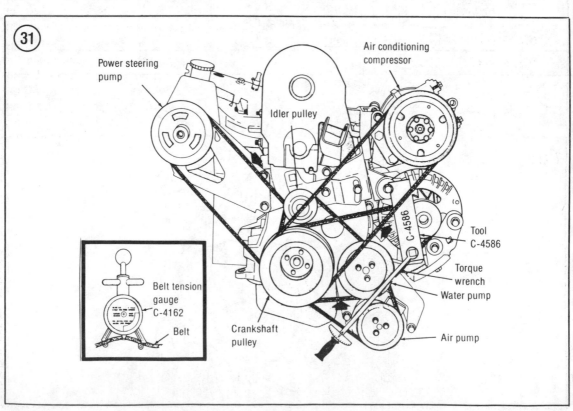

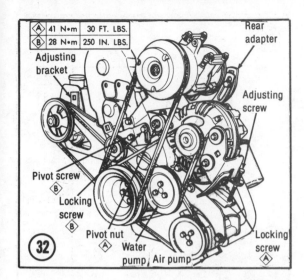

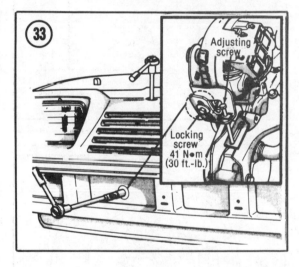

2. Remove the plug from the front access hole (**Figure 33**) and loosen the alternator locking screw.

3. Turn the alternator adjusting screw (**Figure 33**) to obtain belt specification in **Table 8**.

4. Tighten the alternator locking screw and pivot nut to 30 ft.-lb. (1.4 mkg).

5. Install the front access hole plug (**Figure 33**).

**Alternator Belt
Tension Adjustment
(1.6 Liter)**

1. Loosen the pivot nut at the bottom of the alternator.

2. Turn the alternator adjusting screw at the rear of the pivot nut to obtain belt specification in **Table 8**.

3. Tighten alternator pivot nut to 250 in.-lb. (28 N•m).

Air Conditioner

Every 6 months, as a minimum, the air conditioner controls should be checked to see that they are functioning properly. Check the compressor belt for proper tension as described in this chapter and adjust if required. Start the engine and turn on the air conditioner. Observe the sight glass (**Figure 34**). The presence of bubbles or white foam

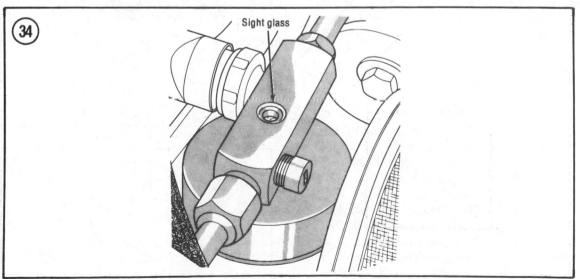

usually indicates that the system needs charging with refrigerant.

On 1978-1979 models, check the oil level in the compressor if there are signs of oil leakage. Before checking the oil level, loosen or remove the compressor drive belt and orient the compressor so that the oil plug is at the top of the unit (**Figure 35**). Clean the plug and the surrounding area, then slowly remove the plug. This allows refrigerant to separate from the oil. Rotate the front plate of the clutch so that the notch is 110° from the bottom as shown in **Figure 36**. In this position, the ball end of the top piston rod is aligned with the oil fill port (**Figure 37**). Insert the dipstick (special tool part No. C-4504) as shown in **Figure 38** until the stop contacts the compressor surface at the filler hole, then remove the dipstick. The dipstick has 8 marks, each representing one ounce. Add oil, if necessary, to bring the level up between the 3 and 4 ounce marks. If the dipstick is not available, refer this check to your Chrysler dealer.

On 1980 and later models, procedures for checking the air conditioner compressor oil level are not required. If an oil leak is detected, indicated by the presence of a wet, shiny surface at one of the compressor component joints (**Figure 39**), refer further service to a Chrysler dealership or air conditioning specialist.

Windshield Wiper Blades

Long exposure to weather and road film hardens the rubber wiper blades and destroys their effectiveness. When blades smear or otherwise fail to clean the windshield, they should be replaced.

ENGINE TUNE-UP

In order to maintain a car in perfect running condition, the engine must receive periodic tune-ups. The procedures outlined here are performed every 15,000 miles (Schedule F) or 22,500 miles (Schedule G) on 1978 cars. The procedures should be performed every 15,000 miles on all 1979 and later models. **Table 9** summarizes tune-up specifications. Since different systems in an engine interact to affect overall performance,

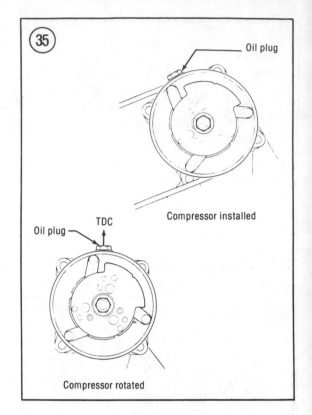

Oil plug

Compressor installed

Oil plug   TDC

Compressor rotated

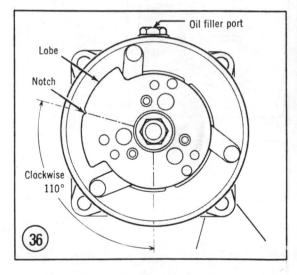

Oil filler port

Lobe

Notch

Clockwise 110°

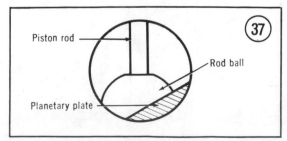

Piston rod

Rod ball

Planetary plate

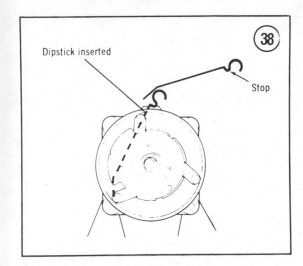

Dipstick inserted

Stop

③⑧

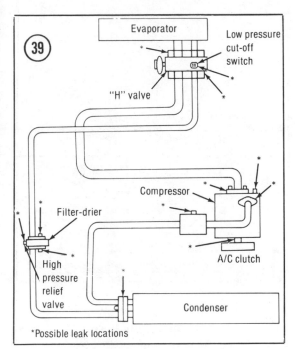

③⑨

Evaporator

Low pressure
cut-off
switch

"H" valve

Compressor

Filter-drier

High
pressure
relief
valve

Condenser

A/C clutch

*Possible leak locations

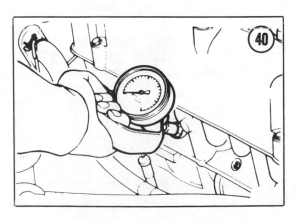

④⓿

3

engine tune-up must be accomplished in the following order:

  a. Compression check
  b. Valve clearance adjustment (1.6 and 1.7 liter engine).
  c. Spark plug replacement
  d. Distributor inspection
  e. Ignition timing
  f. Carburetor adjustment

To perform a tune-up on your vehicle, you will need the following tools and parts:

  a. Spark plug wrench
  b. Universal joint for socket wrench
  c. Socket wrench
  d. 12-inch extension for socket
  e. Common screwdriver
  f. Spark plug gapper tool
  g. Compression gauge
  h. Ignition timing light
  i. Tachometer
  j. Phillips screwdriver
  k. Torque wrench
  l. Valve adjusting shims and tool (1.7 liter only)

Firing Order

The cylinder firing order for all engines is 1-3-4-2. The No. 1 cylinder is on the flywheel end of the 1.6 liter engine and on the timing belt end of the 1.7 and 2.2 liter engines.

COMPRESSION TEST

A "dry" compression test and a "wet" compression test must be interpreted together to isolate the trouble in cylinders or valves.

Dry Compression Test

1. Warm the engine to normal operating temperature. Ensure that the choke valve and throttle valve are completely open.
2. Remove the spark plugs.
3. Connect the compression tester to one cylinder following the tester manufacturer's instructions. See **Figure 40**.
4. Have an assistant crank the engine over until there is no further rise in pressure.
5. Remove the tester and record the reading.
6. Repeat Steps 3 through 5 for each cylinder.

When interpreting the results, actual readings are not as important as the difference

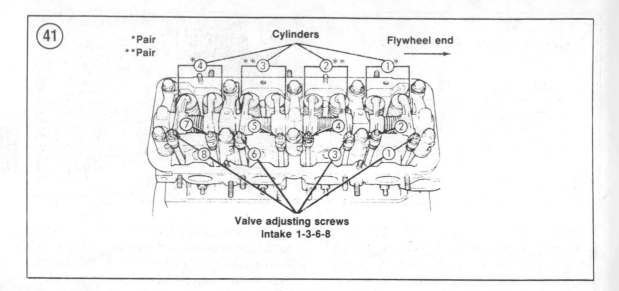

Valve adjusting screws
Intake 1-3-6-8

between readings. All readings should be about 145 psi (1000 kPa). Readings below 100 psi (690 kPa) indicate that an engine overhaul is due. A maximum difference of 21 psi (145 kPa) between any 2 cylinders is acceptable. Greater differences indicate worn or broken rings, leaky or sticky valves or a combination of all. Compare with vacuum gauge reading to isolate the trouble more closely.

Wet Compression Test

Add one tablespoon of heavy oil (at least SAE 30) to any cylinder which checks low. Repeat the procedure above. If compression increases noticeably, the rings are probably worn. If adding oil produces no change, the low reading may be caused by a broken ring or valve trouble. If 2 adjacent cylinders read low during both wet-dry testing, the head gasket may be bad.

Valve Adjustment
(1.6 Liter Engine)

Valve clearance is set when the engine is cold. The piston must be positioned at TDC on the compression stroke.

Before adjusting valves, remove valve cover and all spark plugs. This makes the engine much easier to turn by hand; plugs require replacement at this time anyway.

Intake valve clearance is 0.010 in. (0.25 mm); exhaust valve clearance is 0.012 in.

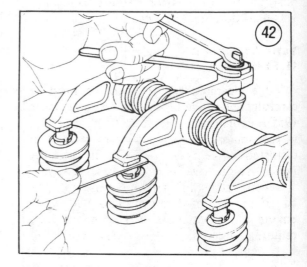

(0.030 mm). Adjust valve clearances in firing order: 1-3-4-2. Refer to **Figure 41** for this procedure.

1. Slowly turn crankshaft with socket wrench while watching movement of exhaust valves. When No. 4 cylinder exhaust valve moves upward (closing) and the intake valve on that cylinder starts to move downward (opening), the No. 1 piston is at TDC on its compression stroke. Stop rotating the crankshaft.

2. Loosen the rocker arm locknut and insert the correct size feeler gauge between the valve stem and rocker arm. Turn the adjusting screw until the feeler gauge is a sliding fit, then tighten the locknut while holding the adjusting screw. See **Figure 42**.

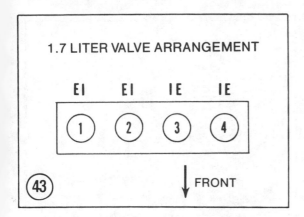

1.7 LITER VALVE ARRANGEMENT

EI   EI   IE   IE

(1)   (2)   (3)   (4)

(43)   ↓ FRONT

3. Repeat Step 1 watching the No. 2 cylinder valves to position the No. 3 piston; watch the No. 1 cylinder valves to position the No. 4 piston and watch the No. 3 cylinder valves to position the No. 2 piston. Adjust each set of valves as described in Step 2.

Valve Adjustment
(1.7 Liter Engine)

Valve clearance for your engine must be carefully determined while the engine is warm (95° F coolant temperature). If the clearance is too small, the valves may be burned or distorted. Large clearance results in excessive noise. In either case, engine power is reduced.

Before adjusting valves, remove valve cover and all spark plugs. This makes the engine much easier to turn by hand; plugs require replacement at this time anyway.

NOTE
After cylinder head repairs, the valve adjustment should be rechecked after 600 miles. Readjust if necessary.

To adjust the valve clearance:

NOTE
Valve clearances are to be adjusted in firing order: 1-3-4-2. Valve arrangement is shown in Figure 43.

1. Turn crankshaft with socket wrench until the cam lobes for cylinder No. 1 no longer rest on the tappets, i.e., intake and exhaust valve for cylinder No. 1 are closed.

2. Insert feeler gauge between cam lobes and tappets (**Figure 44**) and measure clearance very carefully. Quickly write measured clearance on a piece of paper or on cylinder head with a felt tip marker or crayon.

3. Turn crankshaft until intake and exhaust valves for cylinder No. 3 are closed. Measure and record valve clearance as in Step 2, above.

4. Rotate crankshaft as necessary to measure valve clearance for cylinder No. 4, then cylinder No. 2, in the same manner.

5. For each valve, compare measured clearance with specified clearance in **Table 9**. If difference is within the specified limits, no adjustment is necessary. If not within limits, replace tappet clearance disc with a different one to bring clearance with specifications.

Here is an example to determine which size clearance disc must be installed. Suppose that measured clearance for exhaust valve is 0.012 in. (0.30 mm). Subtracting this from the minimum specified clearance, (0.016 in./0.40 mm), yields a difference of 0.004 in. (0.1 mm). If the present disc is 4.05 mm thick, replace it with a new disc 3.95 mm thick, i.e., 0.1 mm thinner. **Table 10** shows tappet clearance discs available.

CAUTION
Special tools are required to change the tappet discs. Due to the possibility of damage, improvised tools are not recommended. Your dealer can order special tool part No. L-4417 (or see NOTE regarding special tools in Chapter One). The other required tool is a pencil-type magnet that can be obtained from most tool shops.

To change the tappet clearance discs:

1. Press valve tappet down with special tool (L-4417).

2. Lift the clearance disc up with a narrow screwdriver and the pencil magnet and remove it from the tappet (**Figure 45**).

3. Installation is the reverse of these steps. Recheck clearance after each new disc is installed.

SPARK PLUGS

Removal

1. Blow out any foreign matter from around spark plugs with compressed air.

> *CAUTION*
> *When spark plugs are removed, dirt around the plug can fall into the spark plug hole. This could cause expensive engine damage.*

> *NOTE*
> *Small cans of compressed, inert gas used to blow off photographic equipment are available at photo supply stores.*

2. Mark spark plug wires with cylinder number so that you can reconnect them properly. A small strip of masking tape numbered in sequence works well. See **Figure 46** (1.6 liter), **Figure 47** (1.7 liter) or **Figure 48** (2.2 liter).

3. Disconnect the spark plug wires. Pull off by grasping the connector, *not* the spark plug wire. See **Figure 49**. If you pull on the wire, it could break.

> *CAUTION*
> *If the boots seem to be stuck, twist them a half turn by hand to break the seal. Do not pull boots off with pliers. The pliers could cut through the silicone material and permit the spark to arc to ground.*

4. Remove the spark plugs. Keep plugs in order so that you know which cylinder they came from.

5. Examine each spark plug and compare its condition to **Figure 50**. Condition of spark plugs is an indication of engine condition and can warn of developing trouble.

6. Discard the plugs. Although they could be cleaned, gapped and reused if in good

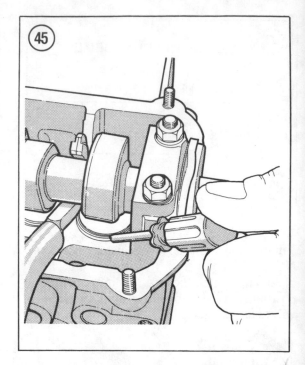

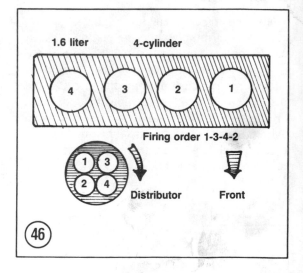

condition, they rarely last very long; new plugs are not very expensive and will be far more reliable.

Gapping and Installing the Plugs

New plugs should be carefully gapped to ensure a reliable, consistent spark. You must use a special spark plug gapping tool with a wire gauge.

1. Refer to **Table 9** and insert the proper size gauge wire between the center and side

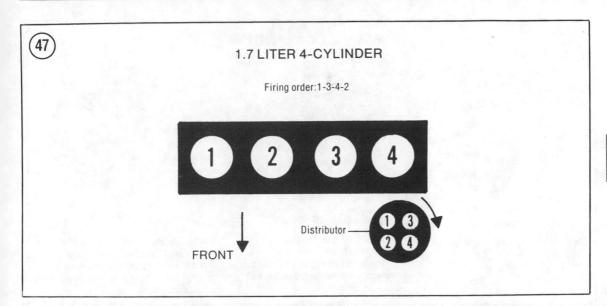

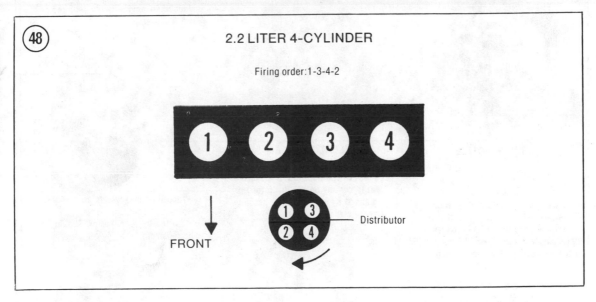

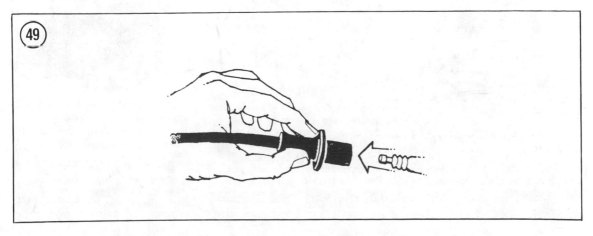

(50) SPARK PLUG CONDITION

NORMAL
• Identified by light tan or gray deposits on the firing tip.
• Can be cleaned.

GAP BRIDGED
• Identified by deposit buildup closing gap between electrodes.
• Caused by oil or carbon fouling. If deposits are not excessive, the plug can be cleaned.

OIL FOULED
• Identified by wet black deposits on the insulator shell bore electrodes.
• Caused by excessive oil entering combustion chamber through worn rings and pistons, excessive clearance between valve guides and stems, or worn or loose bearings. Can be cleaned. If engine is not repaired, use a hotter plug.

CARBON FOULED
• Identified by black, dry fluffy carbon deposits on insulator tips, exposed shell surfaces and electrodes.
• Caused by too cold a plug, weak ignition, dirty air cleaner, defective fuel pump, too rich a fuel mixture, improperly operating heat riser, or excessive idling. Can be cleaned.

LEAD FOULED
• Identified by dark gray, black, yellow, or tan deposits or a fused glazed coating on the insulator tip.
• Caused by highly leaded gasoline. Can be cleaned.

WORN
• Identified by severely eroded or worn electrodes.
• Caused by normal wear. Should be replaced.

FUSED SPOT DEPOSIT
• Identified by melted or spotty deposits resembling bubbles or blisters.
• Caused by sudden acceleration. Can be cleaned.

OVERHEATING
• Identified by a white or light gray insulator with small black or gray brown spots and with bluish-burnt appearance of electrodes.
• Caused by engine overheating, wrong type of fuel, loose spark plugs, too hot a plug, low fuel pump pressure, or incorrect ignition timing. Replace the plug.

PREIGNITION
• Identified by melted electrodes and possibly blistered insulator. Metallic deposits on insulator indicate engine damage.
• Caused by wrong type of fuel, incorrect ignition timing or advance, too hot a plug, burned valves, or engine overheating. Replace the plug.

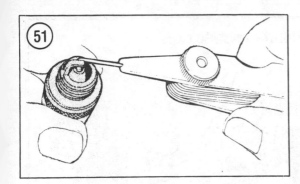

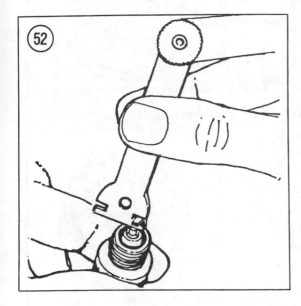

5. Install the spark plug wires. Make sure each is connected to the proper spark plug. Refer to **Figure 46** (1.6 liter), **Figure 47** (1.7 liter) or **Figure 48** (2.2 liter) for spark plug wire routing.

Rotor and Distributor Cap

As part of each tune-up, wipe off any dirt or corrosion on the distributor cap. Examine the inside of the cap for wear and signs of carbon tracks (arcing). Replace the cap if carbon tracks are evident. Remove the rotor and inspect for excessive wear or burning around the metal contact surfaces. Replace rotor if damaged. See **Figure 53**. Always replace cap and rotor as a set if either is damaged.

Spark Plug Wires

Each time the ignition system is serviced the spark plug wires and the high-tension wire between the ignition coil and the distributor center tower should be checked for good connections. Nipples and spark plug covers should be in good condition and should fit tightly around the towers and spark plugs. Clean the wires with a non-flammable solvent and check for brittle or broken insulation. Check the resistance of the wires by removing the distributor cap and connecting an ohmmeter between the spark plug end terminal and the proper terminal inside the cap. If resistance is greater than 50,000 ohms, remove the wire from the distributor cap and recheck the resistance of the wire. If still greater than 50,000 ohms, replace the wire. Check the resistance of the coil high-tension wire by connecting an ohmmeter between the center terminal inside the distributor cap and at either primary terminal at the coil. If resistance is greater than 25,000 ohms, remove the wire and check its resistance. If greater than 15,000 ohms, replace the wire.

NOTE
Do not remove the spark plug wires from the distributor cap towers or the coil high-tension wire from either the coil or distributor cap towers unless the nipples are damaged or it is necessary to check wire resistance as described above. To do so may disturb proper sealing.

electrode of each spark plug. See **Figure 51**. If the gap is correct, you will feel a slight drag as you pull the wire through. If there is no drag or the gauge won't pass through, bend the side electrode *with the gapping tool* (see **Figure 52**) to set the proper gap.

2. Put a *small* drop of oil or anti-seize compound on the threads of each spark plug.

3. Screw each spark plug in by hand until it seats. Very little effort is required. If force is necessary, you have the plug cross-threaded; unscrew it and try again.

4. Tighten the spark plugs finger-tight. If you have a torque wrench, tighten them to 20 ft.-lb. (28 N•m). If you don't have a torque wrench, tighten them an additional 1/4-1/2 turn with a spark plug socket and wrench.

NOTE
Do not overtighten. This prevents the plug from sealing.

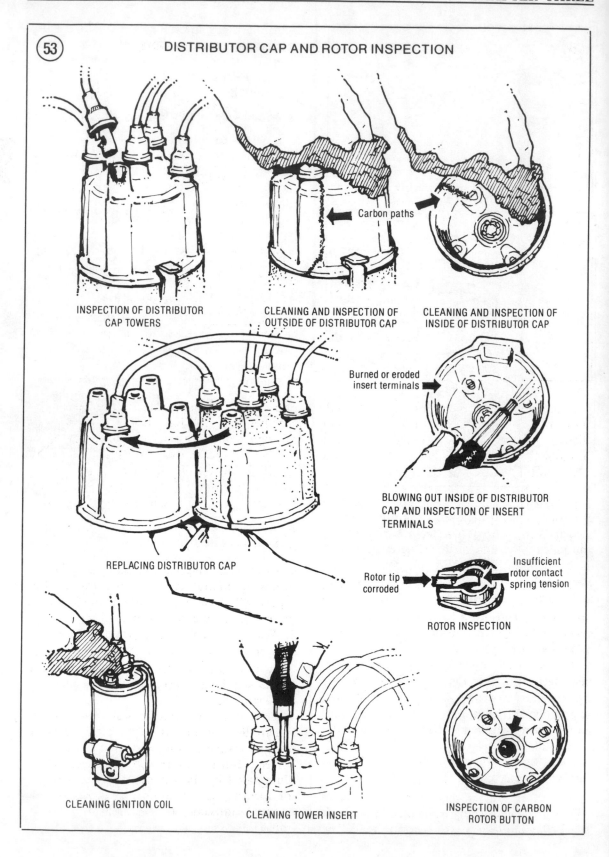

DISTRIBUTOR CAP AND ROTOR INSPECTION

Carbon paths

INSPECTION OF DISTRIBUTOR
CAP TOWERS

CLEANING AND INSPECTION OF
OUTSIDE OF DISTRIBUTOR CAP

CLEANING AND INSPECTION OF
INSIDE OF DISTRIBUTOR CAP

Burned or eroded
insert terminals

BLOWING OUT INSIDE OF DISTRIBUTOR
CAP AND INSPECTION OF INSERT
TERMINALS

REPLACING DISTRIBUTOR CAP

Rotor tip
corroded

Insufficient
rotor contact
spring tension

ROTOR INSPECTION

CLEANING IGNITION COIL

CLEANING TOWER INSERT

INSPECTION OF CARBON
ROTOR BUTTON

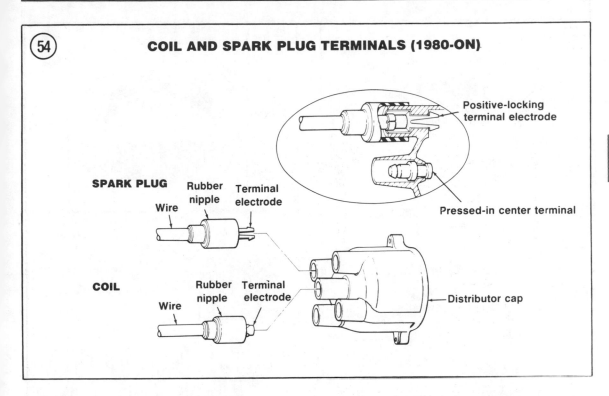

COIL AND SPARK PLUG TERMINALS (1980-ON)

54

Positive-locking terminal electrode

Pressed-in center terminal

SPARK PLUG

Wire — Rubber nipple — Terminal electrode

COIL

Wire — Rubber nipple — Terminal electrode

Distributor cap

3

If the spark plug wires must be replaced, they can be removed from 1978-1979 distributor caps with a twisting, pulling motion. The wire attachment method used on 1980 and later distributor caps differs. A positive-locking terminal electrode is attached to the wire end instead of the distributor cap (**Figure 54**).

Spark plug wires of this type must be removed by pinching the terminal ends together with pliers from inside the cap and pushing them out of the cap tower. The coil wire continues to use a slip-on connector that fits over a permanently mounted cap tower electrode; it can be removed with a twisting, pulling motion.

To install new positive-locking wires, pinch the electrode ends together and fit into the appropriate cap tower. Rotate the rubber nipple over the tower with a downward motion until you hear the terminal electrodes click into place.

IGNITION TIMING

The distributor must be aligned to fire each spark plug at precisely the right moment. The emission control sticker under the hood specifies this time for different combinations of engine and optional equipment and for different locations. Always use the specifications on the sticker on your own car when setting the ignition timing. If the sticker is missing, use the specifications in **Table 9**.

Ignition Timing Adjustment (1978)

1. Connect timing light to spark plug No. 1, following manufacturer's instructions. See **Figure 47**. Connect a portable tachometer, following manufacturer's instructions.

2. Warm engine to normal operating temperature (oil temperature: 176° F, 80° C).

3. Run engine at 900 rpm with vacuum transducer hose disconnected and plugged. See **Figure 55**.

4. Loosen the distributor hold-down screw (**Figure 56**) and turn it until the timing mark on the transmission case aligns with the correct timing mark on flywheel when illuminated by the timing light. See **Table 9** for timing specifications. See **Figure 57** (manual transaxle) or **Figure 58** (automatic transaxle).

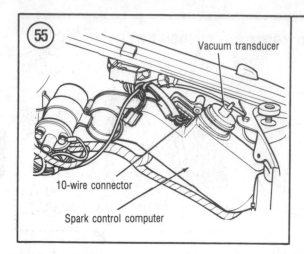

Vacuum transducer

10-wire connector

Spark control computer

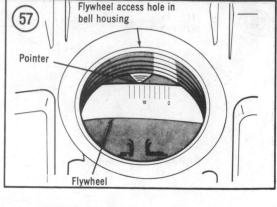

Flywheel access hole in bell housing

Pointer

Flywheel

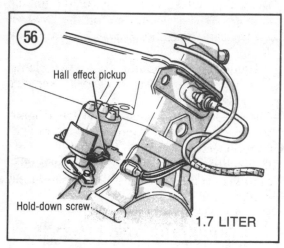

Hall effect pickup

Hold-down screw

1.7 LITER

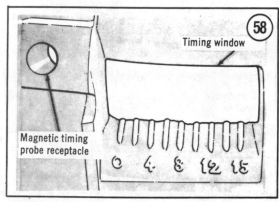

Timing window

Magnetic timing probe receptacle

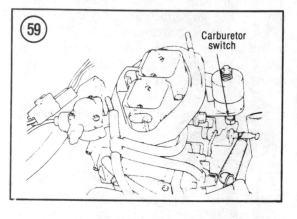

Carburetor switch

5. Tighten the distributor hold-down clamp (**Figure 56**) when adjustment is correct.

6. Unplug and reconnect the vacuum line to the vacuum transducer (**Figure 55**).

Ignition Timing Adjustment (1979-on)

> *NOTE*
> *The basic timing on 1982 1.7 liter engines equipped with a manual transaxle is 20° BTDC. Since the timing indicators are designed to read a maximum of 16° BTDC, the use of an adjustable power timing light or a magnetic timer is necessary to check and/or adjust ignition timing on such vehicles. The basic timing for 1983 1.7 liter engines remains the same, but the transaxle timing indicator is revised to read 20° BTDC.*

1. Connect the timing light to the No. 1 spark plug according to manufacturer's instructions. See **Figures 46-48**.

2. Warm the engine to normal operating temperature (upper radiator hose hot).

3. Connect a tachometer to the engine according to manufacturer's instructions.

4. Start engine and check curb idle speed. Specifications are found on the Vehicle Emission Control Information (VECI) label in the engine compartment. Use the

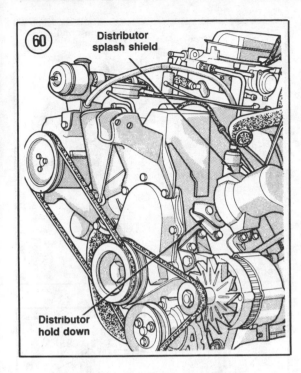

Distributor splash shield

Distributor hold down

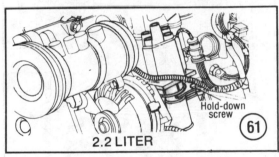

Hold-down screw

2.2 LITER

Timing marks

cover (**Figure 62**). The timing marks for the 1.7 and 2.2 liter engines are on the flywheel and transaxle case. See **Figure 57** and **Figure 58**.

8. Tighten the distributor hold-down clamp screw when adjustment is correct. Recheck timing adjustment.

9. Reconnect the carburetor switch (**Figure 59**) and spark control computer vacuum line, if disconnected.

10. Recheck engine idle speed. If necessary, readjust to correct specifications. Do not reset timing.

CARBURETOR ADJUSTMENTS

Propane-Assisted Idle Speed and Idle Mixture (1978-1979)

An adjustable propane metering valve (tool part No. C-4464 or equivalent; see **Figure 63**), a container of propane and an accurate tachometer are required to perform this procedure.

1. Start the engine and allow it to reach normal operating temperature. Radiator fan should be operating, transmission should be in NEUTRAL, headlights and air conditioning should be off and the idle stop carburetor switch, if so equipped, should be grounded with a jumper wire (See **Figure 64**). Vacuum hoses at the exhaust gas recirculation (EGR) valve, if so equipped, and at the distributor or spark control unit should be disconnected and plugged. If the car is equipped with the Electronic Lean Burn

specifications in **Table 9** if the label is missing or defaced. If adjustment is incorrect, set as described under *Carburetor Adjustments* in this chapter.

5. If equipped with a carburetor switch (**Figure 59**), ground the switch with a jumper wire. Disconnect and plug the spark control computer vacuum line on 1982 and later models.

6. Loosen the distributor hold-down clamp screw. See **Figure 60** (1.6 liter), **Figure 56** (1.7 liter) or **Figure 61** (2.2 liter) for distributor hold-down clamp location.

7. Refer to VECI lable or **Table 9** for timing specifications. Turn the distributor housing until the timing marks align when illuminated by the timing light. The 1.6 liter timing marks are on the crankshaft pulley and timing chain

(ELB) system, wait approximately one minute after the engine returns to idle speed before making any adjustments.

2. After the engine has warmed up, tap accelerator to kick off the fast idle cam. Disconnect the air cleaner supply hose from the carburetor and connect the propane supply hose to the nipple.

3. Connect an accurate tachometer to the engine, using the manufacturer's instructions.

4. Slowly open the propane metering valve until maximum idle speed is obtained. Let the engine idle at this speed with the propane on.

NOTE
If too much propane is flowing, the engine speed will be reduced. Make sure the propane bottle is standing up so a constant flow will be maintained. If engine speed begins to change, check the propane supply.

5. With the engine running and the propane flowing, adjust the curb idle speed screw on top of the idle stop solenoid until the tachometer indicates the specified enriched rpm (taken from the emission control information label in the engine compartment). See **Figure 65** for air conditioned cars and **Figure 66** for cars without air conditioning.

6. Readjust the propane flow for maximum rpm, if necessary. Once the curb idle speed screw has been set to the specified enriched speed, do not reset it.

7. Turn off the propane and adjust the idle air mixture screw (**Figure 67**) to obtain the specified curb rpm speed on the emission control information label. If this speed cannot be obtained within the limits set by the limiter cap on the screw, check the engine basic timing and check for leaks or other malfunctions before removing the limiter cap

8. Turn on the propane and recheck the enriched rpm. If the speed differs by more than 25 rpm from the specification, repeat Steps 1-7.

9. Turn off the propane and remove the metering valve and propane source from the car. Unplug and reinstall the vacuum hose removed and plugged in Step 1.

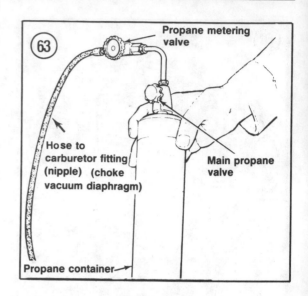

63 Propane metering valve

Hose to carburetor fitting (nipple) (choke vacuum diaphragm)

Main propane valve

Propane container

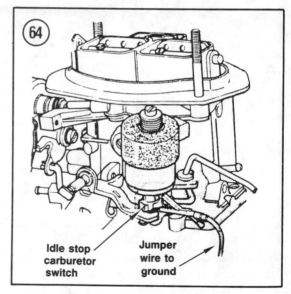

64 Idle stop carburetor switch

Jumper wire to ground

Idle Set RPM Adjustment (1980)

This procedure describes adjustment of the idle set rpm adjustment only. If idle mixture adjustment is required, perform the *Propane-assisted Idle Set and Idle Mixture Adjustment (1980)*, in this section.

1. Set the parking brake and place the transmission in NEUTRAL. Connect a tachometer to the engine, following the manufacturer's instructions. Start the engine and allow it to reach normal operating temperature. Make sure all lights and accessories are turned off.

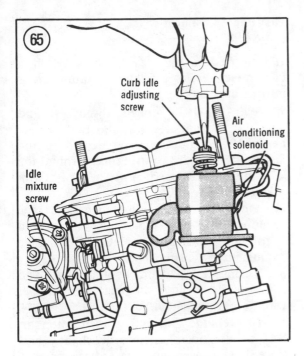

65

Curb idle
adjusting
screw

Air
conditioning
solenoid

Idle
mixture
screw

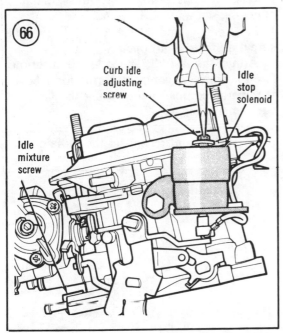

66

Curb idle
adjusting
screw

Idle
stop
solenoid

Idle
mixture
screw

2. Disconnect and plug vacuum hoses at the EGR valve and distributor. Remove the PCV valve from its molded rubber connector. Disconnect the purge-to-vapor canister hose at the carburetor. Leave both hoses open.

3. Disconnect radiator cooling fan and complete the circuit at the plug with a jumper wire to operate the fan.

4. With the engine idling, read the idle speed (RPM) indicated on the tachometer. If the idle speed is not the same as the idle set rpm specified on the emission control information label (in the engine compartment), adjust the idle speed screw until the correct idle set rpm is reached. See **Figure 65** (air conditioning) or **Figure 66** (non-air-conditioning).

**Propane-assisted
Idle Set and Idle
Mixture Adjustment (1980)**

NOTE
An adjustable propane metering valve (tool part No. C-4464 or equivalent) is required, plus a container of propane and an accurate tachometer. You may be able to obtain the propane metering valve from your dealer or a suitable substitute may be available at some auto parts stores. If you are unable to obtain them it is recommended that you take your car to your dealer's service department for adjustment. No other method is accurate enough to meet emission control requirements.

1. Set the parking brake and place the transmission in NEUTRAL. Connect a tachometer to the engine, following the manufacturer's instructions. Make sure all lights and accessories are turned off.

2. Start the engine. Place the fast idle cam on the second highest step and allow engine to warm up to normal operating temperature. Then return engine to idle.

3. Disconnect and plug the EGR vacuum hose. Then disconnect hose leading to distributor, at the 3-way connector. Insert the propane supply hose into the 3-way connector **(Figure 63)**.

4. Check engine timing and adjust if necessary (refer to *Ignition Timing*, in this chapter).

5. Connect a jumper wire to the radiator fan, so that it will run constantly.

6. Disconnect the purge hose from the carburetor and the PCV valve from the rubber connector. (Do not plug either hose.)

7. Open the main propane valve, then slowly open the propane metering valve until the highest rpm is obtained. (When too much propane is added, the rpm will slowly drop.)

3

8. Adjust the idle speed screw until the correct propane rpm specified on the emission label is obtained. Refer to **Figure 65** (cars with air conditioning) or **Figure 66** (cars without air conditioning). Then adjust the propane metering valve again to obtain the highest possible rpm (if necessary, readjust the idle speed screw).

9. Turn off propane and allow engine to idle for a few moments, until it stabilizes. Then adjust the mixture screw to obtain the specified idle set rpm (see emission control information decal in engine compartment). See **Figure 67**.

NOTE
If it is necessary to remove the mixture limiter cap to obtain the correct idle set rpm, first check for possible engine malfunctions and vacuum leaks. Make sure also that all other engine tune-up procedures have been tended to (valve clearance adjustment and ignition service and timing adjustments). When installing new caps, be sure that cap tabs are placed against the "full rich stop" on the carburetor.

10. Turn on the propane metering valve. Repeat adjustment procedures again if engine speed differs more than 25 rpm from the specified propane rpm on the emission control information decal. Then turn off the propane and remove the bottle. Remove jumper wire from radiator fan and reconnect purge hose to carburetor and PCV valve to the rubber connector.

Fast Idle Adjustment
(1978-1980)

1. Remove the air cleaner top. Attach a tachometer following the manufacturer's instructions.

2A. On 1978-1979 models, disconnect and plug the vacuum hoses at the EGR valve. Leave the vacuum line connected to the distributor or spark control unit. Ground the idle stop carburetor switch with a jumper wire (**Figure 64**).

2B. On 1980 models, disconnect and plug vacuum hoses at the EGR valve and distributor. Attach a tachometer following the manufacturer's instructions.

3. Disconnect radiator cooling fan and complete the circuit at the plug with a jumper wire to operate the fan.

4. With engine off and transmission in NEUTRAL, open the throttle slightly and place slowest speed step of fast idle cam under adjusting screw. See **Figure 68**.

5. Start engine and let speed stabilize. Make sure the choke is fully open.

6. Adjust the fast idle speed to specifications (see the emission control information label in the engine compartment), using the fast idle adjustment (**Figure 68**).

7. When adjustment is complete, remove the jumper wires and reconnect the radiator fan.

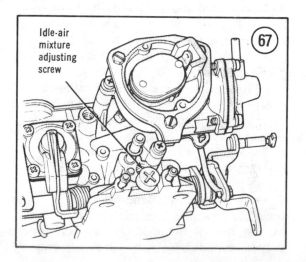

Idle-air mixture adjusting screw

(67)

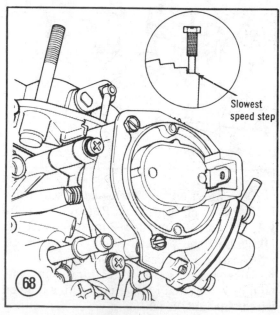

Slowest speed step

(68)

Reconnect vacuum hoses. Reinstall air cleaner.

Carburetor Adjustments (1981-on)

This procedure performs the following adjustments:
  a. Idle speed.
  b. Solenoid idle stop.
  c. Curb idle.
  d. Fast idle speed.

NOTE
Do not remove the air cleaner.

1. Set the parking brake and place the transmission in NEUTRAL. Connect the tachometer to the engine, following the manufacturer's instructions. Make sure all lights and accessories are turned off.
2. Check the ignition timing as described in this chapter and adjust if required.
3. Disconnect and plug the vacuum hoses at the EGR valve. On vehicles equipped with a carburetor switch (**Figure 59**), ground the switch with a jumper wire. Remove the PCV valve from its rubber connector but do not plug. Plug the 3/16 in. diameter PCV control hose at the canister. Disconnect the radiator fan harness and attach a jumper wire to make the fan turn continuously.

4. Turn on the air conditioning (if so equipped) and open the throttle to energize the solenoid. Block the front wheels of automatic transaxle vehicles to prevent the car from creeping forward, then place the gear selector in DRIVE.
5. Remove the adjusting screw and spring at the top of the carburetor-mounted air conditioning solenoid (**Figure 69**).

NOTE
*Carburetors on 1983 2.2 liter engines with air conditioning use either a vacuum kicker (**Figure 70**) or a solenoid kicker (**Figure 71**). These assist devices make it unnecessary to adjust the air conditioning idle speed. Proceed to Step 7.*

6. Insert a 1/8 in. Allen wrench into the solenoid as shown in **Figure 69**. Turn the Allen wrench to adjust the idle speed to specifications shown on the emission control information decal in the engine compartment. Shift the automatic transaxle to PARK. Reinstall the adjusting spring and screw. Turn off the air conditioner (if so equipped). Do not turn off the engine.
7. Wait one minute and read the rpm. If it is not the same as the curb idle rpm specified on the emission control decal, turn the idle speed screw on top of the solenoid until the correct curb idle speed is reached. Turn the engine off.
8. On 2.2 liter engines, disconnect the green wire terminal (1981, if so equipped) or red/tan wire connector (1982) from the carburetor.

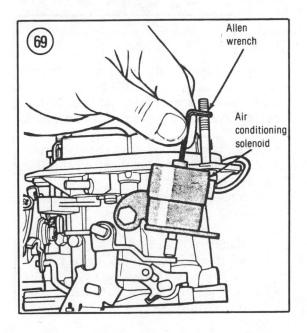

(69) Allen wrench

Air conditioning solenoid

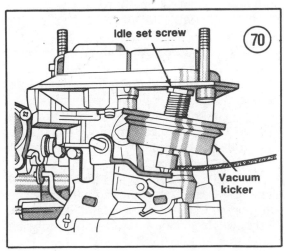

(70) Idle set screw

Vacuum kicker

9. On 1983 vehicles equipped with a feedback carburetor system, disconnect the oxygen system test connector located on the left fender shield near the shock tower.

10. With the engine off, open the throttle slightly. Place the fast idle adjusting screw on the slowest speed step of the cam (**Figure 72**).

11. Start the engine and let the speed stabilize. Make sure the choke valve is fully open. Adjust the fast idle screw to bring the fast idle rpm to the speed specified on the VECI label. Return the carburetor to curb idle speed.

12. Shut the engine off. Remove the jumper wires. Unplug and reconnect all vacuum lines to their components. Reconnect the carburetor wires on 2.2 liter engines. Reconnect the oxygen system test connector on 1983 engines. Reinstall the PCV valve. Remove the tachomter.

Idle Mixture Adjustment (1981-on)

The idle mixture adjusting screw is sealed in accordance with Federal regulations. If an idle mixture adjustment is required, take the car to a dealer or qualified specialist.

Oxygen Sensor Service

At 15,000 mile (1979) or 30,000 mile (1980) intervals, a warning lamp in the instrument panel lights to indicate that the oxygen sensor should be replaced. Sensor replacement is not required on 1981 and later models unless it is defective.

To reset the mileage counter and turn off the warning lamp, locate the mileage counter module box under the instrument panel just above the steering column. Open this box and remove and discard the 9 volt battery inside. This battery provides a memory function for the mileage counter whenever the vehicle battery is disconnected.

Under the 9 volt battery, there is a small hole in the case. Insert the end of a bent paper clip or similar instrument and depress the reset switch. Install a new 9 volt battery and close the module box.

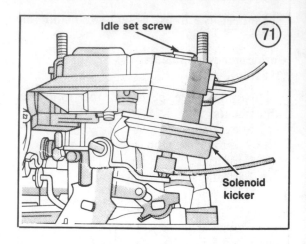

Idle set screw

Solenoid kicker

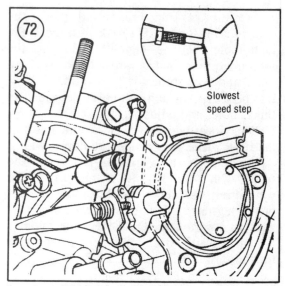

Slowest speed step

Oxygen Sensor Replacement

Remove the sensor when the engine is warm (approximately 120° F) to prevent damage to the exhaust manifold threads. New sensors have an anti-seize compound coating on their threads. If the old sensor is reinstalled for any reason, coat its threads with an electrically conductive anti-seize compound.

1. Disconnect the negative battery cable.
2. Disconnect the oxygen sensor lead.
3. Remove the oxygen sensor with an appropriate size wrench.
4. Install a new sensor and tighten to 30 ft.-lb. (41 N•m).
5. Connect the oxygen sensor lead.
6. Reconnect the negative battery cable.

Table 1   RECOMMENDED MAINTENANCE—ALL SCHEDULES FOR 1978 MODELS

Every Oil Change
- Check power steering fluid level and replenish as required.
- Check brake hoses and repair or replace as required.
- Lubricate door hinges, latches, etc.

Every 6 months
- Inspect fluid level in brake master cylinder and replenish as required.
- Inspect fluid level in transmission and replenish as required.
- Inspect front suspension, steering linkage, and universal joints and repair or replace components as required.
- Check air conditioning belt, sight glass, and operation of controls. Repair or replace as required.

Every 7,500 miles
- Inspect and rotate tires.
- Apply solvent to carburetor choke shaft.
- Check drive belt tension and adjust as required.
- Change engine oil (change oil filter at first 7,500 miles and every second oil change thereafter).
- Apply solvent to fast idle cam and pivot pin.

Every 15,000 miles
- Check automatic choke and adjust as required (Schedule F).
- Check cooling system and service as required (Schedule F).
- Replace fuel filter (replace at first 7,500 miles and every 15,000 miles thereafter).
- Check idle speed and air/fuel mixture (Schedule F).
- Check ignition timing and adjust (Schedule F).
- Check PCV valve and replace if required (Schedule F).
- Replace spark plugs.
- Check valve lash and adjust if required (Schedule F).
- Inspect emission control rubber and plastic hoses in engine compartment (Schedule F).
- Inspect brake linings and replace if required.

Every 22,500 miles (Schedule G)
- Check automatic choke and adjust as required.
- Check cooling system and service as required.
- Check idle speed and air/fuel mixture and adjust as required.
- Check ignition timing and adjust as required.
- Check PCV valve and replace if necessary.
- Replace spark plugs (on cars with catalytic converters). Check spark plug cables and replace if required.
- Check valve lash and adjust if required.
- Inspect emission control rubber and plastic hoses in engine compartment and repair or replace as required.

Every 30,000 miles or 3 years
- Lubricate steering linkage tie rod ends.
- Inspect and lubricate rear wheel bearings.
- Replace carburetor air filter.
- Drain, flush, and refill radiator.
- Replace PCV valve (Schedule F).

Every 45,000 miles
- Replace PCV valve (Schedule G).

Table 2 RECOMMENDED MAINTENANCE (1979)

Every 6 months	•Apply solvent to carburetor choke shaft. •Apply solvent to fast idle cam and pivot pin. •Adjust clutch pedal free play.

Every 7,500 miles	•Replace fuel filter.
	•Check drive belt condition and tension.
	  Replace belts as required.
	•Change engine oil (change oil filter at
	  first 7,500 miles and every second oil change thereafter).

Every 15,000 miles	•Check and adjust automatic choke. •Check and adjust idle speed and air/fuel mixture. •Check ignition timing and adjust if required. •Replace spark plugs. •Check condition of spark plug wires. Replace as required. •Check valve lash and adjust if required. •Check PCV valve and replace if required. •Inspect front brakes.

Every 30,000 miles	•Replace air filter.
	•Replace PCV valve.
	•Inspect rear brakes.
	•Flush and replace cooling system fluid at
	  first 30,000 miles or 24 months (thereafter drain, flush and
	  refill every 12 months).
	•Inspect rear wheel bearings.
	•Lubricate steering linkage tie rod ends.

SEVERE SERVICE MAINTENANCE[1]	
Every 3,000 miles	•Change engine oil (change oil filter at first 3,000 miles and every second oil change thereafter).
Every 9,000 miles	•Inspect and lubricate rear wheel bearings.
Every 15,000 miles	•Lubricate steering linkage tie rod ends. •Change automatic transmission fluid.

1. See Chapter Three introduction on severe service maintenance.

Table 3 RECOMMENDED MAINTENANCE (1980-1982)

Every 7,500 miles	•Change engine oil (change oil filter at first 7,500 miles, then every second oil change thereafter). •Check clutch pedal free play and adjust if required.
Every 15,000 miles	•Check drive belt condition and tension. Replace as required. •Replace spark plugs (vehicles without catalytic converter). •Check valve lash and adjust as required. •Check cooling system and service as required. •Inspect front brake linings.
Every 30,000 miles	•Apply solvent to carburetor choke shaft. •Replace air filter. •Apply solvent to fast idle cam and pivot pin. •Replace oxygen sensor and E.M.R. battery (if equipped). Reset mileage counter. •Replace spark plugs (vehicles with catalytic converter). •Inspect rear brake linings and adjust as required. •Inspect rear wheel bearings. •Lubricate tie rod ends.
SEVERE SERVICE MAINTENANCE[1]	
Every 3,000 miles	•Change engine oil (change oil filter at first 3,000 miles and every second oil change thereafter). •Inspect universal joints.
Every 6,000 miles	•Inspect front brake pads. Replace as required.
Every 12,000 miles	•Inspect rear brake linings. Replace as required. •Inspect and relubricate rear wheel bearings.
Every 15,000 miles	•Change automatic fluid and filter. •Lubricate tie rod ends.

1. See Chapter Three introduction on severe service maintenance.

3

Table 4 RECOMMENDED MAINTENANCE (1983)

Every 7,500 miles	• Change engine oil (change oil filter @ first service then @ every other service) • Check clutch pedal free play and adjust if required (1.7 liter engine) • Check brake hoses
Every 12 months	• Inspect and service cooling system as required
Every 15,000 miles	• Check drive belt condition and tension; replace as required • Replace spark plugs (vehicles without catalytic converter) • Check and adjust valve lash as required
Every 22,500 miles	• Inspect front and rear brake linings; service as required • Inspect rear wheel bearings
Every 30,000 miles	• Apply solvent to carburetor choke shaft • Apply solvent to fast idle cam and pivot pin • Replace spark plugs (vehicles with catalytic converters) • Lubricate ball-joints and steering linkage
Every 52,500 miles	• Replace air cleaner filter • Clean and relubricate crankcase vent module (2.2 liter engine)
First 52,500 miles or 36 months, then @ 30,000 miles or 24 month intervals	• Drain, flush and refill cooling system
SEVERE SERVICE MAINTENANCE*	
Every 3,000 miles	• Change engine oil (change oil filter @ first service and every other service thereafter) • Inspect universal joints and front suspension ball-joints
Every 9,000 miles	• Inspect front brake pads and rear brake linings; replace as required • Inspect and lubricate rear wheel bearings
Every 15,000 miles	• Change automatic transaxle fluid and filter • Lubricate ball-joints and steering linkage

* See Chapter Three introduction on severe service maintenance.

Table 5 RECOMMENDED LUBRICANTS AND FUEL

Application	Temperature Range (° F)	Recommended Type
Engine oil	+32° to above +100° F	20W-40 Service SF 20W-50 Service SF 30W Service SF
	-10° to above +100° F	10W-30 Service SF 10W-40 Service SF 10W-50 Service SF
	-10° to +32° F	10W Service SF
	Below -20° to +32° F	5W-40 Service SF
	Consistently below -10° F	5W-20 Service SF*

(continued)

Table 5 RECOMMENDED LUBRICANTS AND FUEL (continued)

A-412 manual transaxle	Consistently above -10° F	SAE 90W, SAE 80W-90, SAE 85W-90
	As low as -30° F	SAE 80W, SAE 80W-90, SAE 85W-90
	Below -30° F	SAE 75W
A-460 and A-465 manual transaxle	All temperatures	DEXRON II
Automatic transaxle	All temperatures	DEXRON II
Automatic differential	All temperatures	DEXRON II
Power steering	All temperatures	MOPAR power steering fluid.
Fuel	All temperatures	91 octane regular unleaded.

* 5W-20 is not recommended for sustained high-speed operation.

Table 6 APPROXIMATE REFILL CAPACITIES

Application	Capacity*
Engine oil	
1.6 liter	3.5 qt. (3.3 liters)
1.7 and 2.2 liter	4 qt. (3.8 liters)
Manual transaxle	
A-412	1.5 qt. (1.4 liters)
A-460	2.0 qt. (1.8 liters)
A-465	2.3 qt. (2.1 liters)
Automatic transaxle	
1.6 liter	4.0 qt. (3.8 liters)
1.7 and 2.2 liter	2.5 qt. (2.4 liters)
Automatic differential	1.2 qt. (1.1 liters)
Cooling system	
1.6 liter	7.0 qt. (6.6 liters)
1.7 liter	6.0 qt. (5.7 liters)
2.2 liter	
1981-1982	7.0 qt. (6.6 liters)
1983	9.0 qt. (8.5 liters)

* When refilling to approximate capacities, always make final check by observing dipstick or fluid level measurements.

Table 7 DRIVE BELT TENSION SPECIFICATIONS (1978-1980)

	New (ft.-lb)	Used (ft.-lb.)
Tension method (all belts)	120	70
Torque method		
Air conditioning	55	40
Air pump	65	45
Alternator*	70	50
Power steering pump	40	25
*See text on 1980 models.		

Table 8 DRIVE BELT TENSION SPECIFICATIONS (1981-ON)

Tension Method		
	New (ft.-lb.)	Used (ft.-lb.)
Air conditioning		
1.7 liter	90	45
2.2 liter	40	30
Air pump		
2.2 liter	45	35
Air pump/water pump		
1.7 liter	70	40
Alternator/water pump		
1.7 liter	65	40
2.2 liter	110	80
Power steering pump		
1.7 liter	80	50
2.2 liter	75	55
Belt Deflection		
	New	Used
Air conditioning	5/16 in.	3/8 in.
Air pump		
1.6 liter	7/32 in.	5/16 in.
2.2 liter	13/64 in.	1/4 in.
Air pump/water pump		
1.7 liter	3/16 in.	13/64 in.
Alternator/water pump		
1.6 liter	3/16 in.	1/4 in.
2.2 liter	1/8 in.	1/4 in.
Power steering pump		
1.6 liter	3/8 in.	7/16 in.
1.7 and 2.2 liter	1/4 in.	5/16 in.

Table 9 TUNE-UP SPECIFICATIONS

Valve clearance	
1.6 liter*	
Intake	0.010 in. (0.25 mm)
Exhaust	0.012 in. (0.30 mm)
1.7 liter**	
Intake	0.012 in. (0.30 mm)
Exhaust	0.020 in. (0.50 mm)
Ignition timing	
1978-1979	15° BTDC
1980	
1.7 liter	
49-state	12° BTDC
California	10° BTDC
1981	
1.7 liter	
Manual	12° BTDC
Automatic	10° BTDC
2.2 liter	10° BTDC
1982-on	
1.7 liter	
Manual	20° BTDC
Automatic	12° BTDC
1.6/2.2 liter	12° BTDC
Spark plugs	
Type	
1978-1980	Champion RN12Y
1981	
1.7 liter	Mopar 65PR4
2.2 liter	Mopar 65PR
1982-on	Mopar 65PR
Gap	
1978-1980	0.035 in. (0.9 mm)
1981	
1.7 liter	0.048 in. (1.22 mm)
2.2 liter	0.035 in. (0.9 mm)
1982-on	0.035 in. (0.9 mm)
Firing order	1-3-4-2 (No. 1 @ pulley end of 1.7 and 2.2 L; @ flywheel end of 1.6 L)
Idle speed	See Vehicle Emission Control Information label

* Clearance must be set on a cold engine.
** These specifications are for a warm engine. Subtract 0.002 in. (0.05 mm) for cold engine.

3

Table 10 VALVE ADJUSTING DISCS (1.7 LITER)

Thickness (mm)	Part Number	Thickness (mm)	Part Number
3.00	5240946	3.65	5240580
3.05	5240945	3.70	5240581
3.10	5240944	3.75	5240582
3.15	5240943	3.80	5240583
3.20	5240942	3.85	5240584
3.25	5240941	3.90	5240585
3.30	5240573	3.95	5240586
3.35	5240574	4.00	5240587
3.40	5240575	4.05	5240588
3.45	5240576	4.10	5240589
3.50	5240577	4.15	5240590
3.55	5240578	4.20	5240591
3.60	5240579	4.25	5240592

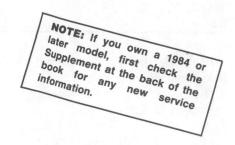

NOTE: If you own a 1984 or later model, first check the Supplement at the back of the book for any new service information.

CHAPTER FOUR

OVERHEAD CAM ENGINES

4

The vehicles covered in this manual are available with a 1.7 or 2.2 liter displacement 4-cylinder engine. Both engines are water-cooled, single overhead camshaft designs with a cast iron cylinder block and aluminum cylinder head. Five main bearings support the cast iron crankshaft. Diecast aluminum housings with hydrodynamic seals are attached to the front and rear of the block for crankshaft oil sealing. A toothed rubber timing belt drives the single camshaft. The timing belt also drives an intermediate shaft which in turn drives the fuel pump, oil pump and distributor. **Table 1** and **Table 2** provide engine specifications. **Table 3** and **Table 4** provide torque specifications. **Tables 1-6** are at the end of the chapter.

SERVICE NOTES

On an inline-mounted engine, the timing gear end of the engine is the front and the flywheel end is the rear, since these ends face that way in the car. Transverse mounting of the engine makes these terms misleading. However, since most mechanics are used to inline terminology, it is used throughout this chapter. "Front" means the timing gear end and "rear" means the flywheel end.

GASKET SEALANT

Gasket sealant is used instead of pre-formed gaskets between numerous mating surfaces on the 2.2 liter engine. See *Gasket Sealant*, Chapter Five, for a description of its use.

ENGINE REMOVAL/INSTALLATION

NOTE
When disconnecting and/or removing wires, hoses, and tubes during the removal procedure, be sure to identify them for easy replacement. A good way to do this is to obtain some small cardboard tags, available at stationery stores, and to tag each side of a connector with identical numbers. Use a permanent-type marker, as the tags may be subjected to oil, grease, etc.

Engine With Manual Transmission

NOTE
The 1.7 liter engine/transaxle must be removed as a unit.

1. Scribe alignment marks directly onto the underside of the hood around the hood hinges then remove the hood.
2. Disconnect negative cable from battery.
3. Drain the engine coolant and engine oil. Remove the oil filter. See Chapter Three.
4. Disconnect the upper and lower radiator hoses at the radiator and the engine, then remove the hoses.

5. Remove the radiator shroud as described in Chapter Seven.

6. Remove the air cleaner assembly as described in Chapter Six.

7. On models equipped with air conditioning, remove the compressor from its mounting brackets and set to one side. See **Figure 1** (1.7 liter) or **Figure 2** (2.2 liter).

WARNING
Never disconnect refrigerant lines. The refrigerant creates freezing temperatures when it evaporates and poisonous gases if discharged near an open flame. If it becomes necessary to disconnect the refrigerant lines, refer the job to a dealer or an air conditioning specialist.

8. On models equipped with power steering, remove the power steering pump from its bracket and remove the drive belt from the pump. Position the power steering pump out of the way. See **Figure 3**.

9. Disconnect electrical connections at the points indicated in **Figure 4** (1.7 liter) or **Figure 5** (2.2 liter).

10. Remove the fuel line, heater hose and accelerator cable connections at points shown in **Figure 6** (1.7 liter) or **Figure 7** (2.2 liter).

11. Remove the alternator and its drive belt as described in Chapter Eight.

12. On the 1.7 liter engine, disconnect the speedometer cable and clutch cable connections shown in **Figure 8**.

13. On the 2.2 liter engine, remove the clutch arm clip from grooves in arm, and pull clutch cable upward and remove (**Figure 9**).

14. Remove starter. See Chapter Eight.

15. Detach exhaust pipe from manifold and remove exhaust pipe support. Remove air pump, bolt and hoses, if so equipped.

NOTE
Steps 16-21 are engine removal steps for the 1.7 liter engine only. Steps 22-27 are for 2.2 liter engine removal only.

16. Raise vehicle and remove drive shafts from transmission and hang them up with wire. See **Figure 10**. See Chapter Eleven.

17. Remove transaxle ground strap between transaxle and body.

18. Remove gearshift linkage from relay lever and short rod at transaxle (**Figure 11**). Lower vehicle.

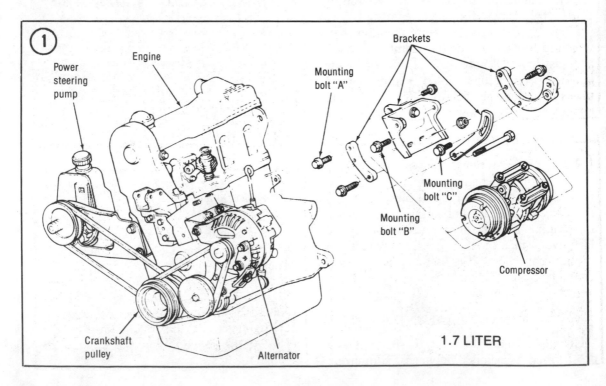

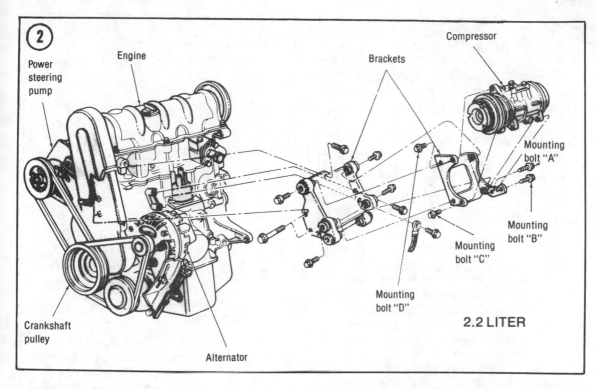

② Power steering pump · Engine · Brackets · Compressor

Mounting bolt "A"

Mounting bolt "B"

Mounting bolt "C"

Mounting bolt "D"

Crankshaft pulley

Alternator

2.2 LITER

4

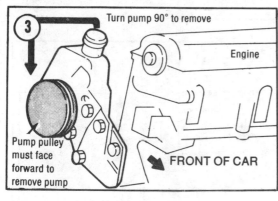

③ Turn pump 90° to remove

Engine

Pump pulley must face forward to remove pump

FRONT OF CAR

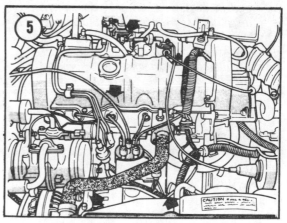

⑤

④

⑥

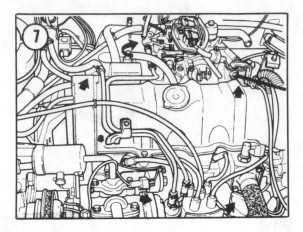

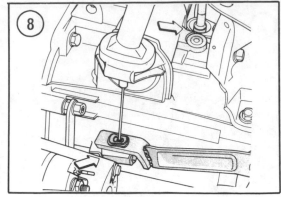

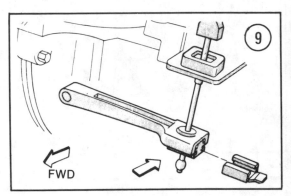

> *WARNING*
> *The engine is very heavy and awkward to handle. It may swing, turn or drop suddenly during removal. Never place any part of your body where a moving engine might trap or crush it. If you have to reposition the engine during removal, push it with a board or similar tool. If the engine is hard to lift, stop and make sure it has been **completely** disconnected from the car. Make sure the engine has not jammed. If necessary, lower the engine back to the mounts and start the lifting process over. Do not try to force the engine loose with the hoist.*

19. Connect chain hoist to engine as shown in **Figure 12**. Lift engine/transaxle just enough so that the hoist bears their weight.

20. Remove front engine mounting bolt (**Figure 13**).

21. Remove right engine mounting bolt (**Figure 14**) and left engine mounting bolt (**Figure 15**).

> *NOTE*
> *Steps 22-27 describe removal of the 2.2 liter engine.*

22. Remove the right inner splash shield (**Figure 16**).

23. Support transaxle with a jack (**Figure 17**). Attach a chain hoist to engine lifting brackets as shown in **Figure 18**. Lift engine/transaxle just enough so the hoist bears their weight.

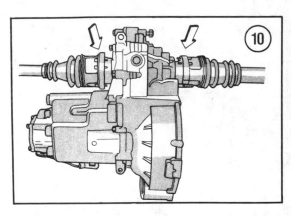

24. Remove the transaxle-to-engine ground strap.

25. Remove the right engine mount screw (A, **Figure 19**).

26. Remove all transaxle housing-to-engine mounting screws.

27. Remove the front engine mount screw and nut (**Figure 20**).

> *NOTE*
> *Steps 28-30 complete engine removal for all engines.*

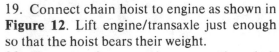

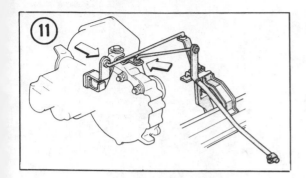

(11)

(12)

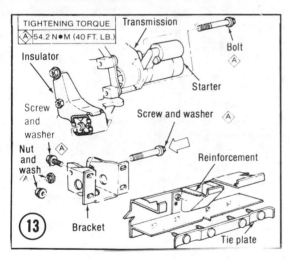

TIGHTENING TORQUE
Ⓐ 54.2 N•M (40 FT. LB.)

Transmission

Insulator

Bolt
Ⓐ

Starter

Screw
and
washer

Screw and washer Ⓐ

Nut
and
wash
Ⓐ

Reinforcement

(13) Bracket

Tie plate

NOTE
Recheck at this point to make sure nothing will hamper engine removal and that all accessories, tubes, hoses and wires are positioned out of the way.

28. Carefully lift engine/transaxle assembly (engine only on 2.2 liter) out of the body.
29. Once the engine is clear of the car, lower it to a suitable support or stand. Secure the engine in the support or stand.

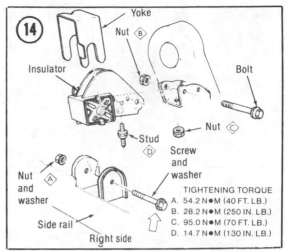

(14)

Yoke

Nut Ⓑ

Insulator

Bolt

Nut Ⓒ

Stud Ⓓ

Screw
and
washer

Nut Ⓐ
and
washer

Side rail

Right side

TIGHTENING TORQUE
A. 54.2 N•M (40 FT. LB.)
B. 28.2 N•M (250 IN. LB.)
C. 95.0 N•M (70 FT. LB.)
D. 14.7 N•M (130 IN. LB.)

4

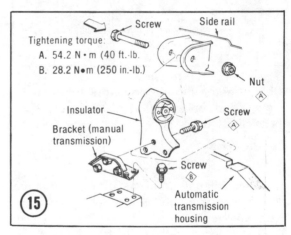

Screw Side rail

Tightening torque:
A. 54.2 N•m (40 ft.-lb.
B. 28.2 N•m (250 in.-lb.)

Nut
Ⓐ

Insulator

Screw
Ⓐ

Bracket (manual transmission)

Screw
Ⓑ

(15) Automatic transmission housing

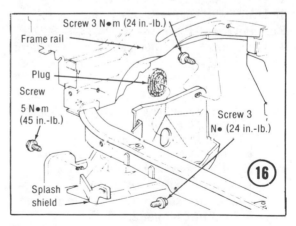

Screw 3 N•m (24 in.-lb.)

Frame rail

Plug

Screw
5 N•m
(45 in.-lb.)

Screw 3
N• (24 in.-lb.)

Splash
shield

(16)

NOTE
*Separate 1.7 liter engine from transaxle as described in this chapter under **Separating Engine/Manual Transaxle (1.7 Liter).***

30. Engine removal is now complete. Inspect

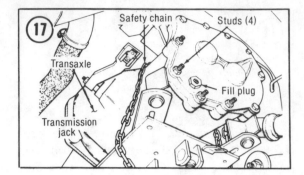

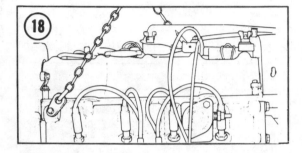

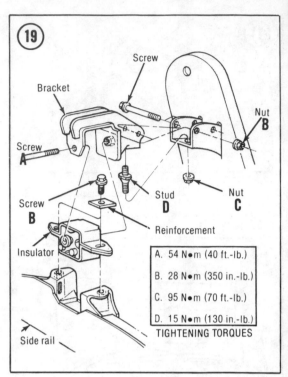

A. 54 N•m (40 ft.-lb.)

B. 28 N•m (350 in.-lb.)

C. 95 N•m (70 ft.-lb.)

D. 15 N•m (130 in.-lb.)

TIGHTENING TORQUES

rubber motor mount insulators for wear or damage and replace before installing engine if these conditions exist.

Engine With Automatic Transmission

1. Scribe alignment marks directly onto the underside of the hood around the hood hinges then remove the hood.
2. Disconnect negative cable from battery.
3. Drain the engine coolant and engine oil. Remove the oil filter.
4. Disconnect the upper and lower radiator hoses at the radiator and the engine, then remove the hoses.

> *NOTE*
> *Disconnect the transmission oil cooler inlet and outlet lines from the bottom of the radiator. The hose sections are secured with small diameter clamps. Plug all lines and fittings to prevent loss of transmission fluid and contamination of lines.*

5. Remove the radiator shroud and radiator as described in Chapter Seven.
6. Remove the air cleaner assembly as described in Chapter Six.
7. On models equipped with air conditioning, remove the compressor from its mounting brackets and set to one side. See **Figure 1** (1.7 liter) or **Figure 2** (2.2 liter).

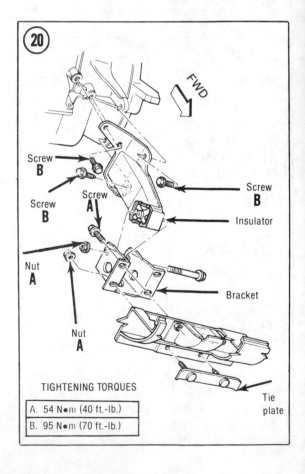

TIGHTENING TORQUES

A. 54 N•m (40 ft.-lb.)

B. 95 N•m (70 ft.-lb.)

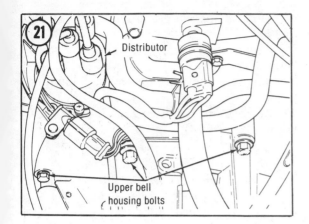

(21)

Distributor

Upper bell
housing bolts

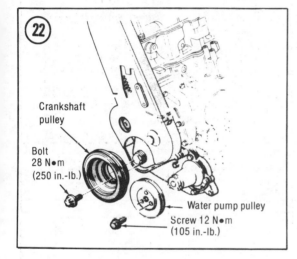

(22)

Crankshaft
pulley

Bolt
28 N•m
(250 in.-lb.)

Water pump pulley

Screw 12 N•m
(105 in.-lb.)

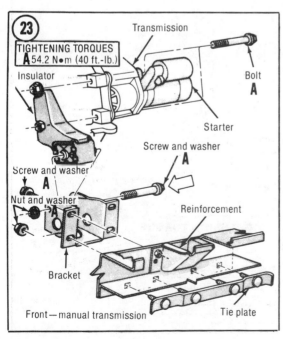

(23)

Transmission

TIGHTENING TORQUES
A 54.2 N•m (40 ft.-lb.)

Insulator

Bolt
A

Starter

Screw and washer
A

Screw and washer
A

Nut and washer
A

Reinforcement

Bracket

Front—manual transmission

Tie plate

WARNING
Never disconnect refrigerant lines. The refrigerant creates freezing temperatures when it evaporates and poisonous gases if discharged near an open flame. If it becomes necessary to disconnect the refrigerant lines, refer the job to a dealer or an air conditioning specialist.

8. On models equipped with power steering, remove the power steering pump from its bracket and remove the drive belt from the pump. Position the power steering pump out of the way. See **Figure 3**.

9. Disconnect electrical wiring at the alternator, carburetor and engine as shown in **Figure 4** (1.7 liter) or **Figure 5** (2.2 liter).

10. Remove the alternator drive belt and alternator. See Chapter Eight.

11. Detach exhaust pipe from manifold.

12. Disconnect and remove starter. See Chapter Eight.

13. Disconnect fuel line from fuel pump.

NOTE
Steps 14-22 describe removal steps unique to the 1.7 liter engine.

14. Remove the upper bell housing-to-engine bolts. See **Figure 21**.

15. Raise vehicle front end and secure with jackstands. Remove both the left and right wheel assemblies. Then remove bolts securing the left and right side splash shields and both splash shields.

NOTE
If a vehicle hoist was used to raise the front end in Step 15, it is not necessary to reinstall front wheels. However, if jackstands are being used, it is necessary at this time to reinstall wheels, remove jackstands and lower vehicle to ground.

16. Support transaxle with a jack.

17. Remove the water pump pulley and crankshaft pulley (**Figure 22**).

18. Attach chain hoist to engine as shown in **Figure 12**. Lift engine just enough so that hoist bears engine weight.

19. Remove the front engine mounting bolt (**Figure 23**).

20. Remove the inspection cover from transaxle. Remove the flex plate bolts.

21. Remove remaining lower bell housing bolts.

22. Remove the right side engine mount and bolt. See **Figure 24** (1978-1980) or **Figure 25** (1981-on).

NOTE
Steps 23-30 describe engine removal procedures unique to the 2.2 liter engine.

23. Remove the transmission case lower cover.

24. Scribe alignment marks on the flex plate-to-torque converter. Then remove screws securing torque converter to flex plate. Attach a C-clamp onto the front bottom of the torque converter housing. This prevents torque converter from coming out.

25. Support the transaxle with a jack. Attach an engine lifting sling to the engine lifting brackets as shown in **Figure 18**. Attach engine sling to a suitable hoist and take up all slack. Make sure the weight of engine is balanced on the sling. Also make sure that you have enough overhead clearance to lift the engine free of the vehicle.

26. Remove the right inner splash shield (**Figure 16**).

27. Remove the engine ground strap at the transaxle.

28. Remove the right engine mount screw (**Figure 19**).

29. Remove transaxle to engine mounting screws.

30. Remove the front engine mount screw and nut (**Figure 20**).

NOTE
Recheck at this point to make sure nothing will hamper engine removal and that all accessories, tubes, hoses and wires are positioned out of the way.

NOTE
Steps 31-33 complete removal for all engines.

31. Carefully lift engine from vehicle.

32. Once the engine is clear of the car, lower it to a suitable support or stand. Secure the engine in the support or stand.

33. Engine removal is now complete. Inspect rubber motor mount insulators for wear or damage and replace before installing engine if these conditions exist.

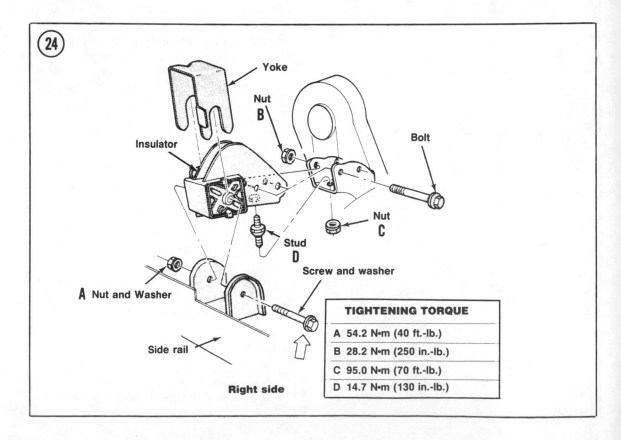

(24)

Yoke

Nut
B

Bolt

Insulator

Nut
C

Stud
D

Screw and washer

A Nut and Washer

Side rail

Right side

TIGHTENING TORQUE		
A	54.2 N•m	(40 ft.-lb.)
B	28.2 N•m	(250 in.-lb.)
C	95.0 N•m	(70 ft.-lb.)
D	14.7 N•m	(130 in.-lb.)

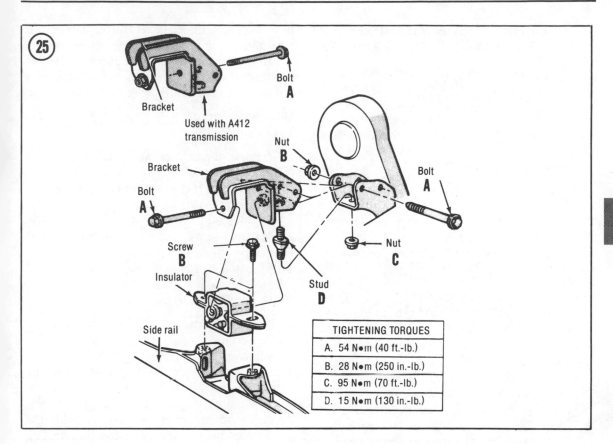

25

Bracket

Bolt
A

Used with A412
transmission

Nut
B

Bracket

Bolt
A

Bolt
A

Screw
B

Insulator

Stud
D

Nut
C

Side rail

TIGHTENING TORQUES	
A. 54 N•m (40 ft.-lb.)	
B. 28 N•m (250 in.-lb.)	
C. 95 N•m (70 ft.-lb.)	
D. 15 N•m (130 in.-lb.)	

4

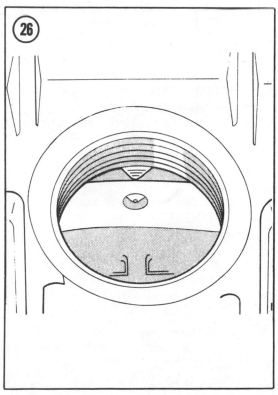

26

SEPARATING ENGINE/MANUAL TRANSAXLE (1.7 LITER)

The engine and manual transaxle on the 1.7 liter vehicles are removed as a unit. Perform the following procedures to separate the engine-to-transaxle unit.

1. Rotate crankshaft with a socket wrench on the pulley nut until the mark shown in **Figure 26** aligns with the transaxle mark.

2. Remove bolts securing engine to transaxle and remove the transaxle cover plate.

3. Pull the transaxle straight away from the engine until the transaxle drive shaft and the clutch pushrod clear the clutch and flywheel.

CAUTION
Do not let the engine tilt or let engine weight put any load on the transaxle drive shaft or clutch pushrod. The drive shaft, pushrod or other clutch parts could be seriously damaged.

JOINING ENGINE/MANUAL
TRANSAXLE (1.7 LITER)

Joining the engine and manual transaxle is the reverse of the separation procedure. Keep these points in mind when joining the two:

    a. Before joining them, rotate the crankshaft so that the flywheel recess is adjacent to the drive shaft flange as shown in **Figure 27**.

    b. Lubricate the drive shaft spline and the end of the clutch pushrod (protruding from the transaxle drive shaft) with multipurpose grease.

    c. Torque bolts which join engine to transaxle to 40 ft.-lb. (5.5 mkg).

ENGINE INSTALLATION

1. To install the engine assemblies, reverse the removal steps noting the following precautions:

    a. Check the wiring harness for damage and correct or replace as necessary.

    b. Check the engine mounts for looseness or damage and tighten or replace as necessary.

2. On 1.7 liter engine with manual transmission, join the engine/transaxle units before installing in vehicle. See *Joining Engine/Manual Transaxle (1.7 Liter)* in this chapter.

3. Refill the engine cooling system; see Chapter Seven.

4. Fill the engine crankcase with engine oil; refer to Chapter Three.

5. Start the engine and let it run at idle; check for fluid leakage.

6. Adjust the following by referring to the appropriate sections in Chapter Three:

    a. Drive belt tensions

    b. Ignition timing

    c. Engine idle

OVERHAUL SEQUENCE

The following sequences are basic outlines that tell how much of the engine needs to be removed and disassembled to perform specific types of service. The sequences are designed to keep engine disassembly to a minimum,

thus avoiding unnecessary work. The major assemblies mentioned in these sequences are covered in detail under their own individual headings within this chapter, unless otherwise noted.

Decarbonizing or
Valve Service

1. Remove the exhaust and intake manifolds (Chapter Six).
2. Remove the rocker arms and camshaft.
3. Remove the cylinder head.
4. Remove and inspect valves. Inspect valve guides and seats, repairing or replacing as necessary.
5. Assemble by reversing Steps 1-4.

Valve and Ring Service

1. Perform Steps 1-4 of Decarbonizing or Valve Service.
2. Remove the oil pan.
3. Remove the pistons together with the connecting rods.
4. Remove the poston rings. It is not necessary to separate the pistons from the connecting rods unless a piston, connecting rod or piston pin needs repair or replacement.
5. Assemble by reversing Steps 1-4.

General Overhaul

1. Remove the engine from the car as described in this chapter.
2. Remove the motor mounts.
3. Remove the fuel pump, carburetor, and intake and exhaust manifolds (Chapter Five).
4. Remove the camshaft timing belt.
5. Remove the water pump and thermostat (Chapter Seven).
6. Remove the distributor and alternator (Chapter Eight).
7. Remove the intermediate shaft.
8. Remove the camshaft.
9. On 1.7 liter engines, remove the valve tappets.
10. Remove the cylinder head.
11. Remove the oil pan.
12. Remove the oil pump.
13. Remove the pistons together with connecting rods.
14. Remove the flywheel.

15. Remove the crankshaft and main bearings.

16. Inspect the cylinder block.

17. Assemble by reversing Steps 1-15.

CAMSHAFT TIMING BELT
(1.7 LITER)

Removal

Refer to **Figure 28** for this procedure.

1. Disconnect negative battery terminal.

2. On models equipped with air conditioning, remove the compressor from its mounting brackets and set to one side. See **Figure 1**.

4

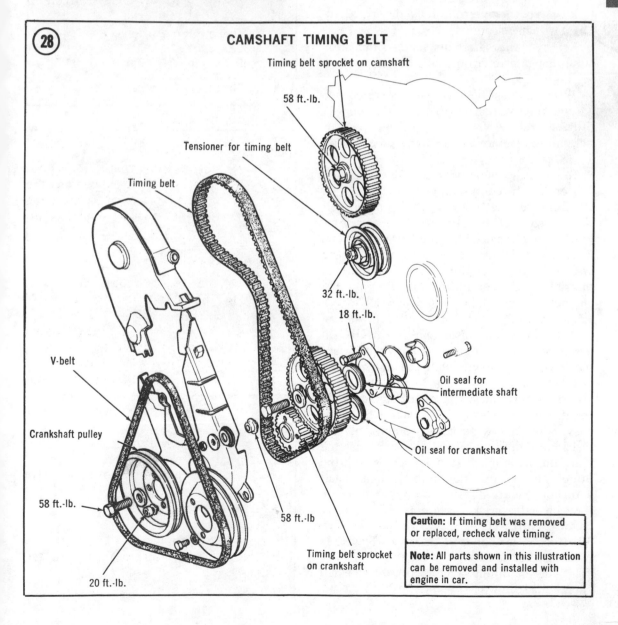

CAMSHAFT TIMING BELT

Timing belt sprocket on camshaft

58 ft.-lb.

Tensioner for timing belt

Timing belt

32 ft.-lb.

18 ft.-lb.

Oil seal for intermediate shaft

V-belt

Crankshaft pulley

Oil seal for crankshaft

58 ft.-lb.

58 ft.-lb

Timing belt sprocket on crankshaft

20 ft.-lb.

Caution: If timing belt was removed or replaced, recheck valve timing.

Note: All parts shown in this illustration can be removed and installed with engine in car.

WARNING
Never disconnect refrigerant lines. The refrigerant creates freezing temperatures when it evaporates and poisonous gases if discharged near an open flame. If it becomes necessary to disconnect the refrigerant lines, refer the job to a dealer or an air conditioning specialist.

3. On models equipped with power steering, remove the power steering pump from its bracket and remove the drive belt from the pump. Position the power steering pump out of the way. See **Figure 3**.

4. Remove the alternator as described in Chapter Eight.

5. Remove the alternator and compressor mounting bracket from the retainer bracket. See **Figure 29**.

6. With accessory components removed, remove all drive belts.

7. Raise vehicle front end and secure with jackstands. Remove the right side splash fender shield.

8. Remove the idler pulley assembly.

9. Remove the crankshaft pulley.

10. Remove the lower plastic timing belt cover (**Figure 28**).

11. Remove jackstands and lower vehicle. Place a jack underneath the engine. Raise engine slightly to remove engine weight from the right engine mounting bolt. Remove the engine mounting bolt.

12. Turn the crankshaft sprocket with a socket wrench until piston No. 1 is at TDC on its compression stroke. This is evident when the TDC mark aligns with the mark in the transmission case opening. At the same time, scribe the position of the distributor rotor on the distributor body and the engine block for easy alignment during assembly of the distributor housing. Finally, ensure that the mark on the crankshaft pulley aligns with the punch mark on the intermediate shaft sprocket (**Figure 30**) and the punch mark on the camshaft sprocket is in line with the valve cover (**Figure 31**).

13. Loosen tensioner as shown in **Figure 32** to release belt tension.

14. Slide the timing belt forward, off camshaft sprocket, as shown in **Figure 33**.

Installation

1. Make certain that punch mark on camshaft sprocket aligns with valve cover (**Figure 31**) and that the intermediate shaft sprocket punch mark aligns with the crankshaft pulley mark (**Figure 30**).

CAUTION
Very accurate alignment of these marks is necessary as this sets the basic valve

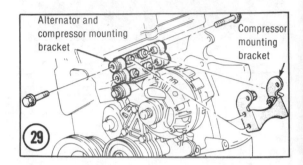

Alternator and compressor mounting bracket

Compressor mounting bracket

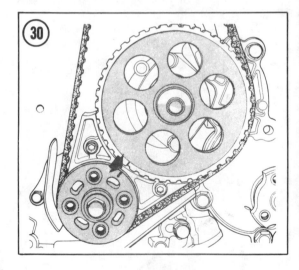

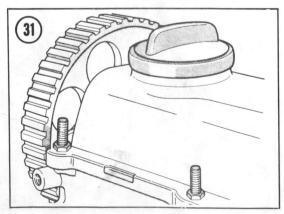

timing of the engine. Failure to align these marks can result in a very poor running engine.

2. Install new timing belt under intermediate shaft sprocket and crankshaft sprocket, then slide it over the top of the crankshaft sprocket.

CAUTION
Be absolutely certain that the sprockets do not move while sliding the belt into place. If necessary, reposition the sprockets as described in Step 1 of this procedure, then reinstall the belt.

3. Turn the belt tensioner until it is just possible to twist the belt about 90° with your thumb and index finger at a point midway between the camshaft and intermediate shaft sprockets. See **Figure 32**. Hold the tensioner in this position and tighten locknut.

4. Reverse Steps 1-10 of *Removal* to complete installation. Start engine and check operation. If a whirring noise is heard at the timing belt, the belt is too tight.

CAMSHAFT TIMING BELT (2.2 LITER)

Removal

Refer to **Figure 34** for this procedure.
1. Disconnect negative battery terminal.
2. On models equipped with air conditioning, remove the compressor from its mounting brackets and set to one side. See **Figure 2**.

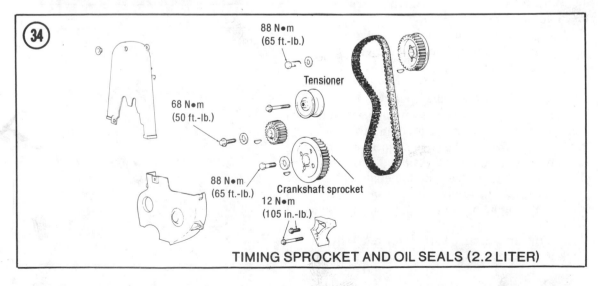

TIMING SPROCKET AND OIL SEALS (2.2 LITER)

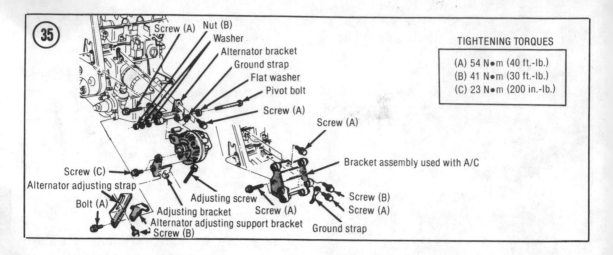

TIGHTENING TORQUES

(A) 54 N•m (40 ft.-lb.)
(B) 41 N•m (30 ft.-lb.)
(C) 23 N•m (200 in.-lb.)

WARNING
Never disconnect refrigerant lines. The refrigerant creates freezing temperatures when it evaporates and poisonous gases if discharged near an open flame. If it becomes necessary to disconnect the refrigerant lines, refer the job to a dealer or an air conditioning specialist.

3. On models equipped with power steering, remove the power steering pump from its bracket and remove the drive belt from the pump. Position the power steering pump out of the way. See **Figure 3**.

4. Remove the alternator as described in Chapter Eight.

5. Remove the alternator and compressor mounting bracket from the retainer bracket. See **Figure 35**.

6. With accessory components removed, remove all drive belts.

7. Raise vehicle front end and secure with jackstands. Remove the front right inner splash shield.

8. Referring to **Figure 22**, remove both the water pump and crankshaft pulleys.

9. Remove bolts securing the upper timing belt cover to the cylinder head and the lower timing belt cover to the engine block. Remove both timing belt cover halves. See **Figure 36**.

10. Place a jack underneath the engine. Raise engine slightly to remove engine weight from the right engine mounting bolt and remove bolt.

11. Turn the crankshaft sprocket with a socket wrench until piston No. 1 is at TDC on

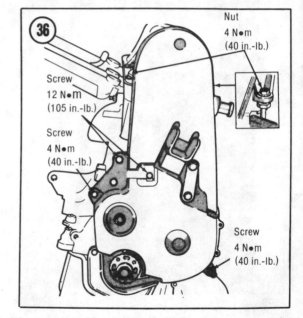

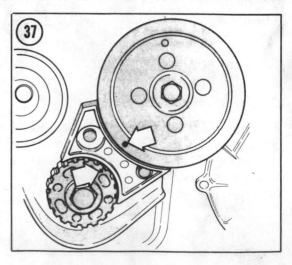

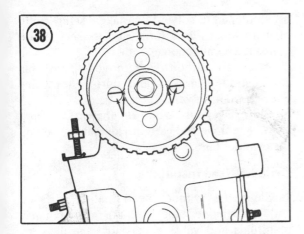

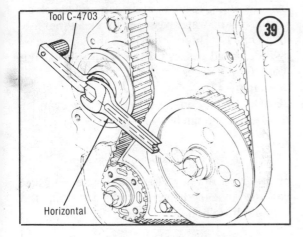

Tool C-4703

Horizontal

its compression stroke. This is evident when the TDC mark aligns with the mark in the transmission case opening. Finally, ensure that the mark on the crankshaft and intermediate shaft sprocket marks are lined up (**Figure 37**) and that the camshaft sprocket timing mark (small hole) is at top of center vertical line (**Figure 38**).

12. Loosen the timing belt tensioner (**Figure 39**), slide the timing belt off the camshaft sprocket and remove completely.

Installation

1. Make certain that the timing marks on the crankshaft and intermediate shaft sprockets are lined up (**Figure 37**) and that the camshaft sprocket timing mark (small hole) is at top of center vertical line (**Figure 38**).

CAUTION
Very accurate alignment of these marks is necessary as this sets the basic valve

timing of the engine. Failure to align these marks can result in a very poor running engine.

2. Install new timing belt under intermediate shaft sprocket and crankshaft sprocket, then slide it over the top of the camshaft sprocket.

CAUTION
Be absolutely certain that the sprockets do not move while sliding the belt into place. If necessary, reposition the sprockets as described in Step 1, then reinstall the belts.

3. Turn the belt tensioner until it is just possible to twist the belt about 90° with your thumb and index finger at a point midway between the camshaft and intermediate shaft sprockets. Hold the tensioner in this position and tighten the locknut.

4. Reverse Steps 1-10 of *Removal* to complete installation. Start engine and check operation. If a whirring noise is heard at the timing belt, the belt is too tight.

CYLINDER HEAD

Some of the following procedures must be performed by a dealer or competent machine shop, since they require special knowledge and expensive machine tools. Others, while possible for the enthusiast mechanic, are difficult or timing-consuming. A general practice among those who do their own service is to remove the cylinder head, perform disassembly except for valve removal and take the head to a machine shop for inspection and service. Since the cost is relatively low in proportion to the required effort and equipment, this may be the best approach even for more experienced owners.

Removal

1. Disconnect the battery ground cable.
2. Drain coolant.
3. Disconnect exhaust header at exhaust manifold flange.
4. Disconnect accelerator cable and carburetor bracket.
5. Remove the carburetor. See Chapter Six.
6. Disconnect coolant hoses from intake manifold and cylinder head.
7. Disconnect wires from temperature sender and oil pressure sender on cylinder head.

8. Remove the alternator (if required).

9. Remove the intake and exhaust manifolds. See Chapter Six.

> *NOTE*
> *Before removing the camshaft timing belt, make sure to turn the camshaft so its sprocket timing mark is straight up. This provides a reference point for later installation.*

10. Remove camshaft timing belt as described in this chapter.

11. Remove the valve cover.

12. Loosen the cylinder head bolts a turn at a time by reversing the sequence shown in **Figure 40**. That is, bolt No. 10 should be loosened first and bolt No. 1 last. The bolts should be loosened in 2 progressive stages to prevent warping of the cylinder head.

> *NOTE*
> *If the cylinder head is difficult to remove, try turning the engine over by hand with the spark plugs installed. The compression in the cylinders should force the cylinder head loose.*

13. Lift the cylinder head away from the block, remove the cylinder head gasket, then place the cylinder head on a soft surface to prevent scratching or otherwise damaging the cylinder head-to-engine mating surface.

Cylinder Head Inspection

1. Check the cylinder head for water leaks before cleaning.

2. Clean the cylinder head thoroughly in solvent. While cleaning, check for cracks or other visible damage. Look for corrosion or foreign material in oil or water passages. Clean the passages with a stiff spiral wire brush, then blow them out with compressed air.

3. Check the cylinder head bottom (block mating) surface for flatness. Place an accurate straightedge along the surface. See **Figure 41**. If there is any gap between the straightedge and cylinder head surface, measure it with a feeler gauge. Have the cylinder head resurfaced by a machine shop if the gap exceeds 0.004 in. (0.1 mm).

Decarbonizing

1. Without removing. valves, remove all deposits from the combustion chambers, intake ports and exhaust ports. Use a wire brush dipped in solvent or make a scraper out of hardwood. Be careful not to scratch or gouge the combustion chambers.

2. After all carbon is removed from the combustion chambers and ports, clean the entire head in solvent.

3. Clean away all carbon on the piston tops. Do not remove the carbon ridge at the top of the cylinder bore.

Cylinder Head Installation

1. Clean the cylinder head mating surfaces and the engine block, intake and exhaust manifolds and valve cover surfaces. Be sure that the cylinder bores are clean and check all visible oil and water passages for cleanliness.

2A. On 1.7 liter engines, install a new cylinder head gasket on the block so that the word OBEN faces toward the cylinder head. See **Figure 42**.

2B. On 2.2 liter engines, install a new cylinder head gasket on the block.

> *NOTE*
> *Never reuse a cylinder head gasket.*

3. After positioning the cylinder head gasket exactly, install the cylinder head and the cylinder head bolts.

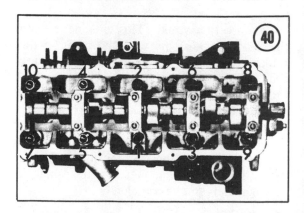

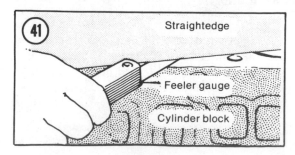

4A. On 1.7 liter engines, first tighten bolts No. 7 and No. 8 finger-tight (**Figure 40**). Then tighten the remaining bolts finger-tight. When torquing the head bolts, tighten in the sequence given in **Figure 40**. Cylinder head bolts should be tightened in 3 steps. First, each bolt should be tightened in the sequence indicated to 30 ft.-lb. (4.0 mkg). Second, each bolt should be tightened to 60 ft.-lb. (8.1 mkg). Third, turn all bolts an additional 1/4 turn.

4B. On 2.2 liter engines, tighten the head

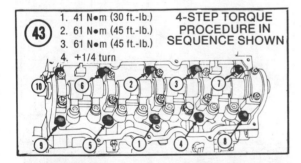

bolts in the sequence given in **Figure 43**. Cylinder head bolts should be tightened in 3 steps. First, each bolt should be tightened in the sequence indicated to 30 ft.-lb. (4.0 mkg). Second, each bolt should be tightened to 45 ft.-lb. (6.1 mkg). Third, tighten all bolts again in sequence to 45 ft.-lb. (6.1 mkg). Fourth, turn all bolts an additional 1/4 turn.

5. Install the camshaft timing belt as described in this chapter.

6. Install the rocker arm cover and spark plugs.

7. Install the alternator if removed. See Chapter Eight.

8. Connect the temperature sender and oil pressure sender wires to connections on cylinder head.

9. Install coolant hoses to intake manifold and cylinder head.

10. Install the carburetor (Chapter Six). Connect the accelerator cable and carburetor bracket.

11. Install the exhaust header to the exhaust manifold flange.

12. Install the air cleaner (Chapter Six).

13. Fill the cooling system with a 50/50 mixture of antifreeze and water. Check the oil level and top up if necessary with a grade recommended in Chapter Three.

14. Run the engine for several minutes and check for leaks. Let engine cool, then recheck head bolt tightness.

VALVE AND VALVE SEATS

Valve Removal (1.7 Liter)

1. Remove the cylinder head as described in this chapter.

2. Remove the camshaft as described in this chapter.

CAUTION
*To prevent bending, the camshaft must be removed exactly as described in the procedure **Camshaft Removal**.*

3. Remove cam follower and valve adjusting disc (**Figure 44**) and store them in a marked holder so they may be reinstalled in their original positions.

4. With special tool (part No. L-4419) or equivalent, push down on the valve spring

retainers and remove the valve locks with needlenose pliers. See **Figure 45**. Slowly release spring tension with tool and remove locking collets (valve keepers). Remove valve retainer and springs. **Figure 46** shows valve and related parts.

> *CAUTION*
> *Remove any burrs from valve stem grooves before removing the valves. Otherwise, the valve guides will be damaged.*

5. Remove the valve stem seal with a pair of needlenose pliers. See **Figure 47**. Then remove the valve spring seats as shown in **Figure 48**.

6. Remove the valves from the cylinder head. Store all parts so they may be reinstalled in their original positions.

Valve Removal (2.2 Liter)

1. Remove the cylinder head as described in this chapter.

2. Remove the camshaft as described in this chapter.

> *CAUTION*
> *To prevent bending, the camshaft must be removed exactly as described in the procedure **Camshaft Removal**.*

3. Remove the rocker arm/valve lash adjuster assembly from its position on the valve. Store each part in a marked holder so it may be reinstalled in its original position.

> *CAUTION*
> *Remove any burrs from valve stem grooves before removing the valves. Otherwise the valve guides will be damaged.*

4. Compress each valve spring with a compressor like the one shown in **Figure 49**. Remove the valve locking collets (valve keepers), then release tension on the valve spring. Remove the valve spring retainers, spring and valve. Label all parts and store for inspection and reassembly.

Valve and Valve Guide Inspection (All Engines)

1. Clean the valves with a wire brush and solvent. Discard cracked, warped or burned valves.

2. Measure the valve stems at the bottom, center and top for wear, using a micrometer.

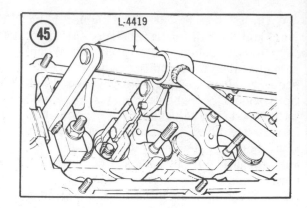

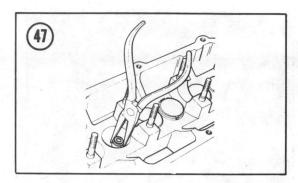

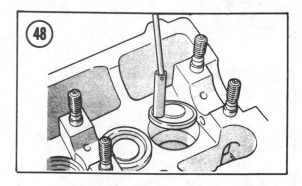

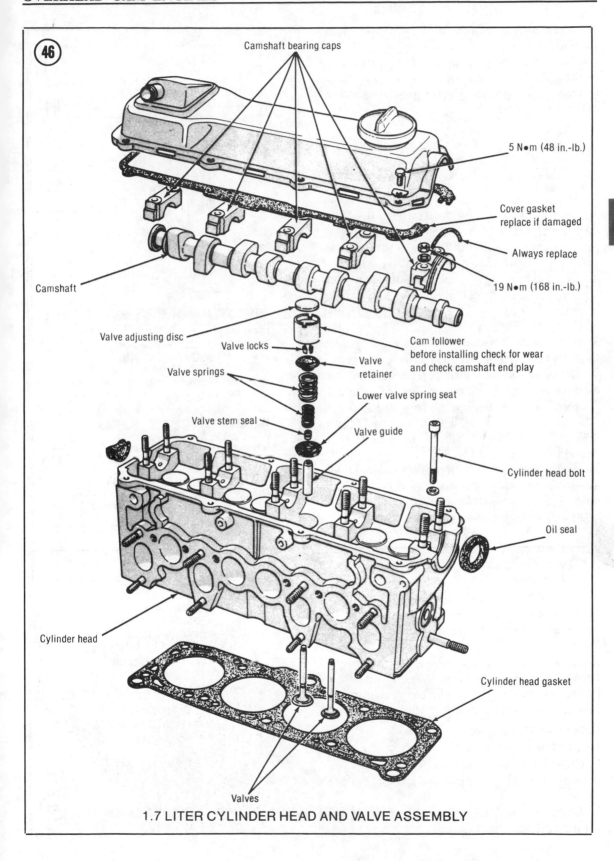

46

Camshaft bearing caps

5 N•m (48 in.-lb.)

Cover gasket
replace if damaged

Always replace

19 N•m (168 in.-lb.)

Camshaft

Valve adjusting disc

Valve locks

Valve springs

Valve stem seal

Valve retainer

Valve guide

Lower valve spring seat

Cam follower
before installing check for wear
and check camshaft end play

Cylinder head bolt

Oil seal

Cylinder head

Cylinder head gasket

Valves

1.7 LITER CYLINDER HEAD AND VALVE ASSEMBLY

A machine shop can do this when the valves are ground. Compare with specifications in **Figure 50** (1.7 liter) or **Figure 51** (2.2 liter).

3. Remove all carbon and varnish from valve guides with a stiff spiral wire brush.

NOTE
The next step assumes that all valve stems have been measured and are within specifications. Replace any valves with worn stems before performing this step.

4. Insert each valve into the guide from which it was removed and hold valve head 0.400 in. (10 mm) above the cylinder head gasket surface. Attach a dial indicator to the valve as shown in **Figure 52**. Rock the valve back and forth in direction of dial indicator and note reading on indicator. If the intake valve rocks more than 0.020 in. (0.5 mm) or the exhaust valve rocks more than 0.027 in. (0.7 mm), the valve guide is worn. Have worn guides replaced by a dealer or repair shop.

5. Measure valve spring free length and compare with specifications (end of chapter). Replace springs that are too long or too short. Measure spring bend with a square (**Figure 53**). Replace springs that are bent more than 0.063 in. (1.6 mm).

6. Have the valve springs tested under load on a spring tester by a dealer or machine shop and compare with specifications (end of chapter). Replace weak springs.

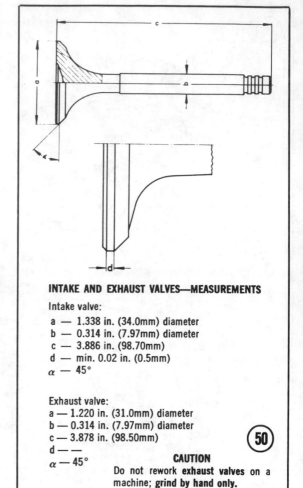

INTAKE AND EXHAUST VALVES—MEASUREMENTS

Intake valve:
a — 1.338 in. (34.0mm) diameter
b — 0.314 in. (7.97mm) diameter
c — 3.886 in. (98.70mm)
d — min. 0.02 in. (0.5mm)
α — 45°

Exhaust valve:
a — 1.220 in. (31.0mm) diameter
b — 0.314 in. (7.97mm) diameter
c — 3.878 in. (98.50mm)
d — —
α — 45°

CAUTION
Do not rework **exhaust valves** on a machine; **grind by hand only.**

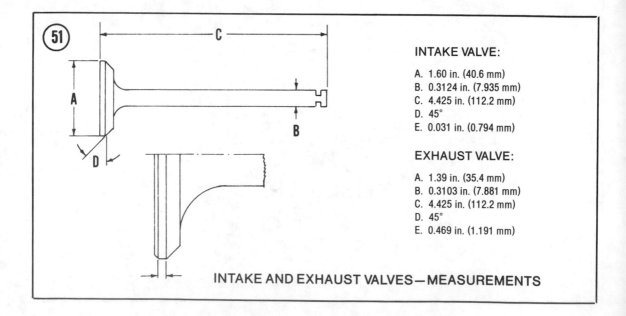

INTAKE VALVE:

A. 1.60 in. (40.6 mm)
B. 0.3124 in. (7.935 mm)
C. 4.425 in. (112.2 mm)
D. 45°
E. 0.031 in. (0.794 mm)

EXHAUST VALVE:

A. 1.39 in. (35.4 mm)
B. 0.3103 in. (7.881 mm)
C. 4.425 in. (112.2 mm)
D. 45°
E. 0.469 in. (1.191 mm)

INTAKE AND EXHAUST VALVES—MEASUREMENTS

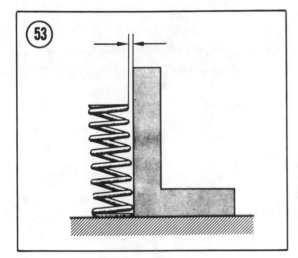

7. Inspect valve seats or valve seat inserts. If worn or burned, they must be reconditioned. This should be done by a dealer or machine shop, although the procedure is described in this section.

Valve Guide Replacement

Valve guide replacement on all engines requires a press and reaming tools. If guides are worn, have a dealer or machine shop remove and install guides.

Valve Seat Reconditioning

This job is best left to your dealer or local machine shop. They have the special equipment and knowledge required for this exacting job. The following procedure is provided in the event you are not near a dealer and the local machine shop is not familiar with the engine.

Valve seats are shrunk into the cylinder heads. Damaged or burned seats may be reconditioned until the bottom edge of the 60 degree chamfer exceeds refinishing depth indicated in **Figure 54** (1.7 liter) or **Figure 55** (2.2 liter). After this point is reached, the cylinder head must be replaced.

1. Using a 45° valve seat cutter or special tool, cut the 45° face. Do not take off any more

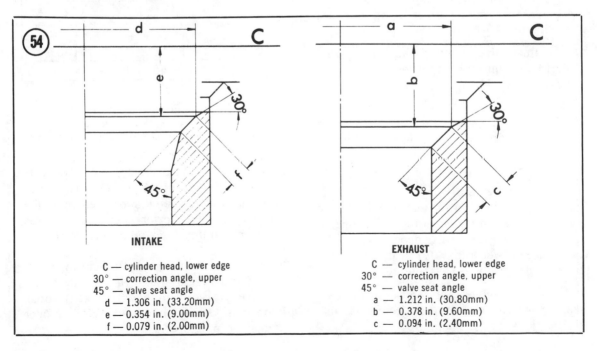

INTAKE

C — cylinder head, lower edge
30° — correction angle, upper
45° — valve seat angle
d — 1.306 in. (33.20mm)
e — 0.354 in. (9.00mm)
f — 0.079 in. (2.00mm)

EXHAUST

C — cylinder head, lower edge
30° — correction angle, upper
45° — valve seat angle
a — 1.212 in. (30.80mm)
b — 0.378 in. (9.60mm)
c — 0.094 in. (2.40mm)

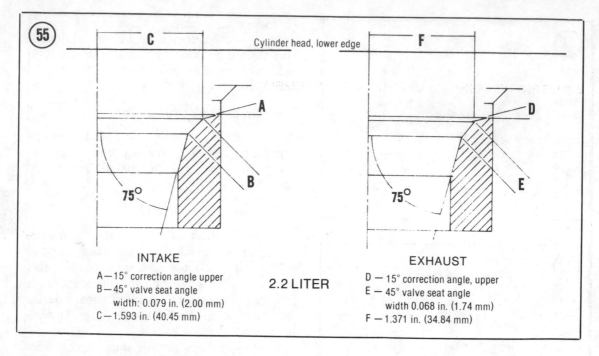

INTAKE

A — 15° correction angle upper
B — 45° valve seat angle
    width: 0.079 in. (2.00 mm)
C — 1.593 in. (40.45 mm)

2.2 LITER

EXHAUST

D — 15° correction angle, upper
E — 45° valve seat angle
    width 0.068 in. (1.74 mm)
F — 1.371 in. (34.84 mm)

metal than necessary to provide a clean, concentric seat. See **Figure 50** and **Figure 54** (1.7 liter) or **Figure 51** and **Figure 55** (2.2 liter).

2. Coat the corresponding valve face with Prussian blue.

3. Insert the valve into the guide.

4. Rotate the valve under light pressure approximately 1/4 turn.

5. Lift the valve out. If the valve seats properly, the blue will transfer to the valve seat face evenly. If not, refer to Step 6A (1.7 liter) or Step 6B (2.2 liter).

6A. On the 1.7 liter engine, if the blue transferred to the bottom or upper valve face edge, cut the top of the seat with a 30° cutter or stone. Repeat Steps 2-5 as required.

6B. On the 2.2 liter engine, if the blue transferred to the bottom edge of the valve face, raise the valve seat with a 75° stone. If the blue transferred to the upper edge of the valve face, lower the valve seat with a 15° stone. Repeat Steps 2-5 as required.

7. When the valve seats are properly cut, measure width of seats and compare with specifications (end of chapter).

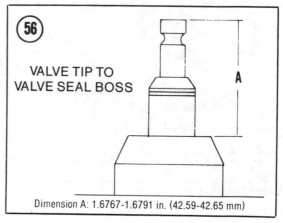

VALVE TIP TO VALVE SEAL BOSS

Dimension A: 1.6767-1.6791 in. (42.59-42.65 mm)

NOTE
The cylinder head must be replaced if valve seats cannot be serviced to provide correct angle and seat width.

8A. On the 1.7 liter engine, if the valve seats are cut too much, intake and exhaust valves are available with stems shortened by 0.020 in. (0.5 mm). The shorter valve stem requires use of minimum thickness valve adjusting discs.

8B. On the 2.2 liter engine, after cutting valve seats, install valve into cylinder head and measure valve tip-to-valve seal boss dimensions. Grind valve tip to provide proper dimensions in **Figure 56**.

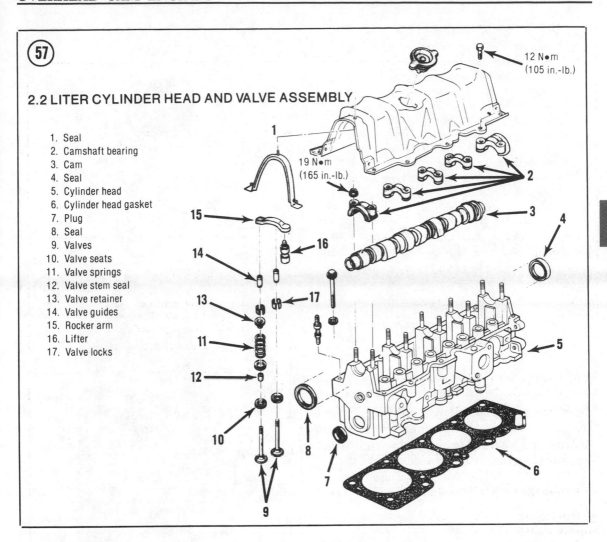

57

2.2 LITER CYLINDER HEAD AND VALVE ASSEMBLY

1. Seal
2. Camshaft bearing
3. Cam
4. Seal
5. Cylinder head
6. Cylinder head gasket
7. Plug
8. Seal
9. Valves
10. Valve seats
11. Valve springs
12. Valve stem seal
13. Valve retainer
14. Valve guides
15. Rocker arm
16. Lifter
17. Valve locks

12 N•m
(105 in.-lb.)

19 N•m
(165 in.-lb.)

Valve Installation

1. Coat the valves with oil and insert them in the cylinder head.

2. Install the valve spring seats, oil seals, springs and spring washers. Compress the valve springs and install the keepers.

CAMSHAFT AND ROCKER ARMS

Figure 46 (1.7 liter) and **Figure 57** (2.2 liter) show the respective engine's camshaft and valve assembly.

Rocker Arm Removal (2.2 Liter)

Rocker arm removal and installation is discussed under *Camshaft Removal* and *Installation* procedures in this section.

Camshaft Removal (All Engines)

It is not necessary to remove the cylinder head in order to remove the camshaft.

1. Remove the camshaft timing belt as described in this chapter.

2. Remove the valve cover.

3. Check camshaft end play. Position a dial gauge as shown in **Figure 58**. Slide the camshaft back and forth against the dial gauge pointer. The reading on the gauge is camshaft end play. Maximum allowable end play is 0.006 in. (0.15 mm). Install shims behind thrust plate if end play is not within specifications.

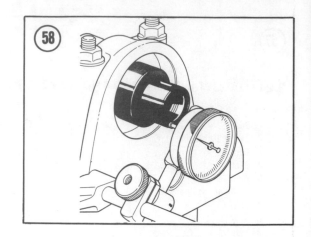

NOTE
On a piece of paper, record the number of each bearing cap and the position it faces for installation purposes. On the 1.7 liter engine, the numbers on the bearing caps will not all align side by side because of off-center bearing positions. On the 2.2 liter engine, caps 1, 2, 3 and 4 have arrows which point toward the timing belt. Each cap must be reinstalled in the same positon to prevent cap breakage during installation.

4A. On the 1.7 liter engine, remove bearing caps 1, 3 and 5. See **Figure 59**. Then loosen diagonally opposite nuts on bearing caps 2 and 4 a turn at a time to gently relieve valve spring pressure.

CAUTION
Camshaft can be bent by spring pressure unless bearing caps are removed exactly as described.

4B. On the 2.2 liter engine, mark rocker arms for proper installation. Then loosen camshaft bearing cap nuts several revolutions. Using a soft-faced hammer, hit end of camshaft to loosen the bearing caps. Further loosen the cap nuts and remove nuts and bearing caps.
5. Lift out the camshaft. On 2.2 liter engines, remove the rocker arms and hydraulic lifters.

Rocker Arm Inspection (2.2 Liter)

Examine the rocker arm for visible wear on its cam contact surface, lifter surface and valve surface. If wear or any defects can be seen, replace the rocker arm.

Camshaft Inspection

1. Check all machined surfaces of the camshaft for nicks or grooves. Minor defects may be removed with a smooth oilstone. Severe damage or wear requires replacement of the camshaft.
2. Measure camshaft bend. Rotate the camshaft between accurate centers (such as V-blocks or a lathe) with a dial indicator contacting the second and third journals. See **Figure 60**. Actual bend is half the reading shown on the gauge when the camshaft is

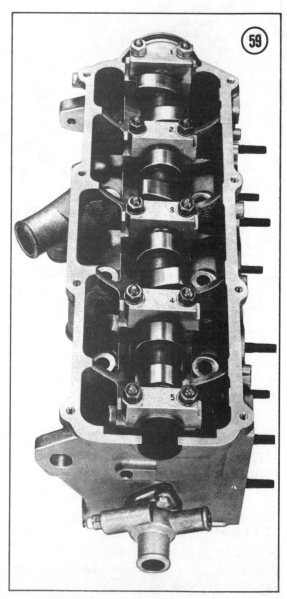

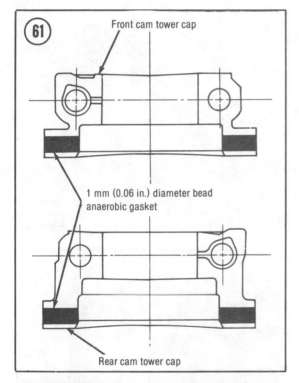

Front cam tower cap

1 mm (0.06 in.) diameter bead
anaerobic gasket

Rear cam tower cap

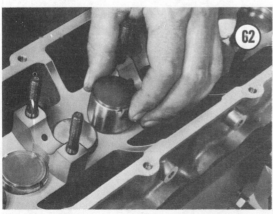

rotated one full turn. Replace the camshaft if
bend exceeds 0.001 in. (0.025 mm).

Camshaft Installation

1. Coat the camshaft journals and bearing
surfaces with clean engine oil.

2. On the 2.2 liter engine, place rocker arms
in position over valve stem end and hydraulic
valve lifter.

3. Carefully lay camshaft in position on lower
journals. Make sure camshaft does not touch
or nick the lower bearing journals.

4A. On the 1.7 liter engine, install bearing
caps in correct order (**Figure 59**). Tighten to
14 ft.-lb. (1.9 mkg).

4B. On the 2.2 liter engine, install caps 2, 3
and 4 with arrow on cap facing toward the
timing belt. On caps 1 and 5, install gasket
sealer part No. 4205918 to the areas shown in
Figure 61. Install cap 1 with arrow facing
toward the timing belt. Cap 5 can only be
installed one way. Tighten to 14 ft.-lb. (1.9
mkg).

5. Apply a 1/8 in. (3 mm) bead of RTV sealer
(part No. 4026070 or equivalent) onto the
cylinder head-to-valve cover contact surface.
Install the valve cover and tighten attaching
screws securely.

6. Install the camshaft timing belt as
described in this chapter.

VALVE TAPPETS
(1.7 LITER)

1. Remove the camshaft as described in this
chapter.

CAUTION
*Follow the camshaft removal and
installation procedure exactly to prevent
distortion of the camshaft.*

2. Lift out tappets as shown in **Figure 62**.
Store them so that they may be reinstalled in
their original positions.

3. When installing tappets, apply a light coat
of oil before insertion in the cylinder head.
Install tappets in their original positions only.

4. Install the camshaft as described in this
chapter. Adjust valve clearance as described in
Chapter Three.

INTERMEDIATE SHAFT

1. Remove the camshaft timing belt as described in this chapter.

2. Remove the timing gear from the intermediate shaft.

3. Remove the fuel pump (Chapter Six) and distributor (Chapter Eight).

4. Remove the intermediate shaft bearing flange and seal.

5. Pull intermediate shaft out of block. See **Figure 63** (1.7 liter) or **Figure 64** (2.2 liter).

6. Pry the old oil seal from the intermediate shaft flange.

7. Coat the intermediate shaft bearings and journals with clean engine oil.

8. Carefully install the intermediate shaft in the engine. Rotate the intermediate shaft slowly while inserting to ease installation. Do not nick or touch the bearings while inserting shaft.

9. *2.2 liter.* Apply a 1/16 in. (1 mm) bead of anaerobic gasket material (part No. 4205918 or equivalent) to the intermediate shaft flange. See **Figure 65**.

> *NOTE*
> *The intermediate shaft flange on the 1.7 liter engine uses an O-ring for*

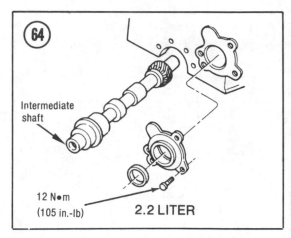

Intermediate shaft

12 N•m (105 in.-lb)

2.2 LITER

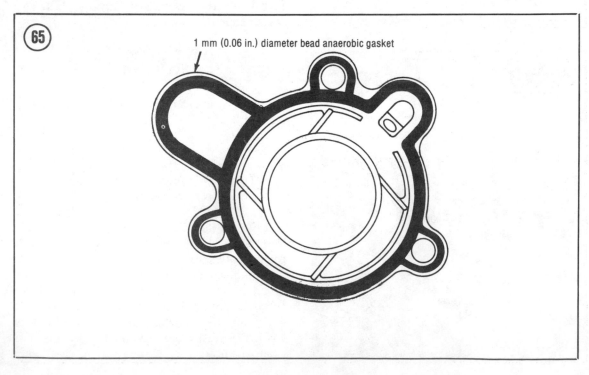

1 mm (0.06 in.) diameter bead anaerobic gasket

flange-to-engine sealing. It would be wise at this time, while the shaft flange is removed, to replace the O-ring.

10. Install the intermediate shaft flange. Tighten to 18 ft.-lb. (1.7 liter) or 8.7 ft.-lb. (2.2 liter).

11. Press a new seal into flange with special tool part No. L-4422 (1.7 liter) or C-4680 (2.2 liter) or equivalent. See **Figure 66** (1.7 liter) or **Figure 67** (2.2 liter).

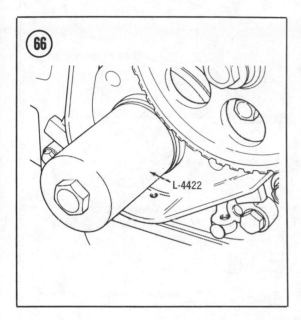

L-4422

12. Place Woodruff key in intermediate shaft keyseat. Align keyway in timing gear with Woodruff key and install timing gear. Tighten to 58 ft.-lb. (7.9 mkg) on the 1.7 liter engine or 50 ft.-lb. (6.8 mkg) on the 2.2 liter engine.

13. Install the fuel pump (Chapter Six) and distributor (Chapter Eight).

14. Install the camshaft timing belt as described in this chapter.

OIL PAN

Removal/Installation

The engine lubrication system is shown in **Figure 68** (1.7 liter) or **Figure 69** (2.2 liter).

1. Raise vehicle front end and secure with jackstands.

2. Drain oil as described in Chapter Three.

3. Remove bolts securing pan to block. Remove pan.

4A. On the 1.7 liter engine, installation is the reverse of these steps. Be sure that you remove all traces of old gasket from the block and the oil pan. Use a new gasket and tighten oil pan bolts to specifications (**Table 3**).

4B. On the 2.2 liter engine, installation is the reverse of these steps. Be sure that all traces of RTV gasket material is removed from the block and the oil pan. Install a 1/8 in. (3 mm) bead of RTV to the oil pan surface (**Figure 70**)

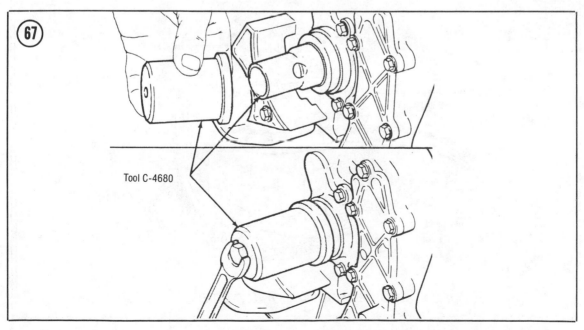

Tool C-4680

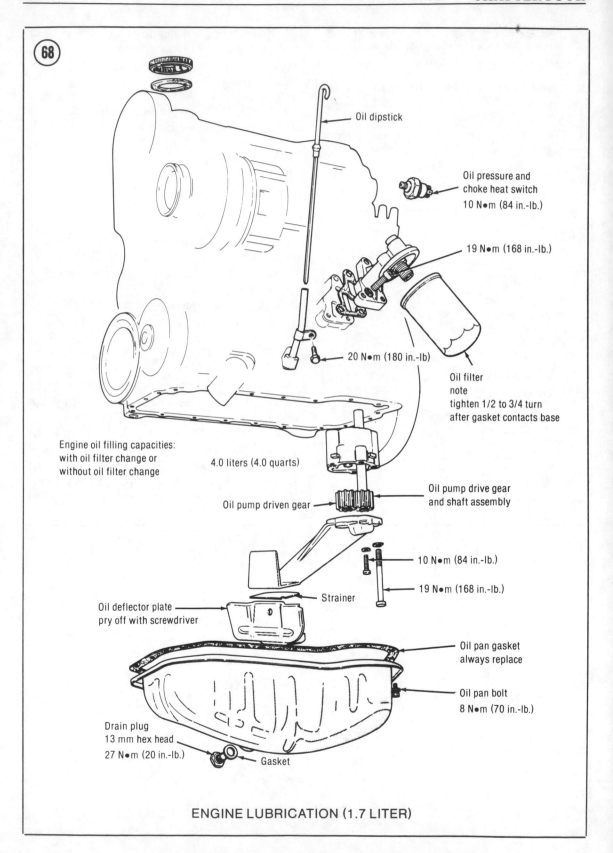

68

Oil dipstick

Oil pressure and
choke heat switch
10 N•m (84 in.-lb.)

19 N•m (168 in.-lb.)

20 N•m (180 in.-lb)

Oil filter
note
tighten 1/2 to 3/4 turn
after gasket contacts base

Engine oil filling capacities:
with oil filter change or
without oil filter change

4.0 liters (4.0 quarts)

Oil pump drive gear
and shaft assembly

Oil pump driven gear

10 N•m (84 in.-lb.)

19 N•m (168 in.-lb.)

Strainer

Oil deflector plate
pry off with screwdriver

Oil pan gasket
always replace

Oil pan bolt
8 N•m (70 in.-lb.)

Drain plug
13 mm hex head
27 N•m (20 in.-lb.)   Gasket

ENGINE LUBRICATION (1.7 LITER)

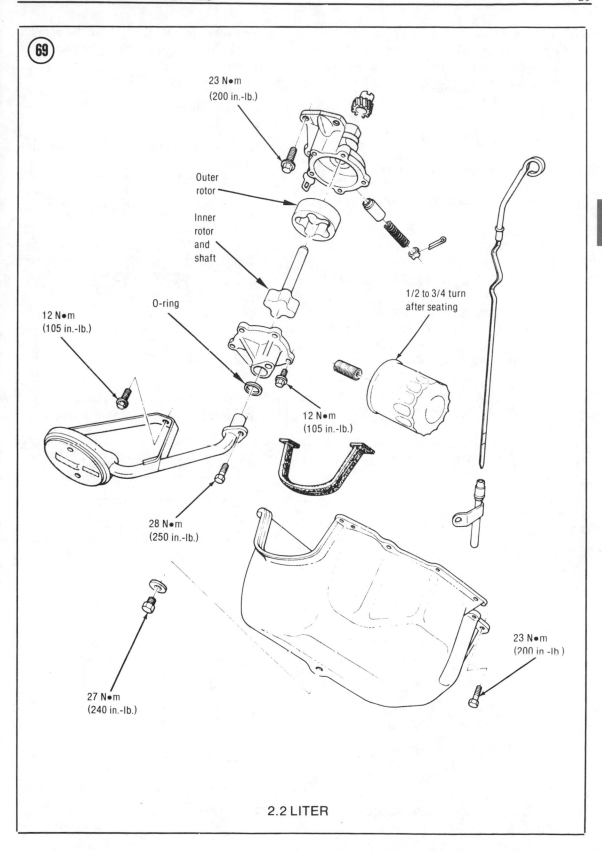

69

23 N•m
(200 in.-lb.)

Outer
rotor

Inner
rotor
and
shaft

O-ring

12 N•m
(105 in.-lb.)

1/2 to 3/4 turn
after seating

12 N•m
(105 in.-lb.)

28 N•m
(250 in.-lb.)

27 N•m
(240 in.-lb.)

23 N•m
(200 in.-lb.)

2.2 LITER

and to the front and rear crankshaft seal retainer at the crankshaft (**Figure 71**). Install the oil pan to the block and tighten the attaching bolts to 20 ft.-lb. (2.7 mkg).

OIL PUMP

The oil pump may be removed and installed without removing the engine. Refer to **Figure 68** (1.7 liter) or **Figure 69** (2.2 liter) for these procedures.

Removal/Installation

1. Remove the oil pan as described in this chapter.
2. *2.2 liter.* Remove the oil pickup tube screw at the No. 3 main bearing cap bolt (**Figure 72**).
3. Remove the screws securing the oil pump to the cylinder block and lower the oil pump.
4. Installation is the reverse of these steps. On 1.7 liter engines, pump indexing is not required. On 2.2 liter engines, perform the following:
    a. Turn the crankshaft until the crankshaft and intermediate shaft marks align as shown in **Figure 73**.

b. The oil pump shaft will then be parallel to the center crankshaft line shown in **Figure 74**.
c. Install the oil pump.

Disassembly/Inspection/Assembly (1.7 liter)

Refer to **Figure 68** (1.7 liter) for this procedure.
1. Remove the oil pump as described in this chapter.
2. Remove the bolts securing the upper and lower pump halves and separate them.

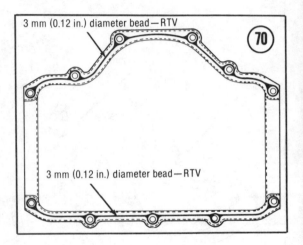

3 mm (0.12 in.) diameter bead—RTV

3 mm (0.12 in.) diameter bead—RTV

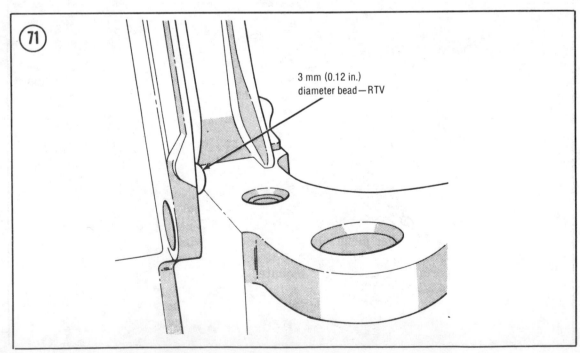

3 mm (0.12 in.) diameter bead—RTV

3. Remove the drive shaft and gear from the upper pump half.

4. Clean all parts with solvent. If very dirty, bend up edges of suction head and remove suction head and filter screen for cleaning.

5. Install pump gears in body. Check backlash by inserting a feeler gauge between gear teeth as shown in **Figure 75**. Backlash should be 0.002-0.008 in. (0.05-0.20 mm).

6. Place a square over the body and insert a feeler gauge as shown in **Figure 76**. Maximum end play allowable is 0.006 in. (0.15 mm).

7. Remove gears from body.

8. Install suction head and filter screen if they were removed.

9. Install drive shaft and gear assembly lubricant and install them in the upper pump half.

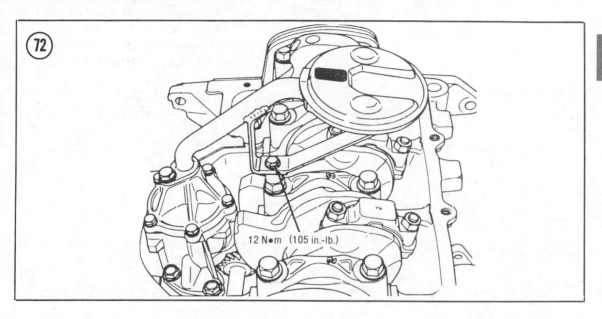

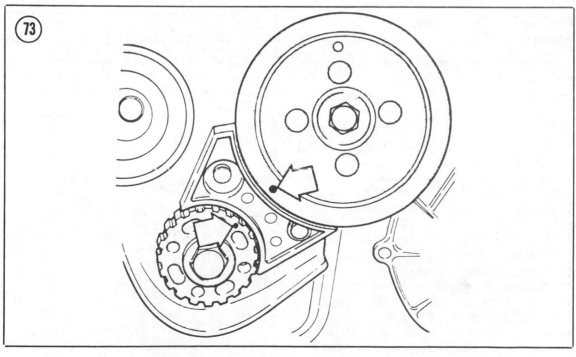

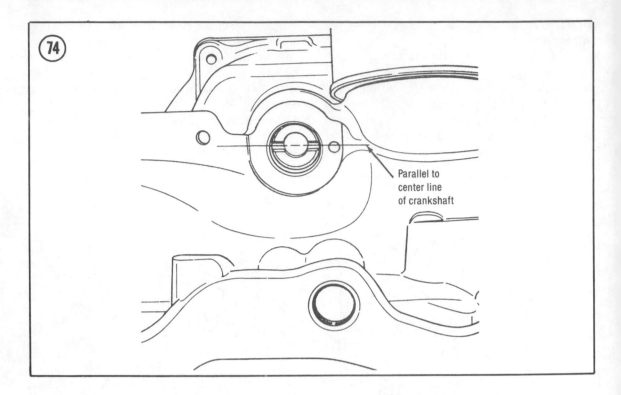

Parallel to
center line
of crankshaft

10. Bolt upper and lower halves together.
Torque short bolt to 7 ft.-lb. (1 mkg) and long
bolt to 14 ft.-lb. (2 mkg).
11. Rotate drive shaft by hand to ensure that
it turns freely and smoothly.

Disassembly/Inspection/Assembly (2.2 liter)

Refer to **Figure 69** (2.2 liter) for this
procedure.
1. Remove the oil pump as described in this
chapter.
2. Remove the oil pickup tube to oil pump
screw on the pump cover and remove the
pickup tube and O-ring.
3. Remove the bolts securing the upper and
lower pump halves and separate them.
4. Remove the inner rotor and shaft and the
outer rotor from the upper pump half.
5. Remove the relief valve cotter key and
remove the cup, spring and relief valve.
6. Clean all parts in solvent.
7. Measure the thickness of the outer rotor
with a micrometer (**Figure 77**). Minimum
allowable thickness is 0.826 in. (20.96 mm).
Measure the outer rotor outer diameter.
Minimum allowable diameter is 2.469 in.

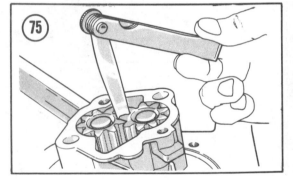

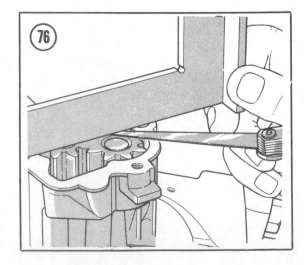

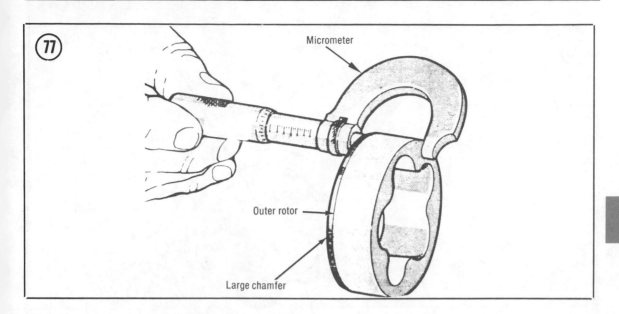

Micrometer

Outer rotor

Large chamfer

4

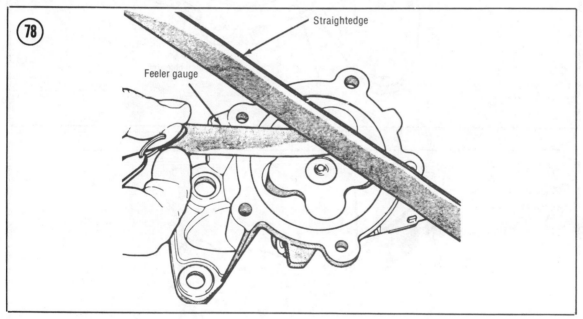

Straightedge

Feeler gauge

(62.7 mm). Replace outer rotor if either measurement is incorrect.

8. Install pump rotors in housing. Check rotor end play with a feeler gauge as shown in **Figure 78**. End play should be between 0.001-0.006 in. (0.03-0.15 mm). Replace rotors if end play is incorrect.

9. Check the clearance between each rotor with a feeler gauge as shown in **Figure 79**. Maximum allowable clearance is 0.01 in. (0.25

mm). Replace both rotors if clearance is incorrect.

10. Check the outer rotor clearance between the housing and rotor with a feeler gauge. See **Figure 80**. Maximum allowable clearance is 0.014 in. (0.35 mm). Replace the housing or rotor as required if clearance is incorrect.

11. Place a straightedge over the pump cover and insert a feeler gauge as shown in **Figure 81**. Maximum clearance allowable is 0.015 in. (0.38 mm). Replace the pump cover if clearance is incorrect.

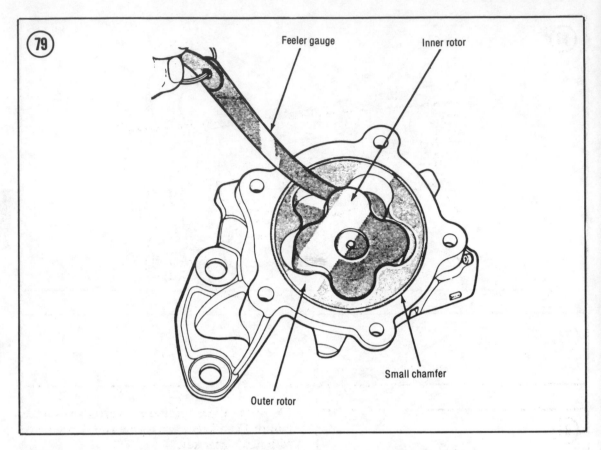

79

Feeler gauge

Inner rotor

Outer rotor

Small chamfer

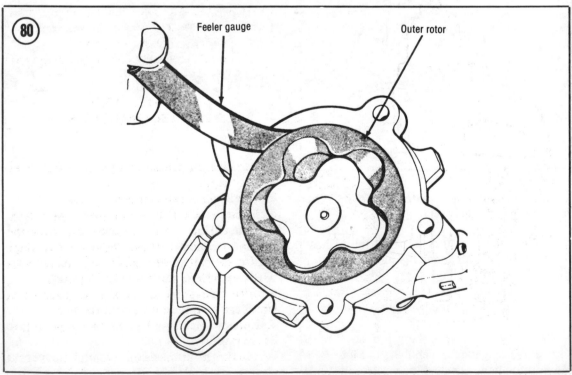

80

Feeler gauge

Outer rotor

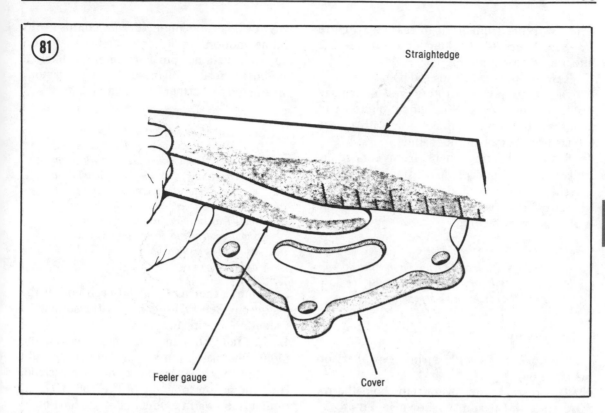

Straightedge

Feeler gauge

Cover

4

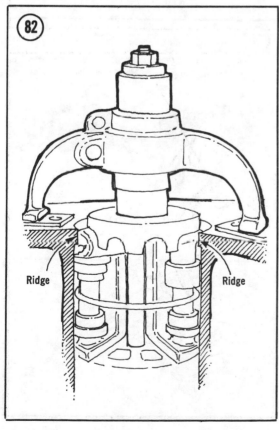

Ridge   Ridge

12. Install the oil pressure relief valve into the pump. Then insert the spring and cup. Secure with new cotter key.

13. Install the rotors into the upper pump half.

14. Bolt upper and lower halves together. Tighten bolts to 16 ft.-lb. (2.3 mkg).

15. Rotate drive shaft by hand to ensure that it turns freely and smoothly.

PISTONS AND CONNECTING RODS

Removal

1. Remove oil pan and oil pump as described in this chapter.

2. Remove the cylinder head.

3. Rotate crankshaft until piston is at bottom of travel. Place an oil-soaked cloth over the piston to collect cuttings, then remove ridge and/or deposits from upper edge of cylinder bore with a ridge remover. See **Figure 82**.

4. Turn crankshaft until piston is at top of its stroke; remove cloth and cuttings.

5. Repeat Steps 3 and 4 for all other pistons to be removed.

6. Mark pistons, connecting rods and connecting rod bearing caps "1" through

"4", working from front to rear. See **Figure 83**. See **Figure 84** (1.7 liter) or **Figure 85** (2.2 liter) for piston marking.

7. Remove the connecting rod bolts.

8. Tape bottom end of rod to prevent damage to cylinder walls and push piston/rod assembly out top of cylinder bore with a piece of hardwood or a hammer handle.

9. Remove bearing shells from connecting rods and bearing caps. Mark the backs of the bearings with the cylinder number from which they were removed and whether they were the upper or lower bearing.

NOTE
Bearing shells may be reused if they are in good condition, but they must be reinstalled in their original positions.

Disassembly

1. Remove rings with a ring expander tool (**Figure 86**).

2. Before removing piston pin, hold the rod and rock the piston as shown in **Figure 87**.

Any rocking movement (do not confuse with sliding motion) indicates wear in the piston pin, rod, bushing, pin bore or more likely a combination of all of these. Mark the piston, pin and rod for further examination later.

NOTE
Removal of piston pins on 1.7 liter engines is described in Steps 3 and 4. Piston pins on all 2.2 liter engines are press-fitted on the connecting rods and slip fit into the pistons. Removal requires an arbor press, or similar device, and a suitable support tool. This is a job for a dealer or machine shop, equipped to fit the pistons and pin, as well as align the pistons with the connecting rods.

3. Remove the snap rings at each end of the piston pin. See **Figure 88**. A drift also may be used for removing the rings.

4. Heat the piston and pin with a small butane torch. The piston pin will probably drop right out, but may need coaxing with a brass rod. Heat the piston to about 140° F (60° C), i.e., until it is too warm to touch, but not too hot.

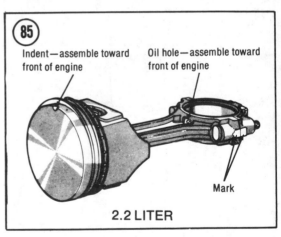

Indent—assemble toward front of engine

Oil hole—assemble toward front of engine

Mark

2.2 LITER

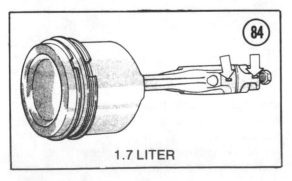

1.7 LITER

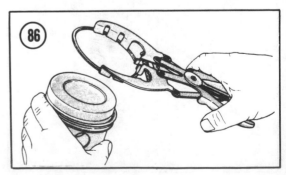

Piston Pin Removal/Installation (2.2 liter)

Piston pins on all 2.2 liter engines are press-fitted on the connecting rods, and slip fit into the pistons. Removal requires and arbor press, or similar device, and a suitable support tool. This is a job for a dealer or machine shop, equipped to fit the pistons and pin, as well as align the pistons with the connecting rods.

Inspection

1. Clean pistons thoroughly in solvent. Scrape carbon deposits from the top of the piston and ring grooves. Do not damage the pistons.

CAUTION
Do not wire brush piston skirts.

2. Examine each ring groove for burrs, dented edges and side wear. Pay particular attention to top compression ring groove, as it usually wears more than the others.
3. Measure piston-to-cylinder clearance as described in this chapter.

4. If damage or wear indicates piston replacement, select a new piston as described under *Piston Clearance* procedure.
5. Measure all parts marked in Step 2 of the piston disassembly procedure with a micrometer and dial bore gauge to determine which part or parts are worn. Any machinist can do this for you if you do not have micrometers. Replace piston/pin set as a unit if either or both are worn.

Piston Clearance

1. Make sure the piston and cylinder walls are clean and dry.
2. Measure the inside diameter of the cylinder bore at a point 1/2 in. (13 mm) from the upper edge with a bore gauge (**Figure 89**).
3A. On the 1.7 liter engine, measure the outside diameter of the piston at a point 7/16 in. (11 mm) from the lower edge of the piston, 90° to the piston pin axis. See **Figure 90**. Record the measurement. Proceed to Step 4.

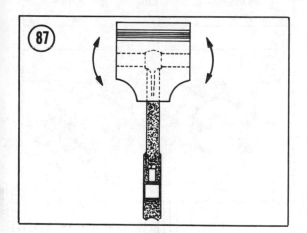

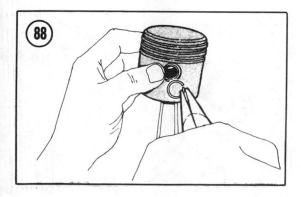

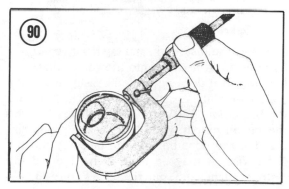

3B. On the 2.2 liter engine, measure the piston, following Step 1 and Step 2 in **Figure 91**. Determine results as follows:

   a. Step 1: The elliptical piston shape should be 0.011-0.013 in. (0.279-0.330 mm) less at diameter A than at diameter B.

   b. Step 2: The piston crown area should be 0.021-0.028 in. (0.533-0.711) less than diameter C. Measuring at the piston skirt area, diameter D should be 0.0000-0.0005 in. (0.0000-0.0152 mm) larger than diameter C.

Replace any piston which does meet these comparison specifications, then proceed to Step 4.

4. Subtract the piston diameter from the cylinder bore diameter. If the difference in the 2 readings exceeds 0.0027 in. (0.07 mm), piston must be replaced.

Assembly

> *NOTE*
> *Steps 1-5 describe 1.7 liter piston/piston pin installation. On 2.2 liter engines, piston pin installation is a job for a dealer or machine shop, as explained under **Disassembly**.*

1. Insert snap ring in either end of piston.

2. Coat the connecting rod bushing, piston pin and piston holes with assembly lubricant.

3. Place the piston over the connecting rod with the top arrow pointing toward the front of the engine and the cast bosses on the connecting rod toward the fuel pump side of the engine. Connecting rod cast bosses are indicated (arrows) in **Figure 92**.

> *NOTE*
> *Two types of rods are used. Bearing end caps on Type A are attached with studs and nuts, while Type B use bolts. See **Figure 92**.*

4. Insert the piston pin and tap it with a plastic hammer until it starts into the connecting rod bushing. If it does not slide in easily, heat the piston until it is warm to the touch, but not too hot (about 140°/60° C). Continue to drive the piston pin in while holding the piston so that the rod does not have to take any shock. Otherwise, it may be bent. Drive the pin in until it touches the snap ring. See **Figure 93**.

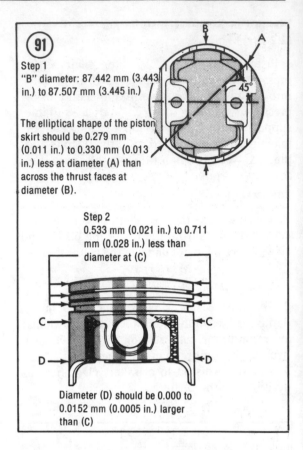

91

Step 1
"B" diameter: 87.442 mm (3.443 in.) to 87.507 mm (3.445 in.)

The elliptical shape of the piston skirt should be 0.279 mm (0.011 in.) to 0.330 mm (0.013 in.) less at diameter (A) than across the thrust faces at diameter (B).

Step 2
0.533 mm (0.021 in.) to 0.711 mm (0.028 in.) less than diameter at (C)

Diameter (D) should be 0.000 to 0.0152 mm (0.0005 in.) larger than (C)

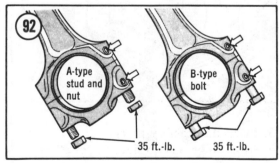

92

A-type stud and nut

B-type bolt

35 ft.-lb.   35 ft.-lb.

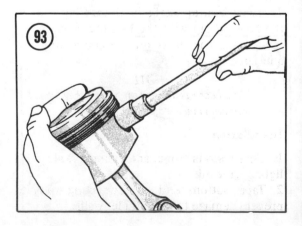

93

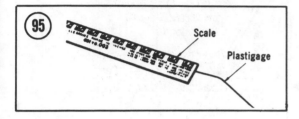

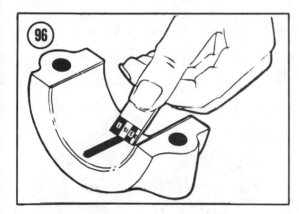

5. Insert the other snap ring.

6. Install rings as described under *Piston Ring Replacement.*

7. Insert bearing shells in connecting rods in the bearing cap with the locating tangs facing toward the cast boss on the connecting rod and cap.

NOTE
If old bearings are reused, be sure they are installed in their exact original locations.

Installation

1. Coat pistons, rings and cylinder walls with light engine oil.

2. Tape bottom end of connecting rods to prevent damage to the cylinder walls.

3. Insert piston/rod assemblies in their respective bores. On 1.7 liter engines, install piston with arrows pointing toward the front of the engine (**Figure 83**). On 2.2 liter engines, install pistons with notch on piston top facing toward front of engine (**Figure 85**).

4. Compress rings with a ring compressor tool and press pistons into bores with a hammer handle. See **Figure 94**.

5. Remove tape from connecting rod end and guide connecting rod into journal.

6. Loosely install bearing caps, matching marks made during removal.

7. Check bearing clearances as described under *Bearing and Crankpin Inspection* in this chapter.

CONNECTING ROD BEARINGS

Bearing and Crankpin Inspection

1. Remove oil pan and oil pump as described in this chapter.

2. Remove connecting rod bearing caps. Be sure to mark them so they may be reinstalled in their original positions.

3. Push piston/rod assembly toward cylinder head just far enough to gain access to crankpin.

CAUTION
Do not force piston high enough so that top ring contacts ridge at top of cylinder.

4. Wipe bearing inserts and crankpins clean. Check bearing inserts and crankpins for evidence of wear, abrasions or scoring.

5. Cut a piece of Plastigage (**Figure 95**) the width of the bearing.

6. Place a piece of Plastigage on one crankpin parallel to the crankshaft.

7. Install rod cap and tighten connecting rod bolts or nuts evenly to specifications (end of chapter).

CAUTION
Do not place Plastigage over oil hole. Do not rotate crankshaft while Plastigage is in place.

8. Remove bearing cap.

9. Measure width of flattened Plastigage according to the manufacturer's instructions. See **Figure 96**. Measure at both ends of the

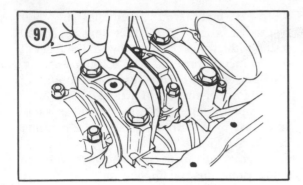

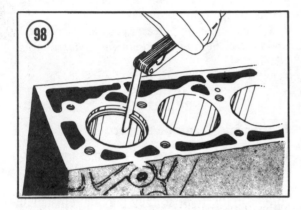

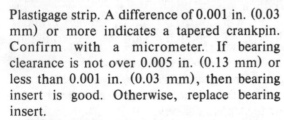

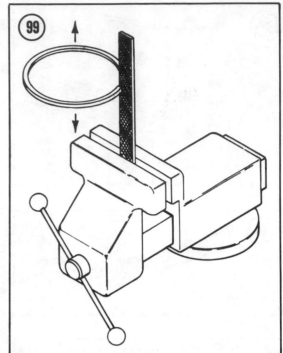

Plastigage strip. A difference of 0.001 in. (0.03 mm) or more indicates a tapered crankpin. Confirm with a micrometer. If bearing clearance is not over 0.005 in. (0.13 mm) or less than 0.001 in. (0.03 mm), then bearing insert is good. Otherwise, replace bearing insert.

10. Remove Plastigage strip.

11. Repeat Steps 5-10 for each of the other rods.

12. Lubricate bearings and crankpins and install rod caps. Tighten the bolts or nuts to specifications (end of chapter).

13. Rotate crankshaft to be sure bearings are not too tight.

14. Insert feeler gauge between connecting rods and crank shoulders. Axial clearance should be less than 0.015 in. (0.037 mm). See **Figure 97**.

PISTON RINGS

1. Remove old rings with a ring expander tool.

2. Carefully remove all the carbon from ring grooves. Inspect grooves carefully for burrs, nicks or broken and cracked lands. Recondition or replace piston if necessary.

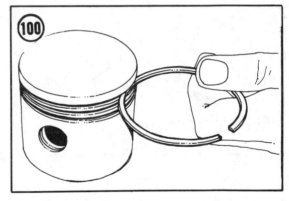

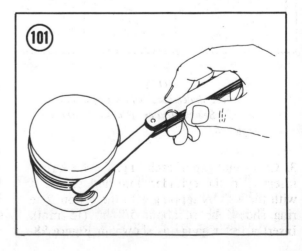

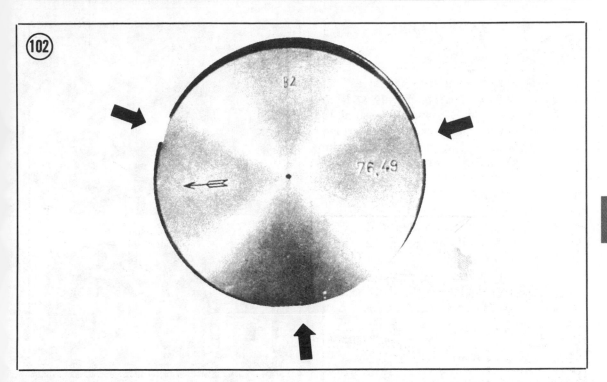

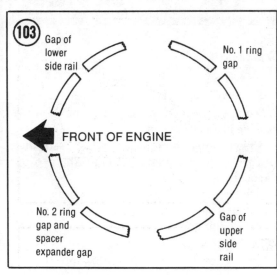

FRONT OF ENGINE

Gap of lower side rail

No. 1 ring gap

No. 2 ring gap and spacer expander gap

Gap of upper side rail

NOTE
*Measure cylinder bore before performing Step 3. See **Cylinder Block**, in this chapter.*

3. Check end gap of each ring. To check ring, insert it in the cylinder bore and square it with the wall by tapping with the piston. The ring should be in about 5/8 in. (15 mm). Insert a feeler gauge as shown in **Figure 98**.

Compare gap with **Table 5**. If the gap is smaller than specified, hold a file in a vise, grip the ends of the ring with your fingers and enlarge the gap. See **Figure 99**.

4. Roll each ring around its piston groove as shown in **Figure 100** to check for binding. Minor binding may be cleaned up with a fine cut file. If the binding is severe, indicating a damaged piston groove, the piston must be replaced.

5. Install oil ring in oil ring groove with a ring expander tool.

6. Install compression rings carefully with a ring expander tool.

NOTE
The top 2 compression rings on 2.2 liter engines must be installed with TOP mark on ring facing upward.

7. Check side clearance of each ring as shown in **Figure 101**. Compare with specifications in **Table 6**. Replace rings as required.

8. Distribute ring gaps around piston as shown in **Figure 102** (1.7 liter) or **Figure 103** (2.2 liter).

CRANKSHAFT

Bearing and Journal Inspection

Generally, the lower bearing halves wear more rapidly than the upper halves. If the lower halves are good, it is safe to assume the upper halves are good also. If new lower halves are required, replace corresponding upper halves at the same time.

1. Remove rear bearing cap and wipe oil from journal and bearing cap.
2. Check bearing insert in journal for evidence of wear, abrasion and scoring.
3. Place a piece of Plastigage on the journal, parallel to the crankshaft.
4. Install bearing cap and tighten retaining bolts evenly to specifications (end of chapter).

CAUTION
Do not place Plastigage over oil hole. Do not rotate the crankshaft while Plastigage is in place.

5. Remove bearing cap.
6. Measure the width of the flattened Plastigage according to manufacturer's instructions. See **Figure 96**. Measure at both ends of Plastigage strip. A difference of 0.001 in. (0.03 mm) or more indicates a tapered journal. Confirm with a micrometer. If bearing clearance is not over 0.005 in. (0.13 mm), the bearing insert is good. Otherwise, replace bearing insert.
7. Remove Plastigage strip.
8. Repeat Steps 1-7 for all other bearings.
9. Install all bearing shells and caps and tighten to specifications (end of chapter).
10. Force crankshaft as far forward as possible by using a screwdriver inserted between a main bearing cap and the crankshaft. Insert a feeler gauge between the cap for main bearing No. 3 and the crankshaft as shown in **Figure 104**. End play should be 0.003-0.007 in. (0.07-0.18 mm). If greater than 0.015 in. (0.37 mm), replace bearing No. 3 (thrust bearing).

Main Bearing Replacement

Main bearings may be replaced with the engine installed or not. Replace bearings in sets.

Engine installed

1. Remove oil pan as described in this chapter.
2. Remove rear bearing cap and remove bearing insert from cap.
3. Insert long cotter pin into crankshaft journal oil hole. Rotate the crankshaft to roll the bearing out.
4. Clean crankshaft journal and insert unnotched side of bearing into notched side of block. Using same technique as for removal, roll new bearing insert into place.
5. Install new bearing insert into cap.
6. Install cap with strip of Plastigage and measure clearance as described in Steps 3-7, *Bearing and Journal Inspection.*
7. If bearing clearance is satisfactory, lubricate the journal and the bearing halves with assembly lubricant.
8. Install bearing cap and tighten to 10-12 ft.-lb. (1.4-1.6 mkg).
9. Repeat Steps 2-8 for other main bearings.
10. Tap crankshaft rearward with a lead hammer to locate bearing caps in bearings.

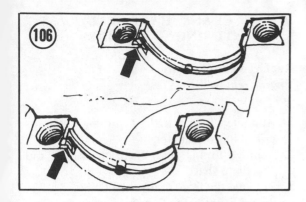

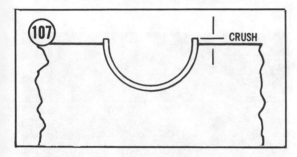

11. Tighten main bearing cap bolts to specifications (end of chapter).

12. Force crankshaft as far forward as possible by using a screwdriver inserted between a main bearing cap and the crankshaft. Insert a feeler gauge between the cap for main bearing No. 3 and the crankshaft as shown in **Figure 104**. End play should be 0.003-0.007 in. (0.07-0.18 mm). If greater than 0.015 in. (0.37 mm), replace bearing No. 3 (thrust bearing).

13. Install oil pan and refill with engine oil.

Engine removed

If engine is removed, simply follow the *Crankshaft Removal* and *Crankshaft Installation* procedures in this chapter.

Crankshaft Removal

1. Remove oil pan and oil pump.

2. Mark all main bearing caps and connecting rod caps so that they will be reinstalled in exactly the same location. See **Figure 105**.

3. Remove connecting rod bearing caps. Push piston/rod assemblies toward the cylinder head.

4. Remove main bearing caps.

5. Remove front and rear seal flanges from cylinder block.

6. Carefully remove the crankshaft from the cylinder block.

7. Remove main bearing inserts from cylinder block and main bearing caps. If they are reusable, mark their location on the back of the insert with a pencil.

8. Remove connecting rod bearing inserts from rods and rod caps. If they are reusable, mark their location on the back of the insert with a pencil.

Crankshaft Inspection

1. Check connecting rod side clearance and bearing clearance as described in this chapter.

2. Clean crankshaft thoroughly with solvent. Clean oil holes with rifle cleaning brushes; flush thoroughly and blow dry with air. Lightly oil all journal surfaces immediately to prevent rust.

3. Carefully inspect each journal for scratches, ridges, scoring, nicks, etc. Very small nicks and scratches may be removed with crocus cloth. More serious damage must be removed by grinding; this is a job for a machine shop.

4. If the surface finish on all journals is satisfactory, take the crankshaft to your dealer or local machine shop. They can check out-of-roundness, taper and wear on the journals. They can also check crankshaft alignment and inspect for cracks.

Crankshaft Installation

1. Make sure the cylinder block bearing saddles, bearing cups, bearing inserts and crankshaft journals are perfectly clean. A small piece of grit behind a bearing insert could deform the bearing and lead to very early failure.

2. Install new upper main bearing inserts in cylinder block. Upper halves have an oil hole. The lower halves do not. Make sure that the bearing tang fits in the cutout in the block. See **Figure 106**.

> *CAUTION*
> *Do not file bearings or bearing saddles to get a better fit. The ends of the bearings normally protrude slightly. This bearing crush causes the bearings to be forced tightly against the saddle and cap when the caps are tightened down. See **Figure 107**, which is exaggerated for clarity.*

3. Install lower bearing inserts in the main bearing caps. Make certain that the bearing tang fits in the cutout in the cap and observe the CAUTION above.

4. Install new bearing inserts in connecting rod caps.

5. Carefully lower crankshaft into place. Be careful not to damage the bearing or journal surfaces.

6. Check clearances of each main bearing following steps in *Bearing and Journal Inspection.*

7. If bearing clearance is satisfactory, lubricate the journal and bearing halves with assembly lubricant.

8. Install bearing caps and tighten to specifications (end of chapter).

9. Tap crankshaft rearward with a lead hammer to locate bearing caps in bearings.

10. Tighten main bearing cap bolts to specifications (end of chapter).

11. Force crankshaft as far forward as possible by using a screwdriver inserted between a main bearing cap and the crankshaft. Insert a feeler gauge between the cap for main bearing No. 3 and the crankshaft as shown in **Figure 104**. End play should be 0.003-0.007 in. (0.07-0.18 mm). If greater than 0.015 in. (0.37 mm), replace bearing No. 3 (thrust bearing).

12. Install rods on crankshaft as described under *Pistons and Connecting Rods* in this chapter.

CRANKSHAFT SEAL (FLYWHEEL SIDE)

Replacement (All Engines)

Seal replacement can be performed with the engine installed or removed from the vehicle.

1. If replacing with the engine installed in the vehicle, remove the transaxle as described in Chapter Nine.

2. Remove the flywheel.

3. Pry old seal out with a screwdriver as shown in **Figure 108**.

4. Clean the seal cavity in the flange thoroughly.

5. Place the new seal in position and tap into the bearing flange.

6. If removed, install the transaxle as described in Chapter Nine.

CRANKSHAFT SEAL (TIMING GEAR SIDE)

Replacement (1.7 Liter)
Engine removed

1. Remove the camshaft timing belt as described in this chapter.

2. Remove timing gears from crankshaft and intermediate shaft.

3. Remove the front crankshaft flange.

4. Press old seal from flange.

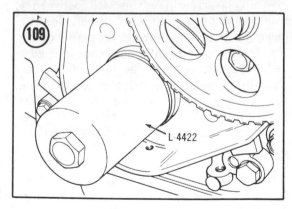

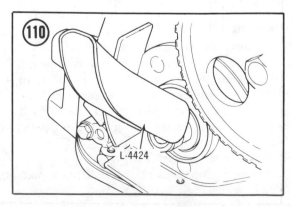

5. Clean flange and mating surface on cylinder block thoroughly. Remove all traces of the old gasket.

6. Install the flange on the cylinder block with a new gasket.

7. Install new seal in flange with special tool (part No. L-4422) as shown in **Figure 109**. Press it in until it is flush with the flange.

Engine in Vehicle

1. Remove camshaft timing belt as described in this chapter.

2. Hold crankshaft at TDC, using a screwdriver against the flywheel (accessible through an opening in the transaxle case).

3. Remove the crankshaft pulley bolt.

4. Remove the pulley.

5. Pry old seal out with special tool (part No. L-4424). See **Figure 110**.

> *CAUTION*
> *The special tool must not fit between the seal and the crankshaft. Instead, the special tool cuts through the dust lip and over the inner edge of the support ring of the seal.*

6. Clean out the seal cavity thoroughly.

7. Press in new seal with special tool (part No. L-4422) until it is flush. See **Figure 109**.

8. Install crankshaft pulley but do not tighten mounting bolt.

9. Install camshaft timing belt exactly as described in this chapter. Tighten the crankshaft pulley bolt after the timing belt is in place.

Replacement (2.2 Liter)

The seal can be removed with the engine in or out of the vehicle.

1. Remove the camshaft timing belt as described in this chapter.

2. Remove the crankshaft sprocket using tool part No. C-4685 (or equivalent) as shown in **Figure 111**.

3. Remove the crankshaft oil seal retainer screws, then remove the retainer. See **Figure 112**.

4. Remove the oil seal using tool part No. C-4679 (**Figure 113**).

5. Clean out the seal cavity thoroughly.

6. Coat the new seal O.D. with Loctite Stud N' Bearing Mount (part No. 4057987).

7. Press in new seal with special tool part No. C-4680 until it is flush. See **Figure 114**.

8. Install camshaft timing belt exactly as described in this chapter.

CYLINDER BLOCK

Inspection

1. Check cylinder block for cracks in the cylinder walls, water jacket and main bearing webs.

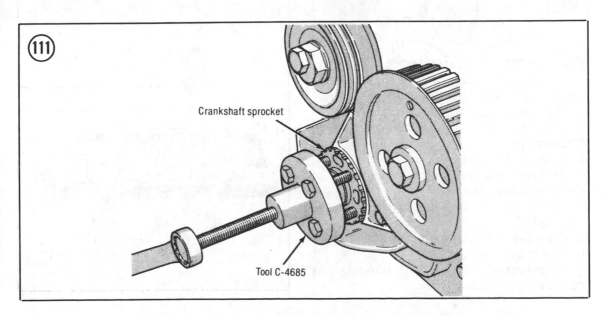

(111)

Crankshaft sprocket

Tool C-4685

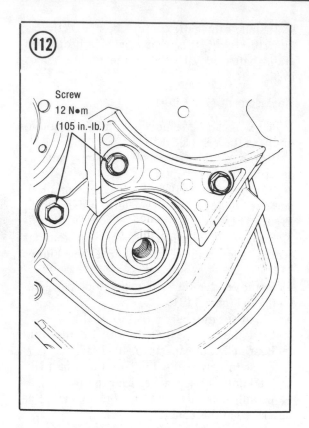

(112)

Screw
12 N•m
(105 in.-lb.)

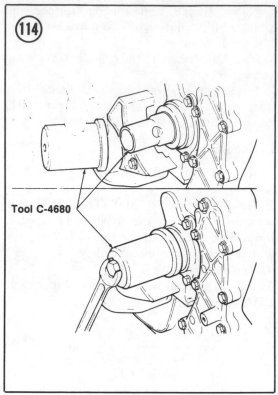

(114)

Tool C-4680

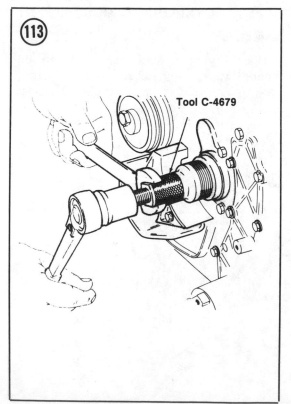

(113)

Tool C-4679

(115)

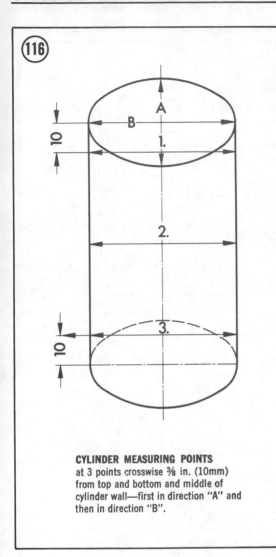

CYLINDER MEASURING POINTS
at 3 points crosswise ⅜ in. (10mm)
from top and bottom and middle of
cylinder wall—first in direction "A" and
then in direction "B".

2. Check cylinder walls for taper, out-of-roundness or excessive ridge at the top of ring travel. Use a dial gauge as shown in **Figure 115**. Check points shown in **Figure 116**.

Reconditioning

Cylinder walls may be reconditioned by honing only or boring and honing to correct out-of-round and taper.

If only slight wear is evident, bores may be lightly honed and high-limit standard size pistons fitted to maintain proper piston-to-cylinder clearance. Measure piston clearance as described in this chapter.

If wear is more excessive, cylinder should be bored and honed for oversize pistons. Measure piston clearance as described earlier.

FLYWHEEL

Removal

Remove flywheel and clutch as described in Chapter Nine.

Inspection

1. Check ring gear teeth for wear or damage.
2. Check clutch friction surface of flywheel for cracks and grooves. If necessary, recondition or replace flywheel.

Installation

Mount flywheel and clutch disc as described in Chapter Nine.

Tables are on the following pages.

Table 1 1.7 LITER ENGINE SPECIFICATIONS

General	
Bore	3.13 in. (79.5 mm)
Stroke	3.40 in. (86.4 mm)
Displacement	104.7 cc (1700 cc)
Minimum compression	107 psi
Maximum variation between cylinders	42 psi
Compression ratio	8.2:1
Firing order	1-3-4-2
Fuel grade	Unleaded (minimum 91 RON)
Oil pressure	
Minimum (at idle)	4 psi (0.3 kg/cm^2) at 176° F/80° C
Minimum (at 2,000 rpm)	28 psi (2.0 kg/cm^2) at 176° F/80° C
Cylinder Head	
Distortion (maximum)	0.004 in. (0.10 mm)
Valve guide wear limit	
Intake	0.020 in. (0.5 mm)
Exhaust	0.027 in. (0.7 mm)
Valve seat width	
Intake	1.306 in. (33.20 mm)
Exhaust	1.212 in. (30.80 mm)
Valve Springs	
Valve spring installed height	1.28 in. (32.6 mm)
Valve spring pressure	38.8 lb. @ 1.28 in.
	(17.6 mkg @ 32.6 mm)
Valves	
Head diameter	
Intake	1.338 in. (34.0 mm)
Exhaust	1.220 in. (31.0 mm
Stem diameter, standard	0.314 in. (7.970 mm
Stem-to-guide clearance (minimum)	
Intake	0.020 in. (0.5 mm)
Exhaust	0.027 in. (0.7 mm)
Valve angles	
Seat	45°
Face	45°
Tappet clearance	
Intake	
Warm	0.008-0.012 in. (0.20-0.30 mm)
Cold	0.006-0.010 in. (0.15-0.25 mm)
Exhaust	
Warm	0.016-0.020 in. (0.40-0.50 mm)
Cold	0.014-0.018 in. (0.35-0.45 mm)
Camshaft	
Runout (maximum)	0.0004 in. (0.01 mm)
End play (maximum)	0.006 in. (0.15 mm)

(continued)

Table 1 1.7 LITER ENGINE SPECIFICATIONS (continued)

Crankshaft	
Main bearing journal diameter	2.125 in. (54 mm)
Maximum out-of-round	0.001 in. (0.03 mm)
End play	0.003-0.007 in.
	(0.07-0.18 mm)
Connecting rod journal diameter	1.81 in. (46 mm)
Connecting rod bearing clearance	0.0004-0.0025 in.
	(0.010-0.064 mm)

Table 2 2.2 LITER ENGINE SPECIFICATIONS

General	
Bore	3.44 in. (87.5 mm)
Stroke	3.62 in. (92 mm)
Displacement	135.00 cc (2200 cc)
Compression pressure	130/150 psi (standard)
Maximum variation between cylinders	20 psi
Compression ratio	8.5:1
Firing order	1-3-4-2
Fuel grade	Unleaded (minimum 91 RON)
Oil pressure	
Minimum (at idle)	45 psi (310 kPa) — engine cold
Minimum (at 2,000 rpm)	50 psi (345 kPa) at
	176° F/80° C
Cylinder Head	
Distortion (maximum)	0.004 in. (0.10 mm)
Valve guide wear limit	
Intake	0.020 in. (0.5 mm)
Exhaust	0.027 in. (0.7 mm)
Valve seat width	
Intake	0.069-0.088 in. (1.75-2.25 mm)
Exhaust	0.059-0.078 in. (1.5-2.0 mm)
Valve Springs	
Valve spring pressure	
Valves open	@ 1.22 in. (30.99 mm)=168-182 lb. (748-808 N.m)
Valves close	@ 1.65 in. (41.91 mm)=99-108 lb. (442-482 N.m)
Valve spring free length	2.28 in. (57.9 mm)
Valves	
Head diameter	
Intake	1.60 in. (40.6 mm)
Exhaust	1.39 in. (35.4 mm
Stem diameter (minimum)	
Intake	0.3124 in. (7.935 mm)
Exhaust	0.3103 in. (7.881 mm)
Stem-to-guide clearance (minimum)	
Intake	0.020 in. (0.5 mm)
Exhaust	0.027 in. (0.7 mm)
Valve angles	
Seat	45°
Face	45°
Tappet clearance	Hydraulic
Camshaft	
Runout (maximum)	0.0004 in. (0.01 mm)
End play (maximum)	0.020 in. (0.50 mm)

(continued)

Table 2 2.2 LITER ENGINE SPECIFICATIONS (continued)

Crankshaft	
Main bearing journal diameter	2.362-2.363 in. (59.987-60.013 mm)
Maximum out-of-round	0.001 in. (0.03 mm)
End play (maximum)	0.014 in. (0.35 mm)
Connecting rod journal diameter	1.968-1.969 in. (49.987-50.013 mm)
Connecting rod bearing clearance	0.0004-0.0026 in. (0.011-0.067 mm)
Connecting rod side clearance	0.005-0.013 in. (0.13-0.32 mm)

Table 3   ENGINE TIGHTENING TORQUES (1.7 LITER)

	Ft.-lb.	Mkg
Cylinder head-to-engine block	60	8.3
Crankshaft bearing caps-to-engine block	47	6.5
Flywheel-to-crankshaft	36	5.0
Sprocket-to-intermediate shaft	58	8.0
Connecting rod	35	5.0
Water pump-to-engine block	14	2.0
Flange-to-engine block	7	1.0
Fuel pump-to-engine block	14	2.0
Intermediate shaft guide-to-engine block	18	2.5
Pulley-to-crankshaft	58	8.0
Distributor clamp-to-engine block	14	2.0
Alternator bracket-to-engine block	24	3.3
Alternator-to-bracket	18	2.5
Alternator adjuster-to-cylinder head and alternator	14	2.0
Water drain plug	25	3.5
Pulley-to-cam belt pulley	18	2.5
Oil pump cover	7	1.0
Oil pump-to-engine block	14	2.0
Oil pan plug	22	3.0
Oil pan-to-engine block (Allen head screws)	7[1]	1.0[1]
Oil filter bracket-to-engine block	14	2.0
Oil filter-to-oil filter bracket	1 turn after contact	
Bearing housing-to-water pump housing	7	1.0
Water pump pulley-to-hub	14	2.0
Cover-to-water pump housing	14	2.0
Carburetor stud-to-intake manifold	14	2.0
Bracket-to-intake manifold	14	2.0
Exhaust manifold stud-to-cylinder head	17	2.3
Camshaft bearing cap-to-cylinder head	13	1.8-2.2
Exhaust manifold-to-cylinder head	14	2.0
Intake manifold-to-cylinder head	18	2.5
Sprocket-to-camshaft	58	8.0
Tensioner-to-cylinder head	32	4.5
Cylinder head cover-to-cylinder head	4	0.6
Carburetor-to-intake manifold	14	2.0
Water adapter-to-cylinder head	7	1.0

(continued)

Table 3 ENGINE TIGHTENING TORQUES (1.7 LITER) (continued)

	Ft.-lb.	Mkg
Heater flange-to-cylinder head	7	1.0
Guard-to-exhaust manifold	14	2.0
Intake manifold support-to-intake manifold	14	2.0
Oil pressure switch	7	1.0
Spark plug	22	3.0
Intake manifold support-to-exhaust manifold	18	2.5
Cam belt guard	7	1.0
Clutch-to-flywheel	14	2.0
Engine-to-transmission	40	5.5
Engine support-to-engine block	32	4.4
Clutch pressure plate-to-flywheel	23	3.2

1. 14 ft.-lb. (2.0 mkg) if hex head screws are used.

4

Table 4 2.2 LITER ENGINE TIGHTENING TORQUES

	Ft.-lb.	Mkg
Cylinder head cover screw	8	1.2
Cylinder head bolt (4 turn sequence)	30	4.1
	45	6.1
	45	6.1
	+ 1/4 turn	+ 1/4 turn
Camshaft sprocket bolt	65	8.8
Camshaft bearing cap nut	14	1.9
Air pump pulley bolt	21	2.8
Crankshaft sprocket bolt	50	6.8
Main bearing cap nolt	30 + 1/4 turn	4.1 + 1/4 turn
Connecting rod bearing cap nut	40 + 1/4 turn	5.4 + 1/4 turn
Front crankshaft oil seal retainer screw	8	1.2
Rear crankshaft oil seal retainer screw	8	1.2
Intermediate shaft sprocket bolt	65	8.8
Intermediate shaft retainer screw	8	1.2
Upper timing belt cover screw	8	1.2
Lower timing belt cover screw	40 in.-lb.	4.0 N.m
Intake manifold bolt	16	2.3
Water crossover screw	8	1.2
Exhaust manifold nut	16	2.3
Thermostat housing screw	21	2.8
Upper water pump housing screw	21	2.8
Lower water pump housing screw	40	5.4
Oil pan screw	16	2.3
Oil pump mounting screw	16	2.3
Oil pump cover screw	8	1.2
Oil pump strainer support mounting screw	8	1.2
Oil pan drain plug	20	2.7
Spark plug	26	3.5

Table 5 RING GAPS

	Ring Gap	Wear Limit
1.7 liter		
Upper piston ring	0.012-0.018 in.	0.039 in.
Lower piston ring	0.012-0.018 in.	0.039 in.
Oil control ring		
1978	0.012-0.018 in.	0.039 in.
1979-on	0.016-0.055 in.	0.074 in.
2.2 liter		
Upper piston ring	0.011-0.021 in.	0.039 in.
Lower piston ring	0.011-0.021 in.	0.039 in.
Oil control ring	0.015-0.055 in.	0.074 in.

Table 6 RING SIDE CLEARANCES

	Groove Clearance	Wear limit
1.7 liter		
Upper piston ring	0.0016-0.0028 in.	0.004 in.
Lower piston ring	0.0008-0.002 in.	0.004 in.
Oil control ring		
1978	0.0008-0.002 in.	0.004 in.
1979-on	Oil ring should rotate free in groove but side clearance should not exceed 0.008 in.	
2.2 liter		
Upper piston ring	0.0015-0.0031 in.	0.004 in.
Lower piston ring	0.0015-0.0037 in.	0.004 in.
Oil control ring	Oil ring should rotate free in groove but side clearance should not exceed 0.008 in.	

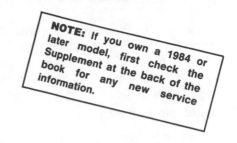

NOTE: If you own a 1984 or later model, first check the Supplement at the back of the book for any new service information.

CHAPTER FIVE

PUSHROD ENGINE

A 1.6 liter 4-cylinder overhead valve engine replaced the 1.7 liter overhead cam engine in mid-1983 production. The water-cooled engine uses a cast iron block with an aluminum cylinder head. Five main bearings support the forged steel crankshaft, with the No. 3 bearing taking the thrust. Rubber-lipped seals are used at the front and rear of the block for crankshaft oil sealing.

The cast iron camshaft is supported by 3 bearings and driven by a dual timing chain. The camshaft is located at the left of the crankshaft (toward front of car). Camshaft end play is controlled by a thrust plate positioned in front of the No. 1 bearing and bolted to the block. A helical gear ·on the camshaft drives the distributor and oil pump while an eccentric operates the fuel pump.

The valve train uses mechanical tappets, pushrods and adjustable rocker shafts.

A "siamese" bore design is used, with piston numbering from *rear-to-front*, the reverse of normal practice.

Table 1 (specifications) and **Table 2** (tightening torques) are at the end of the chapter.

SERVICE NOTES

On an inline-mounted engine, the timing gear end of the engine is the front and the flywheel end is the rear, since these ends face that way in the car. Transverse mounting of the engine makes these terms misleading.

However, since most mechanics are used to inline terminology, it is used throughout this chapter. "Front" means the timing gear end and "rear" means the flywheel end.

GASKET SEALANT

Gasket sealant is used instead of pre-formed gaskets between numerous mating surfaces on the 1.6 liter engine. Two types of gasket sealant are used: room temperature vulcanizing (RTV) and anaerobic. Since these 2 materials have different sealing properties, they cannot be used interchangeably.

Room Temperature Vulcanizing Sealant

This black silicone gel is supplied in tubes and is available from your dealer. Moisture in the air causes RTV to cure. Always place the cap on the tube as soon as possible when using RTV. RTV has a shelf life of one year and will not cure properly when the shelf life has expired. Check the expiration date on RTV tubes before using and keep partially used tubes tightly sealed.

Applying RTV sealant

Clean all gasket residue from mating surfaces with a degreaser and putty knife. Surfaces must be clean and free of oil and dirt or RTV will not seal properly. Remove all sealant material from blind attaching holes.

Apply RTV sealant in a continuous bead about 0.12 in. (3 mm) thick. Apply the sealant on the inner side of all mounting holes. Torque mating parts within 10 minutes after application.

Anaerobic Sealant

This is a red gel supplied in tubes and available from your dealer. It cures only in the absence of air, as when squeezed tightly between 2 machined mating surfaces. For this reason, it will not spoil if the cap is left off the tube. It should not be used if one mating surface is flexible.

Applying anaerobic sealant

Clean all sealant residue from mating surfaces with degreaser and a putty knife. Surfaces must be clean and free of oil and dirt. Remove all sealant from blind attaching holes.

Apply anaerobic sealant in a 0.04 in. (1 mm) or less bead to one sealing surface. Apply the sealant on the inner side of all mounting holes. Torque mating parts within 15 minutes after application.

ENGINE REMOVAL/INSTALLATION

1. Scribe alignment marks directly on the underside of the hood around the hood hinges, then remove the hood.
2. Disconnect the negative battery cable.
3. Drain the engine coolant and engine oil. Remove the oil filter. See Chapter Three.
4. Disconnect the upper and lower radiator hoses at the radiator and engine, then remove the hoses.
5. Remove the radiator shroud, radiator and fan assembly. See Chapter Seven.
6. Remove the air cleaner. See Chapter Six.
7. If equipped with power steering, remove the power steering pump from its bracket (**Figure 1**). Place pump to one side out of the way.
8. Disconnect all electrical connections at the alternator, carburetor and engine.
9. Disconnect the fuel line, heater hoses and throttle cable. Plug the fuel line to prevent leakage.
10. Remove alternator mounting bolts (**Figure 2**). Place alternator to one side out of the way.

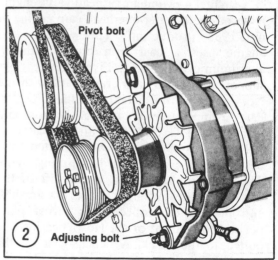

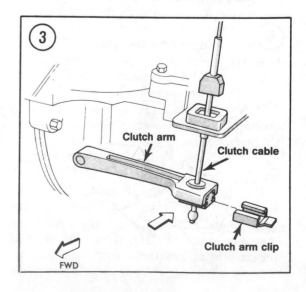

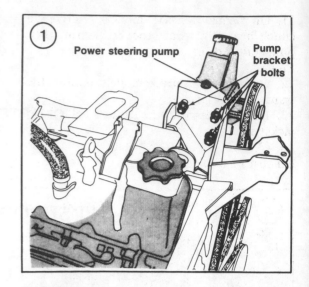

11. On manual transaxle models, remove the clutch arm clip from grooves in arm, then pull clutch cable upward and remove. See **Figure 3**.

12. On manual transaxle models, remove the transaxle case lower cover.

13. Raise the front of the car and place it on jackstands.

14. Disconnect the exhaust pipe at the exhaust manifold.

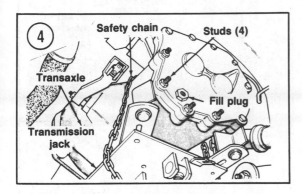

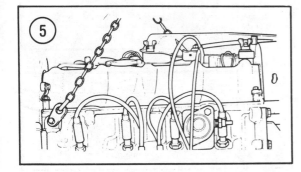

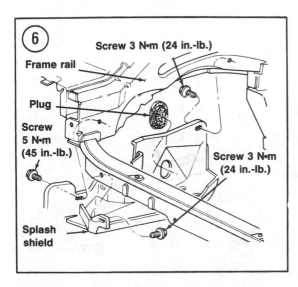

15. Remove the starter. See Chapter Eight.

16. If equipped with automatic transaxle:

  a. Remove transaxle lower case cover and mark flex plate to converter position.

  b. Remove screws holding converter to flex plate, then install a C-clamp on bottom front of converter housing to prevent converter from falling out.

  c. Install a transaxle holding fixture.

WARNING
*The engine is very heavy and awkward to handle. It may swing, turn or drop suddenly during removal. Never place any part of your body where a moving engine might trap or crush it. If you have to reposition the engine during removal, push it with a board or similar tool. If the engine is hard to lift, stop and make sure it has been **completely** disconnected from the car. Make sure the engine has not jammed. If necessary, lower the engine back to the mounts and start the lifting process over. Do not try to force the engine loose with the hoist.*

17. Support the transaxle with a jack (**Figure 4**). Attach a chain hoist to engine lifting brackets as shown in **Figure 5**. Lift engine/transaxle just enough so the hoist bears their weight.

18. Remove the right inner splash shield (**Figure 6**).

19. Disconnect and remove ground strap.

20. Disconnect right engine mount by removing the long bolt from the yoke bracket and insulator. See **Figure 7**.

21. Remove all transaxle housing-to-engine mounting screws.

22. Remove the front engine mount bolt and nut holding the insulator support bracket to the crossmember bracket. See **Figure 8**.

23. Remove the anti-roll strut bolts. See **Figure 9**.

NOTE
Recheck at this point to make sure that all accessories, tubes, hoses and wires are positioned out of the way and that nothing will hamper engine removal.

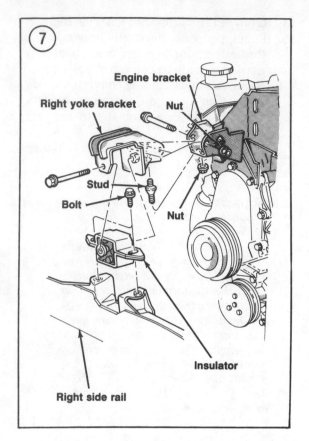

⑦

Engine bracket

Right yoke bracket

Nut

Stud

Bolt

Nut

Insulator

Right side rail

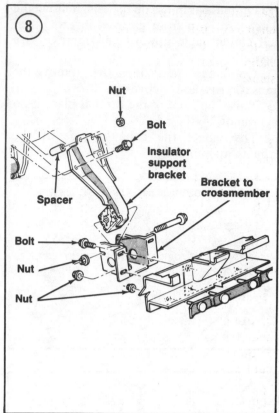

⑧

Nut

Bolt

Insulator
support
bracket

Bracket to
crossmember

Spacer

Bolt

Nut

Nut

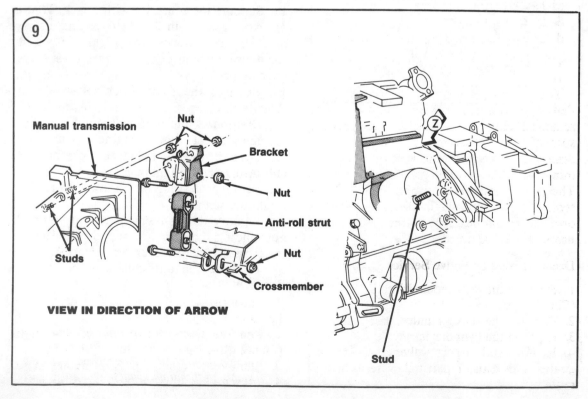

⑨

Manual transmission

Nut

Bracket

Nut

Anti-roll strut

Nut

Studs

Crossmember

VIEW IN DIRECTION OF ARROW

Stud

24. Carefully lift engine assembly out of the engine compartment. Once the engine is clear of the car, lower it to a suitable support or stand. Secure the engine in the support or stand.

ENGINE INSTALLATION

1. Installation is the reverse of removal. Note the following precautions:
   a. Check the wiring harness for damage and correct or replace as necessary.
   b. Check the engine mounts for looseness or damage and tighten or replace as required.
   c. Install engine in engine compartment and tighten mounting bolts finger-tight. Pry engine to the right or left as required to assure correct drive shaft positioning.
2. Install oil filter. Refill the cooling system and crankcase. See Chapter Three.
3. Start engine and run at idle. Check for fluid leaks.
4. Adjust the following by referring to the appropriate sections in Chapter Three:
   a. Valve clearance.
   b. Drive belt tension.
   c. Ignition timing.
   d. Engine idle speed.

OVERHAUL SEQUENCE

The following sequences are basic outlines that tell how much of the engine needs to be removed and disassembled to perform specific types of service. The sequences are designed to keep engine disassembly to a minimum, thus avoiding unnecessary work. The major assemblies mentioned in these sequences are covered in detail under their own individual headings within this chapter, unless otherwise noted.

Decarbonizing or Valve Service

1. Remove the exhaust and intake manifolds (Chapter Six).
2. Remove the rockers and rocker shafts.
3. Remove the cylinder head.
4. Remove and inspect valves. Inspect valve guides and seats, repairing or replacing as required.

5. Assemble by reversing Steps 1-4.

Valve and Ring Service

1. Perform Steps 1-4 of *Decarbonizing or Valve Service*.
2. Remove the oil pan.
3. Remove the pistons together with the connecting rods.
4. Remove the piston rings. It is not necessary to separate the piston from the connecting rod unless a piston, connecting rod or piston pin needs repair or replacement.
5. Assemble by reversing Steps 1-4.

General Overhaul

1. Remove the engine from the car as described in this chapter.
2. Remove the motor mounts.
3. Remove the fuel pump, carburetor and intake/exhaust manifolds (Chapter Six).
4. Remove the camshaft timing chain.
5. Remove the water pump and thermostat (Chapter Seven).
6. Remove the distributor and alternator (Chapter Eight).
7. Remove the cylinder head.
8. Remove the oil pan, oil pump and pump drive shaft.
9. Remove the camshaft and tappets.
10. Remove the pistons together with the connecting rods.
11. Remove the flywheel/drive plate.
12. Remove the crankshaft and main bearings.
13. Inspect the cylinder block.
14. Assemble by reversing Steps 1-12.

CAMSHAFT TIMING COVER, SPROCKETS AND CHAIN

Removal

1. Raise the front of the car and place it on jackstands.
2. Remove the right inner splash shield (**Figure 6**).
3. Remove the alternator. See Chapter Eight.
4. Loosen air pump and remove drive belt.

5. Remove crankshaft pulley bolt, washer and pulley. See **Figure 10**.

6. Drain cooling system through water pump drain plug (see Chapter Seven) and remove the water pump-to-timing cover hose.

7. Place a jack under the timing cover end of the engine and raise it slightly.

8. Remove the bolts holding the engine mount bracket to the timing cover and engine block. See **Figure 11**.

> *NOTE*
> *The cover-to-block screws pass through locating dowels. Make sure these dowels do not fall into the crankcase extension in Step 9.*

9. Remove crankcase extension-to-cover bolts. Remove cover-to-block bolts. Remove timing cover. See **Figure 12**.

10. Rotate the camshaft sprocket until one of the bolt heads is positioned at the top of a centerline drawn through the camshaft and crankshaft sprockets.

> *NOTE*
> *The crankshaft must not be allowed to rotate while performing Step 11.*

11. Install a torque wrench with appropriate socket on top sprocket bolt. Apply 30 ft.-lb. (40 N•m) torque (head installed) or 15 ft.-lb. (20 N•m) torque (head removed) in the direction of crankshaft rotation to take up any slack.

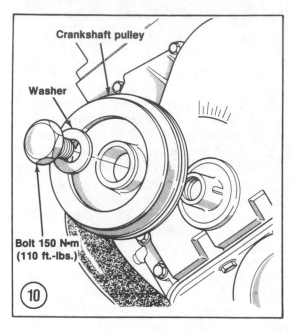

10

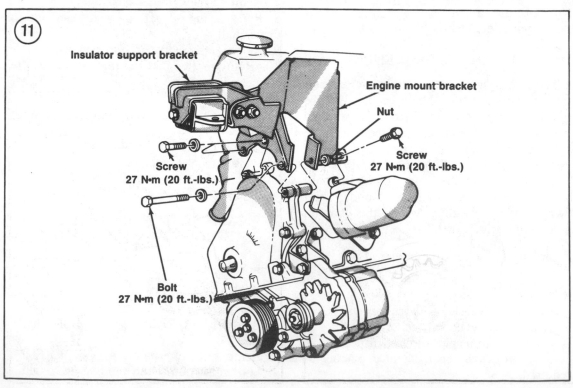

11

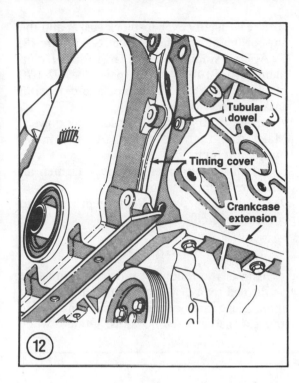

Tubular dowel

Timing cover

Crankcase extension

12

12. Hold a scale even with the edge of one chain link as shown in **Figure 13**. Apply the same amount of torque as in Step 11 in the *reverse* direction. Note how much chain moves. If movement exceeds 1/8 in. (3.175 mm), the chain should be replaced.

13. Remove camshaft sprocket bolts. Remove sprocket and chain. See **Figure 14**.

14. Remove crankshaft sprocket with pilot tool No. C-4760 and puller part No. C-3894-A. See **Figure 15**.

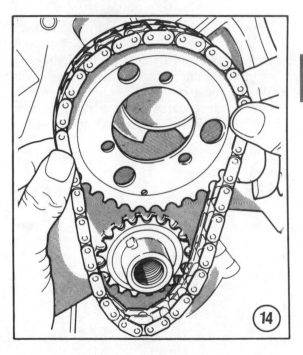

14

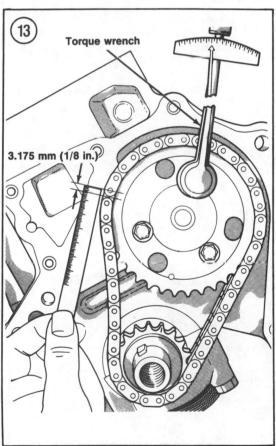

13

Torque wrench

3.175 mm (1/8 in.)

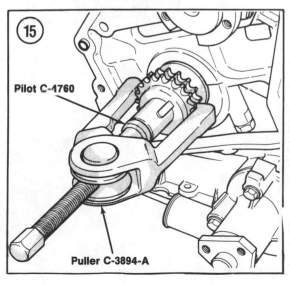

15

Pilot C-4760

Puller C-3894-A

5

Installation

Refer to **Figure 16** for this procedure.

1. Align crankshaft sprocket with key. Drive sprocket firmly onto shaft.

2. Install camshaft sprocket loosely. Rotate sprocket until timing marks on both sprockets are aligned as shown in **Figure 17**.

3. Remove camshaft sprocket without disturbing camshaft position. Fit chain on sprocket and engage chain over crankshaft sprocket. Reinstall camshaft sprocket (**Figure 14**).

4. Recheck timing mark alignment (**Figure 17**) once chain is in place. Install camshaft sprocket bolts and tighten to specifications.

5. Cut about one inch from the timing cover end of a new crankcase extension gasket. Apply a thin coat of quick drying cement (part No. 2299314 or equivalent) to gasket

surfaces. Install cover-to-block gasket and the cut portion of extension gasket. See **Figure 18**.

6. Apply a small drop (not larger than 1/4 in. diameter) of rubber sealer (part No. 4026070 or equivalent) to the block-to-extension gasket corners (**Figure 18**).

7. Install timing cover over locating dowels. Make sure that the gaskets do not move during this step.

8. Install timing cover to block. Tighten all fasteners to specifications.

9. Reverse Steps 1-7 of *Removal* procedure to complete installation.

CYLINDER HEAD

Some of the following procedures must be performed by a dealer or competent machine shop, since they require special knowledge and expensive machine tools. Others, while

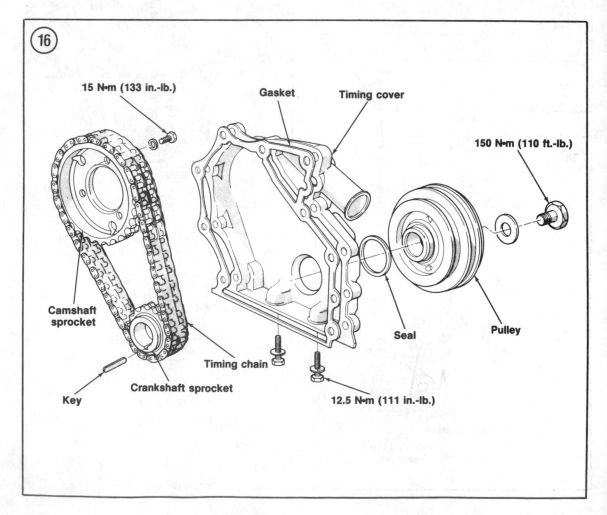

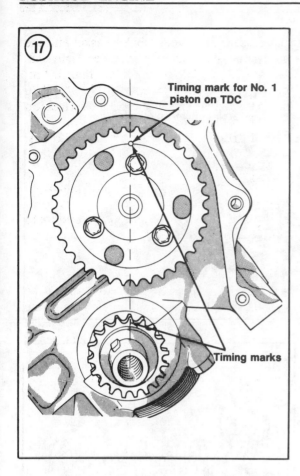

Timing mark for No. 1 piston on TDC

Timing marks

possible for the enthusiast mechanic, are difficult or time-consuming. A general practice among those who do their own service is to remove the cylinder head, perform disassembly except for valve removal and take the head to a machine shop for inspection and service. Since the cost is relatively low in proportion to the required effort and equipment, this may be the best approach even for more experienced owners.

Removal

1. Disconnect the negative battery cable.
2. Drain the cooling system. See Chapter Seven.
3. Disconnect throttle cable and carburetor bracket.
4. Raise the front of the car and place it on jackstands.
5. Disconnect the exhaust pipe at the exhaust manifold.
6. Remove the carburetor. See Chapter Six.
7. Disconnect coolant hoses from intake manifold and cylinder head.
8. Disconnect all electrical wires, connectors and vacuum lines that will interfere with cylinder head removal.

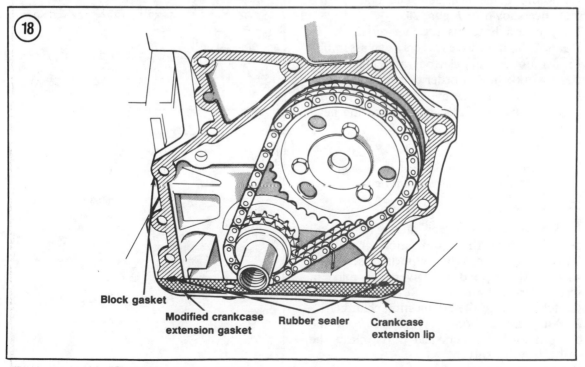

Block gasket

Modified crankcase extension gasket

Rubber sealer

Crankcase extension lip

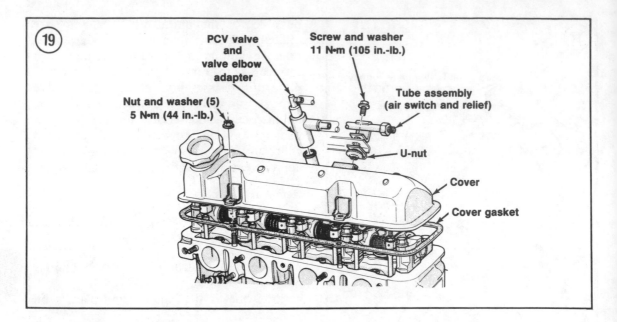

(19)

PCV valve and valve elbow adapter

Screw and washer 11 N•m (105 in.-lb.)

Nut and washer (5) 5 N•m (44 in.-lb.)

Tube assembly (air switch and relief)

U-nut

Cover

Cover gasket

9. Remove the alternator (if required).

10. Remove the intake and exhaust manifolds. See Chapter Six.

11. Disconnect crankcase ventilator system from valve cover. Disconnect diverter hose from bracket. See **Figure 19**.

12. Remove valve cover and gasket. Discard gasket.

13. Remove the cylinder head bolts in the sequence shown in **Figure 20**.

14. Tie end brackets together as shown in **Figure 21** and remove rockers as an assembly.

15. Remove the pushrods and place on a clean workbench in order of removal.

16. Carefully lift the cylinder head from the engine block. Remove and discard the head gasket.

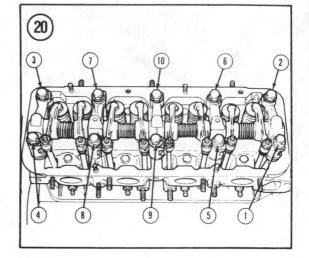

(20)

NOTE
Place the head on its side to prevent damage to the head gasket surface.

Decarbonizing

1. Without removing the valves, remove all deposits from the combustion chambers, intake ports and exhaust ports. Use a fine wire brush dipped in solvent or make a scraper from hardwood. Be careful not to scratch or gouge the combustion chambers.

2. After all carbon is removed from the combustion chambers and ports, clean the entire head in solvent.

(21)

Tie brackets

Dowel

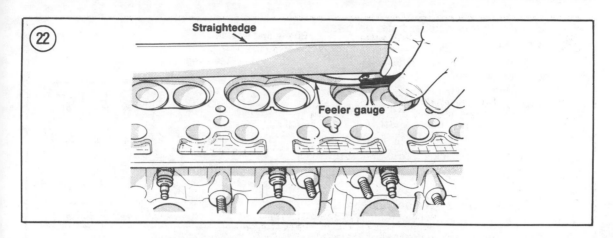

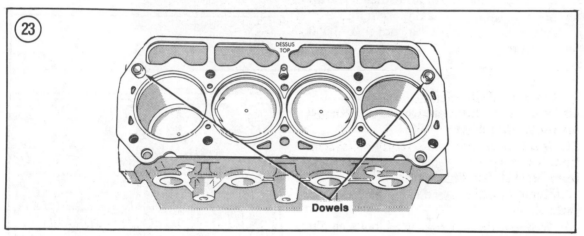

3. Clean away all carbon on the piston tops. Do not remove the carbon ridge at the top of the cylinder bore.

4. Remove the valves as described in this chapter.

5. Clean the pushrod guides, valve guide bores and all bolt holes. Use a cleaning solvent to remove dirt and grease.

6. Clean the valves with a fine wire brush or buffing wheel.

Inspection

1. Check the cylinder head for signs of oil or water leaks before cleaning.

2. Clean the cylinder head thoroughly in solvent. While cleaning, look for cracks or other visible signs of damage. Look for corrosion or foreign material in the oil and water passages. Clean the passages with a stiff spiral brush, then blow them out with compressed air.

3. Check the cylinder head studs for damage and replace if necessary.

4. Check the threaded rocker arm studs or bolt holes for damaged threads. Replace if necessary.

5. Check the flatness of the cylinder head-to-block surface with a straightedge and feeler gauge. See **Figure 23**. If head is warped more than 0.1 in. (0.004 mm), discard it. If warpage is within specifications, the gasket face can be resurfaced to a maximum limit of 0.024 in. (0.6 mm). If this is done, a special 0.070 in. (1.8 mm) gasket must be used to maintain the compression ratio and valve adjustment.

Installation

1. Install a new head gasket over the dowel pins on the block. The word "DESSUS" or "TOP" must face upward. See **Figure 23**.

2. Carefully lower the cylinder head onto the block dowel pins.

3. Insert pushrods in the locations from which they were removed.

4. Place the rocker shaft brackets in position. Wipe the head bolt threads with engine oil and install through the rocker shaft brackets. See **Figure 24**. Screw bolts down finger-tight and make sure each rocker adjusting screw engages its pushrod properly. Remove rocker shaft retaining wire.

5. Tighten head bolts to specifications in the sequence shown in **Figure 25**.

6. Start engine and warm to normal operating temperature (upper radiator hose hot).

7. Shut engine off and let it cool to ambient temperature.

8. Repeat Step 5.

9. Reverse *Removal* Steps 1-12 to complete installation. Refill the cooling system. See Chapter Three. Run the engine for several minutes and check for leaks.

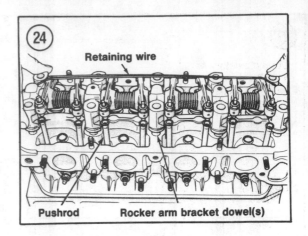

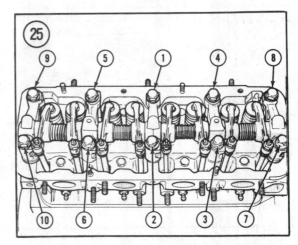

VALVES AND VALVE SEATS

1. Remove the cylinder head as described in this chapter.

2. Compress valve springs with tool part No. C3422-B and adapter part No. C-3422-BB. See **Figure 26**.

3. Remove the valve retainer locks, spring retainer, spring, valve seal and spring seat from each valve. Arrange the parts in order so they can be returned to their original positions when reassembled.

CAUTION
Remove any burrs from the valve stem lock grooves before removing the valves or the valve guides will be damaged.

Valve and Valve Guide Inspection

1. Clean the valves with a wire brush and solvent. Discard cracked, warped or burned valves.

2. Measure the valve stems at the bottom, center and top for wear, using a micrometer. A machine shop can do this when the valves are ground. Compare with specifications in **Figure 27**.

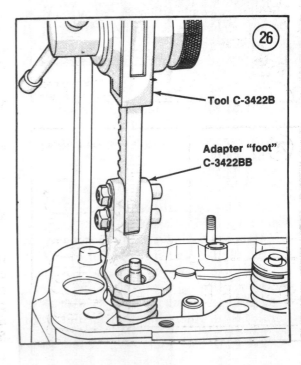

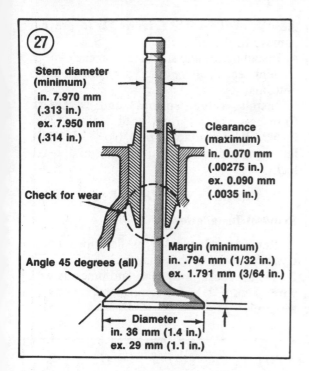

(27)

Stem diameter
(minimum)
in. 7.970 mm
(.313 in.)
ex. 7.950 mm
(.314 in.)

Clearance
(maximum)
in. 0.070 mm
(.00275 in.)
ex. 0.090 mm
(.0035 in.)

Check for wear

Angle 45 degrees (all)

Margin (minimum)
in. .794 mm (1/32 in.)
ex. 1.791 mm (3/64 in.)

Diameter
in. 36 mm (1.4 in.)
ex. 29 mm (1.1 in.)

(28)

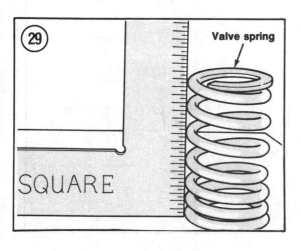

(29)

Valve spring

SQUARE

3. Remove all carbon and varnish from valve guides with a stiff spiral wire brush.

NOTE
The next step assumes that all valve stems have been measured and are within specifications. Replace any valves with worn stems before performing this step.

4. Insert each valve into the guide from which it was removed and hold valve head 0.400 in. (10 mm) above the cylinder head gasket surface. Attach a dial indicator as shown in **Figure 28**. Rock the valve back and forth in the direction of dial indicator and note reading on indicator. If the intake valve rocks more than 0.020 in. (0.5 mm) or the exhaust valve rocks more than 0.027 in. (0.7 mm), the valve guide is worn. Have worn guides replaced by a dealer or repair shop.

5. Measure valve spring free length and compare with specifications (**Table 1**). Replace springs that are too long or too short. Measure spring bend with a square (**Figure 29**). Replace springs that are bent more than 0.063 in. (1.6 mm).

6. Have the valve springs tested under load on a spring tester by a dealer or machine shop and compare with specifications (**Table 1**). Replace weak springs.

7. Inspect the valve seats. If worn or burned, they must be reconditioned. This is a job for a dealer or machine shop, although the procedure is described in this chapter.

Valve Guide Replacement

Valve guide replacement requires a press and reaming tool. If guides are worn, have a dealer or machine shop remove and install guides.

Valve Seat Reconditioning

This job is best left to your dealer or local machine shop. They have the special equipment and knowledge required for this exacting job. The following procedure is provided in the event you are not near a dealer and the local machine shop is not familiar with the engine. Refer to **Figure 30**

5

(intake) or **Figure 32** (exhaust) for valve seat refacing.

1. Cut the valve seats to the specified angle (**Table 1**) with a dressing stone. Remove only enough metal to obtain a good finish.

2. Use tapered stones to obtain the specified seat width when necessary.

NOTE
*Check the thickness of the valve edge or margin after the valves have been ground. See **Figure 27**. Any intake valve with a margin of less than 1/32 in. (0.794 mm) or exhaust valve with a margin of less than 3/64 in. (1.791 mm) should be discarded.*

3. Coat the corresponding valve face with Prussian blue dye.

4. Insert the valve into the valve guide.

5. Apply light pressure to the valve and rotate it approximately 1/4 turn.

6. Lift the valve out. If it seats properly, the dye will transfer evenly to the valve face.

7. If the dye transfers to the top of the valve face, lower the seat. If it transfers to the bottom of the valve face, raise the seat.

Valve Installation

NOTE
Install all parts in the same positions from which they were removed.

1. Coat the valves with oil and install them in the cylinder head.

2. Install spring seats on each guide.

3. Wrap valve stem lock grooves with cellophane tape or place a protector cap over

the end of the valve (**Figure 32**) to prevent damage to the oil seals.

4. Install new valve stem seals on each valve, pushing seal squarely over valve guide until it bottoms.

5. Install valve springs and retainers. Compress valve springs with tool part No. C-3422-B and adapter part No. C-3422-BB far enough to install retainer locks and install locks.

ROCKERS AND ROCKER SHAFTS

Removal/Installation

1. Remove valve cover as described under *Cylinder Head* in this chapter.

2. Tie the rocker arm shaft end brackets with wire (**Figure 21**) and remove rockers as an assembly.

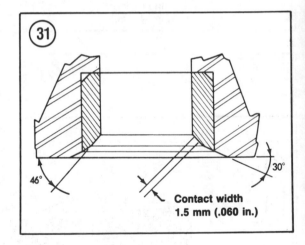

(31)

Contact width 1.5 mm (.060 in.)

46° 30°

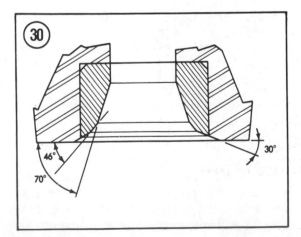

(30)

46° 30°
70°

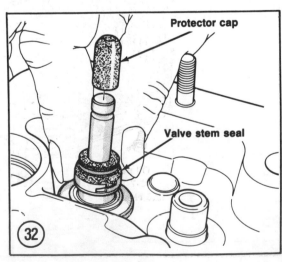

Protector cap

Valve stem seal

(32)

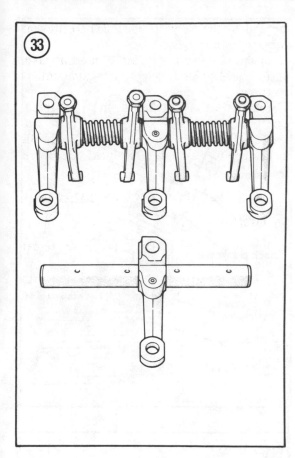

3. Remove retaining wire and slide rocker shaft end brackets, rockers and springs from the shafts. Place all components in the order of removal for proper reinstallation. See **Figure 33**.

4. Installation is the reverse of removal.

Inspection

1. Check rocker fit on shaft and replace if worn or damaged.

2. Inspect shaft lubricating holes to make sure they are not plugged.

OIL PAN

Removal/Installation

Refer to **Figure 34** for this procedure.

1. Raise the front of the car and place it on jackstands.

2. Drain engine oil. See Chapter Three.

3. Remove screws holding pan to crankcase extension. Remove pan and gasket. Discard the gasket.

4. Clean all gasket residue from crankcase extension and oil pan mating surfaces.

5. Install oil pan with a new gasket. Tighten oil pan screws to specifications.

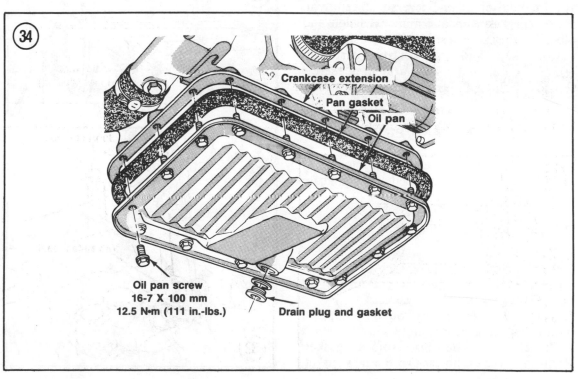

Crankcase extension

Pan gasket

Oil pan

Oil pan screw
16-7 X 100 mm
12.5 N•m (111 in.-lbs.)

Drain plug and gasket

CRANKCASE EXTENSION

The crankcase oil is retained in an aluminum extension bolted to the bottom of the engine block. See **Figure 35**.

Removal/Installation

Refer to **Figure 35** for this procedure.
1. Disconnect negative battery cable.
2. Drain engine oil. See Chapter Three.
3. Drain cooling system through water pump drain plug.
4. Loosen alternator. Remove alternator/ water pump drive belt.
5. Remove water pump. See Chapter Seven.
6. Remove starter. See Chapter Eight.
7. Remove oil pan as described in this chapter.
8. Remove oil pickup attaching screws. Remove oil pickup assembly.

NOTE
Four of the screws to be removed in Step 9 are located inside the extension.

9. Remove crankcase extension attaching screws. Remove extension and gasket. Discard gasket.
10. Installation is the reverse of removal. Clean all gasket residue from extension and block mating surfaces. Install extension with new gaskets and use Loctite (part No. 4057982) on extension attaching screw threads. Tighten all fasteners to specifications.

OIL PUMP AND PICKUP

The oil pump is bolted to the block. Oil pickup removal is described in crankcase extension removal procedure.

Oil Pump Removal/Installation

1. Remove oil filter.
2. Remove oil pump housing/cover assembly mounting bolts (**Figure 36**). Remove oil pump and gasket. Discard gasket.
3. Clean all gasket residue from oil pump and pump mounting surface on block.
4. Install new housing-to-block gasket. Position cover on housing with a new gasket.

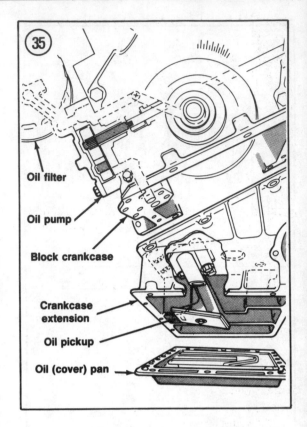

Oil filter

Oil pump

Block crankcase

Crankcase extension

Oil pickup

Oil (cover) pan

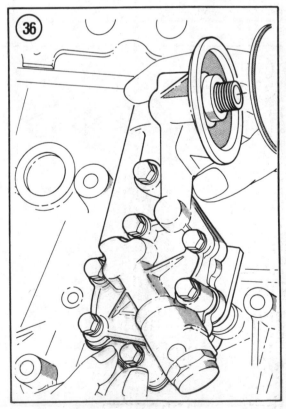

5. Install housing to block, rotating assembly if necessary to engage the drive gear shaft tongue with the driveshaft slot.

6. Align pump housing/cover assembly with block and install attaching bolts. Tighten bolts to specifications.

Disassembly/Inspection/Assembly

The pump body and gears are serviced as an assembly. If one or the other is worn or damaged, replace the entire pump. No wear specifications are provided by the manufacturer. Refer to **Figure 37** for this procedure.

1. Remove oil pump as described in this chapter.

2. Separate housing from cover.

3. Remove the drive and driven gears.

4. Remove the pressure relief valve assembly.

5. Clean all parts in solvent. Brush the inside of the housing and the pressure release chamber to remove all dirt and metal particles. Dry with compressed air, if available.

6. Check the inside of the housing, the drive and driven gears for excessive wear or damage. Inspect the gears for nicks, burrs or scoring. Use an oilstone to remove any minor imperfections.

7. Check the pump housing and cover for cracks or signs of excessive wear.

8. Assemble by reversing Steps 2-4. Use a new cover gasket.

CAMSHAFT AND TAPPETS

The camshaft is located to the left of the crankshaft in the engine block. It has an integral oil pump/distributor drive gear and fuel pump eccentric (**Figure 38**). A thrust

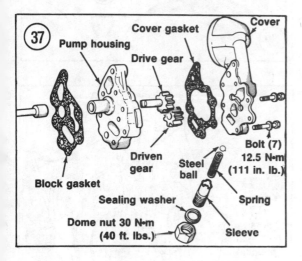

Cover gasket — Cover
(37) Pump housing
Drive gear
Bolt (7) 12.5 N·m (111 in. lb.)
Driven gear — Steel ball
Block gasket
Sealing washer
Dome nut 30 N·m (40 ft. lbs.) — Sleeve — Spring

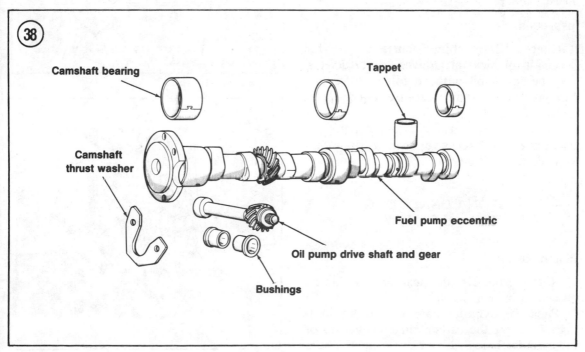

(38)
Camshaft bearing
Tappet
Camshaft thrust washer
Fuel pump eccentric
Oil pump drive shaft and gear
Bushings

plate on the timing chain end of the block controls rearward thrust.

Removal/Installation

1. Remove the engine as described in this chapter.
2. Remove the cylinder head as described in this chapter.
3. Remove the pushrods. Remove the tappets. See **Figure 39**.
4. Remove the timing chain cover and sprockets as described in this chapter.
5. Remove the oil pump as described in this chapter. Remove the oil pump driveshaft.
6. Remove the fuel pump. See Chapter Six.
7. Remove the camshaft thrust plate (**Figure 40**).
8. Carefully withdraw the camshaft from the block (**Figure 41**).
9. Installation is the reverse of removal. Lubricate the camshaft journals and bearing surfaces with clean engine oil. If installing a new camshaft or tappets, add one pint of Chrysler crankcase conditioner (part No. 3419130 or equivalent) to the engine oil.
10. Install a dial indicator as shown in **Figure 42** and measure camshaft end play. If end play is not within specifications (**Table 1**), replace thrust plate.

Inspection

1. Check all machined surfaces of the camshaft for nicks or grooves. Minor defects may be removed with an oilstone. Severe damage or wear requires camshaft replacement.
2. Check tappet skirts and tappet bores in crankcase for excessive scoring or wear. Replace as required.

PISTON/CONNECTING ROD ASSEMBLY

Piston Removal

1. Remove the cylinder head and oil pan as described in this chapter.
2. Pack the cylinder bore with clean shop rags. Remove the carbon ridge at the top of the cylinder bores with a ridge reamer. These

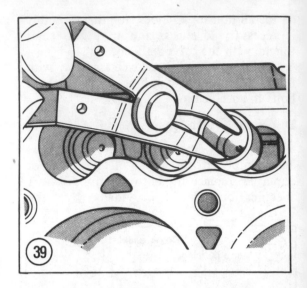
(39)

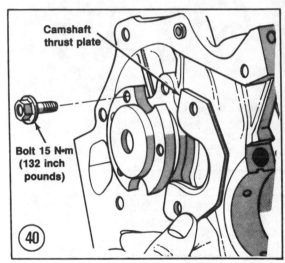
Camshaft thrust plate

Bolt 15 N·m (132 inch pounds)

(40)

(41)

(42)

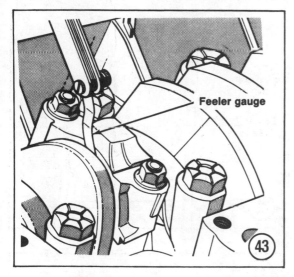

Feeler gauge

(43)

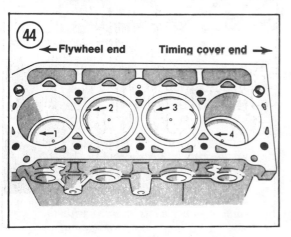

(44) ← Flywheel end   Timing cover end →

can be rented for use. Vacuum out the shavings, then remove the shop rags.

3. Rotate the crankshaft so the connecting rod is centered in the bore.

4. Measure the clearance between each connecting rod and the crankshaft journal flange with a feeler gauge (**Figure 43**). If the big-end clearance exceeds specifications in **Table 1**, replace the connecting rod.

> *NOTE*
> *Mark the cylinder number on the top of each piston with quick-drying paint. Check for cylinder numbers or identification marks on the connecting rod and cap. If they are not visible, make your own (**Figure 44**). Remember that the No. 1 piston is at the flywheel end on this engine.*

5. Remove the nuts holding the connecting rod cap. Lift off the cap, together with the lower bearing insert.

> *NOTE*
> *If the connecting rod caps are difficult to remove, tap the studs with a wooden hammer handle.*

6. Use the wooden hammer handle to push the piston and connecting rod from the bore.

7. Remove the piston rings with a ring remover (**Figure 45**).

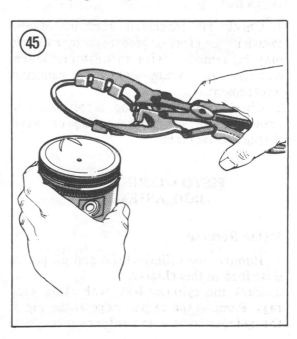

(45)

5

Piston Pin Removal/Installation

The piston pins are press-fitted to the connecting rods and hand-fitted to the pistons. Removal requires the use of a press and support stand. This is a job for a dealer or machine shop equipped to fit the pistons to the pin, ream the pin bushings to the correct diameter and install the pistons and pins on the connecting rods.

Piston Clearance Check

If you do not have precision measuring equipment and know how to use it properly, have this procedure done by a machine shop.
1. Measure the piston diameter with a micrometer as shown in **Figure 46**.
2. Measure the cylinder bore diameter with a bore gauge (**Figure 47**). Measure at the top, center and bottom of the bore, in front- to-rear and side-to-side directions.
3. Subtract the piston diameter from the largest cylinder bore reading. If the difference exceeds specifications (**Table 1**), the cylinder must be rebored and oversized pistons installed.

Piston Ring Fit/Installation

1. Check the ring gap of each piston ring. To do this, position the ring at the bottom of the ring travel area and square it by tapping gently with an inverted piston. See **Figure 48**.

> *NOTE*
> *If the cylinders have not been rebored, check the gap at the bottom of the ring travel, where the cylinder is least worn.*

2. Measure the ring gap with a feeler gauge as shown in **Figure 49**. Compare with specifications. If the measurement is not within specifications, the rings must be replaced as a set.
3. Check the side clearance of the rings as shown in **Figure 50**. Place the feeler gauge alongside the ring all the way into the groove. If the measurement is not within specifications, either the rings or the ring grooves are worn. Inspect and replace as necessary.

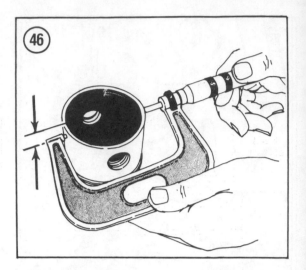

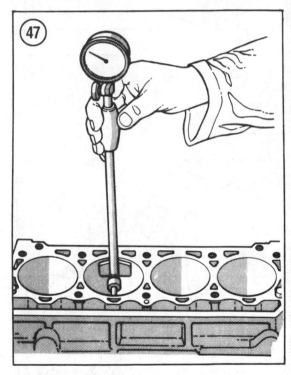

4. Using a ring expander tool (**Figure 45**), carefully install the oil control ring, then the compression rings.

> *NOTE*
> *Oil rings consists of 3 segments. The wavy segment goes between the flat segments to act as a spacer. Upper and lower flat segments are interchangeable. The top side of the No. 2 compression ring is marked with the word "TOP" and must face upward.*

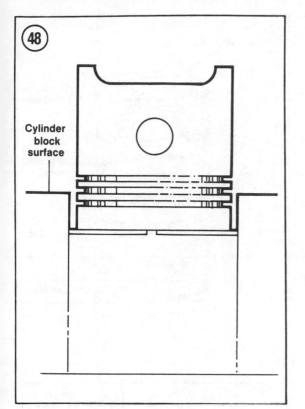

Cylinder
block
surface

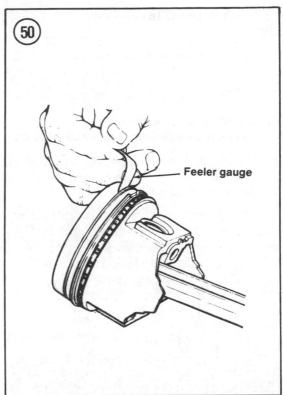

Feeler gauge

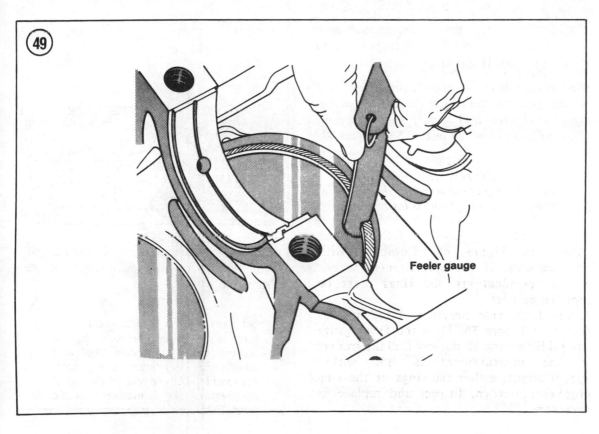

Feeler gauge

5

5. Position the ring gaps 180° apart. See **Figure 51**.

Connecting Rod Inspection

Have the connecting rods checked for straightness by a dealer or a machine shop.

Connecting Rod Bearing Clearance Measurement

1. Place the connecting rods and upper bearing halves on the proper connecting rod journals.
2. Cut a piece of Plastigage the width of the bearing. Place the Plastigage on the journal, then install the lower bearing half and cap.

> *NOTE*
> *Do not place Plastigage over the journal oil hole.*

3. Tighten the connecting rod cap to specifications. Do not rotate the crankshaft while the Plastigage is in place.
4. Remove the connecting rod caps. Bearing clearance is determined by comparing the width of the flattened Plastigage to the markings on the envelope. See **Figure 52**. If the clearance is excessive, the crankshaft must be reground and undersize bearings installed.

Installing Piston/Connecting Rod Assembly

1. Make sure the pistons are correctly installed on the connecting rod.

> *NOTE*
> *The notch on the piston skirt must face the flywheel end on No. 1 and No. 3 pistons. The notch on the No. 2 and No. 4 pistons must face the timing chain end. The connecting rod oil slot must face the camshaft side. See* ***Figure 53***.

2. Make sure the ring gaps are positioned as shown in **Figure 51**.
3. Slip short pieces of hose over the connecting rod studs to keep them from nicking the crankshaft. Tape will work if you do not have the right diameter hose, but it is more difficult to remove.
4. Immerse the entire piston in clean engine oil. Coat the cylinder wall with oil.

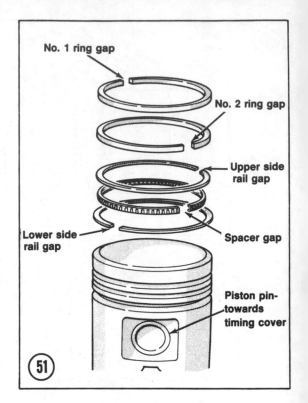

No. 1 ring gap
No. 2 ring gap
Upper side rail gap
Lower side rail gap
Spacer gap
Piston pin-towards timing cover

(51)

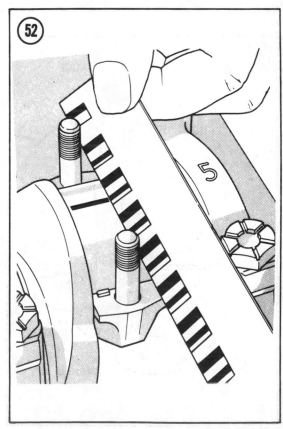

(52)

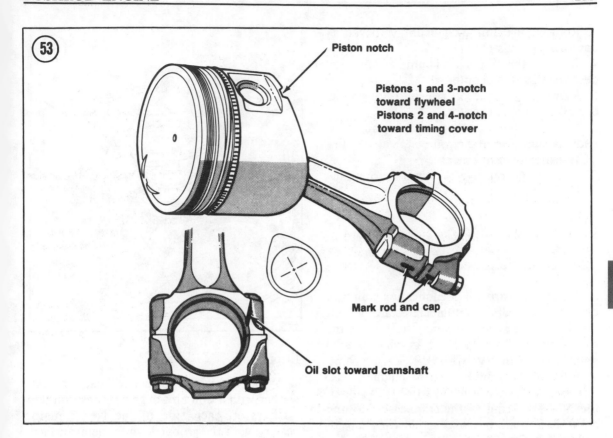

Piston notch

Pistons 1 and 3-notch
toward flywheel
Pistons 2 and 4-notch
toward timing cover

Mark rod and cap

Oil slot toward camshaft

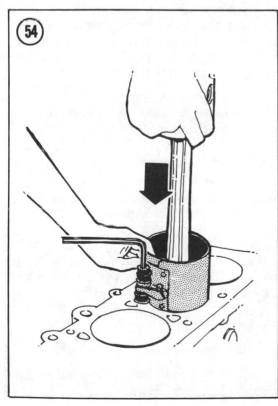

5. Install the piston/connecting rod assembly in its cylinder as shown in **Figure 54**. Make sure the number painted on the top of the piston before removal corresponds to the cylinder number, counting from the *flywheel* end of the engine. See **Figure 44**.

6. Clean the connecting rod bearings carefully, including the back sides. Coat the journals and bearings with clean engine oil. Place the bearings in the connecting rod and cap.

7. Remove the protective hose or tape and install the connecting rod cap. Make sure the rod and cap marks align. Tighten the cap nuts to specifications (**Table 2**).

8. Check the connecting rod big-end play as described under *Piston Removal*.

CRANKSHAFT

Removal

1. Remove the engine from the vehicle as described in this chapter.

2. Remove the spark plugs and the fan/pulley assembly.

3. Remove the timing chain and sprockets as described in this chapter.

4. Remove the oil pan and pump assembly as described in this chapter.

5. Remove the rear oil seal and housing as described in this chapter.

6. Remove the connecting rod bearing caps and bearings. Move the rod/piston assemblies away from the crankshaft.

7. Unbolt and remove the main bearing caps with bearing inserts.

> *NOTE*
> *If the caps are difficult to remove, lift the bolts partway out, then pry the caps from side to side.*

8. Check the caps for identification numbers or marks (the caps are numbered starting from the *flywheel* end). If none are visible, clean the caps with a wire brush. If marks still cannot be seen, make your own with quick-drying paint.

9. Lift the crankshaft from the engine block. Remove the thrust washers from each side of the No. 3 bearing in the crankcase. Lay the crankshaft, main bearings and bearing caps in order on a clean workbench.

Inspection

1. Clean the crankshaft thoroughly with solvent. Blow out the oil passages with compressed air.

> *NOTE*
> *If you do not have precision measuring equipment, have a machine shop perform Step 2.*

2. Check the crankpins and main bearing journals for wear, scoring and cracks. Check all journals against specifications for out-of-roundness and taper. If necessary, have the crankshaft reground.

Main Bearing Clearance Measurement

Main bearing clearance is measured with Plastigage in the same manner as the connecting rod bearing clearance, described in this chapter. Excessive clearance requires that the bearings be replaced, the crankshaft reground or both.

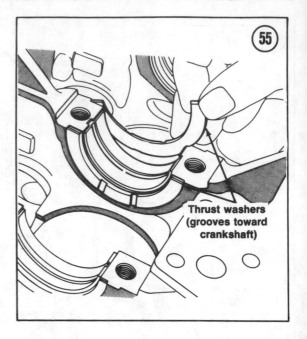

Thrust washers (grooves toward crankshaft)

Installation

1. Wipe the plain surface of each thrust washer with a thin film of grease. Position the washers on each side of the No. 3 main bearing with the grooved white metal surface facing the crankshaft. See **Figure 55**.

2. Install the upper main bearing shells. Make certain the oil holes in the block align with those in the bearing shells and that the bearing tabs seat in the block.

> *NOTE*
> *Remember that the main bearings are numbered from the **flywheel** end of the engine.*

3. Install the grooved bearing shells in the No. 2 and No. 4 bearing caps. Install the plain shells in the No. 1, 3 and 5 bearing caps.

4. Lubricate the bolt threads with SAE 30 engine oil.

5. Install the crankshaft in the block.

6. Install the bearing caps in their marked positions (**Figure 56**) and tighten the bolts finger-tight.

7. Tighten all main bearing cap bolts to specifications.

End Play Measurement

1. Install a dial indicator to the front of the cylinder block. See **Figure 57**.

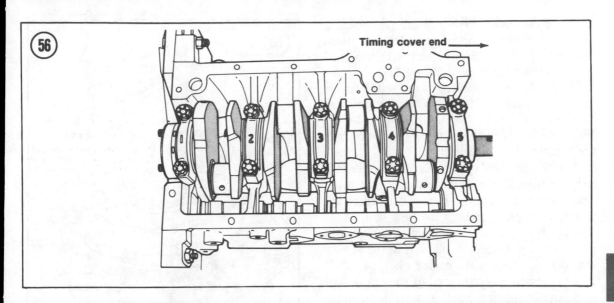

Timing cover end

56

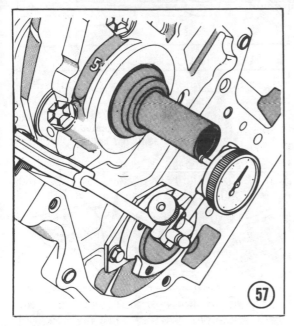

57

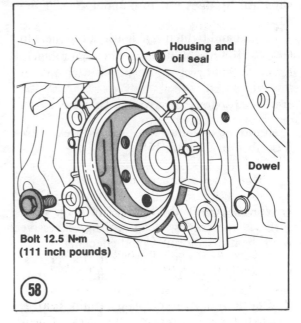

Housing and
oil seal

Dowel

Bolt 12.5 N•m
(111 inch pounds)

58

2. Pry the crankshaft to the rear of the block with a large screwdriver and zero the dial indicator.

3. Pry the crankshaft to the front of the block. Read the dial indicator. The end play is the difference between the high and low measurements. The end play should be between 0.0035-0.011 in. (0.09-0.27 mm).

4. If the end play is not within specifications, check the crankshaft bearing thrust washer faces for wear. If worn, replace the thrust washers and repeat Step 2 and Step 3. If end play is still out of specification, replace the crankshaft.

REAR CRANKSHAFT SEAL

Replacement

1. Remove the engine as described in this chapter.

2. Remove the flywheel/drive plate as described in this chapter.

3. Remove the rear oil seal housing and gasket. Discard the gasket. See **Figure 58**.

4. Place the inner surface of the seal housing on wooden blocks or spacers, leaving room for seal removal. Remove seal with tool part No. C-4759 as shown in **Figure 59**.

5. Place the outer surface of the seal housing on a flat surface. Position a new seal on housing. Reverse tool part No. C-4759 (**Figure 60**) and install seal until it bottoms in the housing.

6. Check crankshaft journal and chamfer that fits into oil seal for damage that might cause seal failure. If damage is found, correct the problem before installing the new seal.

7. Lightly coat a new seal housing gasket with grease and position on block. Lubricate new seal lip with SAE 30W engine oil.

8. Fit the seal over the end of the crankshaft and rotate housing back and forth to make sure seal lip does not turn under. See **Figure 61**.

9. Install and tighten seal housing fasteners to specifications (**Table 1**).

FLYWHEEL/DRIVE PLATE

Removal/installation procedures are described in Chapter Nine.

Inspection

1. Visually check the flywheel or drive plate surfaces for cracks, deep scoring, excessive wear, heat discoloration and checking.

2. Inspect the ring gear teeth for cracks, broken teeth or excessive wear. If severely worn, check the starter motor drive teeth for similar wear or damage. Replace as indicated.

PILOT BUSHING

The pilot bushing is located inside the rear end of the crankshaft on manual transaxle vehicles. It supports the transaxle input shaft.

1. Check the bearing for visible wear or damage. Turn the bearing with a finger and make sure it turns easily.

2. If wear, damage or stiff movement are found, remove the bearing with a puller. These are available from rental dealers.

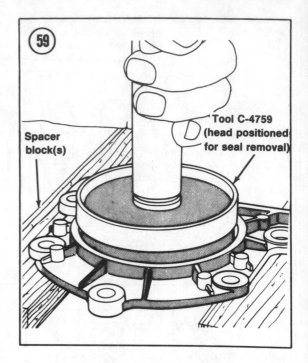

Spacer block(s)

Tool C-4759 (head positioned for seal removal)

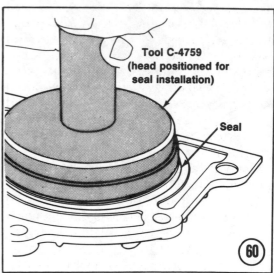

Tool C-4759 (head positioned for seal installation)

Seal

3. Tap a new bearing in place with a drift until fully seated.

CAUTION
Do not tap too hard or you will damage the bearing.

CYLINDER BLOCK

Cleaning and Inspection

1. Clean the block thoroughly with solvent. Remove any RTV sealant residue from the

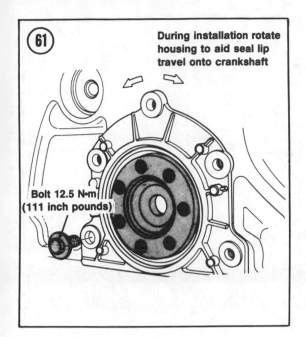

During installation rotate housing to aid seal lip travel onto crankshaft

Bolt 12.5 N•m (111 inch pounds)

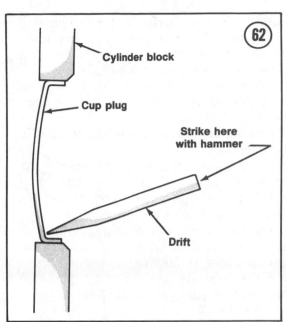

Cylinder block

Cup plug

Strike here with hammer

Drift

machined surfaces. Check all core plugs for leaks and replace any that are suspect. See *Core Plugs* in this chapter. Remove any plugs that seal oil passages. Check oil and coolant passages for sludge, dirt and corrosion while cleaning. If the passages are very dirty, have the block boiled out by a machine shop. Blow out all passages with compressed air. Check the threads in the head bolt holes to be sure they are clean. If dirty, use a tap to true up the threads and remove any deposits.

2. Examine the block for cracks. To confirm suspicions about possible leak areas, use a mixture of 1 part kerosene and 2 parts engine oil. Coat the suspected area with this solution, then wipe dry and immediately apply a solution of zinc oxide dissolved in wood alcohol. If any discoloration appears in the treated area, the block is cracked and should be replaced.

3. Check flatness of the cylinder block deck or top surface. Place an accurate straightedge on the block. If there is any gap between the block and straightedge, measure it with a feeler gauge. Measure from end to end and from corner to corner. Have the block resurfaced if it is warped more than 0.004 in. (0.01 mm).

4. Measure the cylinder bores with a bore gauge (**Figure 47**) as described in *Piston*

Clearance Check in this chapter. If the cylinders exceed maximum tolerances, they must be rebored. Reboring is also necessary if the cylinder walls are badly scuffed or scored.

> *NOTE*
> *Before boring, install all main bearing caps and tighten the cap bolts to specifications.*

CORE PLUGS

The condition of all core plugs in the block should be checked whenever the engine is out of the vehicle for service. If any signs of leakage or corrosion are found around one core plug, replace them all.

Removal/Installation

> *NOTE*
> *Do not drive core plugs into the engine casting. It will be impossible to retrieve them and they can restrict coolant circulation, resulting in serious engine damage.*

1. Tap the bottom edge of the core plug with a hammer and drift. Use several sharp blows to push the bottom of the plug inward, tilting the top out (**Figure 62**).

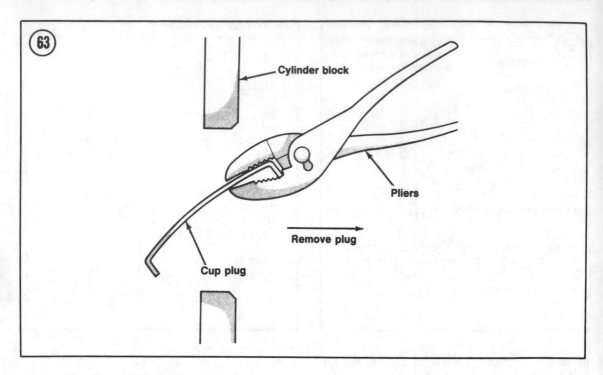

2. Grip the top of the plug firmly with pliers. Pull the plug from its bore (**Figure 63**) and discard.

3. Clean the plug bore thoroughly to remove all traces of the old sealer.

4. Apply a light coat of Loctite Stud N' Bearing mount or equivalent to the plug bore.

5. Install the new core plug with an appropriate size driver or socket. The sharp edge of the plug should be at least 0.02 in. (0.5 mm) inside the lead-in chamfer.

6. Repeat Steps 1-5 to replace each remaining core plug.

Table 1 1.6L ENGINE SPECIFICATIONS

General	
Bore	3.17 in. (80.6 mm)
Stroke	3.07 in. (78 mm)
Displacement	1.6 liter (97.1 cu. in.)
Compression ratio	8.8:1
Firing order	1-3-4-2 (No. 1 @ flywheel end)
Oil pressure (at 3,000 rpm)	58-87 psi
Valve timing	
Intake	
Opens	13° BTDC
Closes	55° ABDC
Exhaust	
Opens	45° BBDC
Closes	13° ATDC
	(continued)

Table 1 1.6L ENGINE SPECIFICATIONS (continued)

Valve clearance	
Cold	
Intake	0.010 in. (0.25 mm)
Exhaust	0.012 in. (0.30 mm)
Hot	
Intake	0.012 in. (0.030 mm)
Exhaust	0.014 in. (0.035 mm)
Valves	
Head thickness (margin)	
Intake	0.794 in
Exhaust	1.791 in
Stem-to-guide clearance	
Intake	0.0015-0.00275 in. (0.037-0.070 mm)
Exhaust	0.00225-0.0035 in. (0.057-0.090 mm)
Stem diameter	
Intake	0.313 in. (7.970 mm)
Exhaust	0.314 in. (7.950 mm)
Valve angles	
Face	45°
Seat	46°
Valve spring free length	1.905 in. (48.4 mm)
Camshaft end play	0.004-0.008 in. (0.010-0.020 mm)
Connecting rod	
Side clearance	0.006-0.009 in. (0.145-0.225 mm)
Bearing clearance	0.001-0.0025 in. (0.025-0.064 mm)
Crankshaft	
Connecting rod journal	1.6061-1.6064 in. (40.957-40.965 mm)
Main bearing journal	2.0382-2.0386 in. (51.975-51.985 mm)
Main bearing clearance	0.0009-0.0031 in. (0.04-0.078 mm)
End play	0.0035-0.011 in. (0.09-0.27 mm)
Piston	
Diameter*	3.168 in. (80.56 mm)
Clearance in bore	0.0016-0.0020 in. (0.041-0.051 mm)
Piston pin	
Outside diameter	0.8624-0.8625 in. (21.991-21.995 mm)
Inside diameter	0.512 in. (13 mm)
Length	2.892 in. (73.9 mm)
Piston ring	
Side clearance	
Compression	0.0018-0.0028 in. (0.305-0.457 mm)
Groove clearance	
Compression	0.02-0.03 in. (0.06-0.08 mm)
Oil	Free in groove, not to exceed 0.008-0.02 mm side clearance
End gap	
Compression	0.012-0.018 in. (0.305-0.457 mm)
Oil	0.010-0.016 in. (0.254-0.406 mm)

* Measure 2.175 in. (55.25 mm) down from top.

5

Table 2 TIGHTENING TORQUES

Fastener	in.-lb.	ft.-lb.	N•m
Camshaft thrust plate bolt	132	15	
Crankcase			
Extension screw-to-block	111	12.5	
Extension oil pan screws	89	10	
Crankshaft			
Main bearing bolts		48	65
Oil seal housing bolts	111	12.5	
Pulley bolt		110	150
Connecting rod nuts		28	37.5
Cylinder head bolts		52	70
Distributor hold-down clamp		15	20
Dipstick mounting guide screw	114	12.9	
Exhaust manifold nuts		15	20
Fuel pump screws		15	20
Intake manifold nuts	133	15	
Oil filter adapter		30	40
Oil pan screw	89	10	
Oil pressure sending unit		15	20
Oil pump			
Mounting screw	111	12.5	
Pickup-to-block screw	111	12.5	
Strainer-to-pickup screw	133	15.	
Rocker adjusting screw locknut	155	17.5	
Spark plug		22	30
Timing chain sprocket screw	133	15	
Timing chain cover			
7 mm bolt	111	12.5	
8 mm bolt		15	20
Valve cover screws	44	5	
Water pump			
Drain plug	155	17.5	
Housing screw	111	12.5	
Pulley nut	133	15	
Water inlet elbow	111	12.5	

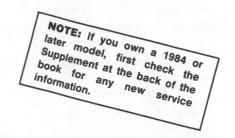
NOTE: If you own a 1984 or later model, first check the Supplement at the back of the book for any new service information.

CHAPTER SIX

FUEL, EXHAUST, AND EMISSION CONTROL SYSTEMS

This chapter contains repair and replacement procedures for the fuel, exhaust, and emission control systems. The fuel system consists of a rear-mounted tank, mechanical fuel pump, and a 2-barrel Holley carburetor. The exhaust system uses a muffler, catalytic converter, and interconnecting pipes. The emission control system includes air injection and exhaust gas recirculation to minimize harmful emissions. In addition, fuel evaporation control prevents emission of gasoline vapor from fuel system. All of these systems are described in detail.

The complexity and interdependence of these systems, and the special tools and knowledge required to work on them, indicate that most emission problems should be referred to your dealer.

FUEL SYSTEM

The fuel system consists of a rear-mounted fuel tank connected through a line to the mechanical fuel pump. An eccentric cam on the camshaft operates the 1.6 liter fuel pump. An eccentric cam on the intermediate shaft, driven by the camshaft drive belt, operates the 1.7 and 2.2 liter fuel pump. All pumps deliver fuel to a 2-barrel Holley carburetor.

AIR CLEANER

The air cleaner should be replaced at the intervals specified in Chapter Three.

Removal (1.7 Liter)

1. Release clips securing cover to air cleaner housing. Remove wingnuts at carburetor.
2. Remove cover and filter element. See **Figure 1**.
3. Replace filter element and reinstall cover. Secure with clips.

> *NOTE*
> *Be sure filter is seated properly to crossover housing. If there is a gap between the filter and air cleaner crossover, dirt and debris will enter the*

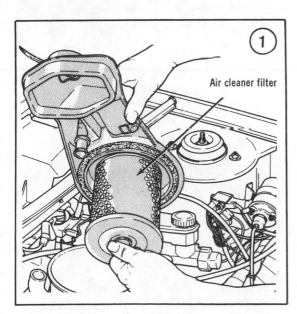
Air cleaner filter

carburetor air horn. This will cause the engine idle to gradually roughen, resulting in poor engine operation.

Removal (1.6 and 2.2 Liter)

The following replacement procedure must be followed exactly to prevent air leaks.

1. Unsnap the air cleaner cover hold-down clips. Remove the wing nuts. See **Figure 2**, typical.

2. Lift the filter from the housing.

3. Install a new filter with the filter element screen facing upward (**Figure 3**, typical). Make sure the filter element fits into the plastic bottom section of the air cleaner housing.

4. Place the air cleaner cover onto the plastic bottom section, making sure to align the 3 hold-down clips while allowing the carburetor and support bracket studs to stick out through their respective stud holes in the cover.

5. Install the plastic wing nuts on both carburetor studs and tighten securely. See **Figure 2**, typical.

6. Install air cleaner tab-to-support bracket wing nut and tighten securely. See **Figure 2**, typical.

7. Snap each of the hold-down clips into position.

CARBURETOR

To work on the carburetor, you must have a clean work area and use the proper tools and cleaning agents. Many of the carburetor passages are small. Any restrictions for the flow of either air or fuel will result in adjustment difficulties and poor engine performance. In some cases, setting the CO and hydrocarbon levels will be impossible. Approach rebuilding and adjustments in the following manner:

1. Read this section through *completely* before starting to work.

2. Select a clean work area. It should have a large flat space, good lighting, and good ventilation. Extinguish any pilot lights within 50 feet of the work area or where gasoline is present.

3. Allow ample time, 3 hours at least.

4. Visually inspect the carburetor prior to removal. Look for fuel leaks at hoses, cracks

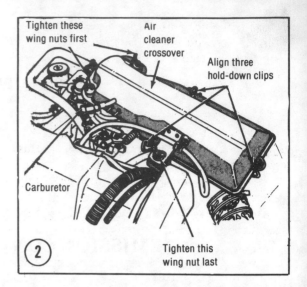

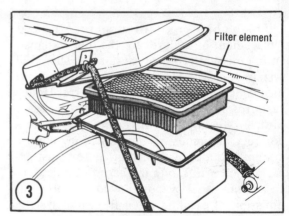

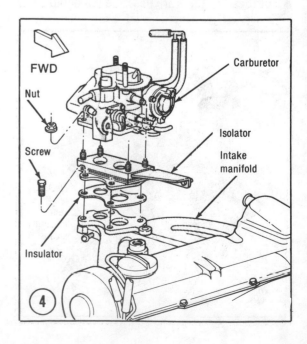

in vacuum lines, obviously worn parts, etc. This will save additional trips for parts.

5. Use only high quality carburetor cleaner and solvent.

Removal

Refer to **Figure 4**, typical.

1. Disconnect the negative battery cable.

2. Remove the air cleaner as described in this chapter.

3. Remove the fuel tank cap to release any pressure in the tank.

4. Place a suitable container under the fuel inlet fitting to catch any spilled fuel.

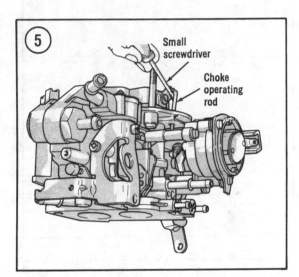

5. Remove the fuel line clamp and fuel line. Cap the line to prevent leakage.

6. Remove the throttle cable linkage.

7. Label and disconnect all vacuum lines and wiring connectors at the carburetor.

8. Remove the 4 carburetor mounting nuts.

9. Lift the carburetor off the gasket (1.6 liter) or isolator (1.7 and 2.2 liter) and place it on a clean workbench. Hold carburetor level to avoid spilling fuel.

CAUTION
Cover the intake manifold openings. Small parts, such as screws or nuts, could fall into the manifold unnoticed and damage the engine.

Installation

1. Install a new gasket (1.6 liter) or the isolator (1.7 and 2.2 liter) on the manifold.

2. Install the carburetor to the manifold. Tighten attaching nuts evenly to 200 in.-lb. (23 N•m).

3. Reconnect the throttle cable linkage.

4. Reconnect all vacuum lines and wiring connectors at the carburetor.

5. Reconnect the fuel line and secure with the fuel line clamp.

6. Reinstall the fuel tank cap.

7. Have an assistant operate the throttle pedal while you watch and make sure the throttle linkage operates properly.

8. Install the air cleaner assembly as described in this chapter.

9. Reconnect the negative battery cable.

HOLLEY 5220 CARBURETOR

Disassembly/Inspection

1. If possible, support the carburetor so that both hands can be used. A bolt held in a vise makes a suitable support.

2. Remove the choke operating rod and choke rod seal. See **Figure 5**.

3. Remove the air horn and electric bowl vent mounting screws. See **Figure 6**. Remove the harness mounting screw.

4. Remove the electric bowl vent cover and separate the air horn assembly from the carburetor body. Remove wiring clip.

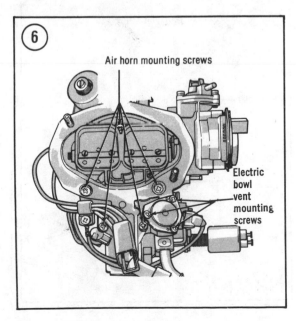

5. Remove the float level pin, float, and float inlet needle. See **Figure 7**.

6. Remove the fuel inlet seat and gasket as shown in **Figure 8**.

7. Remove the power valve diaphragm assembly (3 screws). See **Figure 9**.

8. Remove the electric bowl vent solenoid retaining clip and separate the diaphragm assembly from the air horn. See **Figure 10**.

9. Remove the fuel inlet fitting, fuel filter, and spring. See **Figure 11**.

10. Remove power valve as shown in **Figure 12**.

11. Remove the secondary main metering jet. Note the jet size so it can be reinstalled in its correct position. See **Figure 13**.

12. Remove the primary main metering jet. Note size so jet can be reinstalled in its correct position. See **Figure 14**.

13. Remove the secondary high speed bleed and secondary main well tube. Note sizes for correct reinstallation. See **Figure 15**.

14. Remove the primary high speed bleed and primary main well tube. Note sizes for correct reinstallation. See **Figure 16**.

15. Remove the discharge nozzle screw, nozzle, and gasket. See **Figure 17**.

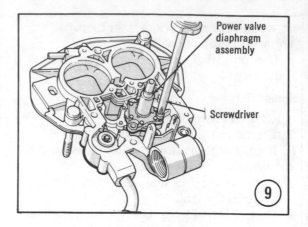

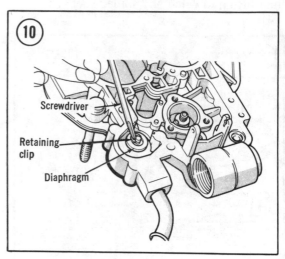

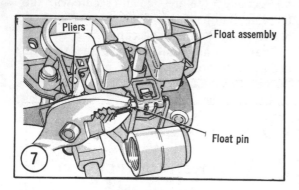

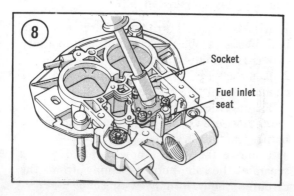

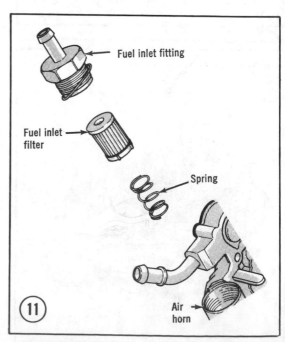

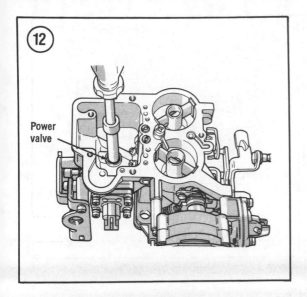

12

Power
valve

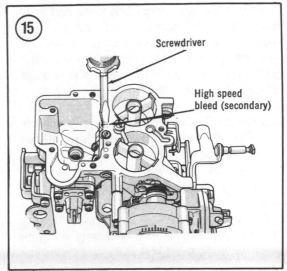

15

Screwdriver

High speed
bleed (secondary)

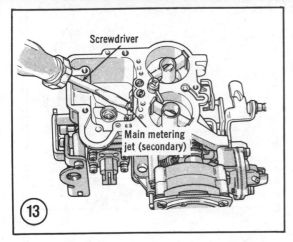

Screwdriver

Main metering
jet (secondary)

13

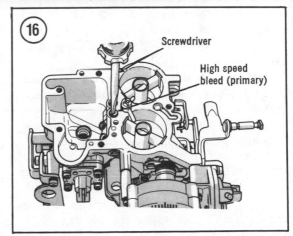

16

Screwdriver

High speed
bleed (primary)

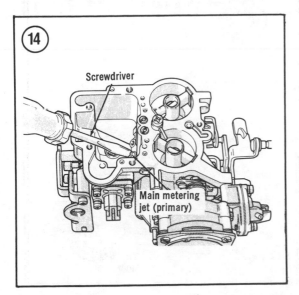

14

Screwdriver

Main metering
jet (primary)

17

Screwdriver

Discharge
nozzle

6

16. Turn the carburetor body over and catch the pump discharge weight ball and the check ball. Both are the same size.

17. Remove cover from the accelerator pump (4 screws) and remove the pump diaphragm and spring. See **Figure 18**.

18. Remove choke cover retaining ring (3 screws), heating element and cover assembly, choke cover ground ring, choke lever sleeve, and choke housing. See **Figure 19**.

19. Remove the choke diaphragm cover (3 screws) and spring. See **Figure 20**.

20. Turn the choke shaft and lever assembly counterclockwise as shown in **Figure 21**, then rotate the choke vacuum diaphragm assembly clockwise and remove it from the carburetor housing.

21. Remove wide open throttle cut-out switch (2 screws). See **Figure 22**. Note the switch location for reassembly.

22. Remove the idle stop solenoid (2 screws). See **Figure 23**.

23. Remove the plastic limiter cap from the idle mixture screw in the base of the carburetor. Take care to avoid damage to the idle mixture screw. Remove the idle mixture screw and spring from the carburetor.

24. Clean all non-electric metal parts in high-quality carburetor cleaning solvent. Make sure all parts are thoroughly clean, paying particular attention to passages in the carburetor body. Blow parts dry with compressed air.

> *CAUTION*
> *Never use wire or other metal objects to clear carburetor passages. To do so could enlarge openings with critical tolerances, causing irreparable damage to the carburetor.*

25. Check choke shaft for freedom of movement in the air horn. Make sure the shaft does not stick and that all deposits are removed from the bearings, the air horn walls, the link between the choke shaft and the thermostat housing, and the sealing block that the link passes through. Reclean if required.

26. Check the throttle shaft for excessive wear. If the shaft does not fit properly, replace the carburetor body assembly rather than trying to fit a new shaft to the old body.

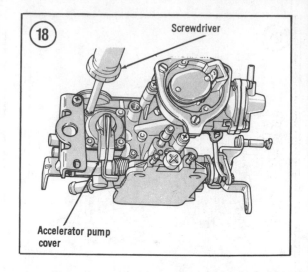

(18) Screwdriver
Accelerator pump cover

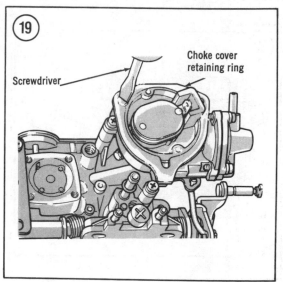

(19) Choke cover retaining ring
Screwdriver

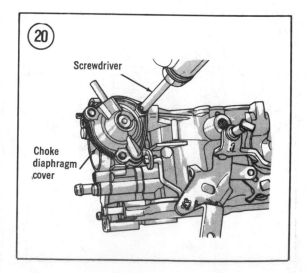

(20) Screwdriver
Choke diaphragm cover

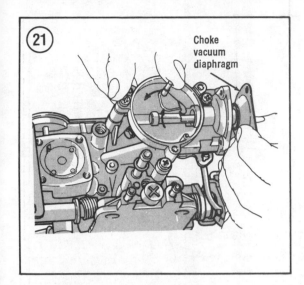

Choke
vacuum
diaphragm

27. Check the idle mixture screw. If the tapered portion is not straight and smooth, replace the screw.

Assembly

> *NOTE*
> *It is recommended that a carburetor overhaul kit be purchased and installed when the carburetor is disassembled and cleaned. Be sure to use all parts in the kit.*

1. Rotate the choke shaft counterclockwise and install the diaphragm (A, **Figure 24**) with a clockwise motion. Install the remaining choke vacuum diaphragm components in alphabetical order as identified in **Figure 24**.

2. Position the choke housing (A, **Figure 25**) on the carburetor body and assemble the remaining components in alphabetical order as identified in **Figure 25**.

> *NOTE*
> *Initial setting of the choke should be 2 notches rich.*

3. Install the spring, diaphragm, and cover (4 screws) in the accelerator pump. See **Figure 18**.

4. Place the accelerator pump discharge check ball in the discharge passage. Check for leakage by holding the ball in place with a length of brass rod and operating the pump plunger by hand. If no resistance is felt, the ball and seat

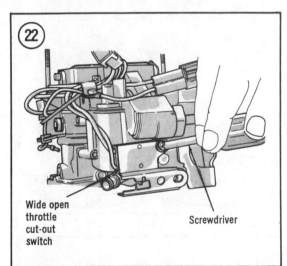

Wide open
throttle
cut-out
switch

Screwdriver

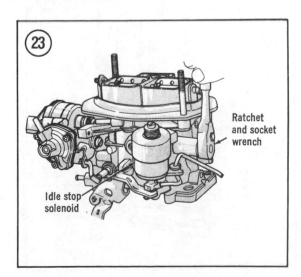

Idle stop
solenoid

Ratchet
and socket
wrench

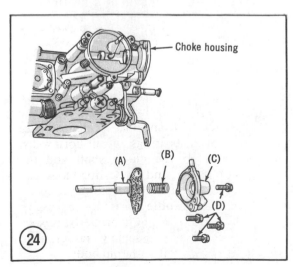

Choke housing

(A)   (B)   (C)

(D)

are leaking. In this case, use drift punch and hammer to gently tap on the old check ball to reform the seat. Take care not to damage the bore. Then remove the old ball, install a new one and recheck for leakage.

5. Install discharge nozzle, using a new gasket. See **Figure 17**.

6. Install the primary main well tube and primary high speed bleed. See **Figure 16**.

NOTE
On this carburetor, the primary and secondary main well tubes are the same size but the primary high speed bleed will have a lower number stamped on it than the number on the secondary high speed bleed.

7. Install the secondary main well tube and the secondary high speed bleed. See **Figure 15** and the NOTE above.

8. Install primary main metering jet (**Figure 14**) and secondary main metering jet (**Figure 13**).

NOTE
The primary main metering jet will have a smaller number stamped on it than the secondary main metering jet.

9. Install the power valve (**Figure 12**).

10. Install the components of the electric bowl vent solenoid in the alphabetical order shown in **Figure 26**.

11. Install the components of the power valve diaphragm assembly in the alphabetical order shown in **Figure 27**.

12. Install the fuel inlet fitting with the fuel filter and spring as shown in **Figure 11**.

13. Install the fuel inlet seat and gasket, float inlet needle, and float lever pin. See **Figure 8** and **Figure 7**.

14. Invert the air horn and check the clearance between the float assembly and the air horn body with a 0.480 in. gauge or drill. See **Figure 28**. If necessary, adjust the dry float level by bending the tang with a small screwdriver as shown in **Figure 29** until this clearance is obtained.

15. Turn the air horn back over and check the float drop with a depth gauge as shown in **Figure 30**. If necessary, use a small screwdriver as shown in **Figure 31** to adjust float drop to 1 7/8 in. (47.6 mm).

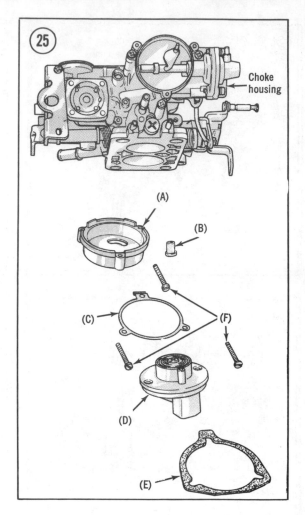

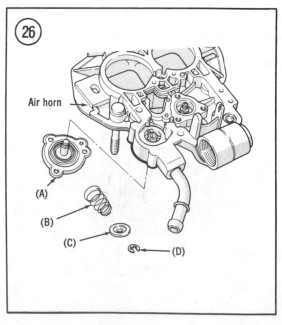

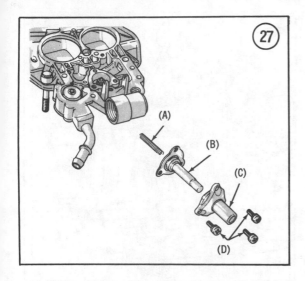

(27)

(A)

(B)

(C)

(D)

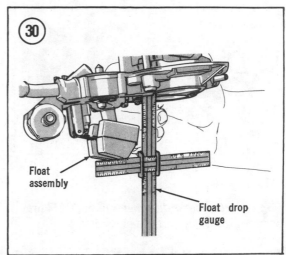

(30)

Float
assembly

Float drop
gauge

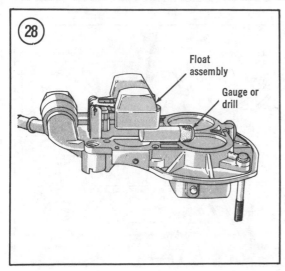

(28)

Float
assembly

Gauge or
drill

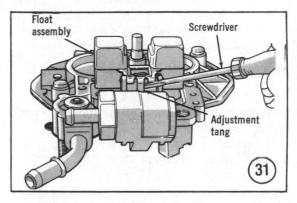

Float
assembly

Screwdriver

Adjustment
tang

(31)

16. Place a new gasket on the air horn and install choke rod seal and choke operating rod.

17. Carefully place the air horn on the carburetor body and install new choke operating rod retainers on the choke shaft and the fast idle cam pickup lever. Connect the choke operating rod.

18. Install the 5 mounting screws to connect the air horn to the body and tighten the screws evenly to 30 in.-lb. (0.35 mkg).

19. Install and tighten the 3 electric bowl vent solenoid screws. See **Figure 6**.

20. Install and tighten the 2 idle stop solenoid screws (**Figure 23**).

21. Install wide open throttle cut-out switch and move switch so air conditioning clutch circuit is open in throttle position of between 10° before wide open to wide open. See **Figure 22**.

22. Install and tighten harness mounting screw.

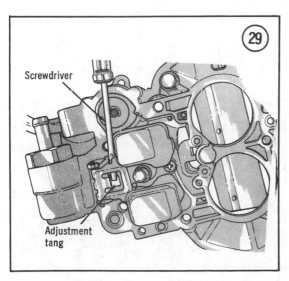

(29)

Screwdriver

Adjustment
tang

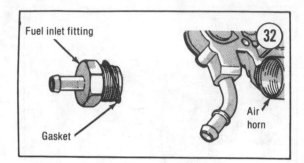

Fuel inlet fitting

Gasket

Air horn

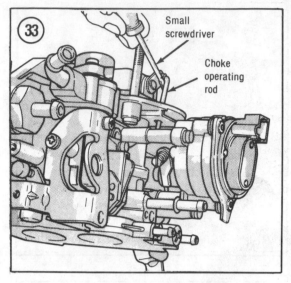

Small screwdriver

Choke operating rod

Adjustment

See *Carburetor Adjustments*, Chapter Three, for carburetor adjustment procedures.

HOLLEY 6520 CARBURETOR

The Holley 6520 carburetor is a staged dual venturi electronic feedback carburetor.

Disassembly

1. If possible, support the carburetor so that both hands can be used. A bolt held in a vise makes a suitable tool.
2. Remove the fuel inlet fitting and gasket from the air horn (**Figure 32**).
3. Disconnect the choke rod retaining circlip from the choke rod with a screwdriver (**Figure 33**). Then remove the choke rod and the choke rod seal.
4. Remove the duty cycle solenoid retaining screws (**Figure 34**) and lift the solenoid up and away from the air horn (**Figure 35**).
5. Remove the anti-rattle spring, 2 idle stop solenoid retaining screws and the idle stop solenoid (**Figure 36**).
6. On air-conditioned vehicles only, remove the 2 wide-open throttle cutout switch mounting screws (**Figure 37**). Then remove the throttle harness mounting screws and retaining clip. Remove the wires from the connector and pass through the clip.
7. Referring to **Figure 38**, remove the air horn mounting screws. Then separate the air horn assembly from the carburetor body.
8. Using a pair of pliers, remove the float level pin, the float and the float inlet needle. See **Figure 39**.
9. With a socket, remove the fuel inlet seat and gasket (**Figure 40**).

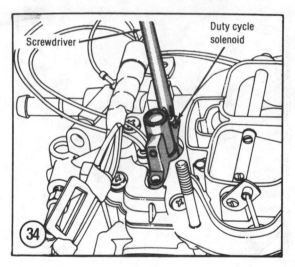

Screwdriver

Duty cycle solenoid

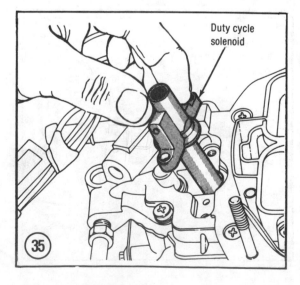

Duty cycle solenoid

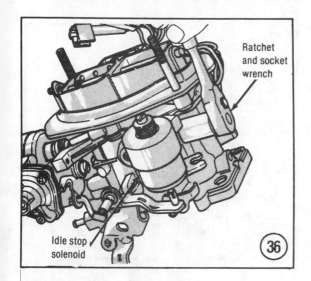

Ratchet and socket wrench

Idle stop solenoid

(36)

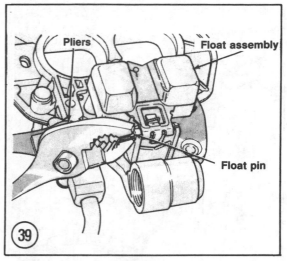

Pliers

Float assembly

Float pin

(39)

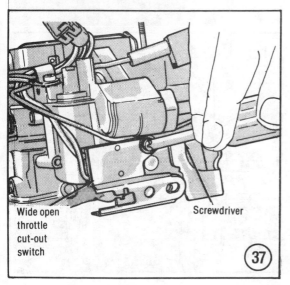

Wide open throttle cut-out switch

Screwdriver

(37)

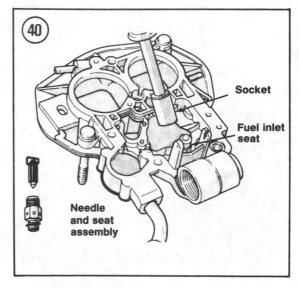

(40)

Socket

Fuel inlet seat

Needle and seat assembly

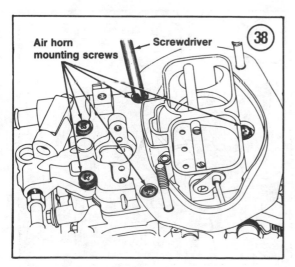

Air horn mounting screws

Screwdriver

(38)

10. Remove the main metering secondary (**Figure 41**) and primary (**Figure 42**) jets. Note the jet size so each can be reinstalled in its correct position.

11. Remove the secondary high speed bleed and secondary main well tube. Note sizes for correct reinstallation. See **Figure 43**.

12. Remove the primary high speed bleed and secondary main well tube. Note sizes for correct reinstallation. See **Figure 44**.

13. Remove the discharge nozzle screw, nozzle and gasket. See **Figure 45**.

14. Turn the carburetor body over and catch the pump discharge weight ball and the check ball. Both are the same size.

6

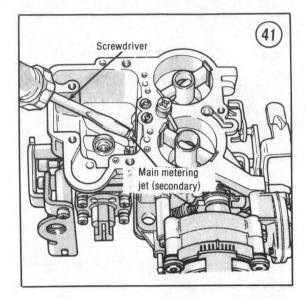

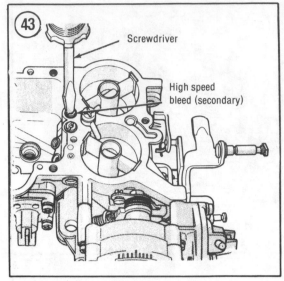

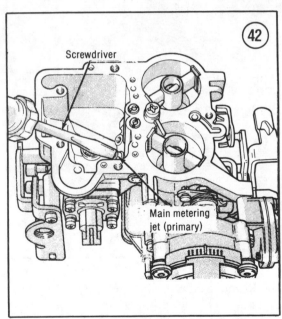

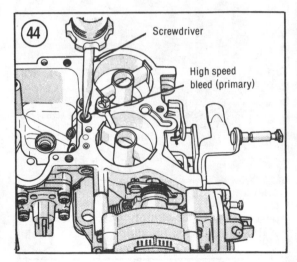

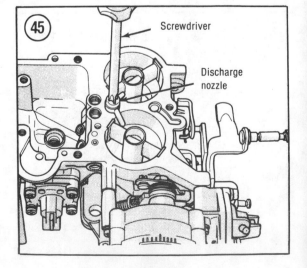

15. Remove the cover from the accelerator pump (4 screws) and remove the pump diaphragm and spring. See **Figure 46**.

16. The choke diaphragm cover is secured with 3 screws. Remove the upper 2 screws with a screwdriver (**Figure 47**). To remove the lower screw, first grind or file away the screw head. Then remove the cover and spring.

17. Turn the choke shaft and lever assembly counterclockwise. Then rotate the choke diaphragm assembly clockwise and remove it

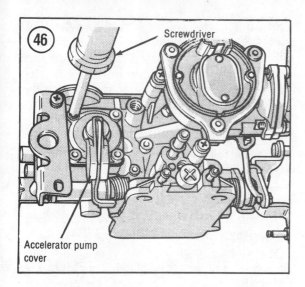

46

Screwdriver

Accelerator pump cover

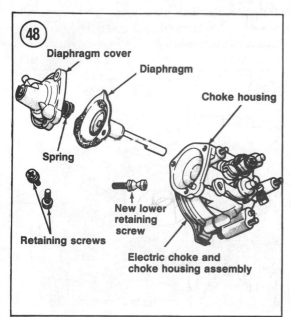

Screwdriver

47

Choke diaphragm cover

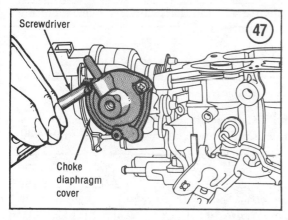

48

Diaphragm cover

Diaphragm

Choke housing

Spring

New lower retaining screw

Retaining screws

Electric choke and choke housing assembly

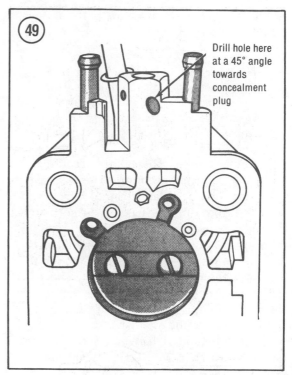

49

Drill hole here at a 45° angle towards concealment plug

6

from the carburetor housing. The lower cover screw can then be removed. See **Figure 48**.

> *NOTE*
> *If replacement of the choke diaphragm is necessary, the diaphragm cover must also be replaced.*

> *NOTE*
> *Steps 18-20 describe removal of the idle mixture screw. The screw should only be removed during carburetor overhaul.*

18. Drill a 0.086 in. pilot hole in the casting at the idle mixture screw (**Figure 49**). Then redrill the hole to 0.120 in.

19. With a blunt edge punch inserted into the hole, drive out the idle mixture concealment plug.

20. Place a sharp punch through the idle mixture screw hole and slide the roll pin out. Remove the idle mixture needle.

Inspection

1. Clean all but electrical parts and diaphragms in high quality carburetor cleaning solvent. Make sure all parts are thoroughly clean, paying particular attention to passages

in the carburetor body. Blow parts dry with compressed air.

CAUTION
Never use wire or other metal objects to clean carburetor passages. To do so could enlarge openings with critical tolerances, causing irreparable damage to the carburetor.

2. Check choke shaft for freedom of movement in the air horn. Make sure the shaft does not stick and that all deposits are removed from the bearings, the air horn walls, the link between the choke shaft and the thermostat housing and the sealing block that the link passes through. Reclean if required.

3. Check the throttle shaft for excessive wear. If the shaft does not fit properly, replace the carburetor body assembly rather than trying to fit a new shaft to the old body.

4. Check the idle mixture screw. If the tapered portion is not straight and smooth, replace the screw.

Assembly

NOTE
It is recommended that a carburetor overhaul kit be purchased and installed when the carburetor is disassembled and cleaned. Be sure to use all parts in the kit.

NOTE
If the entire choke assembly was removed, begin at Step 1. If the choke diaphragm was disassembled, begin at Step 2.

1. Place the choke assembly on the carburetor and install the 3 choke housing screws.

2. Rotate the choke shaft counterclockwise and install the diaphragm (**Figure 48**) with a clockwise motion. Install the choke diaphragm spring and cover. Install the 2 retaining screws into the upper 2 holes. Install the new retaining screw in the bottom hole. Tighten the 2 top screws securely. Tighten the bottom screw as required to break the head of the screw off.

3. Install the spring, diaphragm and cover in the accelerator pump (**Figure 46**).

4. Place the accelerator pump discharge check ball in the discharge passage. Check

accelerator pump and seat by filling the fuel bowl with clean gasoline. Hold the ball in place with a length of brass rod and operate the pump plunger by hand. If no resistance is felt, the ball and seat are leaking. In this case, use a drift punch and hammer to gently tap on the old check ball to reform the seat. Take care not to damage the bore. Then remove the old ball and install a new one (included in rebuild kit) and recheck for leakage.

5. Install discharge nozzle, using a new gasket. See **Figure 45**.

6. Install the primary main well tube and primary high speed bleed. See **Figure 44**.

7. Install the secondary main well tube and the secondary high speed bleed. See **Figure 43**.

8. Install the primary main metering jet (**Figure 42**) and the secondary main metering jet (**Figure 41**).

NOTE
The primary main metering jet will have a smaller number stamped on it than the secondary main metering jet.

9. Install the float inlet seat and gasket, fuel inlet needle and float lever pin. See **Figure 40** and **Figure 39**.

10. Invert the air horn and check the clearance between the float assembly and the air horn body with a 0.480 in. gauge or drill. See **Figure 50**. If necessary adjust the dry float level by bending the tang with a small screwdriver as shown in **Figure 51** until this clearance is obtained.

11. Turn the air horn back over and check the float drop with a depth gauge as shown in **Figure 52**. If necessary, use a small

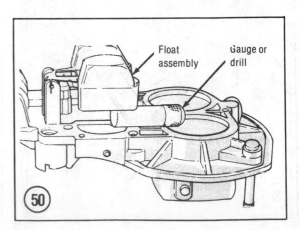
Float assembly   Gauge or drill
(50)

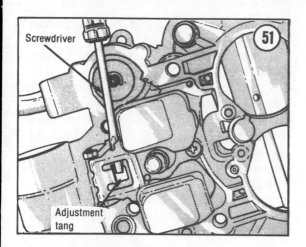

Screwdriver

Adjustment tang

⑤①

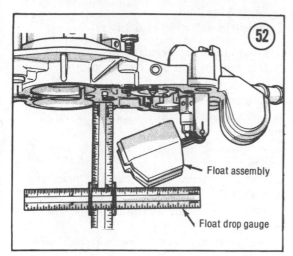

⑤②

Float assembly

Float drop gauge

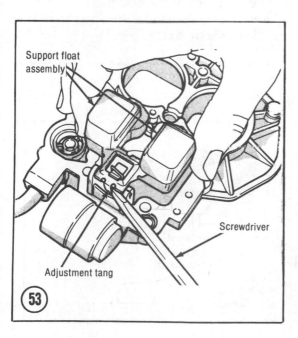

Support float assembly

Screwdriver

Adjustment tang

⑤③

screwdriver as shown in **Figure 53** to adjust the float drop to 1 7/8 in. (47.6 mm).

12. Place a new gasket on the air horn and install choke rod seal and choke operating rod.

13. Carefully place the air horn on the carburetor body and install new choke operating rod retainers on the choke shaft and the fast idle cam pickup lever. Connect the choke operating rod.

14. Install the 5 mounting screws to connect the air horn to the body and tighten the screws evenly to 30 in.-lb. (0.35 mkg). See **Figure 38**.

15. Install and tighten the idle stop solenoid screws. Reinstall the anti-rattle spring.

16. On air-conditioned vehicles, install the wide-open throttle cut-out switch so the air conditioning clutch circuit is open when throttle position is between 10° before wide open to wide open.

17. Install a new duty cycle solenoid gasket on the air horn. Then install a new O-ring seal on the duty cycle solenoid (**Figure 54**). Lightly lubricate the solenoid with petroleum jelly and install into carburetor. Tighten the solenoid screws securely. Route the wiring through clamp.

18. Install and tighten harness mounting screw.

19. Install the fuel inlet gasket and fitting (**Figure 32**).

20. Install carburetor onto vehicle as described in this chapter.

21. Have a Chrysler dealer or qualified specialist adjust the idle mixture.

Adjustments

See *Carburetor Adjustments*, Chapter Three, for carburetor adjustment procedures.

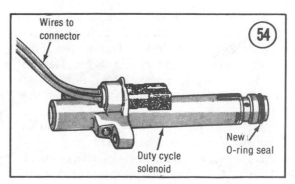

Wires to connector

⑤④

New O-ring seal

Duty cycle solenoid

6

FUEL PUMP

Removal/Installation

The fuel pump used on the 1.7 liter engine is shown in **Figure 55**. The 1.6 and 2.2 liter fuel pump is similar.

1. Disconnect the fuel lines from the fuel pump. See **Figure 56** (1.6 liter), **Figure 57** (1.7 liter) or **Figure 58** (2.2 liter).
2. Remove the pump mounting bolts.
3. Lift the pump from the mounting flange. Remove the spacer block or gasket.
4. Installation is the reverse of removal. Clean the engine and pump mounting flanges of all gasket residue. Use a new gasket or spacer block.

> *NOTE*
> *The fuel pump cannot be repaired. If defective, it must be replaced. See test procedures in Chapter Two. The pump should deliver one quart in one minute at idle at 4-6 psi.*

INTAKE/EXHAUST MANIFOLDS

Intake Manifold
Removal/Installation (1.6 Liter)

1. Disconnect the negative battery cable.
2. Remove the air cleaner as described in this chapter.
3. Label and disconnect all vacuum lines and electrical connectors at the carburetor.
4. Disconnect the fuel line at the carburetor. Cap the line to prevent leakage.
5. Drain the cooling system. See Chapter Seven.
6. Disconnect inlet and outlet hoses at the manifold (**Figure 59**).
7. Disconnect the EGR tube at the manifold (**Figure 59**).
8. Remove the manifold nuts and washers shown in **Figure 60**. Remove the manifold with carburetor attached.
9. Installation is the reverse of removal. Use a new gasket and tighten attaching nuts to 133 in.-lb. (15 N•m).

Exhaust Manifold
Removal/Installation (1.6 Liter)

1. Disconnect the negative battery cable.
2. Disconnect the air heater tubing at the manifold.
3. Disconnect and remove the oxygen sensor.
4. Disconnect the air injection pipe at the manifold.
5. Remove EGR valve assembly from the manifold.
6. Raise the front of the car and place it on jackstands.
7. Disconnect the exhaust pipe at the manifold.
8. Remove the attaching nuts shown in **Figure 61**. Remove the manifold.
9. Remove the carburetor air heater from the manifold (**Figure 61**).

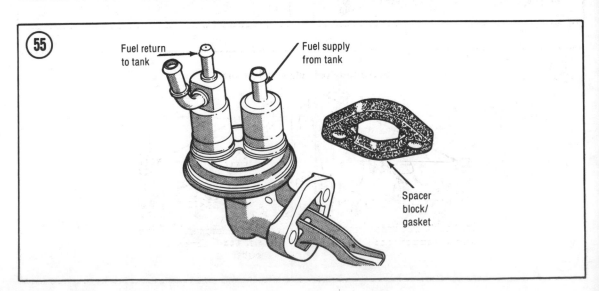

(55) Fuel return to tank   Fuel supply from tank   Spacer block/gasket

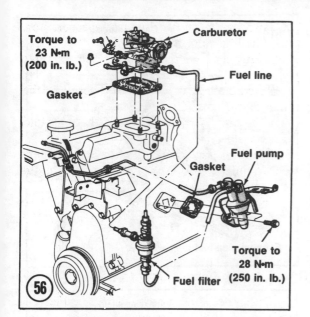

Torque to 23 N·m (200 in. lb.)

Carburetor

Fuel line

Gasket

Gasket

Fuel pump

Torque to 28 N·m (250 in. lb.)

Fuel filter

56

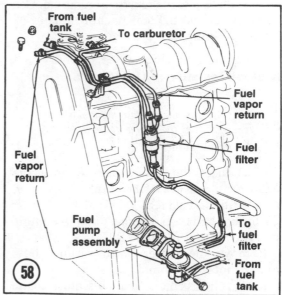

From fuel tank

To carburetor

Fuel vapor return

Fuel filter

Fuel vapor return

Fuel pump assembly

To fuel filter

From fuel tank

58

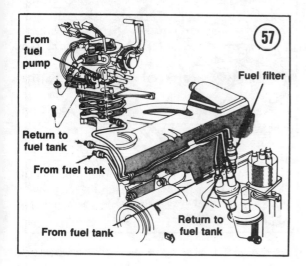

57

From fuel pump

Fuel filter

Return to fuel tank

From fuel tank

From fuel tank

Return to fuel tank

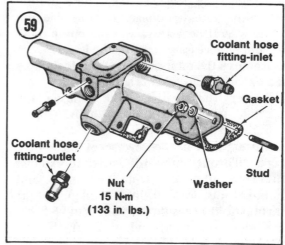

59

Coolant hose fitting-inlet

Gasket

Coolant hose fitting-outlet

Nut 15 N·m (133 in. lbs.)

Washer

Stud

6

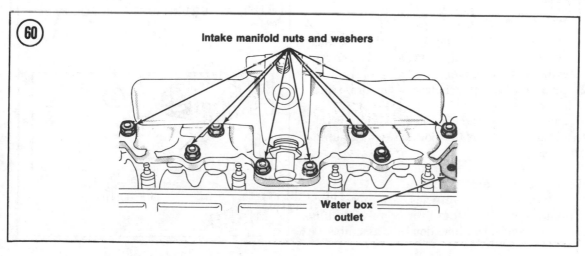

60

Intake manifold nuts and washers

Water box outlet

10. Installation is the reverse of removal. Use a new gasket and tighten attaching nuts to 15 ft.-lb. (20 N•m).

Removal/Installation (1.7 Liter)

NOTE
The intake and exhaust manifolds are removed from the engine as an assembly and then separated.

1. Disconnect the battery and remove the carburetor, as described in *Carburetor, Removal* in this chapter.
2. Loosen the power steering pump mounting bolts and remove the drive belt.
3. Remove the power brake vacuum hose from the intake manifold.
4. Raise the vehicle and disconnect the exhaust pipe from the exhaust manifold.
5. Remove the power steering pump (do not detach the hoses) and place it to one side, out of the way. If necessary, wire the pump up to prevent unnecessary strain on the hoses.
6. Remove the retaining nuts from the intake and exhaust manifolds. **Figure 62**.
7. Lower the vehicle and remove the manifolds from the car as an assembly.
8. Separate the manifolds.
9. Installation is the reverse of the above steps. Torque inboard intake-to-exhaust manifold nut to 13 ft.-lb., (1.8 mkg), and outboard nuts to 17 ft.-lb. (2.4 mkg). Torque the manifold flange attaching nuts to 13 ft.-lb. (1.8 mkg)—exhaust; and to 17 ft.-lb. (2.4 mkg)—intake. See **Figure 62**.

Removal (2.2 Liter)

1. Disconnect the battery and remove the carburetor as described under *Carburetor, Removal*, in this chapter.
2. Open the radiator petcock and drain the radiator.
3. Loosen the power steering pump as required to remove the power steering pump drive belt.
4. Remove the power brake vacuum hose at the intake manifold.
5. On Canadian vehicles, remove the coupling hose from the diverter valve to the exhaust manifold air injection tube assembly.

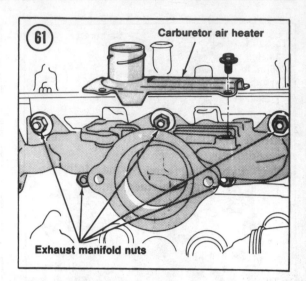
(61) Carburetor air heater

Exhaust manifold nuts

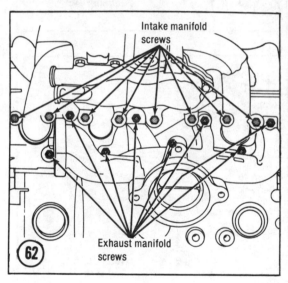
Intake manifold screws

Exhaust manifold screws
(62)

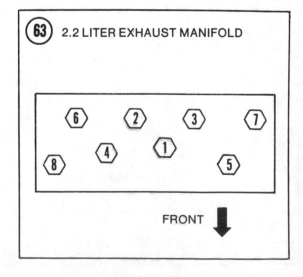
(63) 2.2 LITER EXHAUST MANIFOLD

6 2 3 7
4 1
8 5

FRONT

6. Remove the water hoses from the water crossover cover.

7. Raise the vehicle front end and secure with jackstands.

8. Remove the exhaust pipe at the exhaust manifold.

9. Remove the power steering pump (do not detach the hoses) and place it to one side, out of the way. If necessary, wire the pump up to prevent unnecessary strain on the hoses.

10. Remove the intake manifold support bracket.

11. Remove the EGR tube.

12. On Canadian vehicles, remove the 4 air injection tube bolts and the air injection tube assembly.

13. Remove the retaining fasteners from the intake manifold. See **Figure 62**.

14. Remove the jackstands and lower the vehicle.

15. Remove the intake manifold.

16 Remove the retaining fasteners from the exhaust manifold. See **Figure 62**. Remove the exhaust manifold.

Installation (2.2 Liter)

1. Remove and discard all gaskets. Clean all gasket surfaces on the cylinder head and both manifolds.

2. Lightly coat each gasket on the cylinder head side with Sealer part No. 3419115 or equivalent.

3. Place each gasket onto the cylinder head.

4. Install the exhaust manifold. Tighten the exhaust manifold retaining fasteners to 200 in.-lb. (2.3 mkg) in the sequence shown in **Figure 63**.

5. Install the intake manifold. Tighten the manifold retaining fasteners to 200 in.-lb (2.3 mkg) in the sequence shown in **Figure 64**.

6. Reverse removal procedures Steps 1-12 to complete installation.

7. Fill the cooling system. Start engine and check for leaks.

EXHAUST SYSTEM

The exhaust system consists of a catalytic converter, muffler and interconnecting exhaust pipes. The type of exhaust system used on your car will depend on where the car was originally sold—Canada, California, or elsewhere in the U.S. (Federal).

Catalytic Converter Replacement

The catalytic converter must be replaced when damaged. Periodic service is not required.

1. Raise car on hoist or jackstands.

2. Remove shielding which covers the converter. On some models, the shielding is welded to the front converter.

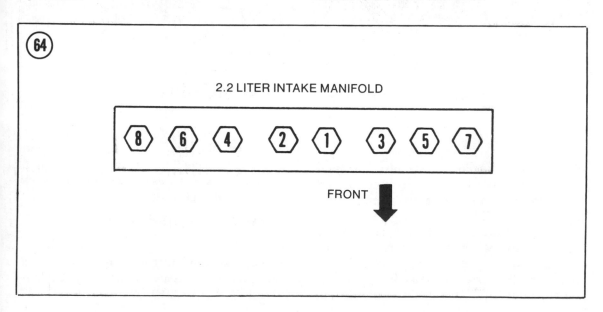

64

2.2 LITER INTAKE MANIFOLD

(8) (6) (4) (2) (1) (3) (5) (7)

FRONT

3. Remove nuts on U-bolt at each end of converter. See **Figure 65**.

4. Remove the converter.

5. Install a new converter.

6. Tighten bolts uniformly.

Muffler Replacement (Typical)

Refer to **Figure 66**.

1. Raise vehicle and secure with jackstands.

2. Loosen clamp at front of muffler or at intermediate pipe. See **Figure 67** (1.6 and 1.7 liter) or **Figure 68** (2.2 liter).

3. Disconnect rubber mountings at front and rear of muffler. **Figure 69** shows the rear muffler mount.

4. Separate defective muffler from system. Use penetrating oil liberally at the connections. If necessary, use a pipe-cutting chisel to free the muffler.

> *NOTE*
> *If muffler is defective, chances are very good that other components are too. Consider replacing the entire system up to the exhaust header.*

5. Install new muffler in place. Tighten clamp.

> *NOTE*
> *Always replace exhaust system components with original equipment parts or their equivalent. This assures proper exhaust system alignment and system operation. Incorrectly fitted parts or those which are not installed properly will eventually break the joining fasteners.*

6. Reconnect rubber mounts. If rubber loops are deteriorated, replace them.

7. Run engine and check for exhaust leaks.

Heat Shields

Heat shields are used at designed points above and below exhaust system components. The shields protect the car and environment from the high temperatures developed by the catalytic converter. The heat shields must never be removed from the car. Likewise, when applying undercoating materials to the bottom of the car, do not apply the material to the heat shields. Undercoating and other such chemicals will

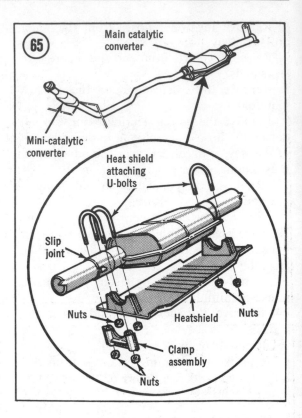

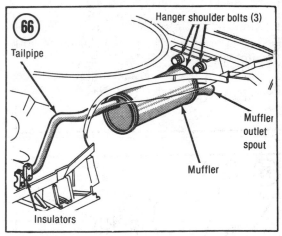

reduce the efficiency of the heat shields and result in excessive floor pan temperatures and exhaust fumes. A series of typical heat shields are shown in **Figure 70**.

EXHAUST GAS RECIRCULATION

The exhaust gas recirculation (EGR) system reduces oxides of nitrogen. **Figure 71** shows the EGR valve. **Figure 72** shows the coolant control EGR (CCEGR) valve.

67

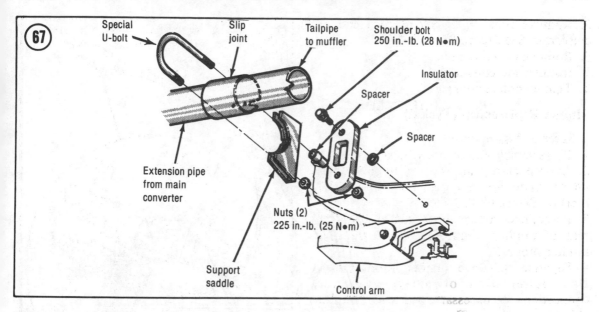

Special U-bolt

Slip joint

Tailpipe to muffler

Shoulder bolt 250 in.-lb. (28 N•m)

Insulator

Spacer

Spacer

Extension pipe from main converter

Nuts (2) 225 in.-lb. (25 N•m)

Support saddle

Control arm

68

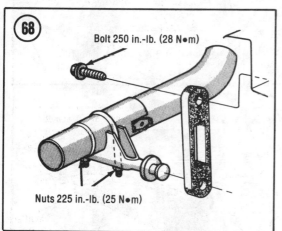

Bolt 250 in.-lb. (28 N•m)

Nuts 225 in.-lb. (25 N•m)

71

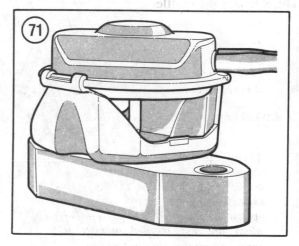

6

69

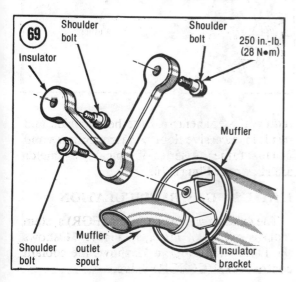

Shoulder bolt

Shoulder bolt

250 in.-lb. (28 N•m)

Insulator

Muffler

Shoulder bolt

Muffler outlet spout

Insulator bracket

72

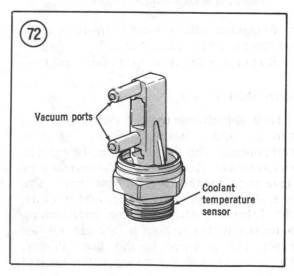

Vacuum ports

Coolant temperature sensor

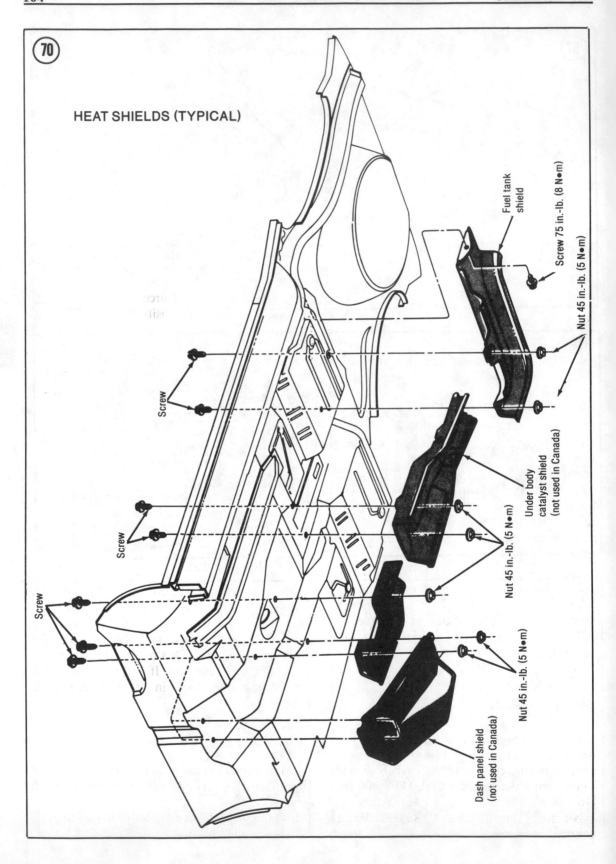

HEAT SHIELDS (TYPICAL)

Fuel tank shield

Screw 75 in.-lb. (8 N•m)

Nut 45 in.-lb. (5 N•m)

Screw

Under body catalyst shield (not used in Canada)

Nut 45 in.-lb. (5 N•m)

Screw

Screw

Nut 45 in.-lb. (5 N•m)

Screw

Dash panel shield (not used in Canada)

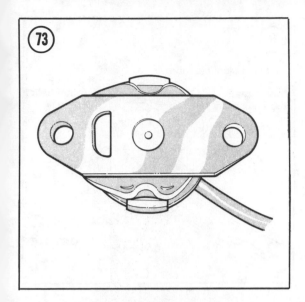

The system is designed to help limit the formation of oxides of nitrogen (NOx) by introducing metered amounts of exhaust gas into the intake manifold where it mixes with the air/fuel mixture. This air/fuel/exhaust gas mixture causes peak flame temperature and pressure in the cylinders to be lowered. Since the production of NOx is directly related to pressure, lowering the peak pressure limits formation of these pollutants. The system does not operate when the engine is cold or under certain operating conditions, such as idling, because the introduction of the exhaust gases under these conditions would cause the engine to run roughly.

During engine warm-up, the CCEGR valve opens when coolant temperature reaches approximately 125° F (52° C) and permits a vacuum to be applied to the EGR valve. The EGR valve then permits exhaust gases to be recirculated.

EGR Valve Check

To check the operation of the EGR system, warm up the engine and allow it to run at idle speed (throttle closed) for at least 70 seconds. Then abruptly accelerate to 2,000-3,000 rpm. Do not exceed 3,000 rpm. Watch the EGR valve stem for movement. Repeat the test several times, if necessary, to verify

movement. If the valve stem moves, the valve is functioning properly. If no movement is detected, see *EGR Valve Service*, this chapter.

EGR Valve Service

1. Remove the EGR valve (2 bolts). Identify hoses so they can be returned to their original positions.
2. Inspect the valve for deposits, paying particular attention to the poppet and seat area. See **Figure 73**.
3. If excessive deposits are present (a thin film is normal), carefully remove them. A manifold heat control valve solvent will speed this operation if care is taken. Open valve with an external vacuum source to allow thorough cleaning. Scrape deposits with a suitable sharp-edged tool.

> *CAUTION*
> *If manifold heat control valve solvent is used, take care to avoid spilling the solvent on the EGR diaphragm. The solvent could damage the diaphragm, thus, causing failure. Also, do not apply force to the diaphragm to operate the valve. Use only an external vacuum source.*

4. If the valve still does not operate properly, or excessive wear is observed on the stem or other moving parts, replace the valve.

CCEGR Valve Test

Remove the CCEGR valve from the housing and place the threaded portion in an ice bath (below 40° F). Connect a vacuum pump to the valve nipple from which the yellow-striped hose was removed and apply a vacuum of 10 in. Hg. If the vacuum drops more than one in. Hg in one minute, replace the valve.

EGR Valve Replacement

1. Disconnect vacuum lines from valve. Mark them so they cannot be interchanged when reinstalled.
2. Remove bolts securing valve to manifold.
3. Installation is the reverse of these steps.

6

AIR INJECTION SYSTEM

All models use an exhaust "after burner" system. See **Figure 74** (1.6 liter), **Figure 75** (1.7 liter) or **Figure 76** and **Figure 77** (2.2 liter). This system reduces pollution by oxidizing hydrocarbons and carbon monoxide as they leave the combustion chamber. Harmful carbon monoxide (CO) changes into harmless carbon dioxide (CO_2) in the process.

The engine-driven air pump compresses air through a check valve to the cylinder head near the exhaust port. This fresh air mixes with the unburned gases in the exhaust and promotes further burning in the catalytic

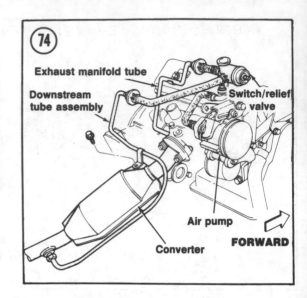

Exhaust manifold tube
Downstream tube assembly
Switch/relief valve
Air pump
Converter
FORWARD

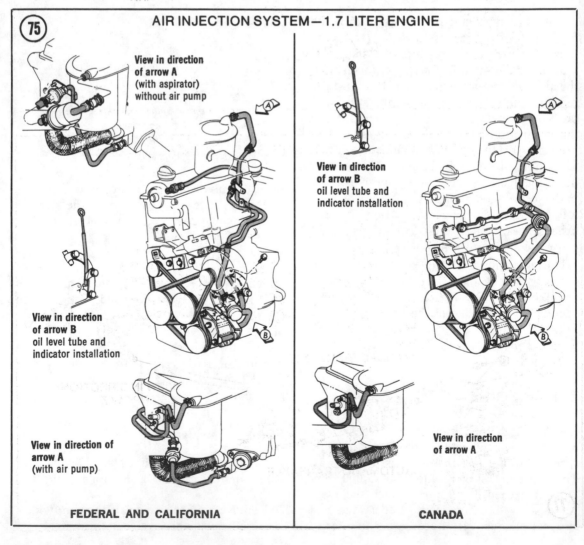

AIR INJECTION SYSTEM—1.7 LITER ENGINE

View in direction of arrow A (with aspirator) without air pump

View in direction of arrow B oil level tube and indicator installation

View in direction of arrow B oil level tube and indicator installation

View in direction of arrow A (with air pump)

View in direction of arrow A

FEDERAL AND CALIFORNIA   **CANADA**

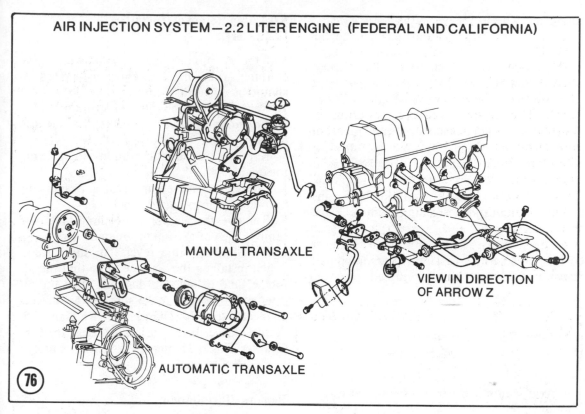

AIR INJECTION SYSTEM—2.2 LITER ENGINE (FEDERAL AND CALIFORNIA)

MANUAL TRANSAXLE

AUTOMATIC TRANSAXLE

VIEW IN DIRECTION OF ARROW Z

76

6

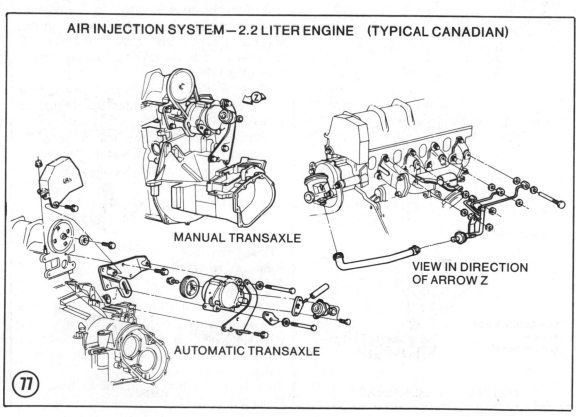

AIR INJECTION SYSTEM—2.2 LITER ENGINE (TYPICAL CANADIAN)

MANUAL TRANSAXLE

AUTOMATIC TRANSAXLE

VIEW IN DIRECTION OF ARROW Z

77

converter. The check valve prevents exhaust gases from entering and damaging the air pump if the pump becomes inoperative, e.g., from a drive belt failure. Under normal conditions, the pump delivers sufficient air pressure to prevent exhaust gases from entering the pump.

The diverter valve senses sharp increases in manifold vacuum such as during closed-throttle deceleration. Increased vacuum opens the control valve, admitting fresh air into the intake manifold. This leans out the air/fuel mixture and prevents exhaust system backfire.

None of the air injection system components can be repaired. If a component proves defective, it must be replaced.

Air Pump Removal/Installation
(1.6 and 1.7 Liter)

If the air pump seizes or makes excessive chirping, rumbling, or knocking noises, it should be replaced.

> *CAUTION*
> *Proper torquing of the air pump attaching screws on the 1.7 liter engine is critical. Failure to tighten all fasteners properly can result in coolant leakage from the water pump or cracking of the pump housing.*

1. Identify vacuum and air hoses for installation and remove them from the pump.
2. Loosen the pivot and adjusting bolts and remove the air pump drive belt.
3. Remove the air pump protection shield and the pump pulley.
4. Remove the attaching bolts and remove the air pump from the engine.
5. Installation is the reverse of these steps. Torque all pulley attaching bolts securely. When installing the air hose, note that the air intake tube is larger in diameter than the air discharge tube and make sure the air hose is connected to the discharge hose. See **Figure 78**. Adjust drive belt tension as described in Chapter Three.

Air Pump Removal/Installation
(2.2 Liter)

If the air pump seizes or makes excessive chirping, rumbling, or knocking noises, it should be replaced.
1. Remove the air hose from the air pump.
2. *Canadian vehicles:* Remove the vacuum and air hoses from the diverter valve.
3. Remove the air pump pulley shield from the engine.
4. Loosen the air pump pivot and adjusting bolts and remove the drive belt.
5. Remove the air pump attaching bolts and remove the pump from the engine.
6. Installation is the reverse of these steps. When installing the air hose, note that the air intake tube is larger in diameter than the air discharge tube and make sure the air hose is connected to the discharge hose. See **Figure 78**. Adjust drive belt tension as described in Chapter Three. Tighten all fasteners securely.

Diverter Valve
Removal/Installation

Replace the diverter valve if it is producing excessive noise, or if air is escaping from the silencer at engine idle speed. See **Figure 79**. On 1981 models, the diverter valve is used on Canadian vehicles only.
1. Remove the air and vacuum hoses from diverter valve and identify them for installation.
2. Remove the diverter valve from the mounting flange on the air pump (2 screws).
3. Clean all gasket material from the flange.
4. Using a new gasket, install the diverter valve and torque securely.
5. Install air and vacuum hoses to valve.

Check Valve
Removal/Installation
(1978-1979 California)

Check valve operation can be verified by removing the air hose from the inlet tube while the engine is operating. If exhaust gas is escaping from the inlet tube, the valve is defective and must be replaced.
1. Release clamp and remove air hose from check valve inlet tube.

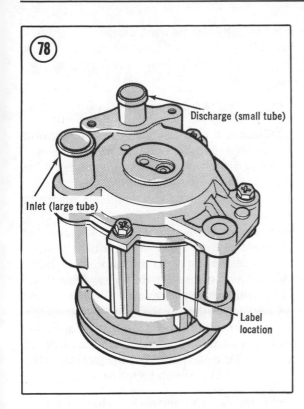

Discharge (small tube)

Inlet (large tube)

Label location

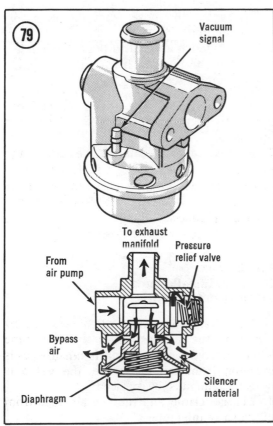

Vacuum signal

To exhaust manifold

Pressure relief valve

From air pump

Bypass air

Silencer material

Diaphragm

2. Remove the nut securing the air injection tube to the exhaust manifold and remove the tube and valve assembly from the engine.

3. Installation is the reverse of these steps. Torque nut to approximately 30 ft.-lb. (4.1 mkg).

Check Valve Removal (1980-On Except Canada)

Check valve operation can be verified by removing the air hose from the inlet tube while the engine is operating. If exhaust gas is escaping from the inlet tube, the valve is defective and must be replaced.

1. Release clamp and remove air hose from inlet tube.

2. Remove the nut securing the air injection tube to the exhaust manifold or catalyst.

3A. On the 1.7 liter engine, remove the top nut on the water valve outlet. Then remove injection tube from the engine.

3B. On the 2.2 liter engine, loosen the starter motor attaching bolt and remove the injection tube from the engine.

4. Remove the catalyst injection tube screw from the catalyst flange and remove the injection tube from the exhaust system.

Check Valve Installation (1980-On Models, Except Canada)

1. Install injection tube into catalyst fitting and tighten tube nut loosely. Install the injection tube attaching screw to the catalyst flange and tighten to 125 in.-lb. (1.4 mkg). Tighten the tube nut to 25-35 ft.-lb. (3.4-4.7 mkg).

2A. On the 1.7 liter engine, install the injection tube bracket onto the water outlet stud and the tube nut into the exhaust manifold fitting. Tighten the tube nut to 25-35 ft.-lb. (3.4-4.7 mkg). Tighten the bracket assembly nut to 124 in.-lb. (1.4 mkg).

2B. On the 2.2 liter engine, install the air injection tube into the exhaust manifold fitting. Install the starter motor bracket and attaching bolt and tighten to 40 ft.-lb. (5.4 mkg). Tighten the injection tube nut to 25-35 ft.-lb. (3.4-4.7 mkg).

3. Connect the air hose to the check valve inlet fitting and secure with clamp.

Check Valve Removal/Installation (Canada 1.7 Liter)

Remove the air hose from the check valve inlet tube to verify operation. If exhaust gas escapes from the inlet tube while the engine is running, the valve is defective and must be replaced.

1. Release clamp and disconnect the air hose from the air inlet tube on the check valve.
2. If the car has air conditioning, remove the compressor and brackets and place to one side in an upright position without tilting.
3. Drain the cooling system until coolant level is below the thermostat housing. Remove the thermostat housing from the engine.
4. Remove the 4 hollow bolts attaching the injection tube assembly to the cylinder head. Remove the injection tube assembly from the engine.
5. Installation is the reverse of these steps. Be sure to use copper washers between each bolt head and the injection tube, and torque bolts to 21 ft.-lb. (3 mkg). Use new gasket and torque thermostat housing bolts to 7 ft.-lb. (1 mkg). Adjust tension of drive belt as described in *Drive Belt Tension*, Chapter Three. Refill cooling system and connect air hose to inlet tube.

Check Valve Removal/Installation (Canada 2.2 Liter)

Remove the air hose from the check valve inlet tube to verify operation. If exhaust gas escapes from the inlet tube while the engine is running, the valve is defective and must be replaced.

1. Release clamp and disconnect the air hose from the air inlet tube on the check valve.
2. On vehicles equipped with power steering, remove the power steering pump bracket.
3. Remove the air cleaner assembly as described earlier in this chapter.
4. Remove the carburetor air heater assembly. See **Figure 80**.
5. Remove the 4 hollow bolts attaching the injection tube assembly to the cylinder head. Remove the injection tube assembly from the engine.
6. Installation is the reverse of these steps. Install 4 plated washers between the injection

tube and the exhaust manifold. Install the 4 hollow bolts to the engine with plated washers between the bolt head and the injection tube. Tighten bolts to 25 ft.-lb. (3.4 mkg).

AIR ASPIRATOR VALVE

Failure of the air aspirator valve is indicated by excessive exhaust noise when the engine is idling and by hardening of the rubber hose between the valve and the air cleaner. The valve cannot be repaired, and replacement is required if it is faulty. All 1978 and 1979 Federal models produced after January 23, 1978, are equipped with the air aspirator valve instead of the air injection pump. The valve uses exhaust pressure pulsation to draw fresh air into the exhaust system.

Check operation of the valve by removing the hose from the valve's air inlet tube. Allow engine to warm up and operate at idle speed. If exhaust gas is escaping from the air inlet tube, the valve is defective and must be replaced.

Aspirator Valve Removal/Installation

1. Disconnect the hose from the aspirator valve inlet tube.
2. Use a wrench applied to the hex shoulder of the valve to unscrew it from the aspirator tube assembly. See **Figure 81**.
3. Installation is the reverse of these steps. Torque the valve to 25 ft.-lb. (3.5 mkg). If the inlet hose has hardened, install a new one.

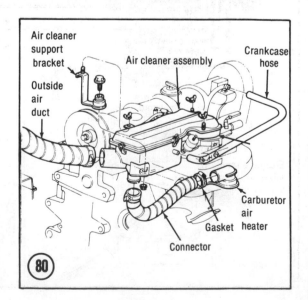

Air cleaner support bracket

Outside air duct

Air cleaner assembly

Crankcase hose

Carburetor air heater

Gasket

Connector

(80)

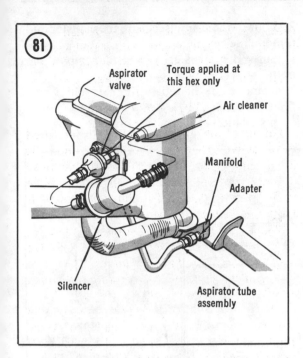

81

Aspirator valve

Torque applied at this hex only

Air cleaner

Manifold

Adapter

Silencer

Aspirator tube assembly

FUEL EVAPORATIVE CONTROL SYSTEM

The fuel evaporative control system prevents the release of fuel vapor into the atmosphere. See **Figure 82** (1.7 liter) or **Figure 83** (2.2 liter). The 1.6 liter system is similar.

Fuel vapor from the fuel tank passes through the separator to the activated charcoal filter. When the engine runs, the fuel vapor is drawn into the air cleaner. Instead of being released into the atmosphere, the fuel vapor takes part in the normal combustion process.

Service to the fuel evaporative system consists mainly of replacing the filter located in the bottom of the charcoal canister if the vehicle is operated frequently in dusty areas.

6

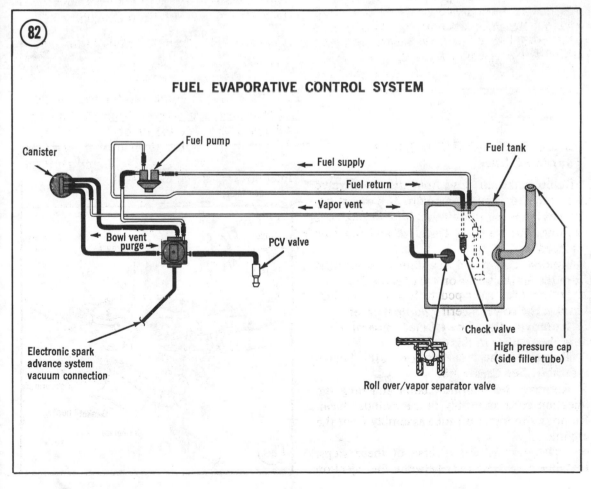

82

FUEL EVAPORATIVE CONTROL SYSTEM

Canister

Fuel pump

Fuel tank

← Fuel supply

Fuel return →

← Vapor vent →

← Bowl vent purge →

PCV valve

Electronic spark advance system vacuum connection

Check valve

High pressure cap (side filler tube)

Roll over/vapor separator valve

Charcoal Canister Filter Replacement

Refer to **Figure 84** for this procedure.

1. Label and disconnect the vent hoses from the top of the canister.

2. Loosen the clamp securing the canister and remove the canister.

3. Turn the canister over and remove the bottom cover.

4. Remove the fiberglass filter. Install a new filter.

5. Installation is the reverse of these steps.

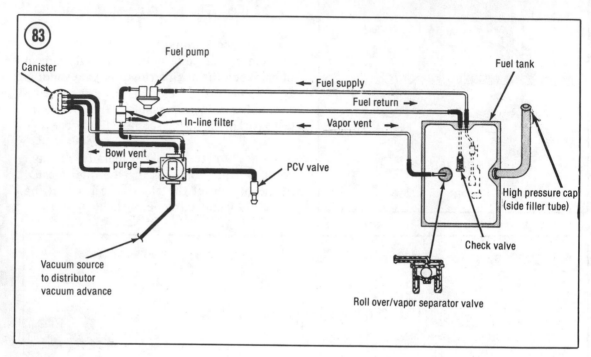

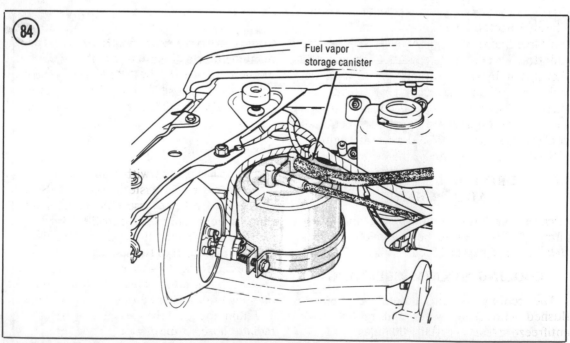

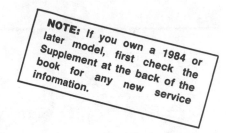
CHAPTER SEVEN

COOLING AND HEATING SYSTEMS

The cooling system is shown in **Figure 1**. Engine coolant is cooled by the radiator and an electric fan. A thermoswitch governs the fan motor, turning it on when engine coolant reaches approximately 194° F (90° C) and off at about 185° F (85° C). The fan can only be energized when the ignition is ON. Engine coolant is circulated by a water pump bolted to the lower front crankcase extension (1.6 liter) or mounted on the side of the engine block (1.7 and 2.2 liter). A single drive belt drives both the water pump and alternator. The thermostat, also mounted on the side of the block, controls coolant flow through the radiator. When the engine is cold, the thermostat bypasses the coolant around the radiator. When the engine is warm, the thermostat opens and directs coolant through the radiator. **Figures 2-4** show the direction of coolant flow for a cold and a warm engine.

Table 1 is at the end of the chapter.

DRIVE BELT TENSION ADJUSTMENT

The procedure for tensioning the water pump/alternator drive belt is given in *Drive Belt Tension*, Chapter Three.

COOLING SYSTEM CLEANING

The cooling system should be drained, flushed with clean water and refilled with antifreeze at least every 30,000 miles.

Cleaning

1. Open draincock and allow cooling system to drain.

2. Fill system with clean water, install radiator cap, and run engine until upper radiator hose becomes hot to the touch.

3. Stop engine and drain cooling system.

4. If water is still dirty, fill, run, and drain system again. Repeat until water drains clear.

5. After final draining, close draincock and fill system with solution of water and ethylene glycol antifreeze. Follow antifreeze manufacturer's instructions to obtain the proper solution for the temperatures anticipated, but use at least a 50/50 solution to protect the system from rust and corrosion.

Reverse Flushing

If simple cleaning with plain water fails to properly clean the system, the radiator and engine should be reverse flushed using a tool that injects short, controlled bursts of compressed air into the system. You may be able to rent this tool from an equipment rental business. If the tool is not available, use a chemical radiator cleaner, following the manufacturer's instructions.

1. Drain the cooling system and detach the radiator hoses at the engine.

7

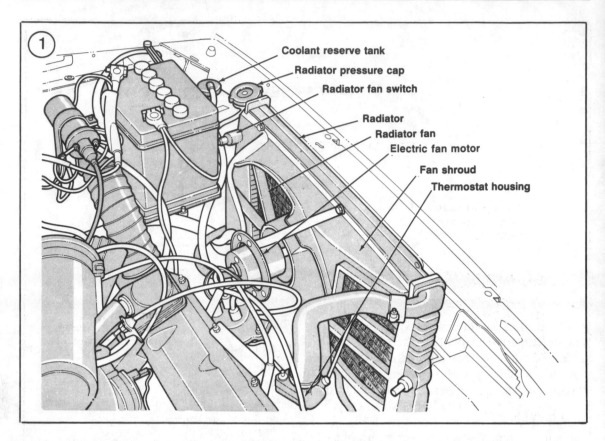

(1)

Coolant reserve tank
Radiator pressure cap
Radiator fan switch
Radiator
Radiator fan
Electric fan motor
Fan shroud
Thermostat housing

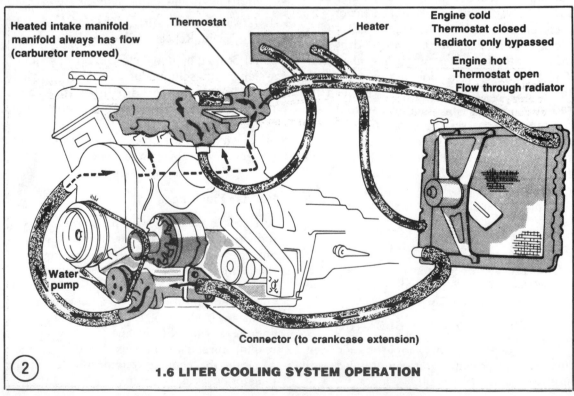

Heated intake manifold
manifold always has flow
(carburetor removed)

Thermostat

Heater

Engine cold
Thermostat closed
Radiator only bypassed

Engine hot
Thermostat open
Flow through radiator

Water pump

Connector (to crankcase extension)

(2)   **1.6 LITER COOLING SYSTEM OPERATION**

1.7 LITER COOLING SYSTEM OPERATION

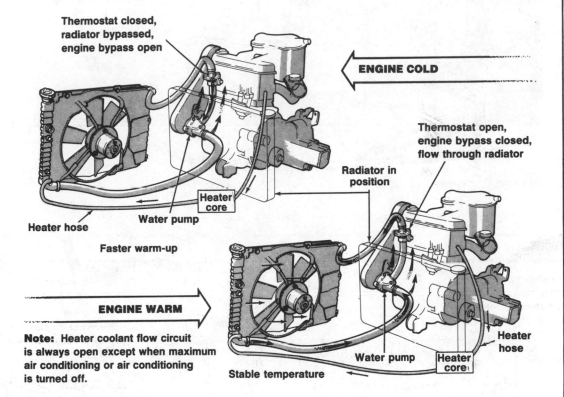

Thermostat closed, radiator bypassed, engine bypass open

ENGINE COLD

Thermostat open, engine bypass closed, flow through radiator

Radiator in position

Heater core

Heater hose

Water pump

Faster warm-up

ENGINE WARM

Note: Heater coolant flow circuit is always open except when maximum air conditioning or air conditioning is turned off.

Heater hose

Water pump

Heater core

Stable temperature

7

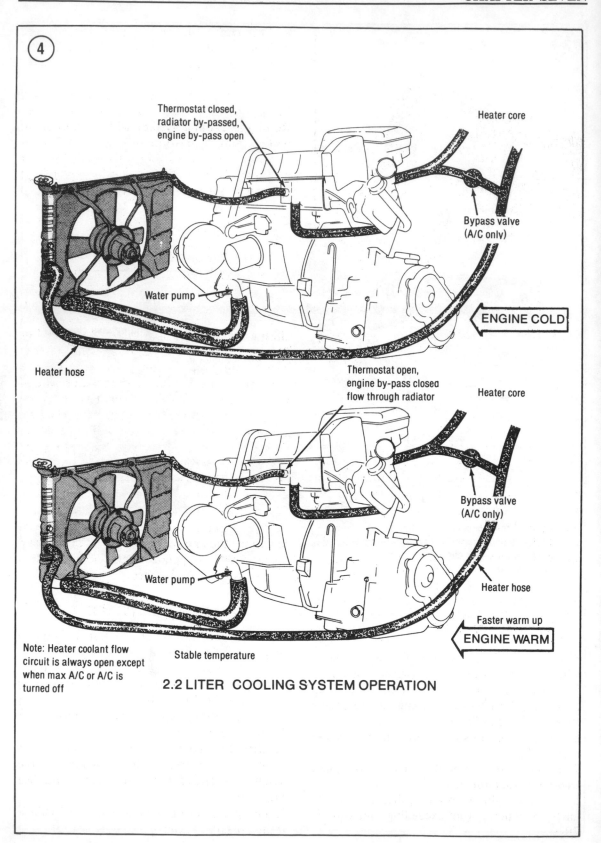

Thermostat closed, radiator by-passed, engine by-pass open

Heater core

Bypass valve (A/C only)

Water pump

ENGINE COLD

Heater hose

Thermostat open, engine by-pass closed flow through radiator

Heater core

Bypass valve (A/C only)

Water pump

Heater hose

Faster warm up

ENGINE WARM

Note: Heater coolant flow circuit is always open except when max A/C or A/C is turned off

Stable temperature

2.2 LITER COOLING SYSTEM OPERATION

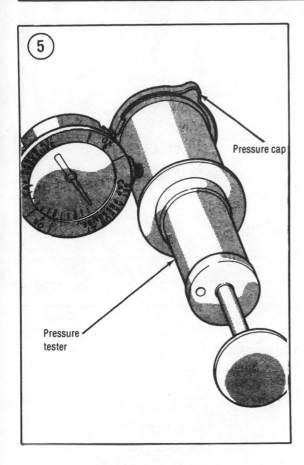

Pressure cap

Pressure tester

2. Install a suitable flushing gun in the lower radiator hose. Connect the gun water hose to a pressurized water source and the air hose to a compressed air source.

3. Fill the radiator with clean water, then turn on the air in short bursts.

CAUTION
Internal radiator pressure must not exceed 20 psi. High pressures can cause radiator damage.

4. Continue filling with water and blasting with compressed air until the water runs clean.

5. Allow the radiator to drain and then reconnect the hoses to the engine and detach them from the radiator.

6. Install the flushing gun in the lower radiator hose.

7. Remove the engine thermostat and replace the thermostat housing.

8. Fill the engine with water, then turn on the air in short bursts (not exceeding a pressure of 20 psi).

9. Continue filling with water and blasting with air until the water running from the engine runs clear.

10. Drain the water from the system, remove the gun, and reconnect the radiator hoses. Install the thermostat, using a new gasket. Refill the cooling system with a solution of water and ethylene glycol antifreeze, following the manufacturer's instructions for anticipated temperatures (solution must be at least 50/50 for engine protection).

System Refilling

When refilling the cooling system with coolant solution, open the heater coolant control valve and fill the system until the coolant level reaches the pressure cap seat. Use an ethylene glycol-type antifreeze that has silicate inhibitor (such as MOPAR 4106784 or Prestone II) in at least a 50/50 solution with clean water. Follow the antifreeze manufacturer's instructions to determine if more antifreeze is required for the anticipated temperatures. Install the radiator cap, start the engine, and allow it to run until the upper radiator hose feels hot. Stop the engine and add coolant as required to completely fill the radiator. Add the same coolant solution to the reserve tank to bring the level in the tank to between the **MIN** and **MAX** marks. Check the fluid level in the tank carefully during the next few times the engine is warmed up because air sometimes is trapped in the cooling system when it is drained and filled.

PRESSURE CHECK

If the coolant system requires frequent topping up, chances are that there is a leak. Not only may coolant be lost, but without proper pressure, the coolant recovery system cannot function properly.

To check the system, proceed as follows:

1. Remove the radiator cap.

2. Dip the cap in water and attach to a cooling system pressure tester, using suitable adapters supplied with the instrument. See **Figure 5**.

3. Pump pressure to that specified in **Table 1**. If the cap fails to hold pressure, replace it.

4. Attach the pressure tester to the filler hole on the radiator. See **Figure 6**.

5. Pump the system to the pressure specified in **Table 1**. There should be no noticeable pressure drop in 30 seconds. If pressure falls off, there is a leak which must be found and sealed.

THERMOSTAT

Removal and Testing

1. Drain the radiator by disconnecting lower radiator hose at water pump.
2. Remove the 2 bolts securing the thermostat housing.
3. Remove thermostat and seal.
4. To test, slip a 0.002 in. feeler gauge between the valve and its seat.
5. Submerge the thermostat in water with a thermometer as shown in **Figure 7**
6. Heat the water and hold a slight tension on the feeler gauge.
7. When the valve opens and the feeler gauge slips out read the thermometer. Compare to specifications in **Table 1**. Note temperature at which thermostat fully opens.
8. If the thermostat opens at the wrong temperature, or does not open at all, replace it.

Installation

1. Test the new thermostat as described above.
2. Install the thermostat in position in the housing.
3. Position the thermostat housing using a new gasket.
4. Tighten 1.6 liter engine cap screws to 200 in.-lb. (23 N•m). Tighten 1.7 and 2.2 liter engine cap screws to 250 in.-lb. (30 N•m).
5. Connect the lower radiator hose. Fill the system with a 50/50 mixture of ethylene glycol and water.

WATER PUMP

A defective water pump is usually evident when the engine overheats and there is no other apparent reason. Quite often, the water pump will give some warning before it fails completely. When the water pump begins to make noise or fails, replace with a new pump.

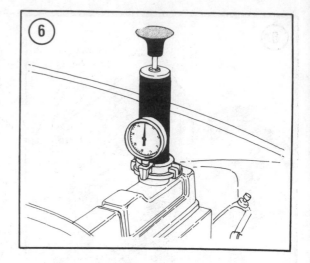

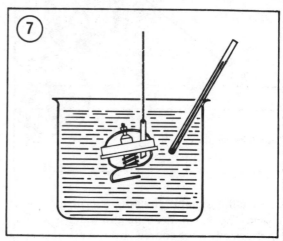

The pump should not be rebuilt since there is considerable risk of cracking the aluminum pump housing when replacing the seals. However, the water pump may be disassembled to replace the sealant between the water pump body and cover.

Removal/Installation
(1.6 Liter)

Refer to **Figure 8** for this procedure.
1. Remove radiator cap. Loosen the drain plug at the bottom of the water pump and drain the cooling system.
2. Disconnect the water pump-to-engine block hose at the water pump.
3. Loosen the alternator adjusting bolt. Pivot the alternator toward the engine and remove the drive belt.

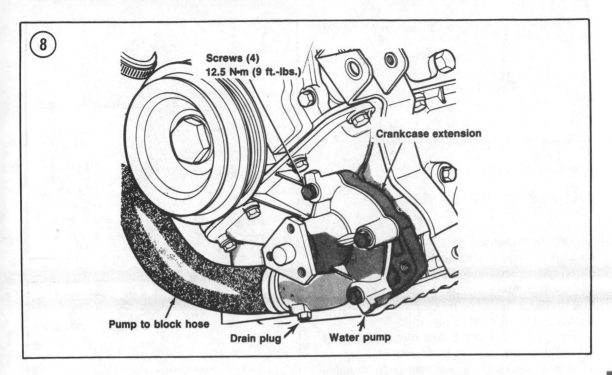

Screws (4)
12.5 N•m (9 ft.-lbs.)

Crankcase extension

Pump to block hose

Drain plug

Water pump

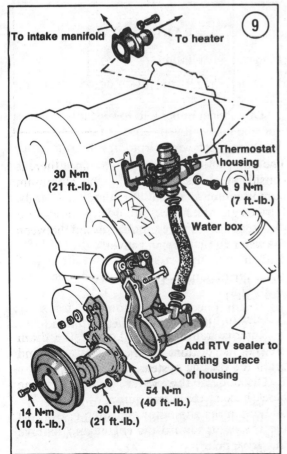

To intake manifold

To heater

Thermostat housing

30 N•m (21 ft.-lb.)

9 N•m (7 ft.-lb.)

Water box

Add RTV sealer to mating surface of housing

54 N•m (40 ft.-lb.)

14 N•m (10 ft.-lb.)

30 N•m (21 ft.-lb.)

4. Remove the water pump pulley.

5. Remove the pump attaching screws. Remove the water pump and discard the gasket.

6. Installation is the reverse of removal. Use a new gasket and tighten pump screws to 9 ft.-lb. (12.5 N•m). Tighten drain plug to 13 ft.-lb. (17 N•m).

Removal/Installation (1.7 Liter)

> *CAUTION*
> *Whenever the water pump is serviced on the 1.7 liter engine, proper torquing of the air pump and alternator bracket-to-water pump screws is critical. Failure to tighten all fasteners properly can result in coolant leakage from the water pump or cracking of the pump housing.*

Refer to **Figure 9**.

1. Drain coolant and remove upper radiator hose.

2. Remove the alternator as described in Chapter Eight. Remove water pump pulley.

3. Remove air conditioner compressor, if so equipped, and place it erect to one side with hoses still connected.

4. Disconnect coolant hoses from water pump.

5. Remove timing belt cover and 2 top water pump mounting bolts.

6. Lift water pump out.

7. Installation is the reverse of these steps. Use a new seal between the water pump and the block and be sure it is seated properly.

Cover Gasket Replacement (1.7 Liter)

The cover sealant can be replaced if it is leaking. Further disassembly of the water pump is not recommended.

1. Remove the water pump as described in this chapter.

2. Remove the drive pulley.

3. Remove the water pump cover shown in **Figure 9**. Clean mating surfaces.

4. Apply new RTV gasket sealer to housing gasket groove.

5. Loosely install water pump cover and allow sealer to set up. Then torque the bolts to 21 ft.-lb. (3 mkg).

6. Install the drive pulley and torque the bolts to 10. ft.-lb. (1.5 mkg).

Removal/Installation (2.2 Liter)

Refer to **Figure 10** for this procedure.

1. Drain coolant and remove the upper radiator hose.

2. *Air conditioned vehicles:* Remove the air conditioning compressor from its brackets and set aside. Do not disconnect the compressor.

3. Remove the alternator as described in Chapter Eight.

4. Disconnect the coolant hoses from the water pump.

5. Remove the water pump attaching screws and remove the pump.

6. Installation is the reverse of these steps. Tighten the top 3 screws to 250 in.-lbs. (30 N•m); tighten the lower screw to 40 ft.-lb. (55 N•m).

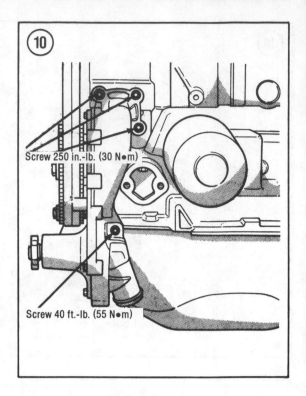

Screw 250 in.-lb. (30 N•m)

Screw 40 ft.-lb. (55 N•m)

RADIATOR

Removal/Installation

1. Drain engine coolant as described in this chapter.

2. Disconnect upper and lower radiator hoses and the heater return hose at the radiator.

3. Disconnect wires from the thermoswitch located on the left side of the radiator. See **Figure 11**, typical.

4. Disconnect overflow line to coolant recovery bottle at the radiator.

5. Disconnect the fan motor plug (**Figure 11**). Remove the fan upper support/shroud bolts. Lift the fan support/shroud from the bottom attachment clips and remove the assembly with fan.

6. If equipped with automatic transaxle, disconnect the oil cooler lines at the radiator. Cap the lines to prevent leakage.

7. Remove upper mounting brackets. On 1.7 and 2.2 engines, loosen lower mounting brackets. See **Figure 12**.

8. Lift radiator from engine compartment.

9. Installation is the reverse of removal. Tighten upper mounting bracket bolts to 105 in.-lb. (11.9 N•m).

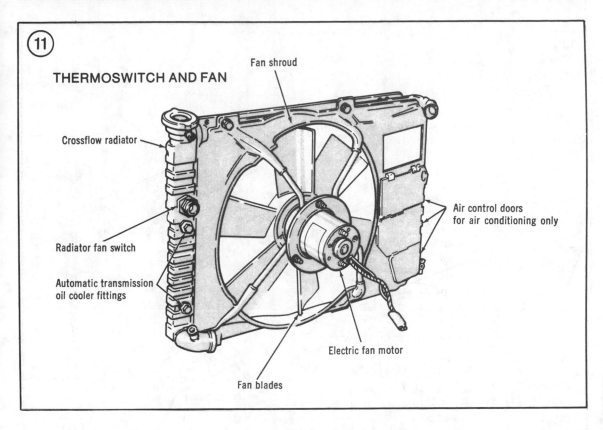

(11)

THERMOSWITCH AND FAN

Fan shroud

Crossflow radiator

Radiator fan switch

Automatic transmission
oil cooler fittings

Air control doors
for air conditioning only

Electric fan motor

Fan blades

7

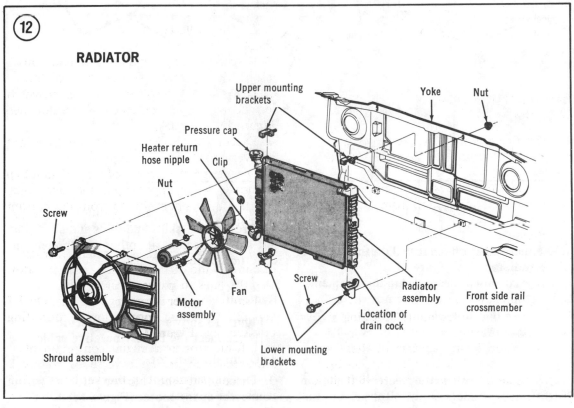

(12)

RADIATOR

Upper mounting
brackets

Pressure cap

Heater return
hose nipple

Clip

Nut

Screw

Yoke   Nut

Screw

Radiator
assembly

Front side rail
crossmember

Location of
drain cock

Fan

Motor
assembly

Shroud assembly

Lower mounting
brackets

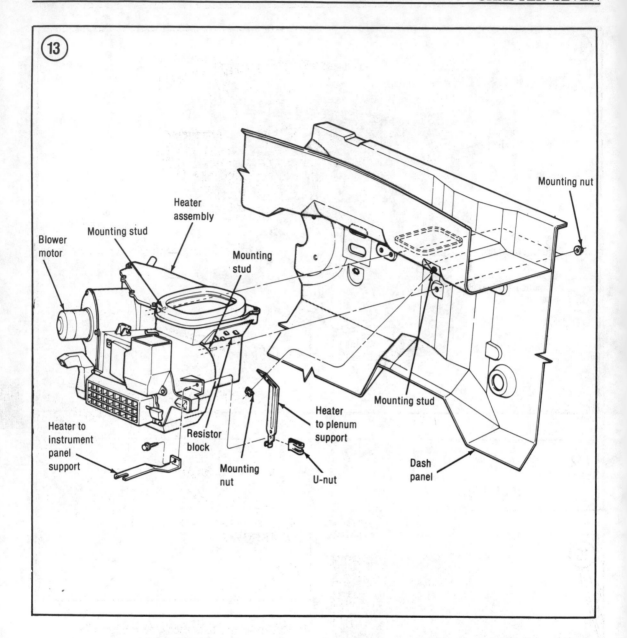

Blower motor · Mounting stud · Heater assembly · Mounting stud · Mounting nut · Heater to instrument panel support · Resistor block · Mounting nut · U-nut · Heater to plenum support · Mounting stud · Dash panel

THERMOSWITCH REPLACEMENT

The thermoswitch is located on the left side of the radiator. See **Figure 11**.

1. Drain coolant as described in this chapter.
2. Disconnect wires from thermoswitch.
3. Unscrew thermoswitch from radiator.
4. Installation is the reverse of these steps.

HEATER

This section covers the heater on non-air conditioned models only. Repair of the integral heater on air conditioned models requires special skills and tools and should be left to a dealer or other competent air conditioning repair shop.

Removal

Figure 13 shows the heater assembly.

1. Disconnect the battery negative cable.

2. Drain the radiator.

3. Disconnect the blower motor wiring connector at the motor (**Figure 14**).

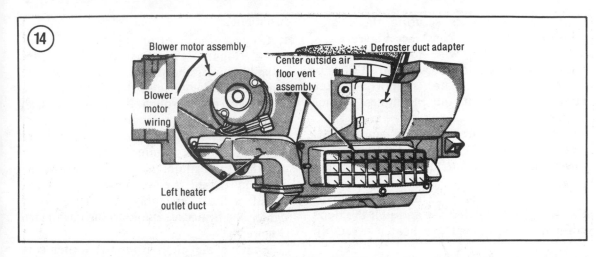

14

Blower motor assembly

Defroster duct adapter

Center outside air floor vent assembly

Blower motor wiring

Left heater outlet duct

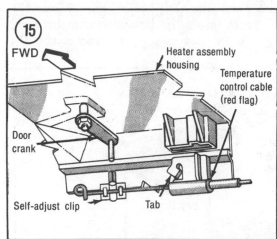

15

FWD

Heater assembly housing

Temperature control cable (red flag)

Door crank

Self-adjust clip

Tab

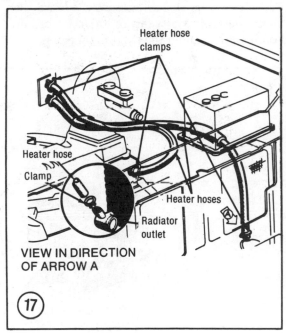

Heater hose clamps

Heater hose

Clamp

Heater hoses

Radiator outlet

VIEW IN DIRECTION OF ARROW A

17

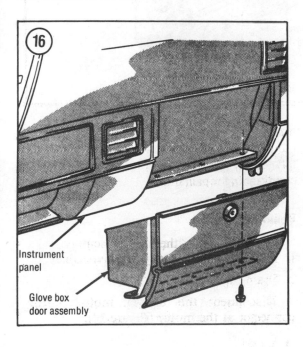

16

Instrument panel

Glove box door assembly

4. Remove the ash receiver receptacle.

5. Referring to **Figure 15**, depress the temperature control cable flag tab and pull temperature control cable out of the receiver on the heater assembly.

6. Remove the screws securing the glove box to the instrument panel **(Figure 16)**. Lower the glove box and remove.

7. Disconnect the heater hoses where they connect to the heater assembly in the engine compartment **(Figure 17)**. Plug the heater core tubes to prevent coolant spillage into the passenger compartment when the heater assembly is removed.

7

8. Remove the nuts securing the heater assembly to the dash panel. See **Figure 18**.

9. Disconnect the wire connector at the blower motor resistor block (**Figure 18**).

10. Remove the heater support bracket attaching screw at the instrument panel (**Figure 18**).

11. Remove the heater support bracket nut. Then disconnect the strap from the stud and lower the heater from the instrument panel (**Figure 18**).

12. Referring to **Figure 19**, depress the tab on the door control cable flag and pull the door control cable out of the heater assembly receiver.

13. Move the heater assembly toward the right side of the vehicle, then lower and remove from under the instrument panel.

Installation

1. Connect the control cable to the door crank (**Figure 19**). Position the heater assembly under the plenum panel. Slide the heater forward enough so that the heater core tubes protrude through the holes in dash panel and that the top mounting studs line up.

2. Install the heater support bracket (**Figure 18**) and tighten as required to hold the heater assembly in position.

3. From inside the engine compartment, install the heater assembly attaching nuts and tighten the heater assembly to the dash panel (**Figure 18**).

4. Remove the plugs from the heater core tubes and attach the heater hoses (**Figure 17**).

5. From inside the passenger compartment, tighten the heater support bracket and the

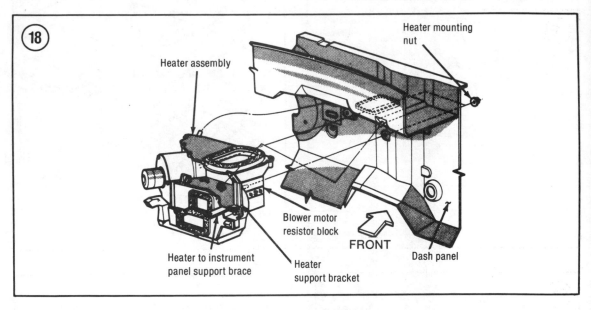

Heater mounting nut

Heater assembly

Blower motor resistor block

FRONT

Dash panel

Heater to instrument panel support brace

Heater support bracket

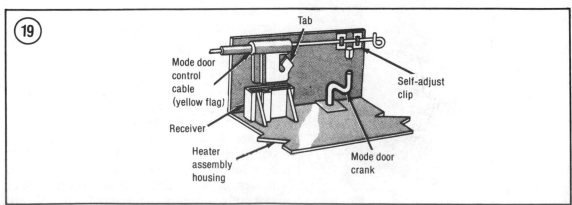

Tab

Mode door control cable (yellow flag)

Self-adjust clip

Receiver

Heater assembly housing

Mode door crank

heater-to-instrument panel support brace (**Figure 18**).

6. Connect the temperature control cable as shown in **Figure 15**.

7. Connect the blower motor wiring connector to the blower motor (**Figure 14**).

8. Place the defrost duct flexible connector onto the defroster duct adapter.

9. Install the ash receiver receptacle.

10. Position the glove box underneath the instrument panel and secure with the glove box attaching screws (**Figure 16**).

11. Refill the cooling system as described under *Cooling System Cleaning*, in this chapter.

Heater Blower Removal

Refer to **Figure 14** for this procedure.

1. Disconnect the blower motor wiring connector at the blower motor.

2. Remove the left heater outlet duct at the heater assembly.

3. Remove the blower mounting plate screws at the heater assembly and remove the blower motor from the heater assembly (**Figure 20**).

4. To remove the blower wheel from the motor shaft, remove the retaining clamp from the blower wheel hub (**Figure 21**). Slide the wheel off the shaft.

5. Installation is the reverse of these steps. If installing the blower wheel, make sure to install the clamp on the blower wheel after installing wheel onto shaft.

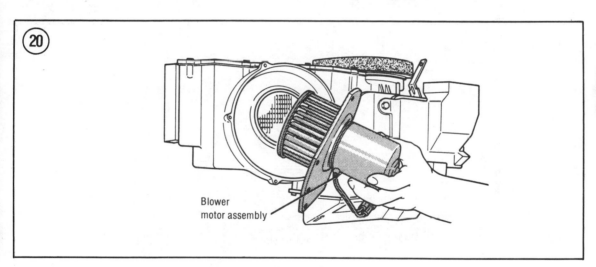

Blower
motor assembly

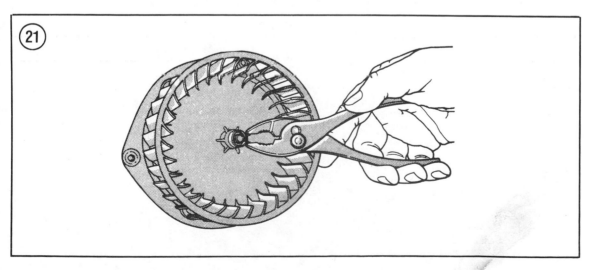

Table 1 COOLING SYSTEM SPECIFICATIONS

System pressure	14-17 psi (0.95-1.16 bar)
Approximate capacity	
1.6 liter	7.0 qt. (6.6 liter)
1.7 liter	
1978	6.5 qt. (6.2 liter)
1979-on	6.0 qt. (5.6 liter)
2.2 liter	9.0 qt. (8.5 liter)
Thermostat	
Opening begins	195° F (91° C)
Fully open	219° F (104° C)
Electric fan	
On	193-207° F (89-97° C)
Off	185° F (85° C)

NOTE: If you own a 1984 or later model, first check the Supplement at the back of the book for any new service information.

CHAPTER EIGHT

ELECTRICAL SYSTEM

This chapter includes service procedures for the battery, starter, charging system, horn, turn signals, fuses and circuit breakers, windshield wipers, lighting system and ignition system. **Tables 1-5** are at the end of the chapter.

BATTERY

The battery is located in the engine compartment. See **Table 1** for battery specifications.

> *NOTE*
> *Make sure battery ground connections are properly made (**Figure 1**). Poor connections can cause illumination of brake warning lamp, or result in speedometer needle not returning to zero, because of improper current flow. When disconnecting battery, always remove ground cable at battery (Z, **Figure 1**) first. When connecting ground cables, make X-Y connection first, then make connection Z. Make certain that all contact surfaces are clean, bright, bare metal, and that all connector bolts are tightened securely.*

Removal/Installation

The following procedures pertain to both open-cell and maintenance-free batteries.
1. Disconnect both battery cables. Use a battery cable puller, if necessary. See **Figure 2**.

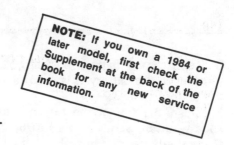

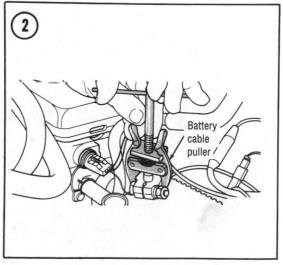

2. Remove the battery hold-down clamp at the rear of the battery (**Figure 3**) and remove the battery.

3. Clean the top of the battery with baking soda solution. Scrub with a stiff bristle brush. Wipe the battery clean with a cloth moistened in ammonia or baking soda solution.

> *CAUTION*
> *Keep cleaning solution out of battery cells or the electrolyte will be seriously weakened.*

4. Clean battery terminals with a stiff wire brush or one of the many tools made for this purpose.

5. Examine entire battery case for cracks. Replace battery if cracks are detected.

6. Install the battery and reconnect the cables.

> *NOTE*
> *Observe polarity when reconnecting cables. Make sure the positive cable is connected to the positive battery terminal.*

7. Coat battery connections with light mineral grease or Vaseline after tightening.

8. On non-maintenance-free batteries, check the electrolyte level and top up if necessary.

Common Causes of Battery Failure

All batteries eventually fail. Their life can be prolonged, however, with a good maintenance program. Some of the reasons for premature failure are listed below.

1. Vehicle accessories left on overnight or longer, causing a discharged condition.

2. Slow driving speeds on short trips, causing an undercharged condition.

3. Vehicle electrical load exceeding the alternator capacity.

4. Charging system defects, such as high resistance, slipping alternator belt or faulty alternator or regulator.

5. Abuse of the battery, including failure to keep battery top and terminals clean, failure to keep cable attaching bolts clean and tight, and failure to add water when needed or habitually adding too much water.

Testing (Open Cell)

Hydrometer testing is the best way to check battery condition. Use a hydrometer with numbered graduations from 1.100 to 1.300 rather than one with color-coded bands. To use the hydrometer, squeeze the rubber ball,

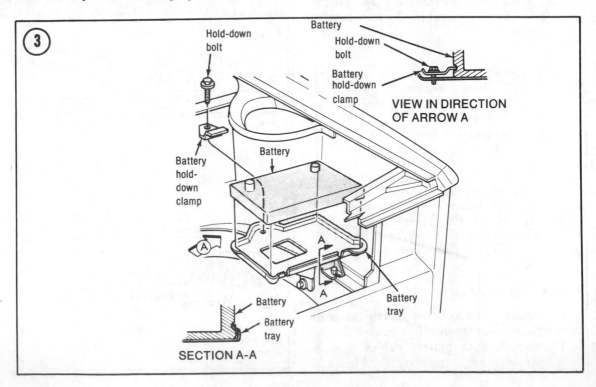

VIEW IN DIRECTION OF ARROW A

SECTION A-A

insert the tip in the cell and release the ball (**Figure 4**). Draw enough electrolyte to float the weighted float inside the hydrometer. Note the number in line with the surface of the electrolyte; this is the specific gravity for this cell. Return the electrolyte to the cell from which it came.

The specific gravity of the electrolyte in each battery cell is an excellent indication of that cell's condition. A fully charged cell will read 1.275-1.380 while a cell in good condition may read 1.250-1.280. A cell in fair condition reads 1.225-1.250, and anything below 1.225 is practically dead.

If the cells test in the poor range, the battery requires recharging. The hydrometer is useful for checking progress of the charging operation. A reading from 1.200 to about 1.225 indicates a half charge; 1.275-1.380 indicates a full charge.

NOTE
For every 10° above 80° F electrolyte temperature, add 0.004 to specific gravity reading. For every 10° below 80° F, subtract 0.004.

CAUTION
Always disconnect both battery connections before connecting charging equipment.

MAINTENANCE-FREE BATTERIES

A sealed or maintenance-free battery is optional on 1979-1982 models and is standard on 1983 models. See **Figure 5**. Except for small vent holes in the cover, the battery is completely sealed, thus making it unnecessary to service the battery water level.

8

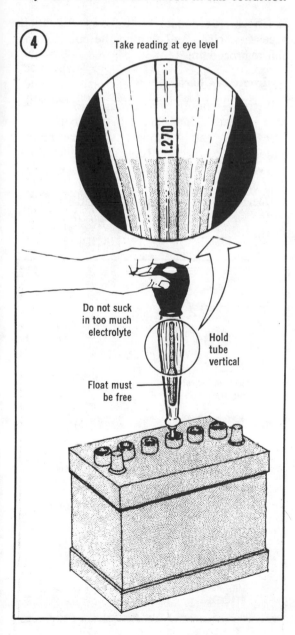

4

Take reading at eye level

1.270

Do not suck in too much electrolyte

Hold tube vertical

Float must be free

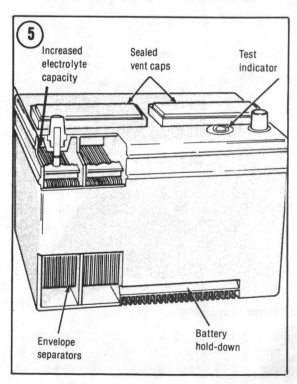

5

Increased electrolyte capacity

Sealed vent caps

Test indicator

Envelope separators

Battery hold-down

Battery Hydrometer

To determine the battery's charge, a built-in hydrometer test indicator is located in the battery's top (**Figure 5**). By observing the hydrometer indicator, it can be determined whether the battery is good and usable, requires recharging or should be replaced.

> *NOTE*
> *Before observing the hydrometer, ensure that the battery top is clean. In poorly-lit conditions, an accessory light may be required to read the hydrometer indicator.*

In reading the built-in hydrometer, 3 different color indications are possible. Refer to **Figure 6** for an example of each.

1. ***Dark green dot visible***: Battery is in good condition and can be tested if necessary.
2. ***Dark green dot not visible***: Battery charge condition is low, battery should be load tested.
3. ***Yellow color visible***: Battery must be replaced.

> *NOTE*
> *On rare occasions, the green dot may still be visible following prolonged cranking. Should this condition occur, charge battery as described under **Charging** in this section.*

> *WARNING*
> *When the hydrometer displays a yellow color, do not charge or load test the battery or jump start the vehicle. Failure to observe this warning could result in personal injury or vehicle damage from battery explosion.*

Testing

Use of the following test procedures will provide a basis for deciding whether a battery is good and usable, requires recharging or should be replaced. A complete analysis of battery condition requires a visual inspection, a hydrometer check and a battery load test.

Visual Inspection

1. Inspect the battery case for damage, chafing and cracks. Pay particular attention to moisture on the outside of the case; often this is an indication that the case is damaged to the extent that the battery is leaking electrolyte. If any such damage is present, replace the battery.

> *NOTE*
> *If battery is leaking electrolyte, a pair of rubber gloves (not the household type) should be worn to protect hands when removing battery. In addition, place old newspapers or other disposable items around the battery to protect the vehicle's body surface from electrolyte.*

2. Check for loose cable connections. If necessary, clean and tighten the connections before proceeding.

Hydrometer Check

If troubleshooting procedures in Chapter Two indicate a low charge battery condition, first observe the hydrometer to determine the battery's condition. Refer to guide lines previously discussed under *Battery Hydrometer*. See **Figure 6**.

1. ***Dark green dot visible***: Load test the battery as discussed under *Load Test* in this section.

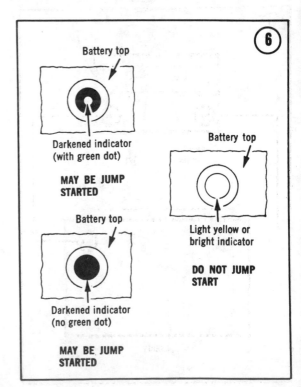

Battery top

Darkened indicator
(with green dot)

MAY BE JUMP STARTED

Battery top

Darkened indicator
(no green dot)

MAY BE JUMP STARTED

Battery top

Light yellow or bright indicator

DO NOT JUMP START

2. ***Dark green dot not visible***: Charge the battery as discussed under *Charging*, then load test the battery as discussed under *Load Test*.

3. ***Clear or yellow dot visible***: Replace the battery.

Load Test

Battery load testing will require a voltmeter and an instrument with battery testing capabilities. Have this done by a qualified specialist if you do not have such equipment.

1. Connect a voltmeter and battery load tester to the battery, following equipment manufacturer's instructions.

2. Apply a 300 amp load to the battery for 15 seconds to remove any surface charge, then remove amp load.

3. Wait 15 seconds to allow battery to recover from Step 2, then apply a 210 amp load. Read voltage after 15 seconds and remove load. Interpret results as follows:

    a. Refer to **Table 2** and estimate outside temperature battery was exposed to before testing.

    b. Referring to **Table 2**, determine the minimum voltage as corrected for

temperature. If battery voltage is less than the minimum listed in **Table 2**, battery should be replaced.

For example, if estimated battery temperature is 70° (21° C) and the minimum battery voltage is 9.6 volts, battery can be considered good. However, if minimum voltage is 9.5 volts or less, the battery must be replaced.

Charging

> *NOTE*
> *Do not charge a battery in which the color indicator reads green (unless charge immediately follows prolonged cranking).*

There is no need to remove the battery from the vehicle to charge it. Just make certain that the area is well-ventilated and that there is no chance of sparks or open flames being in the vicinity of the battery; during charging, highly explosive hydrogen is produced by the battery.

Disconnect both leads from the battery. Connect the charger to the battery—negative to negative, positive to positive. See **Figure 7**.

The sealed battery can be charged in the same manner as non-sealed batteries. If the charger output is variable, select a low setting (5-10 amps), set the voltage selector to 12 volts and plug the charger in. See **Table 3** for charging rates. Charge the battery until the green dot appears in the hydrometer or until maximum charge is reached (see **Table 3**). It may be necessary to tip the battery from side to side to make the green ball appear after a suitable charging time.

> *WARNING*
> *Do not charge battery if hydrometer indicator is clear or yellow (see **Figure 6**). Replace the battery.*

Jump Starting

Jump starting procedures for sealed batteries are similar to procedures for non-sealed batteries. Do not connect a jumper cable to the negative battery terminal of the dead battery. Instead, after connecting one end of the negative jumper cable to the negative terminal of the booster battery,

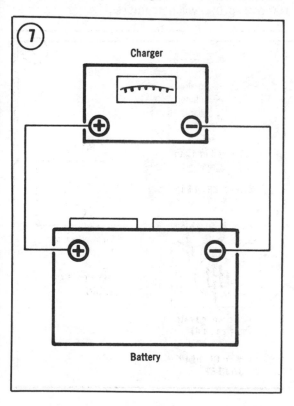

⑦

Charger

Battery

connect the other negative jumper cable to an engine ground, such as the alternator mounting bracket. See **Figure 8**.

Start engine of vehicle providing the jump start. Then start car with discharged battery. Reverse directions exactly to remove jumper cables.

> *WARNING*
> *Do not attempt to jump start a vehicle with a sealed battery if the hydrometer indicator is clear or light yellow. Replace the battery.*

> *NOTE*
> *If hydrometer indicator is dark and has a green dot in the center, failure to start is not due to a discharged battery. The engine cranking system should first be checked. See Chapter Two.*

STARTER

> *NOTE*
> *Five different starters from 3 manufacturers have been used. The 2 Bosch starters are shown in **Figure 9** and the 2 from Nippondenso are shown in **Figure 10**. The 1.6 liter engine uses a Mitsubishi starter. All are similar except for differences in the pinion housing area; service procedures are the same except where noted.*

Removal/Installation

Refer to **Figure 11** for this procedure.
1. Disconnect the battery ground cable.
2. Disconnect the starter wires.
3. On 2.2 liter engines, loosen the air pump tube at the exhaust manifold and move the tube bracket away from the starter.
4. Remove the starter mounting bolts.
5. Remove the heat shield clamp and heat shield at the starter if so equipped.
6. Remove the starter.
7. Installation is the reverse of these steps.

Brush Replacement
(Bosch and Nippondenso)

Starter must be removed and partially disassembled to replace brushes.
1. Remove starter as described in this chapter.
2. Remove end cap and seal shown in **Figure 12**.
3. Pry out the lock ring (**Figure 13**) and remove spring, washer, and seal.

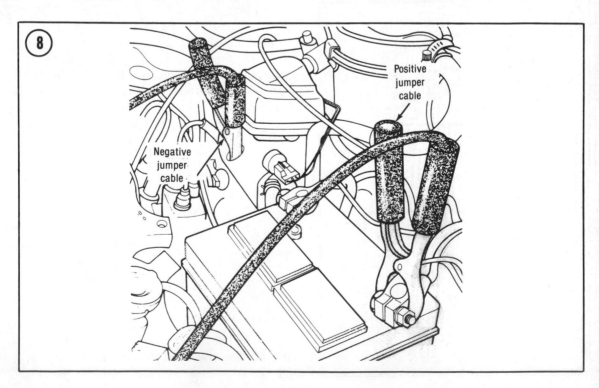

Positive jumper cable

Negative jumper cable

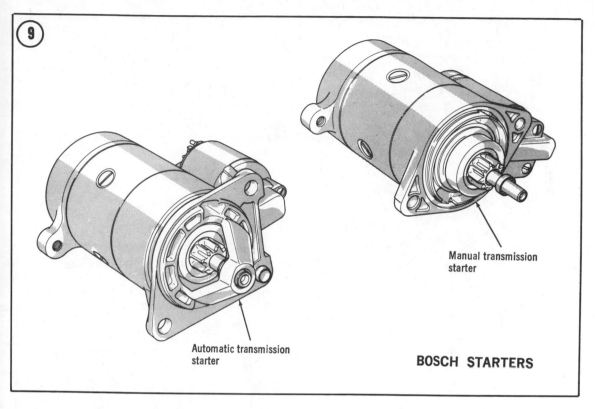

9

Manual transmission
starter

Automatic transmission
starter

BOSCH STARTERS

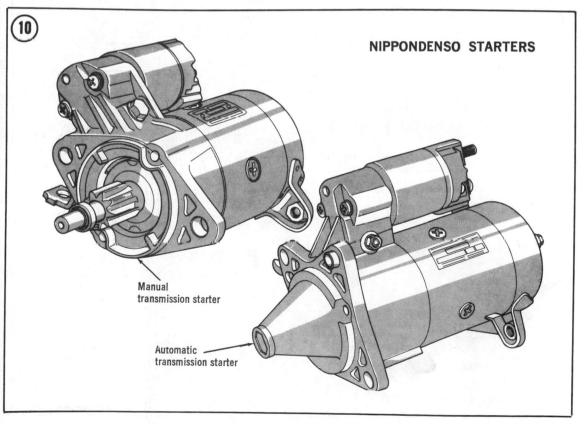

10

NIPPONDENSO STARTERS

Manual
transmission starter

Automatic
transmission starter

8

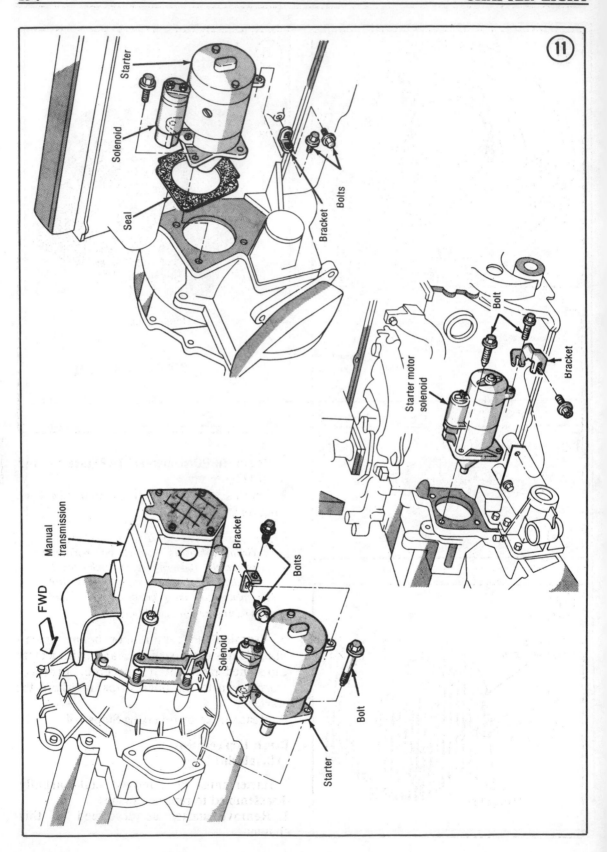

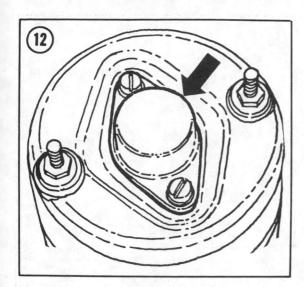

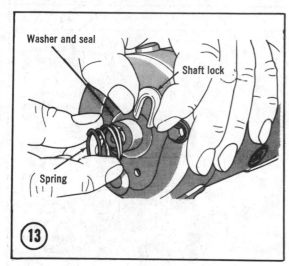

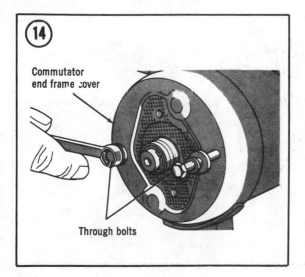

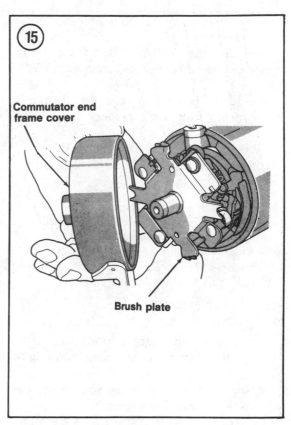

Commutator end frame cover

Brush plate

4. Remove the through bolts (**Figure 14**) and cover (**Figure 15**).

5. Check brush lengths. If less than 11/32 in. long, replace them.

NOTE
Ground brushes cannot be replaced separately. If worn, replace entire brush holder assembly. Field brushes are replaced by unsoldering old ones and soldering new ones in their places.

6. Examine the commutator before assembling. If it is dirty or oily, clean it with a cloth moistened in solvent. If it is scored, burned, or worn down to the mica strips, overhaul the starter.

7. Reassemble by reversing Steps 1-4.

**Brush Replacement
(Mitsubishi)**

Starter must be removed and partially disassembled to replace brushes.

1. Remove starter as described in this chapter.

8

2. Remove the through bolts and mounting bracket (**Figure 16**).

3. Remove the 2 brush plate mounting screws (**Figure 17**). Remove the starter end shield.

4. Pry retaining clips back and slide the 2 field brushes from their holders. See **Figure 18**.

5. Remove the brush plate (**Figure 19**).

6. Check brush lengths. If less than 11/32 in. long, replace them.

> *NOTE*
> *Ground brushes cannot be replaced separately. If worn, replace entire brush holder assembly. Field brushes are replaced by unsoldering old ones and soldering new ones in their places.*

Solenoid Replacement
(All Starters)

1. Disconnect the large connecting wire between the starter and solenoid. See **Figure 20**.

2. Remove 2 screws securing solenoid to the mounting bracket. See **Figure 21**.

3. Lift solenoid pullrod free of the operating lever and remove the solenoid. See **Figure 22**.

4. Place rubber gasket and metal strip on the outer edge of shift fork housing. See **Figure 23**.

5. Pull the drive pinion to bring the operating lever back toward the solenoid opening. Connect the pullrod to the operating lever.

6. Secure solenoid with mounting screws and reconnect large wire from the starter.

ALTERNATOR

The alternator generates alternating current (AC) which is converted to direct current (DC) by six internal silicon diodes. The alternator consists of the rotor, stator, end plate, housing, and drive pulley. Refer to **Table 1** for specifications.

> *CAUTION*
> *Proper torquing of the alternator bracket-to-water pump screws on the 1.7 liter engine is critical. Failure to tighten all fasteners properly can result in coolant leakage from the water pump or cracking of the pump housing.*

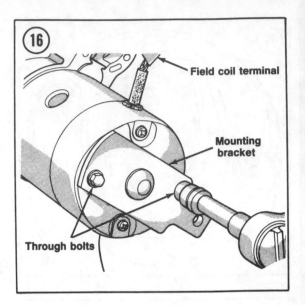

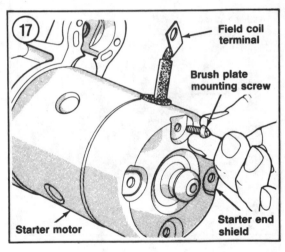

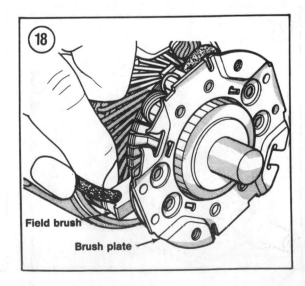

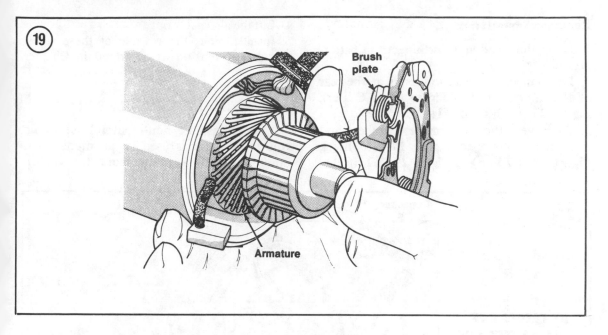

(19)

Brush plate

Armature

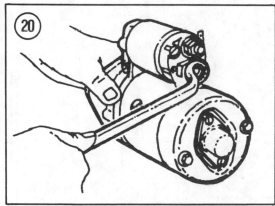

(20)

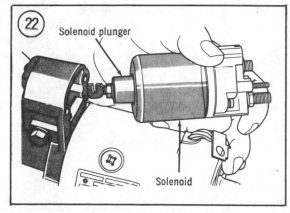

(22)

Solenoid plunger

Solenoid

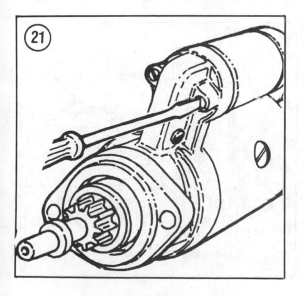

(21)

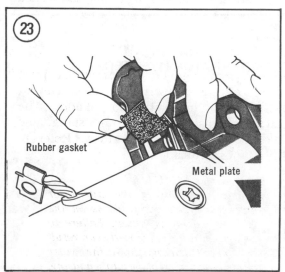

(23)

Rubber gasket

Metal plate

8

Removal/Installation

1. Open the hood and disconnect the battery ground cable.

2. Disconnect the electrical leads at the rear of the alternator. See **Figure 24** (1.6 liter), **Figure 25** (1.7 liter) or **Figure 26** (2.2 liter).

3. Remove the alternator brace and mounting bolts. See **Figure 27** (1.6 liter), **Figure 28** (1.7 liter) or **Figure 29** (2.2 liter).

4. Lift the alternator out.

5. Installation is the reverse of these steps. Adjust belt tension as described in Chapter Three.

VOLTAGE REGULATOR

A non-adjustable, non-repairable electronic voltage regulator is used on all models. On Bosch and Chrysler alternators, the voltage

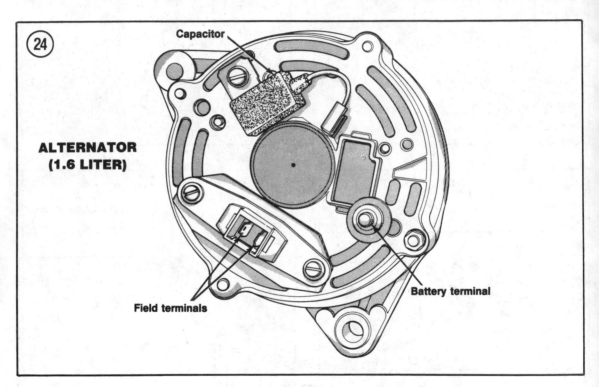

(24)

Capacitor

**ALTERNATOR
(1.6 LITER)**

Field terminals

Battery terminal

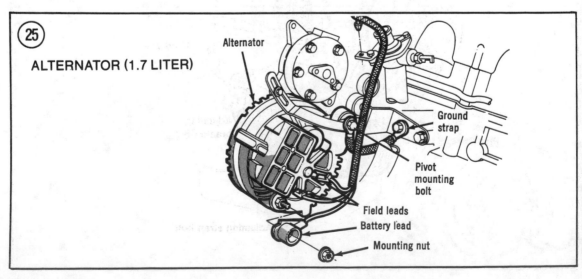

(25)

ALTERNATOR (1.7 LITER)

Alternator

Ground strap

Pivot mounting bolt

Field leads

Battery lead

Mounting nut

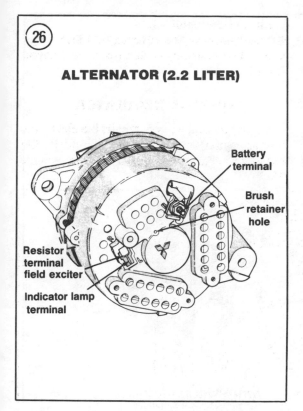

26

ALTERNATOR (2.2 LITER)

Battery terminal

Brush retainer hole

Resistor terminal field exciter

Indicator lamp terminal

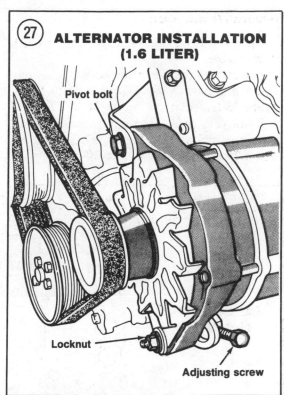

27

ALTERNATOR INSTALLATION (1.6 LITER)

Pivot bolt

Locknut

Adjusting screw

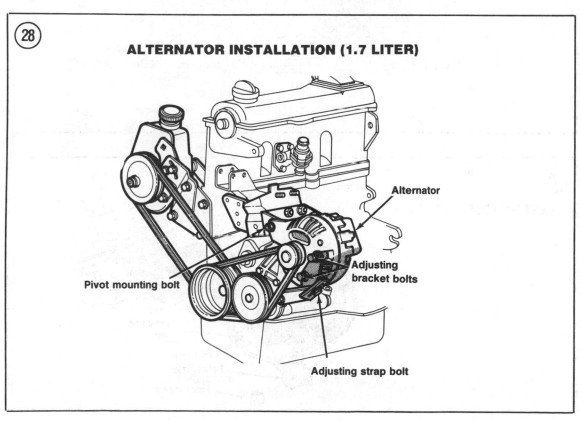

28

ALTERNATOR INSTALLATION (1.7 LITER)

Alternator

Adjusting bracket bolts

Pivot mounting bolt

Adjusting strap bolt

8

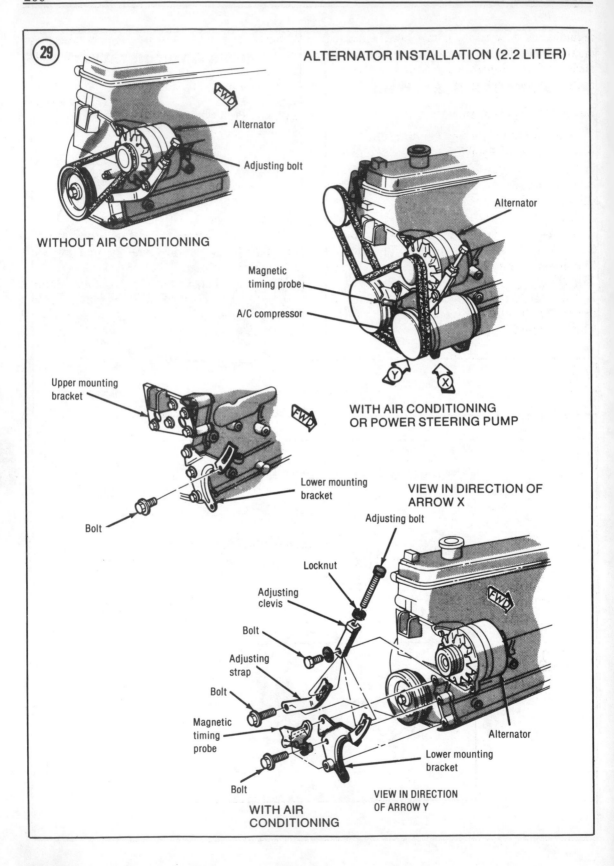

(29)

ALTERNATOR INSTALLATION (2.2 LITER)

Alternator

Adjusting bolt

WITHOUT AIR CONDITIONING

Alternator

Magnetic
timing probe

A/C compressor

WITH AIR CONDITIONING
OR POWER STEERING PUMP

Upper mounting
bracket

Lower mounting
bracket

Bolt

VIEW IN DIRECTION OF
ARROW X

Adjusting bolt

Locknut

Adjusting
clevis

Bolt

Adjusting
strap

Bolt

Magnetic
timing
probe

Bolt

Alternator

Lower mounting
bracket

VIEW IN DIRECTION
OF ARROW Y

WITH AIR
CONDITIONING

regulator is a separate component mounted on the firewall. On Mitsubishi alternators, an electronic IC (integrated circuit) regulator is built into the back of the alternator.

Regulator Test (Chrysler)

Refer to **Figure 30** for this procedure.

1. Clean and inspect the battery as described in this chapter. On open cell type batteries, a specific gravity reading of 1.220 or higher should be maintained when performing the following regulator test. If the specific gravity is below 1.220, the battery should be charged. On maintenance-free batteries, the built-in hydrometer indicator should show green (**Figure 6**).

2. Connect the positive lead of a volmeter to the battery positive terminal and the negative lead to ground. See **Figure 30**.

3. Start the engine and make sure all lights and accessories are off. Operate the engine at 1,250 rpm.

4. Read the voltmeter. Voltage should be between 13-16 volts as indicated in **Table 4**. If voltage is low or fluctuates, check for proper ground at the regulator.

NOTE
Ground at regulator is obtained through the case. Make sure the screws hold the case securely to the car body sheet metal.

5. Turn off ignition and check condition of connector at the regulator to make sure terminals are making good contact.

6. Turn on ignition, but do not start engine. Check for voltage at the blue and green wiring harness terminal leads. Battery voltage should be present at both leads.

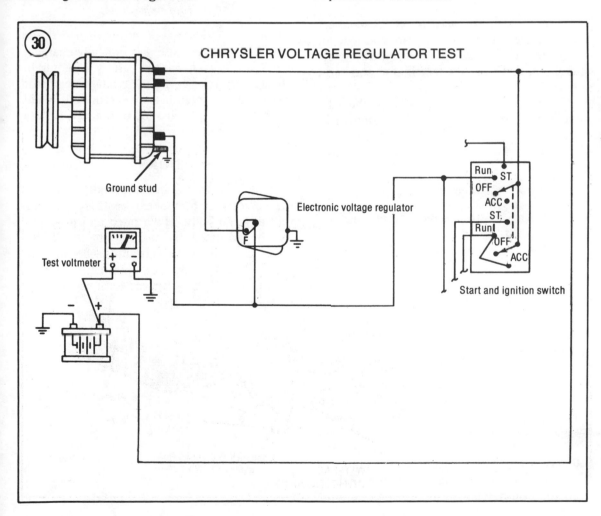

CHRYSLER VOLTAGE REGULATOR TEST

Ground stud

Electronic voltage regulator

Run ST
OFF
ACC
ST.
Run
OFF
ACC

Start and ignition switch

Test voltmeter

8

7. If above checks (see NOTE and Steps 5 and 6) are not satisfactory, replace the voltage regulator with a new one and repeat Steps 3 and 4.

Regulator Test (Mitsubishi)

The voltage regulator is an electronic IC (integrated circuit) type and is built into the back of the alternator. Refer to **Figure 31** for this procedure.

1. Clean and inspect the battery as described in this chapter. On open cell type batteries, a specific gravity reading of 1.220 or higher should be maintained when performing the following regulator test. If the specific gravity is below 1.220, the battery should be charged. On maintenance-free batteries, the built-in hydrometer indicator should show green (**Figure 6**).

2. Turn the ignition switch off. Disconnect the positive battery cable and connect an ammeter between the positive battery cable and the positive battery terminal as shown in **Figure 31**.

3. Connect a voltmeter between the "L" alternator terminal and ground as shown in **Figure 31**.

> *NOTE*
> *When connecting the voltmeter leads, the voltmeter should read 0 volts. If the voltmeter pointer deflects, indicating voltage is present, the alternator is defective or there is a short in the wiring.*

4. Turn on the ignition, but do not start the engine. The voltmeter should read approximately one volt or less. A higher reading indicates a possible defective alternator.

5. Connect a tachometer to the engine, following the manufacturer's instructions.

6. Short circuit the ammeter terminals and start the engine. When the engine is running, remove the short circuit.

7. Operate the engine between 2,000 and 3,000 rpm and record the ammeter reading.

8. If the ammeter reading is 5 amps or less, read the voltmeter with the engine operating between 2,000 to 3,000 rpm. The charging voltage should be 14.1-14.7 volts at 68° F (20° C). If the ammeter reading is more than 5 amps, proceed to Step 10.

> *NOTE*
> *The voltage regulator is temperature compensated. Thus, the temperature at the rear alternator bracket must be measured and the charging voltage corrected to the temperature. For every degree below 50° F (10° C) subtract 0.1 volt.*

9. If the charging voltage is not within the specified range as described in Step 8, the alternator must be replaced.

> *NOTE*
> *Step 10 pertains only to those alternators in which an amp reading of 6 or more amps was recorded during Step 8.*

10. An amp reading of more than 5 amps indicates that the battery is not fully charged. See Step 1 and charge the battery as required. To accurately perform the voltage regulator test, a fully charged battery is required. When the battery is fully charged or if a new battery is installed, perform Steps 6-8.

HORN

If the horn works, but not loudly or not at the correct pitch, make sure that it is not touching the body. Horn pitch and loudness can be adjusted by turning the adjusting screw. See **Figure 32**. To adjust the horn to blow louder, turn the adjusting screw clockwise and test. Repeat until the correct horn loudness is reached.

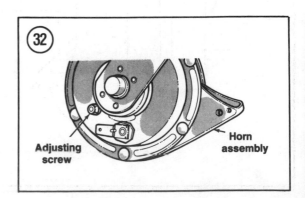
(32) Adjusting screw — Horn assembly

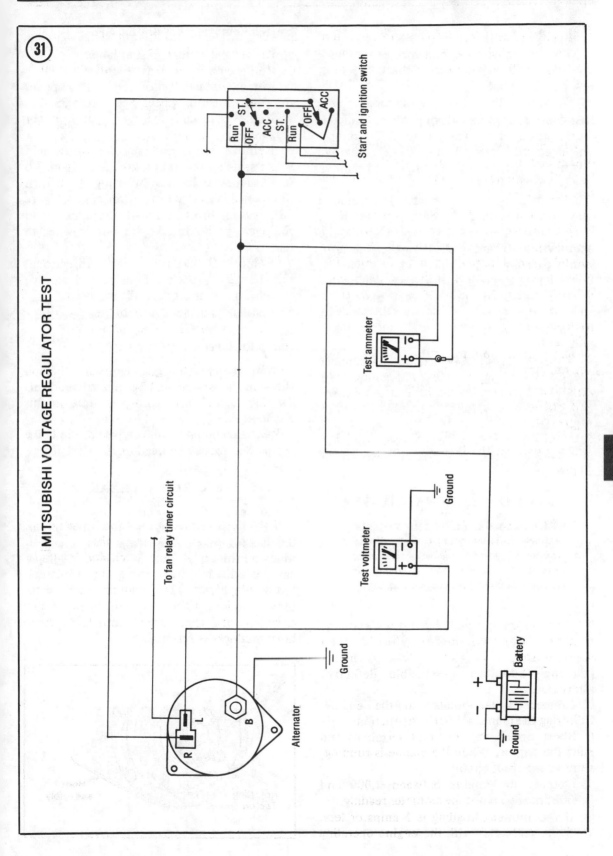

MITSUBISHI VOLTAGE REGULATOR TEST

Horn Switch

When the horn does not work at all, check the wiring to the horn and check the horn switch. To service the horn switch:

1. Disconnect the battery ground cable.

2A. With a 3-spoke steering wheel, pull the horn button outward and remove. Disconnect the electrical lead at the horn switch. Remove the horn switch mounting screws and remove the horn. See **Figure 33**.

2B. With a 4-spoke steering wheel, remove the horn pad/horn switch screws from underneath the steering wheel. Pull the pad/switch upward and disconnect the horn contact terminal. See **Figure 34**.

3. Clean contact points with fine crocus cloth.

4. Installation is the reverse of these steps.

Horn Replacement

The horn is mounted at the front end, near the radiator.

1. Disconnect battery ground cable.

2. Remove nut securing horn to bracket.

3. Disconnect wires from horn.

4. Installation is the reverse of these steps. Make sure that the horn does not touch the body.

DIRECTIONAL SIGNAL SYSTEM

The directional signal system consists of the steering column-mounted switch, flasher, and indicator lamps.

Switch Removal/Installation

1. Disconnect battery ground cable.

2. Remove horn switch as described earlier.

3. Remove steering wheel nut and use puller to remove steering wheel. See **Figure 35**.

4. Remove lower steering column cover (**Figure 36**).

5. Remove screw and set the windshield wiper switch lever to one side. See **Figure 37**.

6. Disconnect hazard warning and turn directional signal wiring connectors (**Figure 38**), unsnap wiring harness from bracket, and remove tape holding key-in buzzer wires to harness.

7. Remove 3 screws securing directional signal switch to switch housing and remove switch from housing. See **Figure 39**.

8. Installation is the reverse of these steps.

Lamp Replacement

Front directional signal lamps are behind the same lenses as parking lights. See *Front Parking Turn Signal Lights* procedure in this chapter.

Rear directional lamps are part of the brake lamps. See *Taillights* procedure in this chapter.

FUSES/CIRCUIT BREAKERS

Whenever a failure occurs in any part of the electrical system always check the fuse box to see if a fuse has blown. If one has, it will be evident by blackening of the fuse or by a break

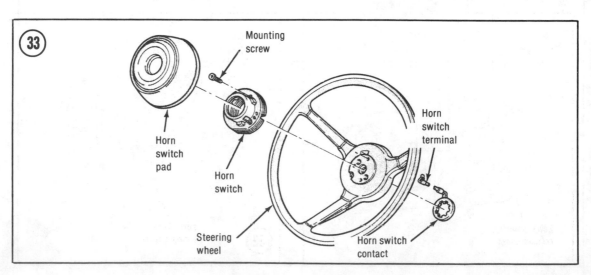

(33) Mounting screw

Horn switch pad

Horn switch

Steering wheel

Horn switch terminal

Horn switch contact

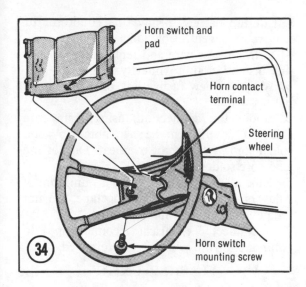

Horn switch and pad

Horn contact terminal

Steering wheel

34 Horn switch mounting screw

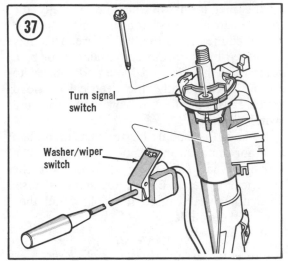

37

Turn signal switch

Washer/wiper switch

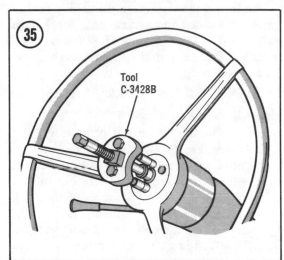

35

Tool C-3428B

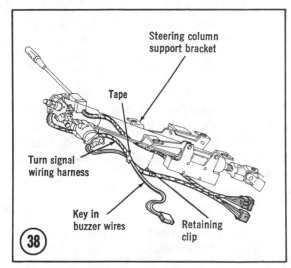

Steering column support bracket

Tape

Turn signal wiring harness

Key in buzzer wires

Retaining clip

38

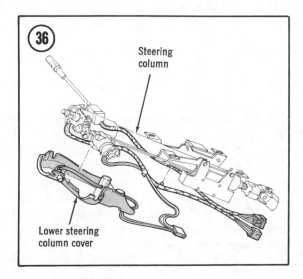

36

Steering column

Lower steering column cover

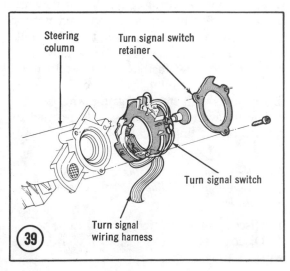

Steering column

Turn signal switch retainer

Turn signal switch

Turn signal wiring harness

39

8

in the metal link in the fuse. Usually the trouble can be traced to a short circuit in the wiring connected to the blown fuse. This may be caused by worn-through insulation or by a wire which has worked loose and shorted to ground. Occasionally, the electrical overload which causes the fuse to blow may occur in a switch or motor.

A blown fuse should be treated as more than a minor annoyance; it should serve also as a warning that something is wrong in the electrical system. Before replacing a fuse, determine what caused it to blow and then correct the trouble.

WARNING
Never replace a fuse with one of a higher amperage rating than that of the one originally used. Never use tinfoil or other metallic material to bridge fuse terminals. Failure to follow these basic rules could result in heat or fire damage to major parts or loss of the entire vehicle.

The fuse panel is located on the left cowl under the dash. **Figure 40** identifies fuse functions for the 1978-1979 models. **Figure 41** identifies fuse functions for the 1980-on models.

Fusible Links

Fusible links provide protection to circuits which are not protected by the circuit breakers and fuses. The links are short pieces of wire smaller than the wiring in the circuit they are protecting. Fusible links are covered with a special high-temperature insulation. If a link burns out, the cause must be isolated and corrected. A new fusible link must then be spliced into the circuit. *Do not* replace blown fusible links with standard gauge wire.

The following procedure should be used to replace fusible links.

NOTE
Replacement links with the correct wire gauge are available from Chrysler dealers.

1. Disconnect the battery ground cable.
2. Disconnect the old fusible link from the wiring harness.

3. Cut the harness behind the connector to remove damaged fusible link.
4. Strip harness wire and replacement fusible link insulation approximately 1 in.
5. Wrap the new fusible link on to the main harness wire.
6. Solder the connection, using rosin core solder. Use sufficient heat to obtain a good solder joint, but do not overheat. Do not use acid core solder.
7. Tape all exposed wires with a minimum of 3 layers of electrical insulating tape. Do not tape over the fusible link.
8. Reconnect electrical connection to component from which it was removed.

FLASHER UNITS

The turn signal and hazard warning flasher units are located in the fuse box. See **Figure 40** (1978-1979) or **Figure 41** (1980-on). To replace a flasher, remove the old flasher and plug in a new one.

WINDSHIELD WIPER SYSTEM

Motor Removal/Installation

Refer to **Figure 42** for this procedure.
1. Disconnect battery ground cable.
2. Remove the wiper arms by raising the arm and pulling the securing latch out of its holding position. Then release the arm. Rock the arm to remove from the pivot.
3. Remove the tie down nuts and washers from the left and right wiper arm pivots.
4. Open the engine hood and remove the wiper motor plastic cover.
5. Disconnect the wiring connector on the wiper motor.
6. Remove mounting bolts near the wiper motor.
7. Detach the left and right side pivots from the cowl top mounting positions.
8. Push wiper assembly down and out of holes in body and remove motor with wiper frame.
9. Installation is the reverse of these steps. When installing the wiper arm assemblies, mount the arms on the pivot shafts, making sure the tips of the blades locate about 1 1/2 inch (38 mm) above the bottom of the windshield moulding. Wet the windshield with water, then check the operation of motor and wiper blades.

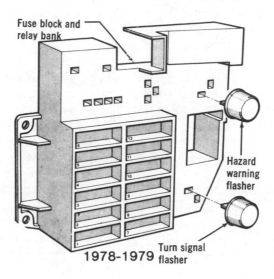

Fuse block and relay bank

Hazard warning flasher

Turn signal flasher

1978-1979

8

FUSES AND CIRCUIT BREAKERS (1978)

Cavity	Fuse (amps)	Item
1	30	Heater blower motor; air conditioning; blower motor
	20	Heater
2	3	Air conditioning; heater switch lamps; ash tray lamps; electrically heated rear window lamp; radio lamp; rear windshield wiper and washer switch lamp; cluster lamps; console gear; selector lamp
3	20	Emergency flasher
4	20	License lamp; parking lamps; side marker lamps; tail lamps
5	20	Cargo lamp; cigar lighter; clock dome lamp; glove box lamp; ignition lamp; key-in buzzer; map lamp; brake lamps
6	Not used	
7	Not used	
8	5	Fuel gauge; oil pressure switch; parking brake lamp; seatbelt warning buzzer; temperature gauge
9	5	Radio
10	20	Air conditioning clutch; turn signal flasher; backup lamps
11	3	Electrically heated rear window
12	6	Rear windshield wiper and washer (c/bkr)

FUSES AND CIRCUIT BREAKERS (1979)

Cavity	Fuse	Item
1	Not used	
2	6 amp c/brkr	Rear washer and wiper Hatch release
3	5 amp	Radio
4	20 amp	A/C clutch; turn signal and back-up lamps and tachometer
5	3 amp	Cluster, radio, air conditioner; heater; ash receiver; gear selector; heater window; rear washer/wiper; hatch release lamps
6	20 amp	Hazard flasher
7	Not used	
8	20 amp	Stop, dome, cargo, glove box, map and ignition lamps; time delay relay; clock; cigar lighter; and key-in buzzer clock; cigar lighter; and key-in buzzer
9	20 amp	Horn and horn relay; park, tail, side marker, license and cluster lamps
10	Not used	
11	5 amp	Seat belt, oil pressure and brake warning lamps; seat belt buzzer, voltage limiter, and fuel and temperature gauge
12	30 amp 20 amp	A/C and heater blower motor Heater blower motor

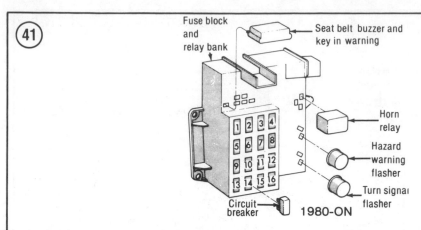

(41) **Fuse block and relay bank**

Seat belt buzzer and key in warning

Horn relay

Hazard warning flasher

Turn signal flasher

Circuit breaker

1980-ON

FUSES AND CIRCUIT BREAKERS (1980-1982)

Cavity	Fuses	Item
1	20 amp	Hazard flasher
2	3 amp	Speed control
3 (1981)	20 amp	A/C radiator fan motor
4	20 amp	Heater blower motor
	30 amp	A/C blower motor
5	Not used	
6	20 amp	Stop, dome, map, glove box, ignition switch and cargo lamps; key-in buzzer; clock; cigar lighter; anti-diesel relay and ignition key lamp time delay relay
7	20 amp	Horn and horn relay; park, tail, side maker, license and cluster lamps
8	Not used	
9	Not used	
10	Not used	
11	5 amp	Seatbelt warning, brake warning, temperature and oil fuel and exhaust sensor lamps, anti-diesel relay coil and voltage limiter
12	Not used	
13	3 amp	Console gear selector; radio; cluster; A/C and heater; heated rear window; rear washer wiper; hatch release and ash receiver lamps
14	6 amp c/brkr	Rear washer/wiper; electric hatch release
15	5 amp	Radio
16*	20 amp	Backup and turn signal lamps; A/C clutch; tachometer; and heater rear window relay

* Cavity 16 on 1981 models also include functions of the solenoid idle stop and the radiator fan relay coil.

FUSES AND CIRCUIT BREAKERS (1983)

Cavity	Fuse (amps)	Item
1	20	Hazard flasher
2	Not used	
3	3	Speed control; heated rear window
4	20	Heater blower motor (without AC)
	30	AC blower motor
5	Not used	
6	20	Cargo lamp; cigarette lighter; clock; dome lamp; glove box lamp; ignition lamp time delay relay; key-in and headlamp on buzzer; map lamp; stop lamp switch; ignition switch lamp; electronically tuned radio memory; console bin lamp
7	20	Horn; license lamp; parking lamp; front side markers; taillamps; radio; rear side markers
8	Not used	
9	Not used	
10	Not used	
11	5	Instrument voltage limiter; oil pressure and engine temperature warning lamp; brake warning lamp; seatbelt buzzer; fuel gauge; seatbelt warning lamp
12	3	AC and heater switch lamps; ashtray lamp; heated rear window switch lamp; radio lamp; rear wiper/washer switch lamp; cluster lamps; console gear selector lamp; liftgate release lamp; cigarette lighter lamp
13	20	Intermittent wiper motor
14	6 (c/bkr)	Rear wiper/washer; liftgate release
15	5	Radio
16	20	Backup lamps; AC compressor clutch; turn signal flasher; tachometer; fast idle solenoid; cooling fan relay; anti-diesel relay; electronic spark advance

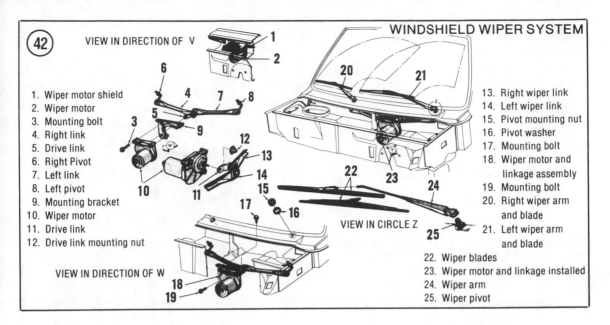

42

VIEW IN DIRECTION OF V

WINDSHIELD WIPER SYSTEM

1. Wiper motor shield
2. Wiper motor
3. Mounting bolt
4. Right link
5. Drive link
6. Right Pivot
7. Left link
8. Left pivot
9. Mounting bracket
10. Wiper motor
11. Drive link
12. Drive link mounting nut

13. Right wiper link
14. Left wiper link
15. Pivot mounting nut
16. Pivot washer
17. Mounting bolt
18. Wiper motor and linkage assembly
19. Mounting bolt
20. Right wiper arm and blade
21. Left wiper arm and blade
22. Wiper blades
23. Wiper motor and linkage installed
24. Wiper arm
25. Wiper pivot

VIEW IN DIRECTION OF W

VIEW IN CIRCLE Z

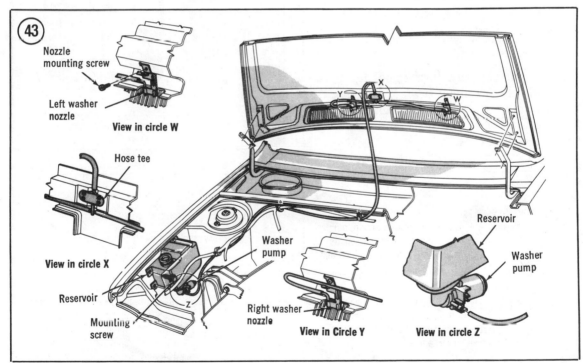

43

Nozzle mounting screw

Left washer nozzle

View in circle W

Hose tee

View in circle X

Reservoir

Mounting screw

Washer pump

Right washer nozzle

View in Circle Y

Reservoir

Washer pump

View in circle Z

8

Switch Removal/Installation

The wiper switch is part of the directional signal switch. See *Directional Switch Removal/Installation.*

Washer Pump Replacement

Refer to **Figure 43** for this procedure.

1. Disconnect the wiring harness from the reservoir pump.
2. Remove the reservoir attaching screws and remove reservoir. Then disconnect the washer hose at the reservoir and immediately block the hose outlet port to prevent liquid from running out while removing the reservoir from the engine compartment.

3. Using a suitable size socket through the liquid filler opening, loosen the pump filter and nut.

4. Disconnect the outside portion of the pump. Then remove the inner and outer portions of the pump.

5. Installation is the reverse of these steps.

LIGHTING SYSTEM

See **Table 5** for lamp bulbs used.

Headlight Replacement

1. Remove headlight bezel.

2. Remove screws securing retaining ring. Do not disturb the aiming screws.

3. Pull sealed beam out.

4. Disconnect plug from sealed beam.

5. Installation is the reverse of these steps.

6. Adjust headlights according to the local traffic regulations. Use the aiming screws.

Front Parking and Turn Signal Lights (Sedan)

Front parking and turn signal lights are located in the headlight bezel. To replace the lamp, remove screws securing the bezel and lift it off. Replace the lamp and secure the bezel. See **Figure 44**.

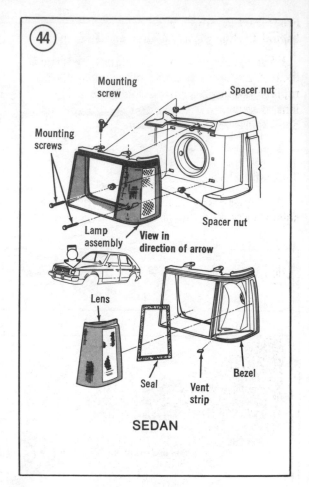

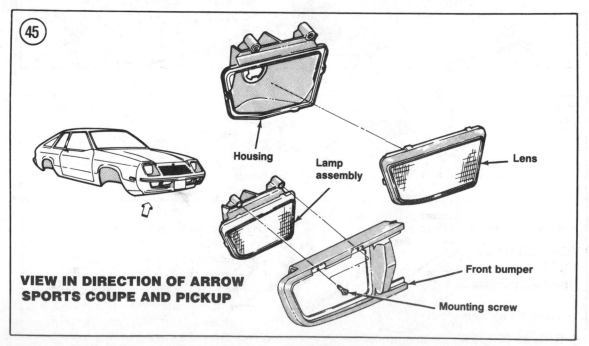

Front Parking and Turn
Signal Lights (Sports Coupe and Pickup)

Front parking and turn signal lights are located underneath the bumper assembly. To replace the lamp, remove screws securing the lens. Replace the lamp and secure the lens. See **Figure 45**.

Taillights (Sedan)

To replace the rear taillight, brake, turn signal or backup lamps, snap or twist out the socket from inside the car and replace the defective bulb. The housing assembly can be removed by depressing 4 tabs and pushing the assembly out of the car. See **Figure 46**.

Taillights (Sports Coupe)

To replace the rear taillight, brake, turn signal or backup lamps, twist out the socket from inside the car and replace the defective bulb. The housing assembly can be removed by removing the 4 mounting nuts in the trunk and pulling the housing away from the body. See **Figure 47**.

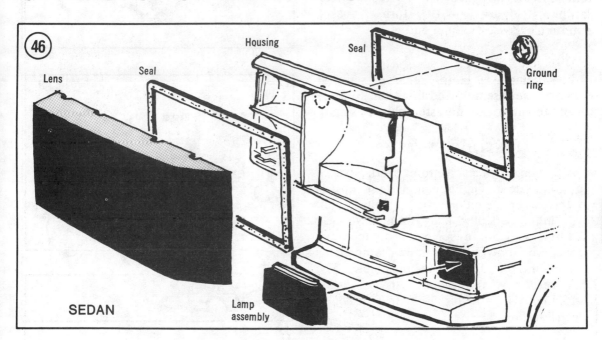

SEDAN

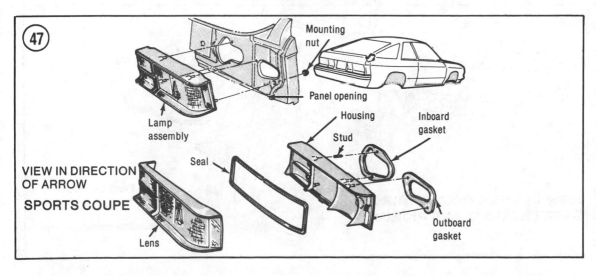

VIEW IN DIRECTION OF ARROW

SPORTS COUPE

8

Taillights (Pickup)

To replace the rear taillight, brake, turn signal or backup lamps, remove 2 screws holding lamp assembly. Remove assembly and twist out the socket(s). Replace defective bulbs(s). Twist in socket(s) and reinstall assembly.

Side Marker Lamps

Side marker lamps are located in the fender mounted assemblies. To replace the front lamps, remove the screws securing the cover and lens and lift them off. To replace rear lamps (**Figure 48**), turn socket counterclockwise and pull out.

License Plate Lights

To replace a lamp, remove screw(s) securing the assembly and lift it off. Replace the lamp and secure the assembly. See **Figure 49**.

IGNITION SYSTEM

All engines use an electronic spark advance ignition system. The ignition system consists of the battery, ignition switch, ignition coil, distributor, spark plugs and associated wiring.

This section describes replacement procedures only. No ignition components except the distributor are repairable. The distributor assembly requires special testing equipment and should be left to a dealer or electrical shop.

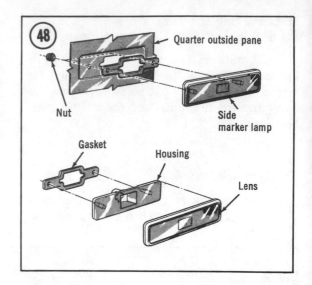

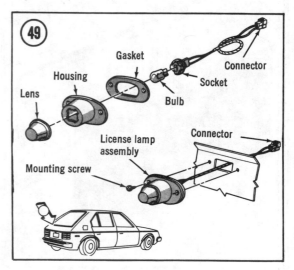

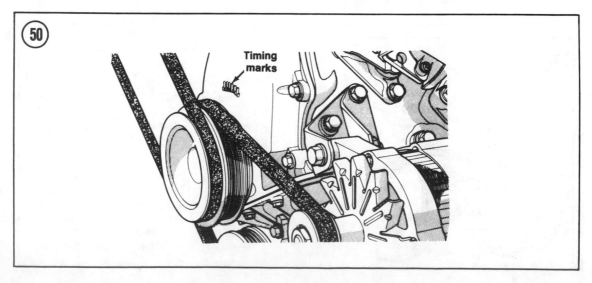

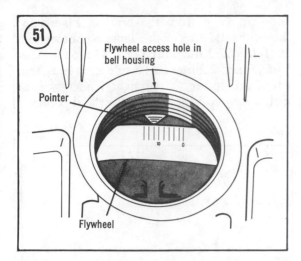

Flywheel access hole in bell housing

Pointer

10 0

Flywheel

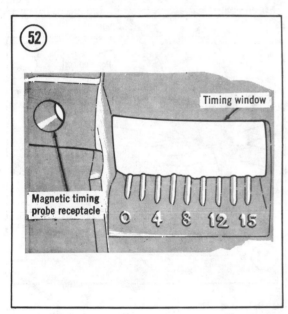

Timing window

Magnetic timing probe receptacle

0 4 8 12 15

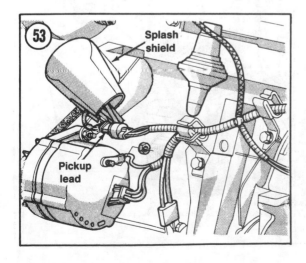

Splash shield

Pickup lead

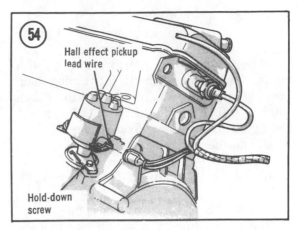

Hall effect pickup lead wire

Hold-down screw

Distributor Removal

1. Remove the splash shield, if so equipped.
2. Remove the distributor cap. If the wires are to be disconnected from cap or spark plugs, label them.
3. Rotate crankshaft until timing marks align. The 1.6 liter timing marks are located on the crankshaft pulley and timing chain cover (**Figure 50**). The 1.7 and 2.2 liter timing marks are located at the flywheel end of the transaxle. See **Figure 51** or **Figure 52**.
4. Make scribe marks on distributor body in line with rotor pointer. Also make a mark on the engine block for installation reference.
5. Disconnect the pickup lead at the wiring harness connector. See **Figure 53** (1.6 liter), **Figure 54** (1.7 liter) or **Figure 55** (2.2 liter).
6. Remove distributor hold-down clamp bolt. See **Figure 54**, typical.
7. Lift distributor from engine.

Distributor Installation

1. Ensure that the No. 1 piston is still at TDC on a compression stroke.
2. Install the distributor so that when the gear engages the camshaft drive gear the rotor and distributor body and engine block are all properly aligned.

NOTE

If the engine was moved while the distributor was removed, it will be necessary to establish proper relationship between the distributor shaft and the No. 1 piston position. If the engine position was moved, proceed to Step 3. If not, proceed to Step 7.

8

3. Remove the distributor.

4. Rotate the crankshaft until the No. 1 piston is at the top of the compression stroke. The crankshaft pulley timing mark will align with the "0" TDC mark on the 1.6 liter timing chain cover (**Figure 50**). The pointer on the clutch housing will align with the "0" (TDC) mark on the flywheel. See **Figure 51** or **Figure 52**.

5. Rotate the rotor to a position just ahead of the No. 1 distributor cap terminal.

6. Install the distributor so that the distributor gear engages with the drive gear on the camshaft. When the distributor is fully seated on the engine, the rotor should be under the No. 1 cap spark plug tower.

7. Tighten the distributor clamp nut.

8. Install distributor cap and adjust ignition timing as described in Chapter Three.

Ignition Coil Replacement

The ignition coil is mounted in the engine compartment. To remove, disconnect the primary and secondary wires from the coil

and remove it from the bracket. **Figure 56** shows the 1.7 liter coil; **Figure 57** shows the 1981-1982 2.2 liter coil. On 1983 models, the 1.6 liter and 2.2 liter coil is relocated from the left shock tower to the right fender shield. Install new coil, tighten bracket and connect the wires.

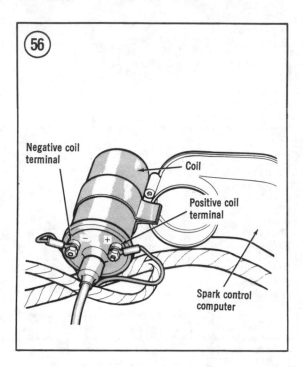

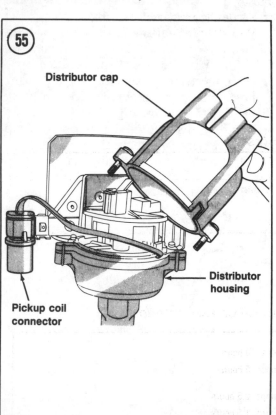

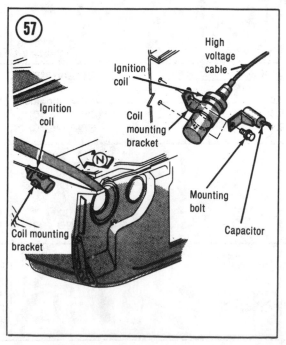

Table 1 ELECTRICAL SPECIFICATIONS

Battery (open cell)	
Voltage	12 V
Ground terminal	Negative
Load test	145 amps
Cranking rating @ 0° F	310 amps
Battery (sealed)	
Voltage	12 V
Ground terminal	Negative
Load test	210 amps
Cranking rating @ 0° F	430 amps
Alternator (Chrysler or Bosch)	
Current	
Yellow tag	60 amps
Brown tag	65 amps
Alternator (Mitsubishi)	
Current output	17-25 amps @ 13.5 volts (500 rpm)
	63-75 amps @ 13.5 volts (1,000 rpm)
	74 amps @ 13.5 volts (2,000 rpm)
Voltage output	14.1-14.7 volts @ 68° F
Temperature compensation	
gradient	-0.1 volts @ 50° F
Starter	
Voltage	12 V
Amps	47 (free running)
Distributor	
Rotation	Clockwise
Firing order	1-3-4-2 (No. 1 @ pulley end of 1.7 L and 2.2 L; @ flywheel end of 1.6 L)

8

Table 2 LOAD TEST

Minimum Voltage	Temperature
9.6	70° F and above (21° C and above)
9.5	60° F (16° C)
9.4	50° F (10° C)

Table 3 CHARGING RATE: MAINTENANCE FREE BATTERY

Slow Charging	5 amps: 10 hours
	10 amps: 5 hours
Fast Charging	20 amps: 2.5 hours
	30 amps: 1.5 hours

Table 4 VOLTAGE CHART: CHRYSLER ALTERNATOR

Ambient Temperature	Voltage
20° F (-30° C)	14.9-15.9
80° F (27° C)	13.9-14.6
140° F (60° C)	13.3-13.9
Above 140° F (60° C)	Less than 13.60

Table 5 BULB CHART

Interior Lamps	Bulb Number (1)
Air conditioner controls	
1978	363
1979-on	161
Ashtray	161
Clock	
1978-1981	168
1982-on	194
Gearshift selector console	194
Rear window defroster control	161
Heater controls	
1978	363
1979-on	158
Instrument cluster	
1978-1981	158
1982-on	194
AM radio	158
AM/FM radio	158
AM/FM stereo radio	
1978	53
1979-on	363
Speedometer	
1978-1981	158
1982-on	194
Switch callouts	
1978	158
1979-on	161
Brake indicator	
1978-1981	158
1982-on	194
Courtesy lamp	562
Dome lamp	211-2
Fasten seat belt lamp	
1978-1981	158
1982-on	194
Glove compartment	1891
Rear window defroster indicator	
1978	74
1979	161
1980-on	LED
High beam indicator	
1978-1981	158
1982-on	194
Ignition switch lamp	1445
Map lamp	562

(continued)

Table 5 BULB CHART (continued)

Interior Lamps	Bulb Number (1)
Oil pressure indicator	
1978-1981	158
1982-on	194
Trunk	912
Turn signal indicator	
1978-1981	158
1982-on	194
Underhood lamp (1978)	912
Oxygen sensor indicator	158

Exterior Lamps	Bulb Number
Headlamps	
1978-1982	6052
1983	H6054
Side marker lamps (front)	
1978-1980	(2)
1981-on	168
Side marker lamps (rear)	
1978-1980	168
1981-on	(3)
Park and turn signal lamp	
1978-1980	1157
1981-1982	2057
1983	1157
Tail and stop lamps	1157
Turn signal lamps	1156
Fender mounted turn signal indicator	
1978-1979	168
License plate lamp	168
Backup lamps	1156

1. All bulbs used should be constructed with a brass or glass wedge base. Aluminum bulbs are not approved and must not be used.
2. Parking lamp serves as front side marker.
3. Tail lamp serves as rear side marker.

8

NOTE: If you own a 1984 or later model, first check the Supplement at the back of the book for any new service information.

CHAPTER NINE

CLUTCH AND TRANSAXLE

CLUTCH

The clutch is a single plate, dry disc type, mounted on the flywheel. The pressure plate has a diaphragm spring.

Transaxle Identification

The 4-speed Chrysler A-412 manual transaxle is used on 1978-on models with the 1.7L engine. During the 1981 model year, the 4-speed A-460 manual transaxle was introduced for use with the 2.2L engine. The 5-speed A-465 manual transaxle was introduced in 1983 and is used with both the 1.6L and 2.2L engines. To determine the transaxle type look for:

a. The A-412 manual transaxle serial number on the top of the transaxle housing between the timing window and the differential. See **Figure 1**.

b. The A-460 or A-465 manual transaxle serial number on a metal tag attached to the front side of the transaxle.

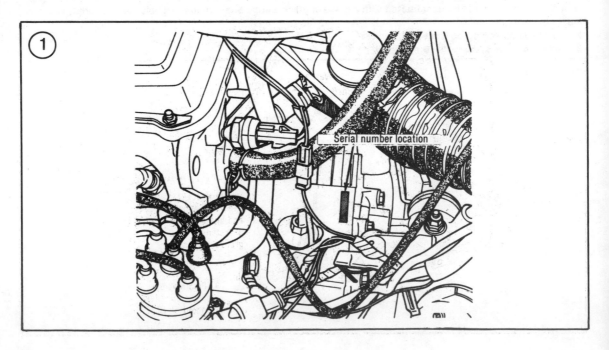
Serial number location

CLUTCH CABLE

Clutch Free Play Adjustment
(A-412 Transaxle)

Clutch adjustment involves taking up cable slack caused by cable stretch and lining wear. To check the clutch free play, measure as shown in **Figure 2**. If free play at the clutch lever is not 1/4 in., pull up on cable and rotate sleeve until free play is correct. Make sure sleeve is seated in rectangular groove in grommet when measuring free play and after adjustment is completed.

Clutch Cable Replacement
(A-412 Transaxle)

1. Lift clutch cable up and remove clutch cable lock. See **Figure 2**.
2. Remove other end of cable from slot in end of clutch pedal.
3. Remove cable from firewall bracket and remove cable from car.
4. Installation is the reverse of these steps. Adjust free play as described in this chapter after installation.

Clutch Cable Mechanism
(A-460 and A-465 Transaxle)

The clutch release mechanism on the A-460 and A-465 transaxles is self-adjusting. The clutch cable cannot be adjusted. When the clutch cable is installed (**Figure 3**), a spring in the clutch pedal holds the cable in the proper position, regardless of clutch disc wear. When the clutch pedal is depressed, the adjuster pivot grabs the positioned adjuster and holds the release cable in position to assure complete clutch release.

Clutch Cable Replacement
(A-460 and A-465 Transaxle)

To replace the clutch cable, remove the old cable from its mounting positions and install a new cable.

CLUTCH REMOVAL

The engine and transaxle must be separated to remove the clutch.

Removal (A-412 Transaxle)

Refer to **Figure 4** for this procedure.
1. Remove the transaxle as described in this chapter.

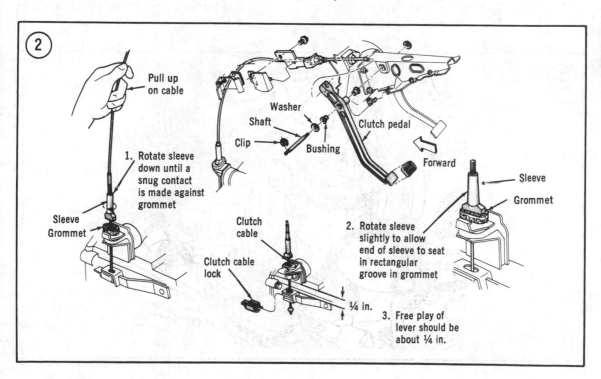

(2)

Pull up on cable

1. Rotate sleeve down until a snug contact is made against grommet

Sleeve
Grommet

Clutch cable

Clutch cable lock

Washer
Shaft
Clip
Bushing

Clutch pedal

Forward

Sleeve
Grommet

2. Rotate sleeve slightly to allow end of sleeve to seat in rectangular groove in grommet

¼ in.

3. Free play of lever should be about ¼ in.

9

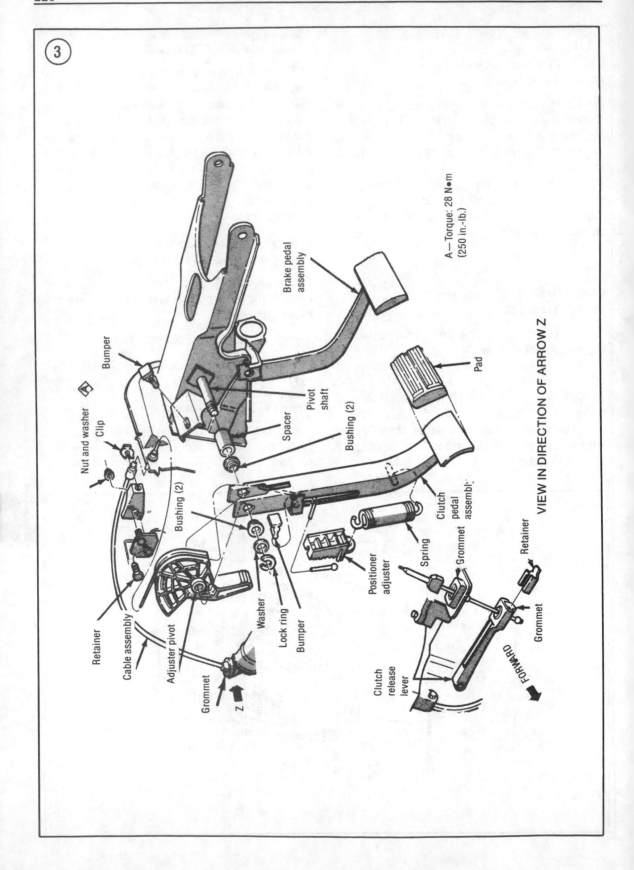

③

Nut and washer
Clip

Bumper

A

Retainer

Cable assembly

Adjuster pivot

Grommet

Z

Washer

Lock ring

Bumper

Bushing (2)

Brake pedal
assembly

Pivot
shaft

Spacer

Bushing (2)

Pad

Positioner
adjuster

Spring

Clutch
pedal
assembly

Grommet

Clutch
release
lever

FORWARD

Retainer

Grommet

A — Torque: 28 N•m
(250 in.-lb.)

VIEW IN DIRECTION OF ARROW Z

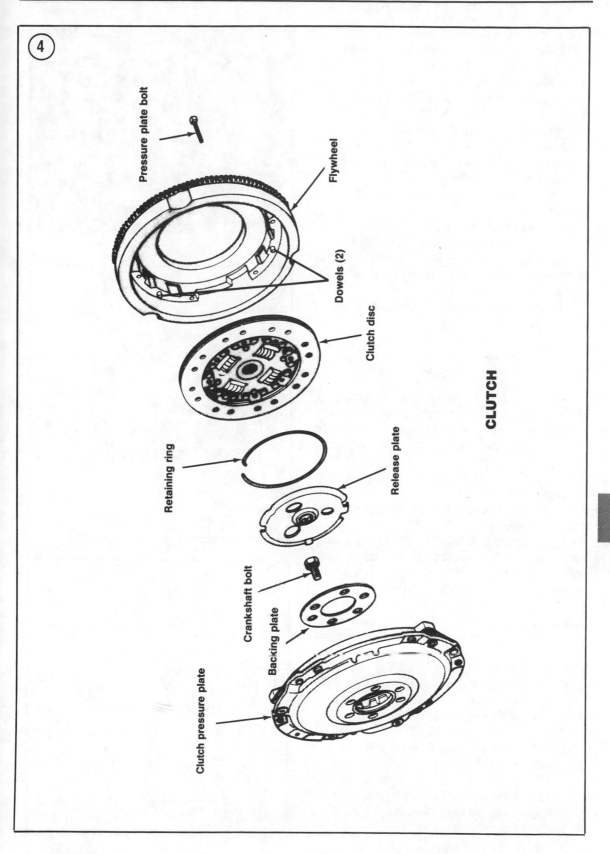

④

Pressure plate bolt

Flywheel

Dowels (2)

Clutch disc

Retaining ring

Release plate

Crankshaft bolt

Backing plate

Clutch pressure plate

CLUTCH

9

2. Prevent the flywheel from turning.

3. Unscrew bolts securing flywheel to pressure plate one turn at a time. Unscrew bolts diagonally opposite from one another, rather than working directly around the flywheel. This ensures that heavy spring pressure will not warp the pressure plate.

4. Once spring tension is relieved, unscrew each bolt entirely and remove the flywheel.

5. Remove the clutch disc.

6. Pry the retaining ring off with a screwdriver.

7. Remove the release plate.

8. Prevent the pressure plate from turning.

9. Remove bolts securing pressure plate to crankshaft and remove pressure plate from engine.

10. Inspect the clutch as described under *Clutch Inspection*.

Installation
(A-412 Transaxle)

1. Wash your hands *clean* before proceeding.

2. Sand the friction surface of the flywheel and pressure plate with medium-fine emery or crocus cloth. Sand lightly across the surfaces, not around, until they are covered with fine scratches. This breaks the glaze and aids seating a new clutch disc.

3. Clean the flywheel and pressure plate with a non-oil based cleaner.

4. Apply Loctite Lock N' Seal to mounting bolts and install pressure plate and backing plate on crankshaft. Tighten diagonally opposite bolts to 55 ft.-lb. (7.5 mkg).

5. Apply multipurpose grease to contact surface and pushrod socket of release plate. Install release plate. Secure with retaining ring. Make sure that ring ends rest between 2 slots as shown in **Figure 5**.

6. Place the clutch disc and flywheel over the pressure plate.

7. Install bolts finger-tight. Center disc with special tool part No. L-4533 as shown in **Figure 6**. This tool is easily improvised. See **Figure 7** for one method.

8. With centering tool in place, tighten diagonally opposite bolts a few turns at a time until they are torqued to 15 ft.-lb. (2.0 mkg).

9. Remove the centering tool.

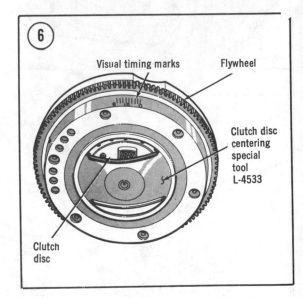

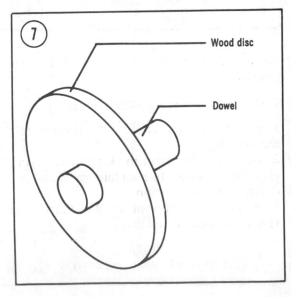

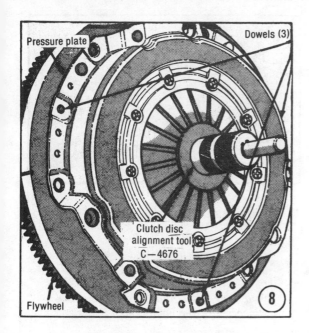

10. Install transaxle as described in this chapter.

Removal (A-460 and A-465 Transaxle)

1. Remove the transaxle as described in this chapter.
2. Scribe an alignment mark on the pressure plate and flywheel to maintain same position during clutch installation.
3. Position a pilot tool in the clutch disc (**Figure 8**) so it will not drop.

NOTE
Inexpensive pilot tools are available at many auto parts stores.

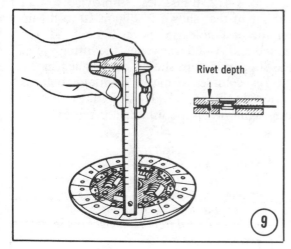

4. Loosen the pressure plate attaching bolts one or two turns at a time in a diagonal pattern until all are removed. This assures that the clutch cover is not bent by the uneven spring pressure.
5. Remove the pressure plate.
6. Inspect the clutch as described under *Clutch Inspection.*

Installation (A-460 and A-465 Transaxle)

1. Wash your hands *clean* before proceeding.
2. Sand the friction surface of the flywheel and pressure plate with medium-fine emery or crocus cloth. Sand lightly across the surfaces, not around, until they are covered with fine scratches. This breaks the glaze and aids seating a new clutch disc.
3. Clean the flywheel and pressure plate with a non-oil based cleaner.
4. Place the disc and pressure plate in position on the flywheel, making sure to align both the marks made before removal and the dowels as shown in **Figure 8**.
5. Center the disc with the pilot tool (**Figure 8**).
6. Install the clutch cover bolts, tightening gradually in a diagonal pattern. Correct torque is 21 ft.-lb. (2.8 mkg).

CLUTCH INSPECTION

Clutch Disc

Check the clutch disc for the following:
a. Oil or grease on the facings
b. Glazed facings
c. Warped facings
d. Loose or missing rivets
e. Facings worn to within 0.015 in. (0.38 mm) of any rivet. Measure with a vernier caliper as shown in **Figure 9**.
f. Broken springs
g. Loose fit or rough movement on transaxle input shaft splines

Small amounts of oil or grease may be removed from the disc with a non-petroleum based cleaner and the facings may be dressed with medium-fine emery or crocus cloth. Sand lightly across the surfaces, not around, until they are covered with fine scratches. This breaks the glaze and aids seating a new clutch

9

disc. However, if the facings are soaked with oil or grease, the disc must be replaced. The disc must also be replaced if any of the other defects are present or if facings are worn and a new pressure plate is being installed.

Pressure Plate

Check pressure plate for:
a. Scoring
b. Burn marks (blue-tinted areas)
c. Cracks

Replace the pressure plate if any of these defects are present. Also, check the friction area of pressure plate for flatness with a straightedge. Replace if not flat within 0.020 in. (0.50 mm).

Flywheel

Check flywheel for any of the following:
a. Scoring
b. Burn marks (blue-tinted areas)
c. Cracks
d. A glazed surface

If any of these defects are present, have the flywheel turned by a machine shop.

MANUAL TRANSAXLE

The A-412 and A-460 4-speed manual tranaxles have four forward speeds and one reverse. The A-465 5-speed manual transaxle is similar to the A-460 but an overdrive 5th gear set is located outside the main case in the rear cover. All gears are in constant mesh and all forward speeds are fully synchronized.

Repairs requiring transaxle disassembly are not possible for home mechanics without special skills and a large assortment of special tools.

The price of these tools far exceeds the price of a professionally rebuilt transaxle.

Considerable money can be saved by removing the old transaxle and installing a new or rebuilt one yourself. This chapter includes removal and installation procedures, plus other simple repairs. See **Table 1** at the end of this chapter for specifications and tightening torques. See Chapter Three for lubrication and preventive maintenance.

Removal/Installation

The transaxle can be removed without removing the engine.

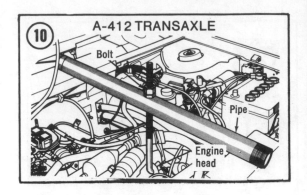

1. Disconnect the battery cables.

> *WARNING*
> *Be certain the improvised holding tool is strong enough to support the weight of the engine. Never place any part of your body beneath the engine while it is supported by the holding tool.*

2. On A-412 transaxles, improvise a tool similar to that shown in **Figure 10** to lift up on the cast holes in the cylinder head. On A-460 and A-465 transaxles, the lifting eye of the support fixture should be installed in the No. 4 cylinder exhaust manifold bolt as shown in **Figure 11**. These fixtures support the engine when the transaxle is removed.

> *CAUTION*
> *Make sure that the improvised tools in Step 2 bear on the inside of the fenders as shown in **Figure 10** or **Figure 11** and not on the tops of the fenders which could be dented from the weight of the engine.*

3. Turn the engine over until the drilled mark on the flywheel is aligned with the pointer on the clutch housing. See **Figure 12**.
4. Disconnect the shift linkage rods at the transaxle.

> *NOTE*
> *The linkage cannot be reconnected properly with the original fasteners. New fasteners are required to assure safe and proper operation. The gearshift control rod connector used with 1980 and later models differs from previous ones in that the rod is designed to use a rod retention circlip. Whenever*

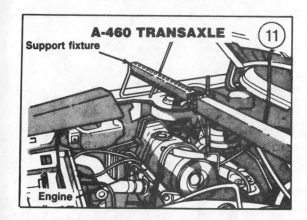

A-460 TRANSAXLE

Support fixture

Engine

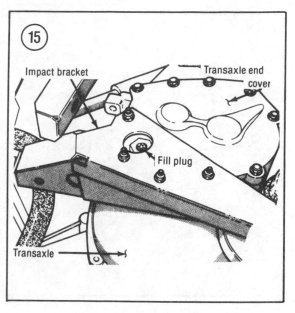

Impact bracket

Transaxle end cover

Fill plug

Transaxle

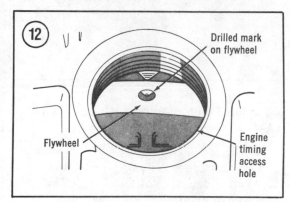

Drilled mark on flywheel

Flywheel

Engine timing access hole

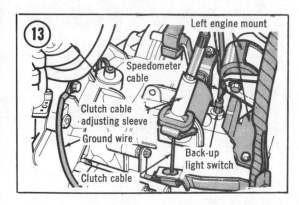

Left engine mount

Speedometer cable

Clutch cable adjusting sleeve

Ground wire

Back-up light switch

Clutch cable

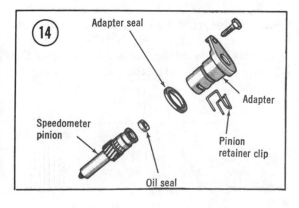

Adapter seal

Adapter

Speedometer pinion

Pinion retainer clip

Oil seal

the transaxle shift connector is disconnected on 1978-1979 models, install a new grommet and retention clip connector.

5. Disconnect the starter wire and the ground wire (**Figure 13**).

6. Disconnect the wire from the back-up switch (**Figure 13**).

7. Remove the starter from the engine. See Chapter Eight.

8. Disconnect the clutch cable from the transaxle. See **Figure 2** or **Figure 3**.

9. Refer to **Figure 14** and remove bolt holding speedometer cable adapter to transaxle. Carefully work adapter and pinion out of transaxle. Cable housing should remain connected.

10. Loosen the left-hand and right-hand front wheel hub nuts, then raise the vehicle and secure the front end with jackstands.

11. Remove the left-hand drive shaft from the vehicle. Disconnect the right-hand drive shaft and tie it out of the way. See Chapter Eleven.

12. Remove the left-hand splash shield, then remove the small dust cover from the bell housing. Remove the large dust cover bolts.

13. On A-460 and A-465 transaxles, remove the impact bracket from the transaxle (**Figure 15**) and the anti-rotational link from underneath the vehicle (**Figure 16**).

9

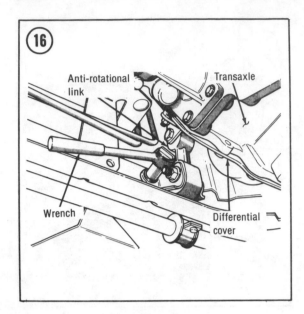

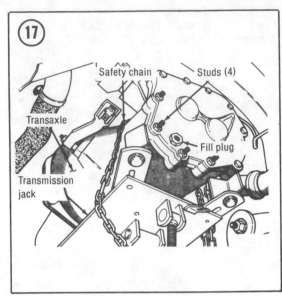

14. Drain the transaxle oil.

15. Position a transmission jack under the transaxle and secure it with a chain (**Figure 17**).

16. Remove the left-hand engine mount bolts and the bolts securing the transaxle to the engine.

17. Slide the transaxle to the left and rear until the main shaft clears the clutch, then lower the jack and remove the assembly from the car.

18. Installation is the reverse of these steps. Tighten transaxle-to-engine and motor mount bolts to specifications in **Table 1**.

CAUTION
Two types of attaching screws are used with the left front engine mount. Two of the 3 screws used are a pilot type with an extended tip and must be installed in the locations shown in Figure 18 when reattaching the A-460 or A-465 manual transaxle. If the screws are installed incorrectly, difficult shifting or damage to the shift cover may result.

19. On A-412 transaxles, adjust the clutch cable as described in this chapter. Adjust shift linkage as described in this chapter. Fill transaxle with lubricant. See Chapter Three for type and amount.

Gearshift Linkage Adjustment (A-412 Transaxle)

1. With gearshift in NEUTRAL between 3rd and 4th gears, loosen clamp on shift tube.

2. Align slider tab with blocker bracket hole as shown in **Figure 19**.

3. Insert a spacer between the slider and the blocker bracket as shown in **Figure 20**. See **Table 1** for spacer dimensions. Apply pressure as shown and tighten the shift tube clamp. Remove the spacer.

Gearshift Linkage Adjustment (A-460 and A-465 Transaxle)

1. Remove the transaxle selector shaft housing lock pin from the left-hand side of the engine compartment. See **Figure 21**.

2. Reverse the lock pin (so that the long end is facing down) and screw the lock pin into the threaded hole from which it was removed (Step 1) while at the same time pushing the selector shaft into the selector housing (**Figure 21**).

NOTE
A hole in the selector shaft will align with the lock pin, thus allowing the lock pin to be screwed into the housing.

⑱

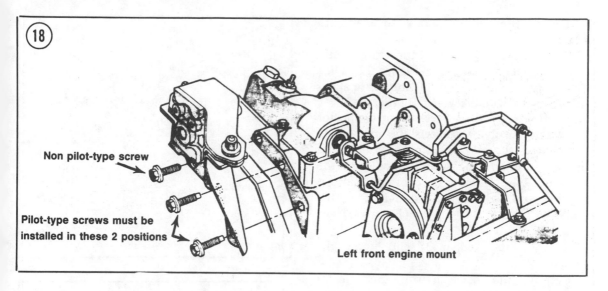

Non pilot-type screw

Pilot-type screws must be
installed in these 2 positions

Left front engine mount

⑲

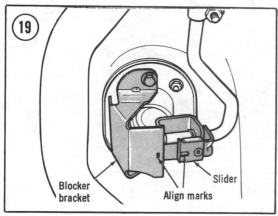

Blocker
bracket

Align marks

Slider

⑳

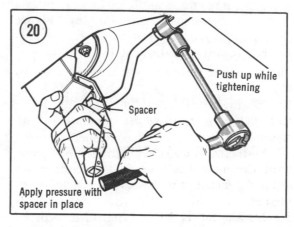

Push up while
tightening

Spacer

Apply pressure with
spacer in place

9

㉑

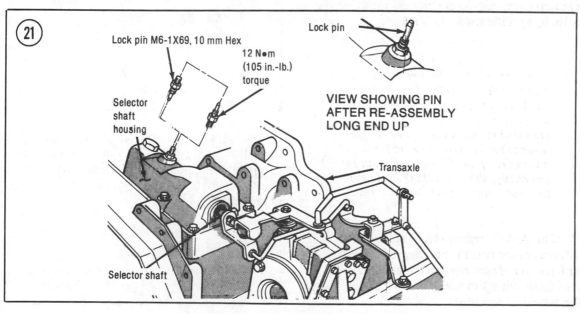

Lock pin M6-1X69, 10 mm Hex

12 N•m
(105 in.-lb.)
torque

Lock pin

VIEW SHOWING PIN
AFTER RE-ASSEMBLY
LONG END UP

Selector
shaft
housing

Transaxle

Selector shaft

3. Raise the vehicle and secure with jackstands.

4. Loosen the gearshift tube-to-gearshift connector clamp bolt. See **Figure 22**. Then check to see that the gearshift connector slides and turns freely in the gearshift tube.

5. Position the shifter mechanism connector so that the isolator contacts the upstanding flange and that the rib on the isolator is aligned fore and aft with the hole in the block-out bracket. Hold the clamp bolt in this position and tighten the clamp bolt on the gearshift tube to 170 in.-lb. (1.9 mkg). See **Figure 22**.

6. Remove the jackstands and lower the vehicle.

7. Remove the lock pin from the selector shaft housing and reinstall the lock pin upside down in the selector shaft housing (**Figure 21**). Tighten lock pin to 105 in.-lb. (1.2 mkg).

8. Check shift into FIRST and REVERSE.

AUTOMATIC TRANSAXLE

The automatic transaxle contains a fully automatic, hydraulically controlled 3-speed transmission with a torque converter. Gearshifts are automatic, depending on engine speed and throttle position.

Automatic transmission overhaul requires special skills, tools, and high standards of cleanliness not possessed by the average home mechanic. Considerable money can be saved by removing the old transaxle and installing a new or rebuilt one yourself. This chapter includes removal and installation procedures, plus other simple repairs. See Chapter Three for lubrication and preventive maintenance.

Removal/Installation

The automatic transaxle can be removed without removing the engine. Transaxle and torque converter must be removed as an assembly, however.

1. Disconnect battery cables at battery.

2. Improvise a tool similar to that shown in **Figure 23** to lift up on the cast hole in the cylinder head and support the engine.

3. Disconnect throttle and shift linkage from transaxle.

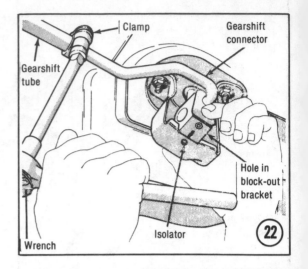

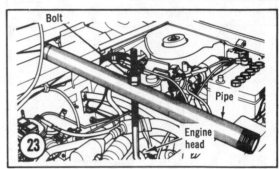

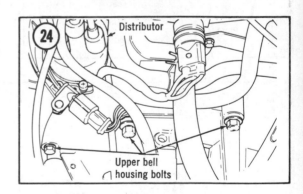

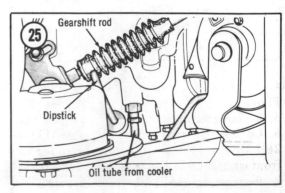

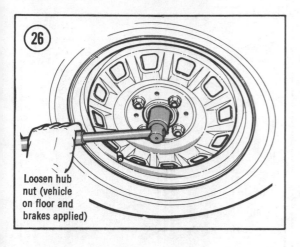

26
Loosen hub nut (vehicle on floor and brakes applied)

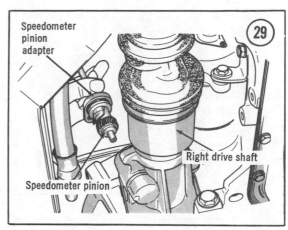

29
Speedometer pinion adapter
Right drive shaft
Speedometer pinion

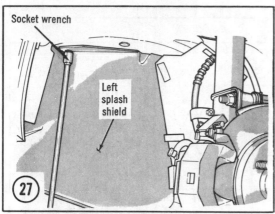

Socket wrench
Left splash shield
27

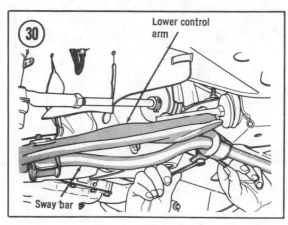

30
Lower control arm
Sway bar

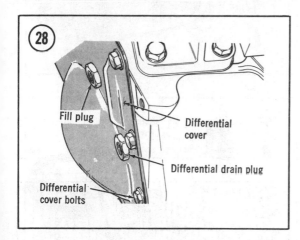

28
Fill plug
Differential cover
Differential drain plug
Differential cover bolts

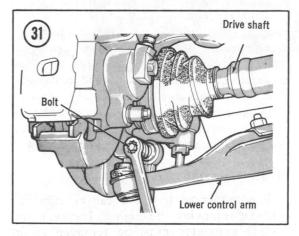

31
Drive shaft
Bolt
Lower control arm

9

4. Remove the upper bell housing bolts. See **Figure 24**.

5. Remove the upper cooler tube (**Figure 25**).

6. Loosen the front wheel hub nuts (**Figure 26**), then raise the vehicle and remove the front wheels.

7. Remove the left splash shield (**Figure 27**).

8. Drain the differential and remove the differential cover (**Figure 28**).

9. Remove the speedometer adapter, cable, and pinion as an assembly. See **Figure 29**.

10. Remove the sway bar (**Figure 30**) and remove the lower ball-joint to steering knuckle bolts (**Figure 31**). Separate the

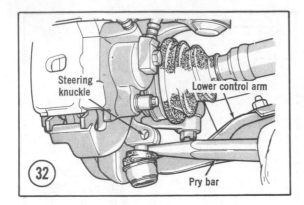

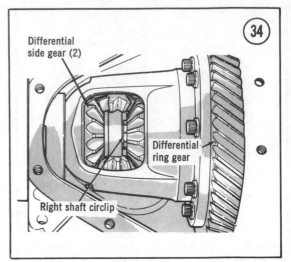

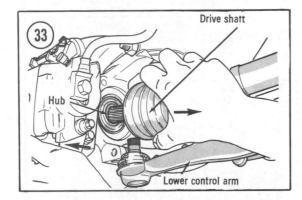

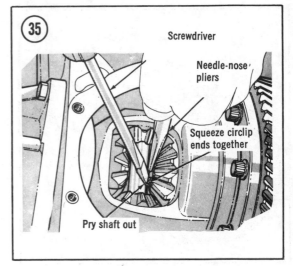

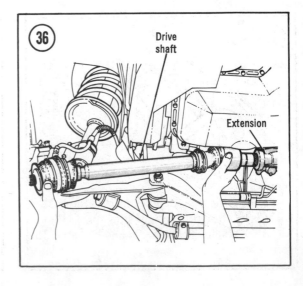

ball-joints and steering knuckles with a pry bar (**Figure 32**).

11. Remove the drive shafts from the hubs (**Figure 33**). Rotate the drive shafts to expose the ends of the circlips (**Figure 34**).

12. Squeeze the circlip ends together and pry the drive shafts out of side gears (**Figure 35**). Remove the drive shafts (**Figure 36**).

13. Mark the torque converter and drive plate as shown in **Figure 37** and remove the torque converter mounting bolts.

14. Remove the plug in the right splash shield and use a wrench to rotate engine (**Figure 38**) if required during removal or installation.

15. Remove the lower cooler tube and the wire to NEUTRAL/PARK safety switch (**Figure 39**).

16. Remove engine mount bracket from the front crossmember (**Figure 40**).

17. Remove through bolt from front engine mount insulator (**Figure 41**) and the bezel housing bolts.

18. Support the transaxle with a transmission jack as shown in **Figure 42** and secure with a chain.

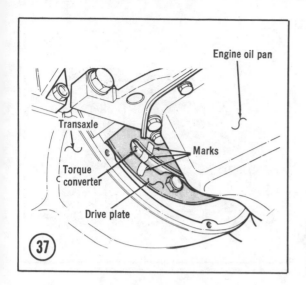

Engine oil pan

Transaxle

Marks

Torque converter

Drive plate

(37)

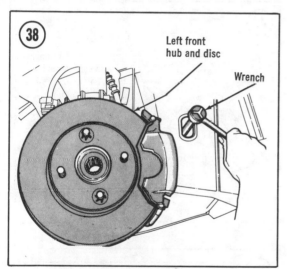

(38)

Left front hub and disc

Wrench

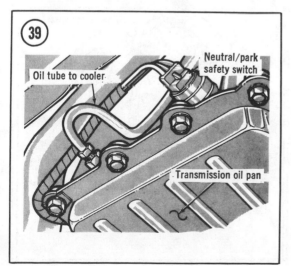

(39)

Oil tube to cooler

Neutral/park safety switch

Transmission oil pan

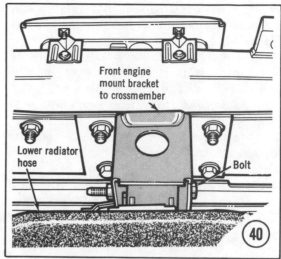

Front engine mount bracket to crossmember

Lower radiator hose

Bolt

(40)

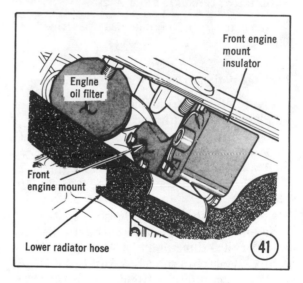

Front engine mount insulator

Engine oil filter

Front engine mount

Lower radiator hose

(41)

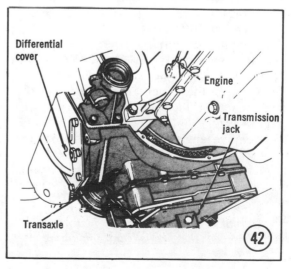

Differential cover

Engine

Transmission jack

Transaxle

(42)

9

19. Remove left engine mount (**Figure 43**). Remove long bolt through mount as shown in **Figure 44**.

20. Use jack to raise or lower transmission and use a lever (large screwdriver. etc.) as shown in **Figure 45** to pry the transaxle/torque converter assembly away from the engine.

21. Use the jack to lower the assembly and remove it from the car.

22. Installation is the reverse of these steps. Before lowering the vehicle, fill with DEXRON automatic transmission fluid. Torque transmission-to-engine and engine mount bolts to 40 ft.-lb. (5.5 mkg).

Automatic Transaxle Fluid

Check level and condition as described in Chapter Three.

Linkage Adjustment

Figure 46 shows the linkage.

1. Place the gearshift selector in PARK.

2. Loosen the cable retaining clamp on the cable mounting bracket.

3. Apply a load as follows while retightening the cable retaining clamp bolt to 90 in.-lb. (10 N•m).

   a. Column shift models: apply a 10 lb. load on the cable housing isolator in the forward direction.

   b. Console shift models: apply a 10 lb. load on the transmission lever at the transmission in a forward direction.

4. Move shift lever through all positions while trying to start the engine. The engine should only start in the PARK and NEUTRAL positions.

NOTE
A high-pitched gear noise may be heard at road speeds between 40-60 mph on some 1981-on vehicles. This noise can be reduced by installing a rubber shift cable sleeve on the gearshift selector cable as shown in **Figure 47**. *Unravel the sleeve from the center and wrap it around the cable at a mid-point between the firewall and mounting bracket.*

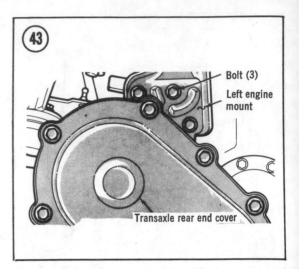

43   Bolt (3)
    Left engine mount
    Transaxle rear end cover

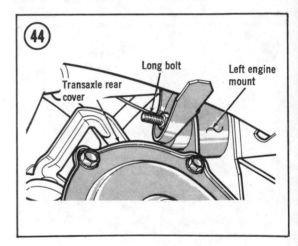

44   Long bolt   Left engine mount
Transaxle rear cover

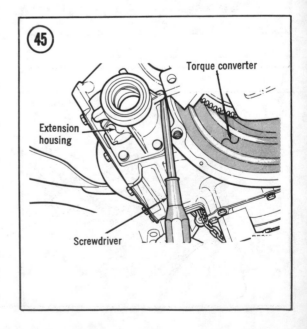

45   Torque converter
Extension housing
Screwdriver

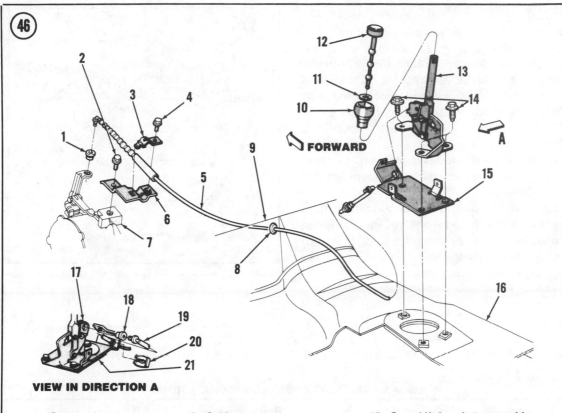

46

12

11

10

13

14

FORWARD

A

1

2

3

4

5

6

7

9

8

15

16

17

18

19

20

21

VIEW IN DIRECTION A

1. Grommet
2. Screw and washer
3. Clamp
4. Bolt
5. Cable assembly
6. Bracket
7. Transaxle

8. Cable grommet
9. Dash panel
10. Knob
11. Retainer clip
12. Button assembly
13. Gearshift lever
14. Screw and washer (3)

15. Gearshift bracket assembly
16. Floor pan
17. Actuator assembly
18. Grommet
19. Cable assembly
20. Clip (cable)
21. Gearshift bracket assembly

9

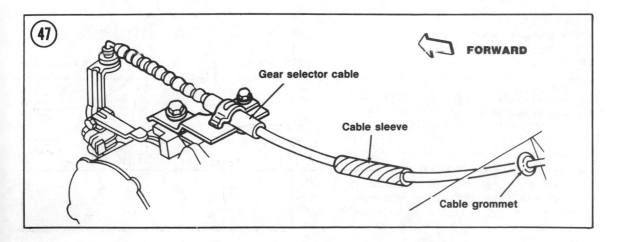

47

FORWARD

Gear selector cable

Cable sleeve

Cable grommet

Throttle Cable Adjustment

Refer to **Figure 48** for this procedure.

1. Warm the engine to normal operating temperature. Connect a tune-up tachometer to the engine. Make sure that the carburetor is not on the fast idle cam and check idle speed (see Chapter Three). Adjust if necessary.

2. Loosen the cable adjustment bracket lock screw.

3. Push the transaxle lever rearward as far as possible. Tighten the cable adjustment bracket lock screw.

4. Have an assistant floor the gas pedal, then slowly release it. Make sure the transaxle throttle lever moves smoothly and returns to idle position by itself.

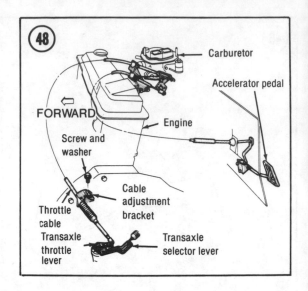

Table 1 MANUAL TRANSAXLE SPECIFICATIONS

	ft.-lb.	N·m
A-412 transaxle		
Drain and fill plugs	14.5	20
Back-up light switch	12	16
Transmission case		
Clutch housing bolt/stud	21	28
Release bearing end cover screw	9	7
A-460 and A-465 transaxle		
Gearshift housing to case bolt	21	28
Shift linkage adjusting pin	9	7
Strut to block or case bolt	70	95
Flywheel to crankshaft bolt		
1.7 liter	60	81
1.6 and 2.2 liter	65	88
Clutch pressure plate to flywheel bolt	21	28
Impact bracket to case stud nut	21	28
Fill plug	24	33
A-412 transaxle		
Gearshift linkage adjustment spacer		
dimension (thickness)		
1978	1/2 in. (13 mm)	
1979-1980	5/8 in. (16 mm)	
1981-on	3/4 in. (19 mm)	

NOTE: If you own a 1984 model, first check the Supplement at the back of the book for any new service information.

CHAPTER TEN

BRAKES

All models use a dual hydraulic brake system with disc brakes at the front and drum brakes at the rear. The brake system is diagonally split, with the right front and left rear brakes on one circuit and the left front and right rear on the other circuit. See **Figure 1.**

A pressure differential valve contains a brake warning switch. If a pressure loss occurs in either brake circuit, a warning light on the instrument panel illuminates to warn the driver.

Vehicles with power brakes have a vacuum booster to reduce braking effort.

A cable-operated mechanical handbrake expands the rear brake shoes to provide parking brakes when the hand lever is drawn up.

Table 1 (specifications) and **Table 2** (tightening torques) are at the end of the chapter.

MASTER CYLINDER

Removal/Installation

1. Place rags under the master cylinder to protect the body paint.
2. Remove brake fluid from reservoir with a siphon used exclusively for brake fluid.
3. Disconnect tubes from primary and secondary tube ports. See **Figure 2.** Install plugs in ports.

NOTE: *On models without power brakes, disconnect stop lamp switch mounting bracket under dash, and pull brake pedal backward to disengage pushrod from the master cylinder piston. This will destroy the grommet. Make sure all pieces of old grommet are removed, and use a new grommet when installing.*

4. Remove master cylinder mounting nuts and remove master cylinder from brake booster on firewall.
5. Installation is the reverse of these steps.
6. Fill the brake fluid reservoir with clean brake fluid.
7. Bleed entire brake system as described later.

Disassembly (1978-1982)

NOTE
No overhaul kit is provided for 1983 master cylinders. The unit is serviced as a complete assembly.

Refer to **Figure 3** for the following procedure.

1. Drain any remaining fluid and hold the master cylinder in a vise. Pull the brake fluid reservoir straight up with both hands. See **Figure 4.** Remove the reservoir grommets **(Figure 5).**

10

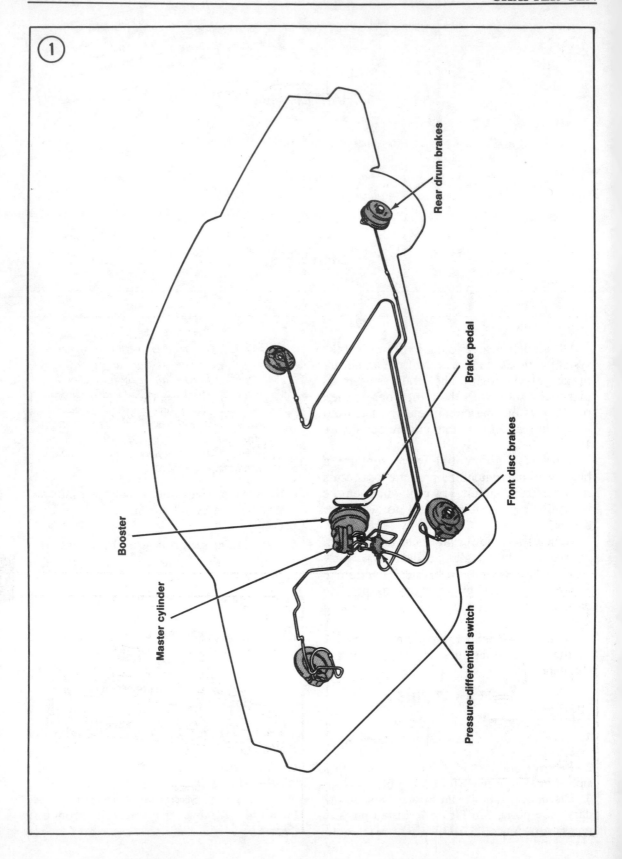

①

Rear drum brakes

Brake pedal

Front disc brakes

Booster

Master cylinder

Pressure-differential switch

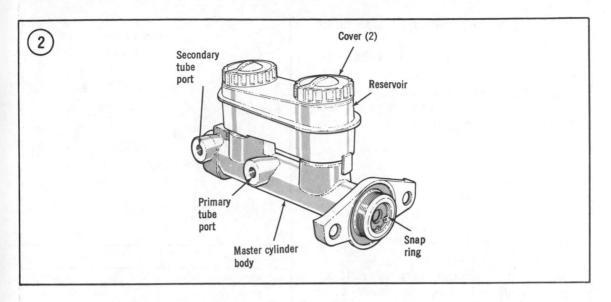

(2)

Cover (2)

Secondary
tube
port

Reservoir

Primary
tube
port

Master cylinder
body

Snap
ring

(3)

Cover

Cover seal

Reservoir

Seat (2)

Body to
reservoir
grommet

Piston
retainer pin

Anodized master
cylinder body

Seal
retainer

Secondary
piston return
spring

Primary cup

Check
flow washer

Primary piston assembly

Piston retainer
snap ring

Secondary cup

Secondary
piston

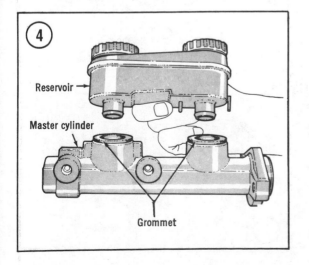

(4)

Reservoir

Master cylinder

Grommet

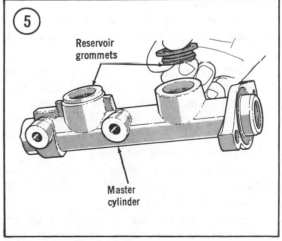

(5)

Reservoir
grommets

Master
cylinder

10

2. Remove secondary piston retaining pin. See **Figure 6**.

3. Remove circlip from master cylinder as shown in **Figure 7**.

4. Remove primary and secondary pistons. See **Figures 8 and 9**. If the secondary piston does not shake out easily, blow it out with compressed air.

> NOTE: *New cups must be installed if air pressure is used in disassembly.*

5. If replacement is planned, remove tube seats as shown in **Figure 10**.

6. Remove cup from secondary piston. If cup on primary piston is worn or damaged, entire piston must be replaced.

Inspection

Clean all parts in clean brake fluid or methylated spirits (denatured alcohol) which does not contain benzene. Do not use gasoline or kerosene. If in doubt about a solvent, do not use it; use brake fluid.

Examine the cylinder walls. If scored or scratched, hone the cylinder with a brake hone, following manufacturer's instructions. Carefully clean the cylinder after honing and be sure all passages are clear.

Assembly

1. Assemble all parts for the secondary piston as shown in **Figure 3**. Use all new parts except for the piston itself. Be sure the seals face in the proper direction.

2. Lubricate the cylinder with brake fluid. Dip the secondary piston assembly in brake fluid. Slide the spring on and insert the secondary piston in the cylinder. See **Figure 9**. Make sure lips of cup enter the bore evenly, and keep them well lubricated with brake fluid.

3. Work the end of secondary cup over the end of the primary piston (**Figure 3**), with larger lip of the cup toward the piston.

4. Center spring retainer of primary piston on secondary piston and push assemblies into

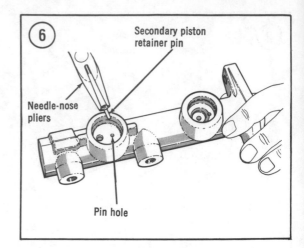
6. Secondary piston retainer pin / Needle-nose pliers / Pin hole

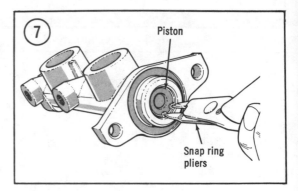
7. Piston / Snap ring pliers

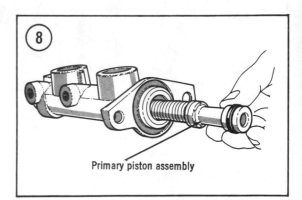
8. Primary piston assembly

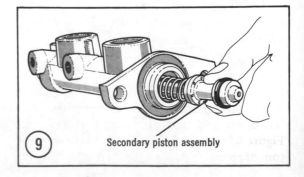
9. Secondary piston assembly

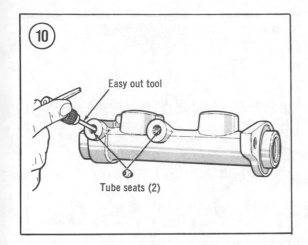

Easy out tool

Tube seats (2)

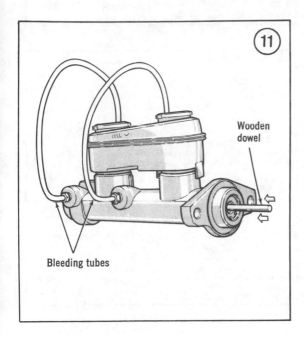

Wooden dowel

Bleeding tubes

Bleeding

1. Clamp the master cylinder in a vise, attach bleeding tubes as shown in **Figure 11**, and fill both tubes with brake fluid. See Chapter Three for correct type.

2. Operate pistons with a wooden dowel. Press in slowly and allow pistons to return several times until all air bubbles disappear from bleed lines.

3. Remove tubes, plug outlets, and install reservoir covers.

4. Remove master cylinder from vise and install in car. Tightening torques are found in **Table 2**.

DISC BRAKES

A single piston, floating caliper design is used on all vehicles. A 2-pin ATE caliper is used on 1978-1982 and some 1983 models. A one-pin Kelsey-Hayes caliper is used on other 1983 models. Brake calipers on 1983 models use a phenolic piston larger in diameter than previous calipers. These pistons are not interchangeable with earlier calipers, nor can the ATE and Kelsey-Hayes pistons be interchanged.

The brake pads should be inspected when recommended in Chapter Three and replaced when the combined lining and pad thickness is less than 0.30 in. (7.62 mm). Never allow the linings to wear to less than this minimum thickness. Always replace pads in complete sets.

Pad Replacement
(All Calipers)

1. Raise the front of the vehicle and place it on jackstands.

2. Remove the front wheels.

3. Remove the caliper guide pins. See **Figure 12** for ATE caliper; Kelsey-Hayes has only one pin. On ATE calipers, remove the anti-rattle spring.

NOTE
It may be necessary to loosen the caliper by prying it away from the adapter with a screwdriver before performing Step 4.

bore up to the primary piston cup. Work cup lips into the bore very carefully, making sure they enter evenly. Continue pushing until pistons are seated.

5. Install the snap ring. See **Figure 7**.

6. Install the retaining pin in the master cylinder. See **Figure 6**.

7. Install grommets in master cylinder. See **Figure 5**.

8. Lubricate mounting areas with brake fluid and install reservoir on master cylinder, pressing down and using a rocking motion. See **Figure 4** for proper orientation. Make sure bottom of reservoir touches top of master cylinder.

10

4. Slowly pull the caliper disc out and away from the disc (**Figure 13**). Tie the calipers up out of the way to relieve strain on the flexible brake hoses.

> *NOTE*
> *The Kelsey-Hayes caliper uses 3 hold-down springs. One is on the outer top of the caliper, one is on the bottom of the outboard lining and one is on the top of the inner lining.*

5. Remove the outboard pad and lining assembly from adapter. See **Figure 14** for ATE and **Figure 15** for Kelsey-Hayes calipers.
6. Slide the brake disc off the axle flange. See **Figure 16**.
7. Remove the inboard pad and lining assembly from the adapter. **Figure 17** shows the ATE caliper; the Kelsey-Hayes is similar.
8. Installation is the reverse of removal. Refer to **Figure 18** (typical). Before-starting, push the piston slowly and carefully back into the caliper bore until it bottoms. Have an assistant watch the master cylinder reservoir to make sure it does not overflow. If necessary, remove some fluid from the reservoir with a clean syringe. Tighten guide pins to specifications. When installation is complete, operate the brake pedal several times to seat the caliper pistons and obtain a firm brake pedal. If the pedal still feels spongy, bleed the system as described in this chapter. Top up the master cylinder reservoir with DOT 3 brake fluid. Install wheels, lower vehicle and take a test drive to make sure the brakes operate properly.

Caliper Disassembly
(All Calipers)

Refer to **Figure 19** (ATE) and **Figure 20** (Kelsey-Hayes) for this procedure.

1. Remove the caliper as described above and support it on the upper control arm with the brake hose still connected. Use shop towels or clean rags to protect the caliper and to catch spilled fluid.

2. Press the piston out of the bore by carefully depressing the brake pedal. Use a suitable wood block to prop the brake pedal in a depressed

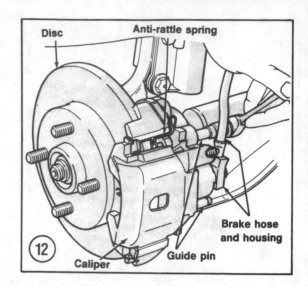

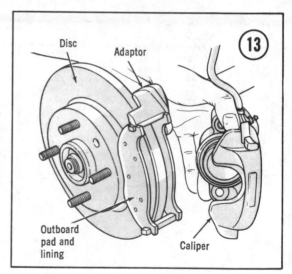

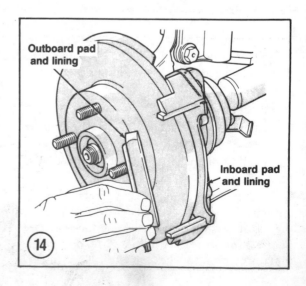

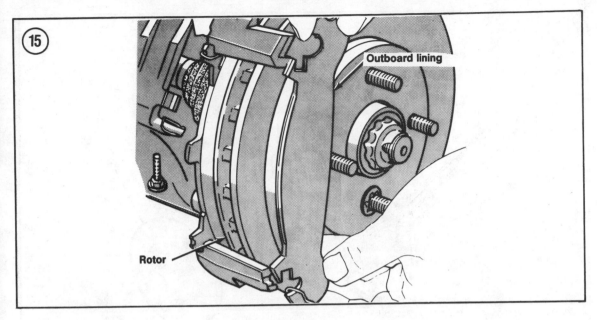

(15) **Outboard lining**

Rotor

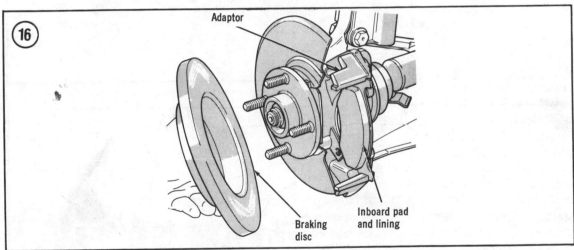

(16) **Adaptor**

Inboard pad and lining

Braking disc

10

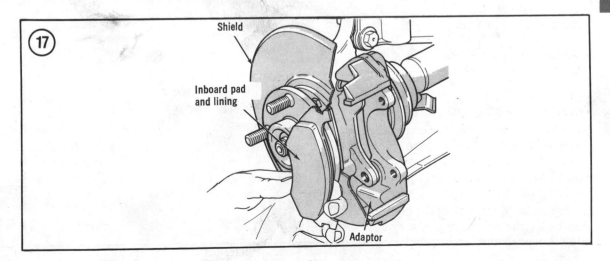

(17) **Shield**

Inboard pad and lining

Adaptor

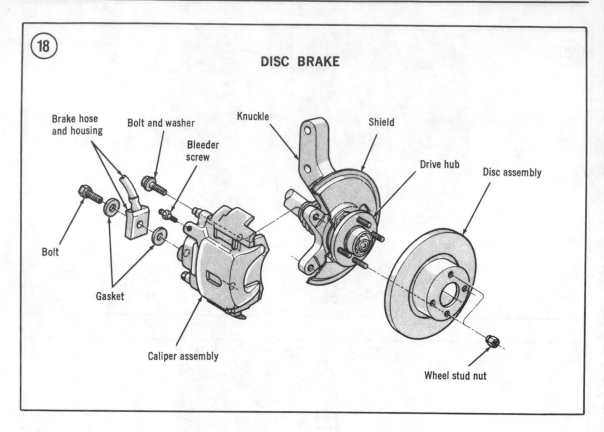

(18)

DISC BRAKE

Brake hose and housing
Bolt and washer
Bleeder screw
Knuckle
Shield
Drive hub
Disc assembly
Bolt
Gasket
Caliper assembly
Wheel stud nut

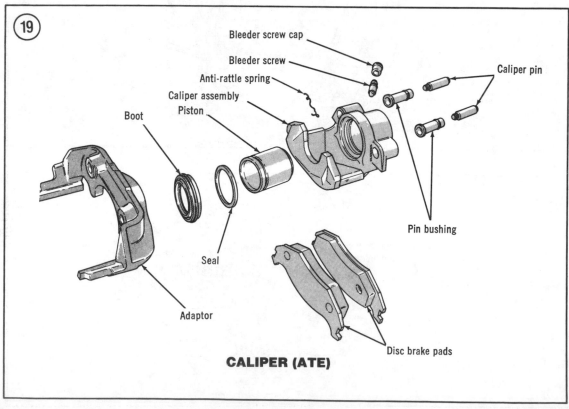

(19)

Bleeder screw cap
Bleeder screw
Anti-rattle spring
Caliper assembly
Caliper pin
Boot
Piston
Pin bushing
Seal
Adaptor
Disc brake pads

CALIPER (ATE)

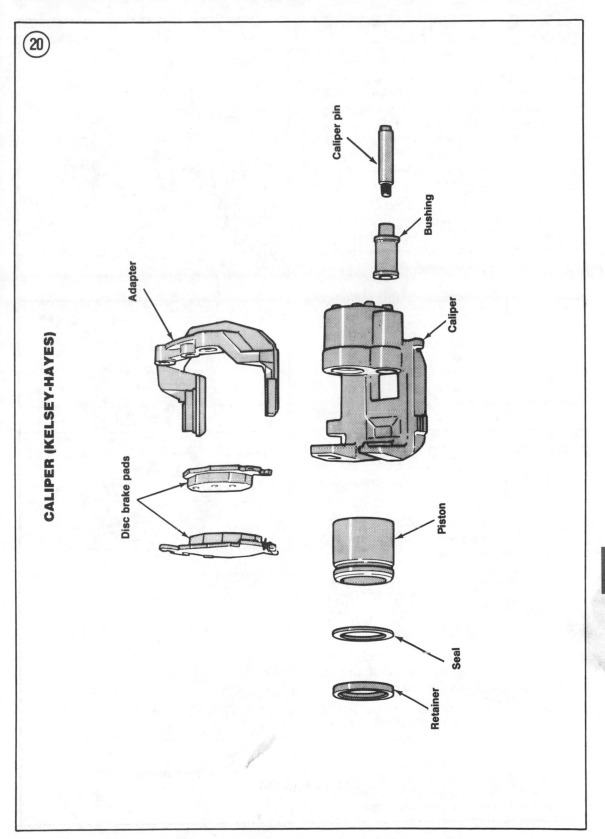

20

CALIPER (KELSEY-HAYES)

Adapter

Caliper pin

Bushing

Caliper

Disc brake pads

Piston

Seal

Retainer

10

position below the first inch of pedal travel. This will help prevent loss of fluid.

> NOTE: *If both caliper pistons are to be removed, remove one caliper and remove the piston with the other caliper still installed. Then disconnect the flexible hose of the detached caliper at the frame bracket and plug the brake tube. Remove the other caliper and remove the piston as previously described.*

WARNING
Do not use compressed air to remove pistons from calipers, as injury or damage to the piston could result.

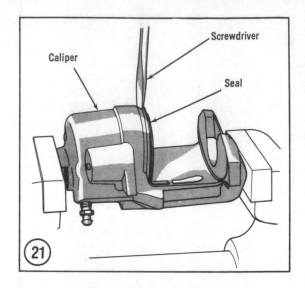

3. Disconnect the flexible hose from the caliper and mount the caliper in a vise with protected jaws.

CAUTION
Do not clamp vise too tightly, as this could cause distortion of the caliper bore and could result in brake failure.

4. Remove and discard the dust seal. See **Figure 21**.
5. Use a pointed wooden or plastic stick to work the piston seal out of the goove in the bore. See **Figure 22**. Discard the seal.

CAUTION
Do not use a metal tool to pry out the seal as this could scratch or otherwise damage the caliper bore.

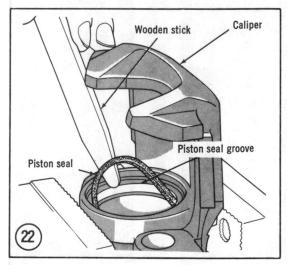

6. Press bushings out of the caliper with a wooden dowel as shown in **Figure 23**. Discard the bushings.

Caliper Cleaning/Inspection

1. Clean all parts in alcohol or clean brake fluid and blow dry with compressed air. Pay particular attention to bores and passages.

2. Inspect the piston bore for scoring, pitting, etc., and clean up corrosion or slight pitting with crocus cloth.

CAUTION
Do not use sandpaper or emery cloth, as either could damage and/or leave residue in the bore that could lead to eventual brake failure.

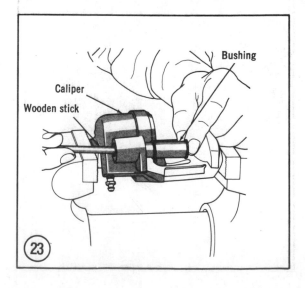

3. If deep scratches or scoring are present, the bore should be honed.

> NOTE: *Unless you have honing experience and own the proper honing tool (C-4095 or equivalent), this job should be referred to your dealer or a specialist.*

CAUTION
No more than 0.001 in. (0.254mm) of metal should be removed during honing. If the bore does not clean up within this limit, a new caliper should be installed. After honing, thoroughly clean the bore, paying particular attention to the seal and boot grooves. Residue in the groove could lead to early brake failure.

4. After honing, flush the bore with clean brake fluid and wipe dry with a clean, lint-free cloth. Then flush and dry a second time.

> NOTE: *Black stains on the piston or in the bore are caused by the piston seal and cause no harm.*

Caliper Assembly
(ATE Caliper)

1. Dip a new piston seal in clean brake fluid and install it in the groove in the bore. Use clean fingers to work the seal into the groove and make sure seal is properly seated. See **Figure 24**. Make sure seal is not twisted or rolled.

2. Dip a new piston boot in clean brake fluid and work the boot into the outer groove in the bore. Using a small steel plate, wooden dowel and hammer as shown in **Figure 25**, drive the seal into the caliper until it is evenly seated. A C-clamp of suitable size also can be used to seat the boot.

4. Use fingers (make sure they are clean) to spread boot and work piston into boot while pressing down on piston. The air trapped below the boot should force the boot around the piston and into its groove as the piston is pressed. See **Figure 26**.

5. Remove the plugs from the hose and bleed valve inlets and push the piston into the bore

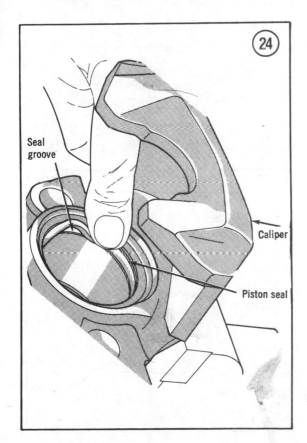

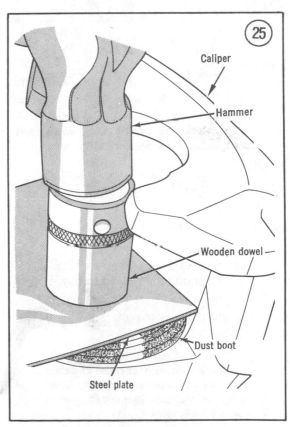

10

until it bottoms. Apply force evenly to avoid cocking the piston.

6. Install new guide pin bushings by compressing the bushing flanges and pushing them into place with the fingertips or a wooden stick. See **Figure 27**. Make sure bushing flanges are not distorted.

7. Install the caliper and bleed the hydraulic system as described elsewhere in this chapter.

Caliper Assembly
(Kelsey-Hayes Caliper)

1. Dip a new piston seal in clean brake fluid and install it in the groove in the bore. Use clean fingers to work the seal into the groove, and make sure seal is properly seated. See **Figure 24**. Make sure seal is not twisted or rolled.

2. Dip a new piston boot in clean brake fluid and position boot over the piston.

3. Work the piston past the seal in the bore and push inward until it bottoms. See **Figure 28**. Apply force evenly to avoid cocking the piston.

4. Position dust boot in counterbore. Use installer (part No. C-4682) with handle (part No. C-4171) as shown in **Figure 29** to drive boot into counterbore.

5. Install new inner and outer guide pin bushings by compressing with fingers and pushing them into place with the fingertips or a wooden stick. See **Figure 27**. Make sure bushing flanges extend over caliper evenly on all sides.

6. Install the caliper and bleed the hydraulic system as described in this chapter.

BRAKE DISC

Inspection

Check the brake disc for deep scratches, excessive runout, and uneven thickness.

Small marks on the disc are not important, but deep radial scratches reduce braking effectiveness and increase pad wear.

To Check disc runout, mount a dial indicator as shown in **Figure 30** and rotate the disc. Runout should not exceed 0.003 in. (0.08 mm) on 1978-1982 models or 0.005 in. (0.127 mm) on 1983 models. This procedure

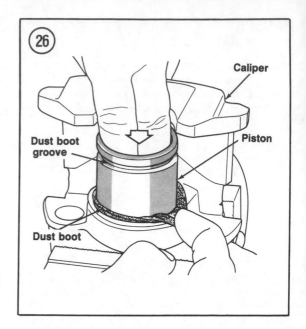

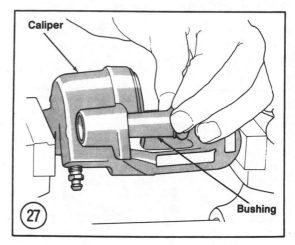

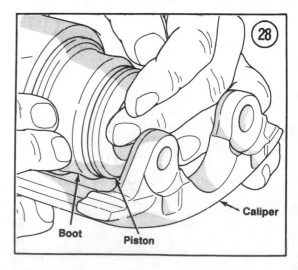

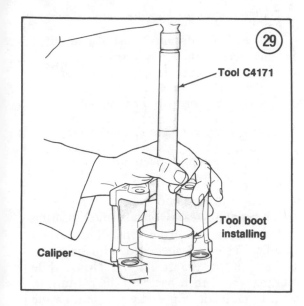

Tool C4171

Tool boot installing

Caliper

assumes that the wheel bearings are in good condition and that the hub is not warped. Check them if in doubt.

Check the thickness of the disc with micrometer. See **Figure 31**. Make about 12 measurements around the disc about one inch from the outer edge. Measurements should not vary more than 0.0005 in. (0.013 mm).

If the disc has excessively deep scratches, excessive runout or variation in thickness, renew or replace the disc. If the disc is renewed, minimum thickness must be at least 0.431 in. (10.95 mm) and an equal amount must be removed from each side. See **Figure 32**.

Removal/Installation

1. Raise front of vehicle on jackstands and remove wheels.

2. Remove caliper as described earlier, except leave brake hose attached and brake pads installed. Hang the assembly up with a piece of wire.

3. Pull off the brake disc. Do not use force, as force could cause damage.

4. Installation is the reverse of these steps.

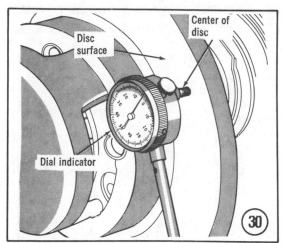

Disc surface

Center of disc

Dial indicator

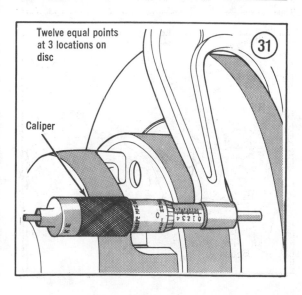

Twelve equal points at 3 locations on disc

Caliper

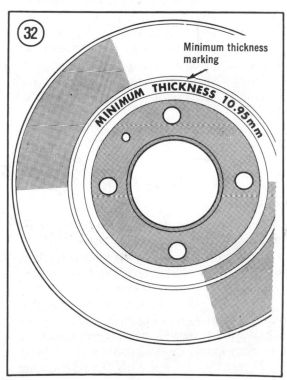

Minimum thickness marking

MINIMUM THICKNESS 10.95 m.m

10

REAR BRAKE DRUMS

Removal/Installation

Refer to **Figure 33** for this procedure.

1. Put transmission in gear (manual) or PARK (automatic) and pull up the handbrake.

2. Loosen the rear wheel lug bolts.

3. Pry off dust cap on the wheel hub.

4. Remove the cotter pin and loosen the castellated nut on the axle stud.

> **CAUTION**
> *Never loosen the nut unless all 4 wheels are firmly on the ground. The force required to loosen the nut is sufficient to knock the car off jackstands.*

5. Raise the rear of the car on jackstands and remove the rear wheels.

6. Remove the castellated nut, hex nut, and washer.

7. Release the parking brake.

8. Pull the brake drum off, making sure that the inner race of the outer bearing is not lost. Remove the inner race from the brake drum.

> NOTE: *Before removing drums, release brake shoes by inserting a thin-bladed screwdriver in the brake adjusting hole and turning the adjuster nut up (left side) or down (right side) until the drum can be removed.*

9. Clean bearings and repack them with wheel bearing grease. Install inner bearing and dust seal in drum. Install drum on spindle. Install washer and adjusting nut. Tighten nut to 25 ft.-lb. (35 N•m) while rotating wheel, then back nut off 1/4 turn to release preload. Finger-tighten nut while rotating wheel. Align nut lock slots with spindle hole and install a new cotter pin.

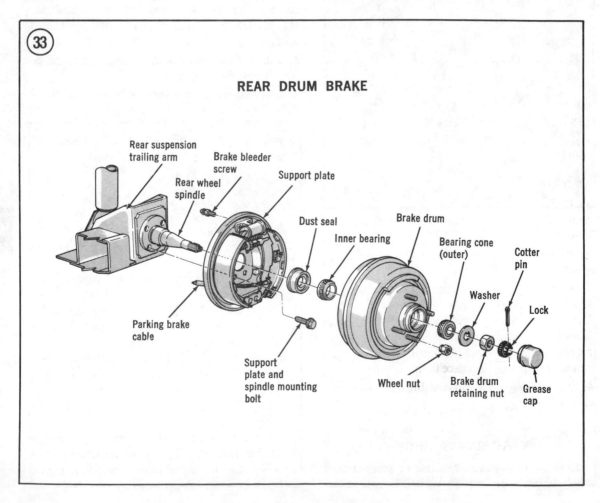

(33)

REAR DRUM BRAKE

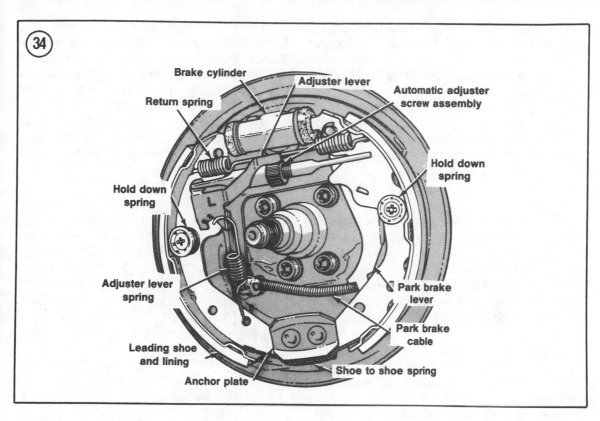

(34)

Brake cylinder

Adjuster lever

Automatic adjuster
screw assembly

Return spring

Hold down
spring

Hold down
spring

Adjuster lever
spring

Park brake
lever

Park brake
cable

Leading shoe
and lining

Shoe to shoe spring

Anchor plate

Check end play. It should be 0.0001-0.003 in. for 1978-1982 models or 0.0001-0.002 in. for 1983 models. Install dust cap and wheel.
10. Adjust brakes as described in this chapter.

Inspection

1. Blow brake dust and dirt from the brake drum. Remove grease and oil with cleaning solvent; blow dry.
2. Clean the drum braking surface with alcohol.
3. Inspect brake drums for scoring, cracking, taper, out-of-roundness, heat evidence, etc. Drums which are scored or worn should be turned by a dealer. Brake shoes must be replaced with oversized shoes. Cracked drums cannot be turned; replace them.
4. Remove glaze on serviceable drums with fine emery cloth.

REAR BRAKE SHOES

Brake shoes require relining or replacement when linings are soaked with oil, grease, or brake fluid. In addition, replace linings worn to less than $\frac{1}{16}$ in. If brake drums have been turned, use oversized linings. Always replace linings on both rear wheels to ensure uniform braking.

Removal/Installation

1983

Refer to **Figure 34** for this procedure.
1. Remove the brake drum as described in this chapter.
2. Disconnect and remove the adjuster lever spring.
3. Depress the shoe hold-down springs with a brake tool. Rotate spring 90° and remove from backing plate pin.
4. Spread the brake shoes to disengage them from the wheel cylinder and remove the entire shoe/adjuster/spring assembly from the backing plate, twisting it to disengage the parking brake cable.
5. If installing new shoes, pry the retainer from the parking brake lever mounting stud on the trailing shoe. Install parking brake lever to new shoe with retainer.

10

6. Lubricate shoe contact areas on support plate with multipurpose lubricant. See **Figure 35**.

7. Connect parking brake cable to parking brake lever and position trailing shoe on backing plate to engage wheel cylinder.

8. Connect leading shoe to trailing shoe with upper return spring, then install adjuster lever assembly between shoes to engage adjuster lever and trailing shoe. See **Figure 36**.

9. Install shoe-to-shoe spring at bottom of shoe assembly.

10. Install hold-down springs to backing plate pins and rotate 90° to secure shoes in place.

11. Install adjusting lever spring (**Figure 37**).

12. Check position of all components against **Figure 34**. If correct, install brake drums as described in this chapter.

1978-1982

1. Remove the brake drum as previously described.

2. Remove parking brake cable. See **Figure 38**.

3. Remove shoe-to-anchor springs. See **Figure 39**. Remove hold-down spring. See **Figure 40**.

4. Spread shoes and remove adjuster screw assembly (**Figure 41**). Make sure nut is fully backed off.

5. Raise the parking brake lever and pull trailing shoe away from support to release tension of pull-back spring. Remove the shoe

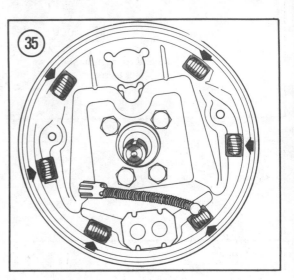

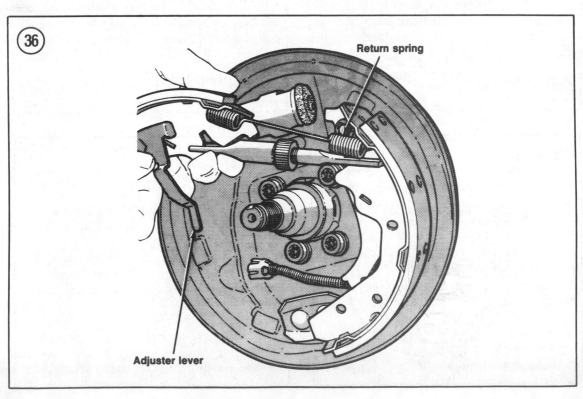

Return spring

Adjuster lever

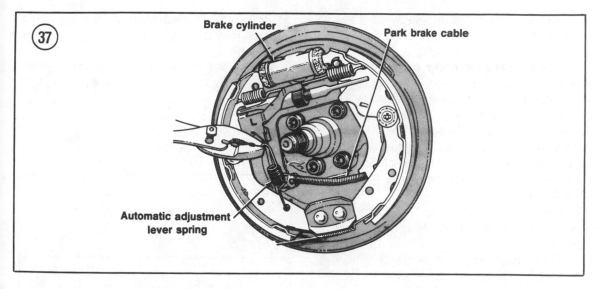

(37) Brake cylinder

Park brake cable

Automatic adjustment
lever spring

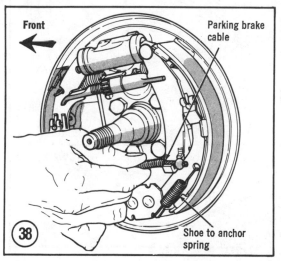

Front

Parking brake
cable

(38)

Shoe to anchor
spring

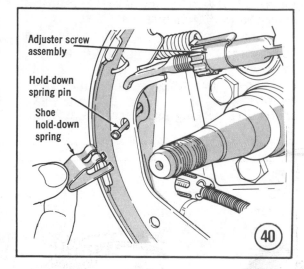

Adjuster screw
assembly

Hold-down
spring pin

Shoe
hold-down
spring

(40)

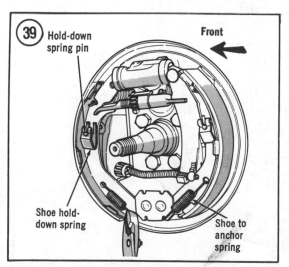

(39) Hold-down
spring pin

Front

Shoe hold-
down spring

Shoe to
anchor
spring

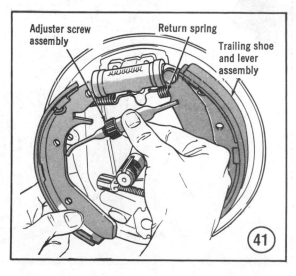

Adjuster screw
assembly

Return spring

Trailing shoe
and lever
assembly

(41)

10

and disengage spring from support. See **Figure 42**.

6. Raise the leading shoe to release tension. Remove shoe and disengage spring from support. See **Figure 43**.

7. Installation is the reverse of these steps. Lubricate shoe contact areas on support plate with multipurpose lubricant. See **Figure 35**.

8. Install brake drum as described earlier.

WHEEL CYLINDERS

Removal/Installation

1. Remove brake drum and brake shoes as described earlier.

2. Depress the brake pedal all the way and hold it with a support to close the compensating port in the master cylinder.

3. Disconnect the brake line at the wheel cylinder and cover it with the rubber cap from the bleeder screw to prevent entry of dirt and moisture.

4. Remove the bolts securing the wheel cylinder to the backing plate. Take the wheel cylinder off. See **Figure 44**.

5. Installation is the reverse of these steps.

Rebuilding

Refer to **Figure 45** for this procedure.

1. Remove rubber boots.

2. Remove pistons, cups, cup expanders, and springs.

3. Remove bleeder valve screw.

4. Clean all parts in alcohol or clean brake fluid.

5. Examine the cylinder bore for scoring, pitting, or heavy corrosion. Very light scratches may be removed with crocus cloth. Flush out with alcohol and blow dry. Replace wheel cylinders which show more extensive damage.

6. Lubricate all parts with brake fluid.

7. Install new cups, cup expanders, and springs provided in repair kit. Do not reuse old parts.

8. Install pistons and new rubber boots.

9. Install bleeder valve screw.

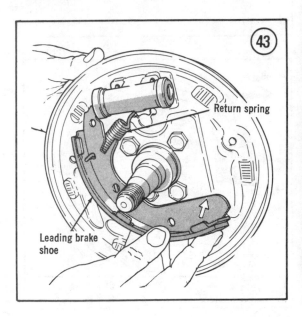

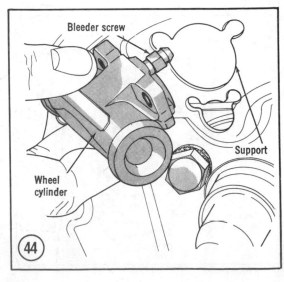

FOOTBRAKE ADJUSTMENT

Only the rear drum brakes on 1978-1982 models require adjustment. All front disc brakes and 1983 rear drum brakes are self-adjusting. Refer to **Figure 46** for this procedure.

1. Raise the car on jackstands and release the handbrake.

2. Depress brake pedal several times to centralize the shoes in the drum.

3. Turn the adjuster nut as necessary until the wheel can no longer be turned by hand. Back off the starwheel until the wheel can just be turned by hand (about 10 clicks).

4. Repeat these steps on the other wheel.

5. Operate footbrake several times and check that all wheels can just be rotated.

6. Check the brake fluid level and top up if necessary.

7. Road test the car. Check pedal free play and ensure that the car does not swerve to one side. If it does, recheck the adjustments.

HANDBRAKE ADJUSTMENT

1. Raise the rear of the car on jackstands and release the handbrake.

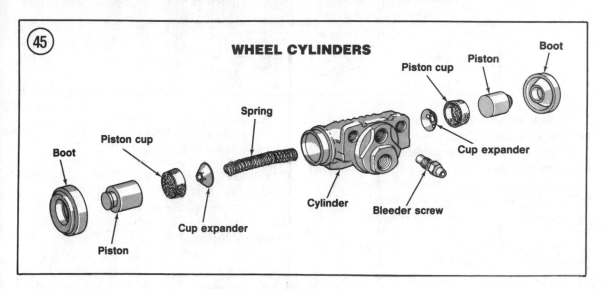

WHEEL CYLINDERS

Boot — Piston cup — Cup expander — Spring — Cylinder — Bleeder screw — Piston cup — Piston — Boot — Cup expander — Piston — Boot

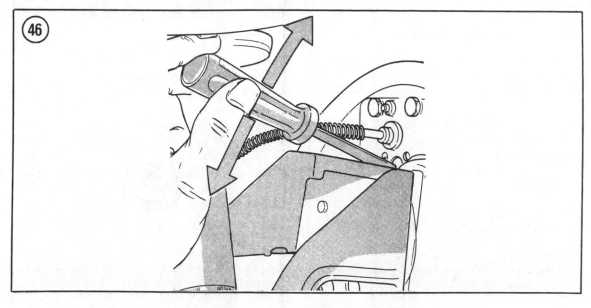

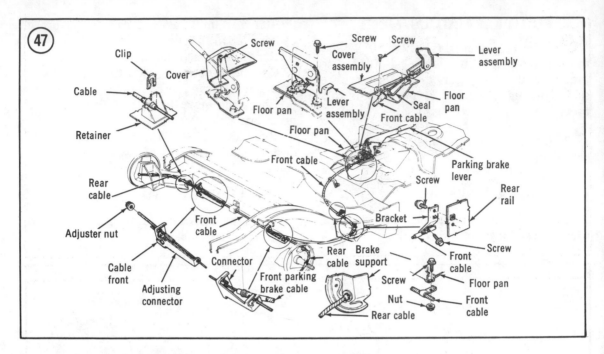

2. Loosen adjusting nut shown in **Figure 47** and back off until there is slack in the cable.

3. Adjust footbrake as described earlier.

4. Tighten adjusting nut until a slight drag is felt when either rear wheel is turned by hand.

5. Loosen nut until both rear wheels can be turned freely, then back nut off another 2 full turns.

6. Apply and release parking brake several times to make sure wheels turn freely.

BRAKE BLEEDING

Brakes require bleeding whenever air enters the system, lowering the effective braking pressure. Air can enter when the master cylinder or wheel cylinders are serviced or if the fluid in the reservoir runs dry. Air can also enter through a leaky brake line or hose. Find the leaking line and replace it before bleeding.

> *CAUTION*
> *Whenever handling brake fluid, do not get any on the brake shoes, brake discs, calipers, or body paint. Brake shoes or brake pads will be permanently damaged, requiring replacement. Body paint*

can also be damaged unless you wipe the area with a clean cloth and wash it with a soapy solution immediately.

1. Make sure that the brake fluid reservoir is full and that the vents in the cap are open.

2. Connect a plastic or rubber tube to the bleeder valve on the right rear wheel. See **Figure 48**. Suspend the other end of the tube in a jar or bottle filled with a few inches of brake fluid. During the remaining steps, keep this end submerged at all times and never let the level in the brake fluid reservoir drop below 1/2 level.

3. Open the bleed valve on the right rear wheel about one turn. See **Figure 48**. Have an assistant depress the brake pedal slowly to the floor. As soon as the pedal is all the way down, close the bleeder valve and let the pedal up. Repeat this step as many times as necessary or until fluid with no air bubbles issues from the tube.

4. Bleed the remaining valves in the same manner as described in the steps above. Follow the sequence shown in **Figure 49**. Keep checking the brake fluid reservoir to be sure it does not run out of fluid.

5. When all wheels are bled, discard the brake fluid in the jar or bottle; never reuse such fluid. Top up the brake fluid reservoir with clean fluid.

(48)

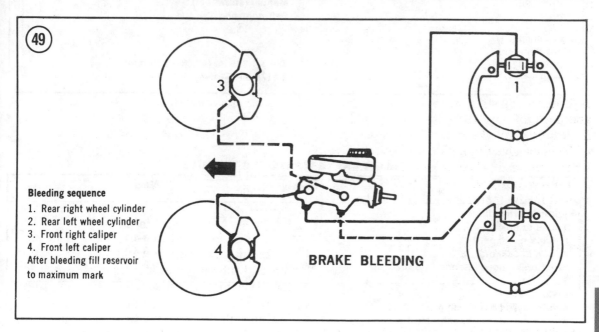

(49)

Bleeding sequence
1. Rear right wheel cylinder
2. Rear left wheel cylinder
3. Front right caliper
4. Front left caliper
After bleeding fill reservoir
to maximum mark

BRAKE BLEEDING

3

4

1

2

10

Tables are on the following page.

Table 1 BRAKE SPECIFICATIONS

Disc brakes	
Diameter	
Except Shelby Charger	9.0 in. (228 mm)
Shelby Charger	10.2 in. (260 mm)
Maximum allowable runout	0.004 in. (0.1016 mm)
Shoe and lining thickness	
New	0.710 in. (18.0 mm)
Minimum	0.300 in. (7.62 mm)
Brake adjustment	Automatic
Drum brakes	
Diameter	
Except Shelby Charger	7.87 in. (200 mm)
Shelby Charger	8.63 in. (220 mm)
Lining thickness	3/16 in. (5 mm)
Drum regrind dimension	Limit marked on drum
Brake adjustment	
1978-1982	Manual (starwheel)
1983	Self-adjusting
Brake caliper	
Bore diameter	
1978-1982	1.893-1.895 in. (48.08-48.13 mm)
1983	2.1176 in. (54 mm)

Table 2 BRAKE TIGHTENING TORQUES

	ft.-lb.	Mkg
Hydraulic brake lines		
Tubes to flexible hoses	6-12	0.9-1.7
Fittings to calipers	19-29	2.6-4.0
Hoses to calipers	19-29	2.6-4.0
Front brake hose intermediate bracket	6-9	0.8-1.3
Master cylinder		
Master cylinder to dash panel	16-21	2.2-2.8
Master cylinder to booster front cover	14-19	1.9-2.6
Power brake		
Power brake assembly to dash panel	1.6-21	2.2-2.8
Lower pivot	30	4.1
Pedal pushrod bolt	30	4.1
Calipers		
Adapter mounting bolts	70-100	9.5-13.6
Caliper retaining plate screws	14-21	1.9-2.9
Guide pins		
1978	25-40	3.5-5.5
1979	18-22	2.5-3.0
1980	25-40	3.4-5.5
1981-1982	18-22	2.5-3.0
1983		
Kelsey-Hayes	25-35	3.4-4.7
ATE	18-26	2.5-3.5

NOTE: If you own a 1984 or later model, first check the Supplement at the back of the book for any new service information.

CHAPTER ELEVEN

FRONT SUSPENSION AND STEERING

Specifications (**Table 1**) are found at the end of the chapter.

WHEEL ALIGNMENT

Several suspension angles affect running and steering. These angles must be properly aligned to maintain directional stability, ease of steering and proper tire wear.

The angles involved define:

a. Caster
b. Camber
c. Toe
d. Steering axis inclination
e. Toe-out on turns

Only camber and toe are adjustable. Neither should be adjusted without a front-end rack.

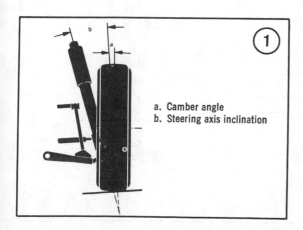

a. Camber angle
b. Steering axis inclination

Other suspension angles, though not adjustable, should be measured on a front-end rack to check for bent suspension parts.

Pre-alignment Check

Several factors influence the suspension angles, or steering. Before any adjustments are attempted, perform the following checks.

1. Check tire pressure and wear.
2. Check the play in wheel bearings. Adjust if necessary.
3. Check the play in ball-joints.
4. Check for broken springs or torsion bar (rear only).
5. Remove any excessive load.
6. Check shock absorbers.
7. Check steering gear adjustments.
8. Check play in tie rod parts.
9. Check wheel balance.
10. Check *rear* suspension for looseness.

A proper inspection of front tire wear can point to several alignment problems. See Chapter Two.

Camber

Camber is the vertical inclination of the wheel, (**Figure 1**). Note that angle (a) is positive camber, i.e., the top of the tire inclines outward more than the bottom.

11

Camber combines with steering axis inclination to determine steering roll radius as described later. Camber is easily adjusted on a front-end rack. Loosen the 2 bolts holding the steering knuckle to the suspension strut. The top bolt is an eccentric. See **Figure 2**. Rotate the upper bolt to move the top of the wheel in or out as required to obtain specified camber, then tighten both bolts without disturbing the adjustment. On 1978-1982 models, tighten the bolts to 85 ft.-lb. (115 N•m). On 1983 models, tighten the bolts to 45

ft.-lb. (61 N•m), then tighten each bolt 1/4 turn (90°) beyond the specified torque.

Caster

Caster is the inclination of the axis through the suspension strut from vertical. Caster helps the wheels to return to a position straight ahead after a turn. It also prevents the car from wandering due to wind, potholes, or uneven road surfaces.

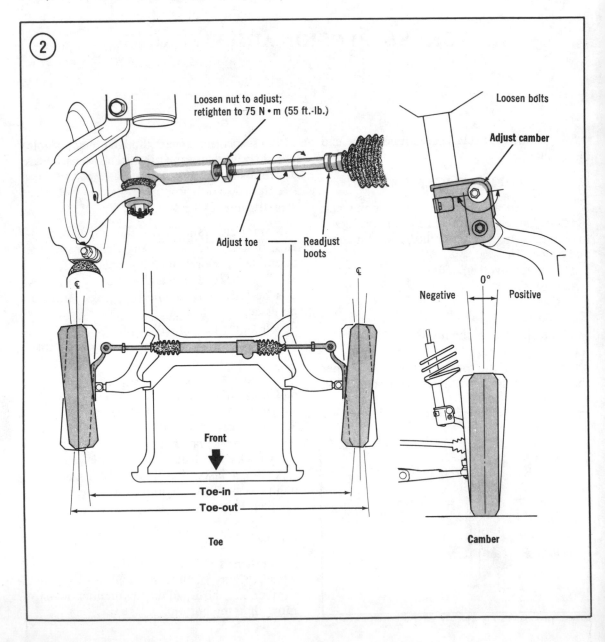

②

Loosen nut to adjust; retighten to 75 N • m (55 ft.-lb.)

Loosen bolts

Adjust camber

Adjust toe — Readjust boots

Negative 0° Positive

Front

Toe-in

Toe-out

Toe

Camber

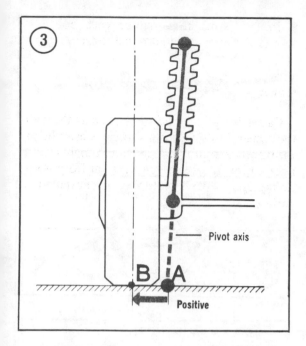

Pivot axis

B A

Positive

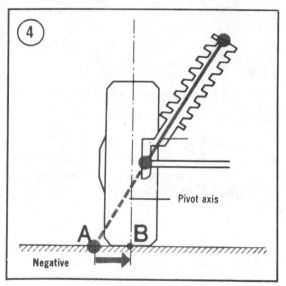

Pivot axis

A B

Negative

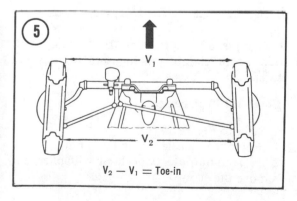

V_1

V_2

$V_2 - V_1 = $ Toe-in

Steering Axis Inclination

On very early automobiles, the front wheels pivoted on a vertical axis. The pivot point was far from the centerline of the tire and caused the wheels to scuff and pull on irregular roads.

To combat this, automobile engineers tilted the steering axis inward (steering axis inclination) and tilted the top of the wheel outward (camber). See **Figure 3**. This placed the pivot point close to the centerline of the wheel.

The actual difference between the pivot point and the wheel is called the scrub radius. If the pivot point is inside the centerline of the wheel, the scrub radius is positive. If the pivot point is outside the wheel centerline, the scrub radius is negative. See **Figure 4**.

Steering axis inclination is a design function and is not adjustable.

Toe

Camber and rolling resistance tend to force the front wheels outward at their forward edge. To compensate for this tendency, the front edges are turned slightly inward or outward when the car is at rest. This is toe. See **Figure 5**.

Toe is adjusted by lengthening or shortening the adjustable tie rod. See **Figure 2**.

STEERING WHEEL

1. Disconnect battery ground cable.
2. Pry horn cover and switch off by hand.
3. Remove steering wheel nut and lockwasher.
4. Remove steering wheel, using a puller. See **Figure 6**.
5. Installation is the reverse of these steps. Tighten steering wheel nut to 60 ft.-lb. (8.3 mkg).

11

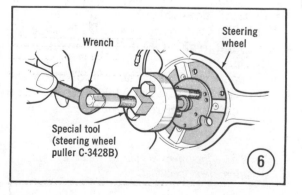

Wrench

Steering wheel

Special tool
(steering wheel
puller C-3428B)

STEERING GEAR

The manual steering gear cannot be repaired. If defective, replace it as described below. Repair of the power steering gear and pump by the amateur mechanic is not recommended, as special skills and tools are required.

Removal/Installation

Refer to **Figure 7** and **Figure 8**.

1. Remove front wheels and both tie rods as described in this chapter.

2. Remove splash and boot seal shields.

3. If equipped with power steering, remove tubes to power steering pump. Drain oil into suitable container.

4. Remove lower roll pin securing drive shaft lower universal joint shaft to steering gear. Remove bolts which mount the steering gear to frame crossmember and remove the assembly from the left side.

5. Installation is the reverse of these steps. After installation, tie rods should be adjusted by a specialist. Tighten crossmember attaching bolts to 21 ft.-lb. (2.9 mkg).

TIE RODS

Outer Tie Rod Replacement

Refer to **Figure 9**.

1. Remove the cotter pin and castle nut and separate the outer tie rod from the steering knuckle.
2. Loosen the jam nut and unthread the outer tie rod from the inner tie rod.
3. To replace, install outer tie rod on inner tie rod, but do not tighten jam nut.
4. Install outer tie rod on steering knuckle and torque nut to about 40 ft.-lb. (5.5 mkg). Install cotter pin.
5. Expand outer boot clamp with pliers and leave clamp loose on rod. Make toe adjustment by turning inner tie rod (do not twist boot).

> *NOTE*
> *Toe adjustment should be made by an alignment specialist.*

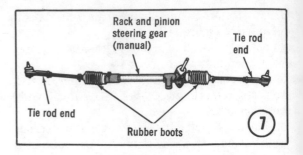

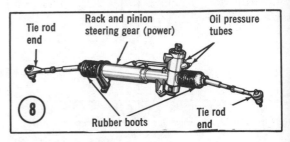

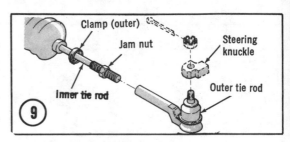

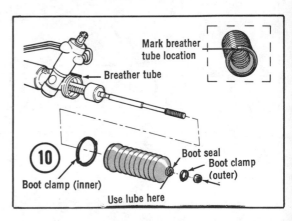

6. Torque jam nut to 50 ft.-lb. (7 mkg). Install outer boot clamp, making sure boot is not twisted.

Boot Seal Replacement

Refer to **Figure 10**.

1. Remove outer tie rod and jam nut.
2. Expand the outer boot clamp with pliers and remove the clamp.

3. Cut, remove, and discard the inner boot clamp. See **Figure 11**.

4. Mark the location of the breather tube on the boot, then remove the boot.

5. To replace, install boot on the inner tie rod and align mark made during removal with breather tube.

6. Place the inner boot seal over the steering gear housing lip, making sure hole in boot lines up with breather tube. Install new inner boot clamp (**Figure 11**).

NOTE
*A special clamping tool (C-4124) is required to install the clamp. See **Figure 11**.*

You may be able to devise a substitute if this tool cannot be obtained.

Inner Tie Rod Replacement

1. Remove the steering gear assembly from the car as described earlier in this chapter.

2. Remove the boot seals as described earlier.

3. Remove the shock dampener ring from the inner tie rod housing and slide it back on the rack. See **Figure 12**.

4. Use 2 wrenches as shown in **Figure 12** and turn inner tie rod housing counterclockwise

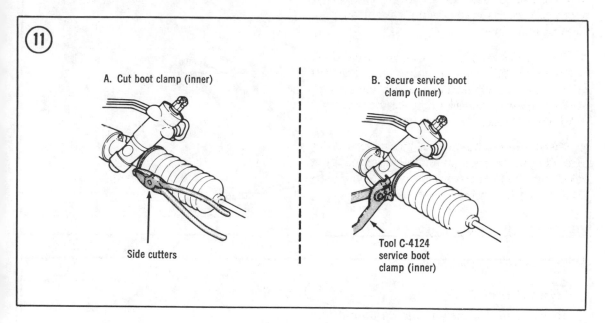

A. Cut boot clamp (inner)

Side cutters

B. Secure service boot clamp (inner)

Tool C-4124 service boot clamp (inner)

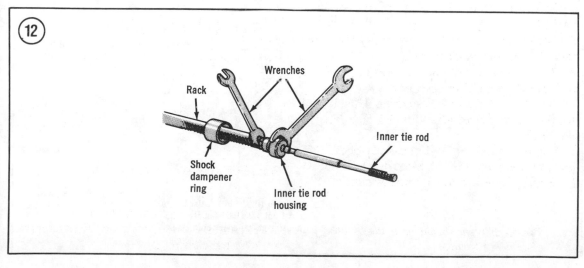

Rack

Wrenches

Shock dampener ring

Inner tie rod housing

Inner tie rod

until the inner tie rod separates from the steering gear rack.

5. To replace, install the inner tie rod on the rack and hand tighten as far as possible.

6. Use a crow's foot and torque wrench as shown in **Figure 13** to tighten housing to 70 ft.-lb. (9.7 mkg). Hold the rack with a wrench as shown to avoid internal damage to the steering gear assembly.

7. Stake the tie rod housing to the rack flat as shown in **Figure 14**. Support the assembly on a vise or anvil as shown, to avoid damage. Stake both sides.

8. Check the clearance between the rack and housing stake on both sides with a 0.010 in. (0.25 mm) feeler gauge. The gauge must not pass between the rack and housing stake.

9. Slip shock dampener ring over inner tie rod housing until it is engaged.

DRIVE SHAFTS

Drive shaft replacement procedures vary according to the transaxle model and drive shaft type (**Figure 15**). The GKN design was introduced as a running change on some 1982 models and is used on all 1983 vehicles.

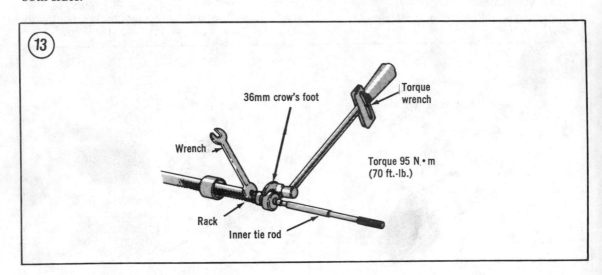

(13)

Wrench

36mm crow's foot

Torque wrench

Torque 95 N•m (70 ft.-lb.)

Rack

Inner tie rod

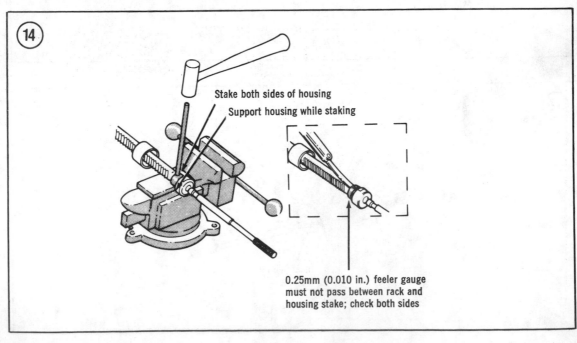

(14)

Stake both sides of housing

Support housing while staking

0.25mm (0.010 in.) feeler gauge must not pass between rack and housing stake; check both sides

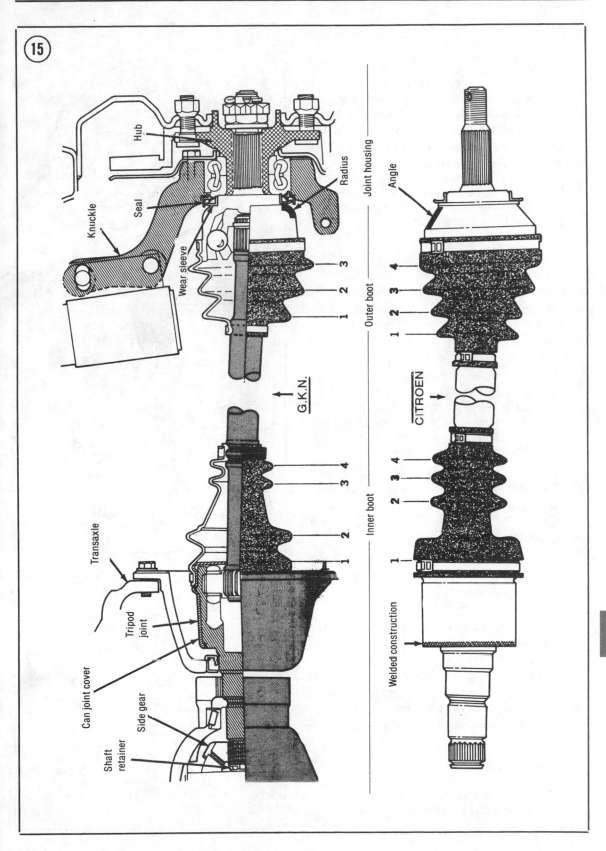

15

Hub

Knuckle

Seal

Wear sleeve

Radius

Joint housing

Angle

Outer boot

1 2 3

1 2 3 4

G.K.N.

CITROEN

Transaxle

Tripod joint

Can joint cover

Side gear

Shaft retainer

Inner boot

1 2 3 4

Welded construction

11

CAUTION
Moving a front-wheel drive vehicle on its wheels with the drive shaft removed will cause bearing damage. The front bearing must be loaded by the outer end of the drive shaft and a properly torqued hub retaining nut if the vehicle is moved on its wheels.

Removal/Installation (A-412 Manual Transaxle)

1. Loosen hub nuts while car is still on the ground, then raise car and remove hub nuts and wheel assemblies. See **Figure 16**.

WARNING
Never loosen hub nuts unless all 4 wheels are firmly on the ground. The force required to loosen a nut could knock the car off a jack or jackstands.

2. Remove the clamp bolt (**Figure 17**) and separate the ball-joint stud from the steering knuckle as shown in **Figure 18**.

CAUTION
Support both ends of the drive shaft during removal to prevent damage to boots. Also exercise care when separating ball-joint from steering knuckle to avoid damage to boots.

3. Hold constant velocity joint housing and pull on knuckle hub assembly to separate outer constant velocity joint splined shaft from hub. See **Figure 19**. Support the drive shaft by tying it to the control arm.

CAUTION
*Take care to avoid bending grease slinger (**Figure 19**). Do not attempt to remove, repair, or replace the slinger.*

4. Remove the 6 Allen head screws attaching the inner constant velocity joint to the transaxle drive flange. See **Figure 20**. On all 1979 and later models, it is necessary to first remove the plastic caps from the Allen head screws by prying under the cap and against the inner joint flange. Wipe the joint and drive flange free of foreign material.

NOTE
Chrysler recommends the use of special tool part No. L-4550 for removing the Allen head screws. An 8 mm Allen wrench or socket with extension could be substituted.

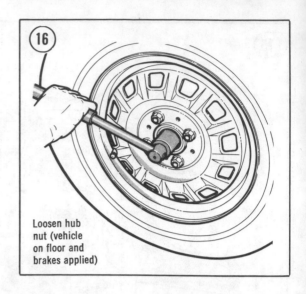

Loosen hub nut (vehicle on floor and brakes applied)

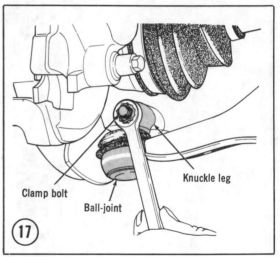

Knuckle leg

Clamp bolt

Ball-joint

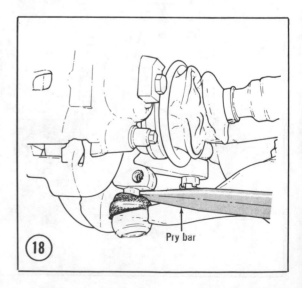

Pry bar

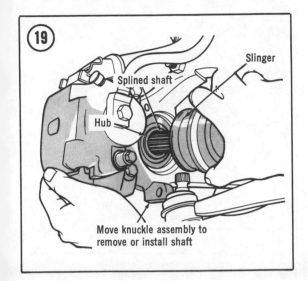

⑲

Slinger

Splined shaft

Hub

Move knuckle assembly to
remove or install shaft

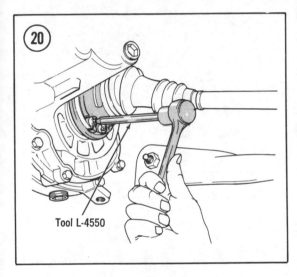

⑳

Tool L-4550

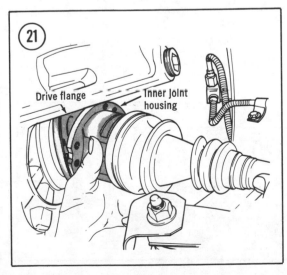

㉑

Drive flange   Inner joint
housing

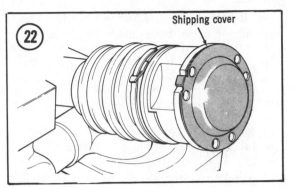

㉒

Shipping cover

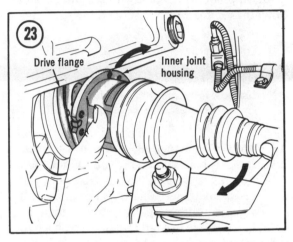

㉓

Drive flange   Inner joint
housing

5. Untie the outer assembly from the control
arm and hold the inner and outer housings
parallel. Rotate the outer housing down while
pivoting the inner housing up at the drive flange
as shown in **Figure 21** to remove the drive shaft
assembly. Following this procedure will prevent
loss of lubricant from the inner constant velocity
joint.

6. Remove the shipping cover, if installed, from
the replacement drive shaft (if new drive shaft is
to be installed). See **Figure 22**. Fill the inner
constant velocity joint with lubricant (part No.
4131389 or equivalent).

7. Before installation, clean all grease from
joint housing, face, screw holes, and transaxle
drive flange.

8. Position the housing to the drive flange as
shown in **Figure 23** and rotate the assembly up
to seat the inner housing in the drive flange.
Support the outer end of the drive shaft, and do
not move the inner constant velocity joint in and
out, as the pumping action could force the
special lubricant out of the joint. See **Figure 23**.

11

9. Install 6 new Allen head screws to attach the inner housing to the drive flange. Torque screws to 18 ft.-lb. (2.5 mkg). See **Figure 24**.

10. Push knuckle hub assembly out and install outer constant velocity joint in hub as shown in **Figure 25**.

11. Install knuckle assembly on ball-joint stud as shown in **Figure 26**. Install the clamp bolt and tighten to 50 ft.-lb. (7 mkg). See **Figure 27**.

12A. For 1978 models, install a new hub nut and torque to 200 ft.-lb. (27.8 mkg) with the brakes applied. See **Figure 28**. Stake hub nut as shown in **Figure 29**.

> *CAUTION*
> *Always use a new hub nut, as use of an old one could lead to improper torque reading and resultant improper preloading. Use a staking tool with the dimensions given in **Figure 29**. Do not use a sharp chisel or a punch.*

12B. On 1979-on models, clean hub threads and install washer and new hub nut (**Figure 30**). With the brakes applied, torque hub nut to 180 ft.-lb. (24.5 mkg). See **Figure 28**. Place the nut lock over the hub nut, making sure to align the nut lock with hole in shaft threads. Install a new cotter pin and secure by bending arms of cotter pins as shown in **Figure 31**.

Removal/Installation
(A-460 and A-465 Manual, All Automatic Transaxles)

> *NOTE*
> *Inner constant velocity joints are splined into the differential side gears. Non-spring loaded (Citroen) shafts are*

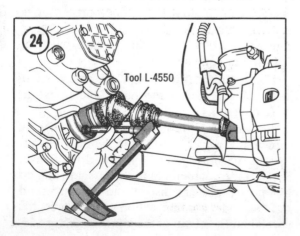

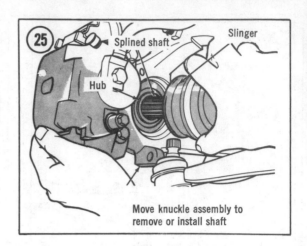

Move knuckle assembly to remove or install shaft

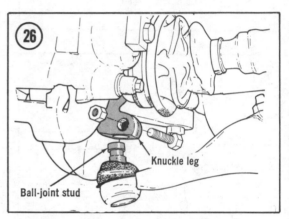

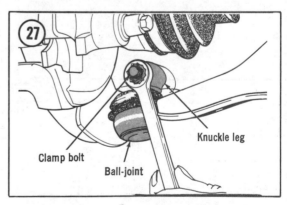

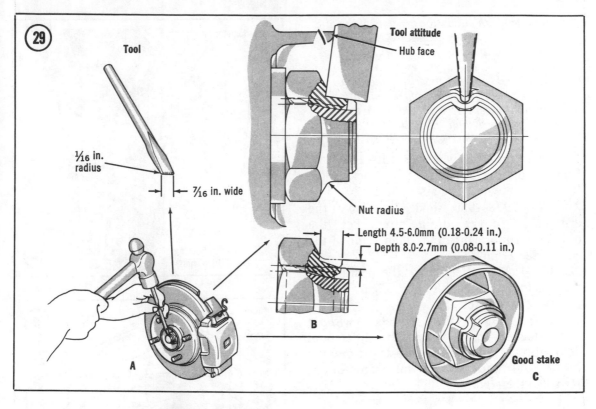

29

Tool

Tool attitude

Hub face

1/16 in. radius

7/16 in. wide

Nut radius

Length 4.5-6.0mm (0.18-0.24 in.)

Depth 8.0-2.7mm (0.08-0.11 in.)

A

B

Good stake

C

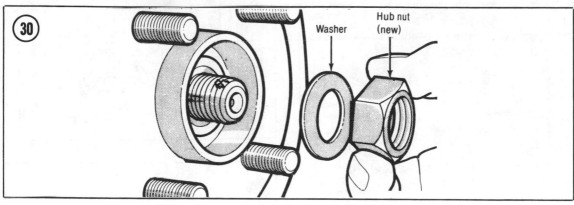

30

Washer

Hub nut (new)

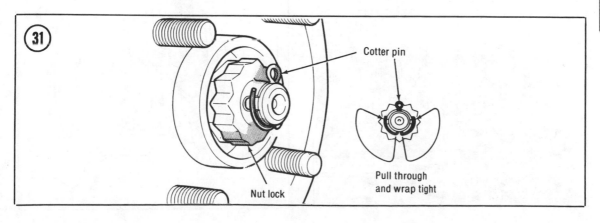

31

Cotter pin

Nut lock

Pull through and wrap tight

11

retained with circlips on the ends of the stub shafts. Spring-loaded GKN shafts are held in place by a spring within the joint. GKN shafts are used on some 1982 and all 1983 models. If the joint can be pried out of the differential, it is spring-loaded. If equipped with this type of drive shaft, omit Steps 2, 3, 7 and 11 of the following procedure.

1. Loosen the front wheel lug nuts. Raise the front of the car and place it on jackstands. Remove the wheel/tire assemblies.

2A. For 1978-1980 models, remove the differential cover drain plug. Let the differential lubricant drain, then remove the cover. See **Figure 32**.

2B. For 1981 models, mark the position of the resistor bracket as shown in **Figure 33** and remove the bracket.

2C. For 1981-1982 models *without* spring-loaded shafts, loosen the differential cover bolts, pull the cover away from the differential and let the lubricant drain. Remove the cover.

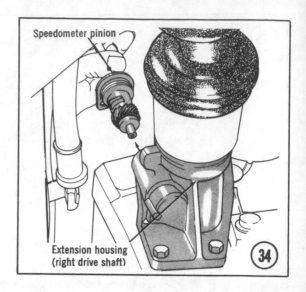

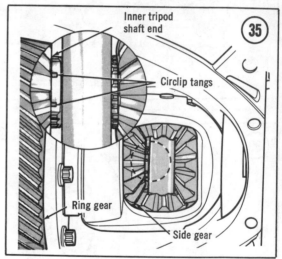

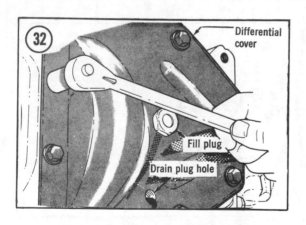

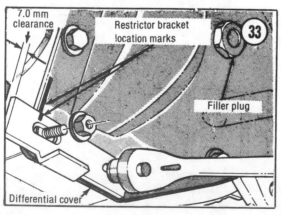

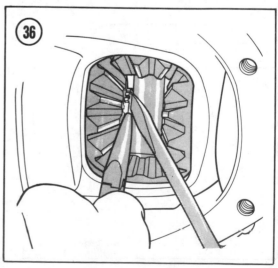

NOTE
If the right side drive shaft is being re-
moved, it is necessary to remove the
speedometer pinion from the right drive
*shaft extension housing. See **Figure 34**.*

3. Rotate drive shaft until the circlip tangs are exposed in the differential opening (**Figure 35**). Compress the tangs with needle-nose pliers and push the drive shaft and compressed circlip into the side gear as shown in **Figure 36**.

4. Remove the clamp bolt (**Figure 37**) and separate the ball-joint from the knuckle as shown in **Figure 38**. Take care not to damage the ball-joint or constant velocity joint boots.

5. Separate the outer constant velocity joint splined shaft from hub as shown in **Figure 39**. Do not pry on or attempt to remove grease slinger on the constant velocity joint.

6. Grasp the assembly at the constant velocity joint housings as shown in **Figure 40** and pull outward on the inner joint housing to remove the drive shaft assembly. Do not pull on the drive shaft or the outer joint. When removing the left drive shaft assembly, use a screwdriver applied between the differential pinion shaft and the end face of the splined stub shaft to assist in removal.

7. Align tangs of circlip with flat side of shaft (**Figure 41**) and grasp shaft assembly by the 2

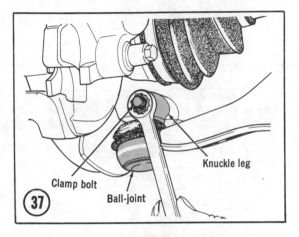

Knuckle leg
Clamp bolt
Ball-joint
(37)

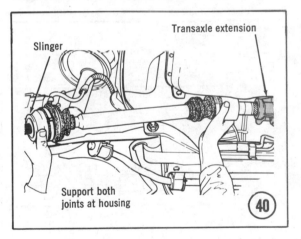

Slinger
Transaxle extension
Support both
joints at housing
(40)

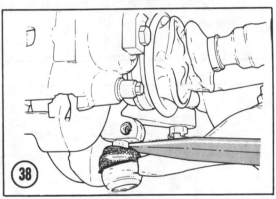

(38)

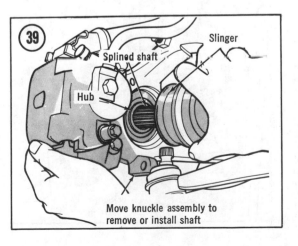

(39)
Splined shaft
Slinger
Hub
Move knuckle assembly to
remove or install shaft

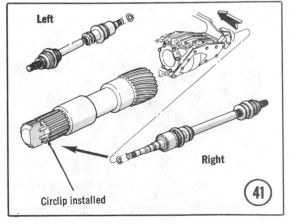

Left
Right
Circlip installed
(41)

11

constant velocity joint housings. Align the splines of the inner stub shaft with those in the differential, compress the circlip, and guide into the transaxle (**Figure 42**). A quick thrust applied to the inner joint housing should cause the stub axle to seat the circlip to lock it in place. Inspect circlip to make sure it is locked in position (**Figure 35**).

8. Push out on the knuckle hub assembly and install the splined stub shaft of the outer constant velocity joint in the hub (**Figure 43**).

9. Install the knuckle on the ball-joint stud (**Figure 44**) and tighten clamp bolt to 50 ft.-lb. (7 mkg). See **Figure 45**.

10. Install the speedometer pinion (**Figure 46**).

11. Apply a ribbon of RTV gasket material to the differential cover and install the cover. Torque retaining screws to 21 ft.-lb. (2.9 mkg). Fill the differential with DEXRON II automatic transmission fluid.

12. For 1981 models only, install the restrictor bracket and align the marks made during re-

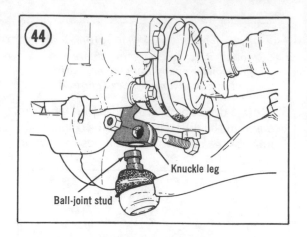

Knuckle leg
Ball-joint stud

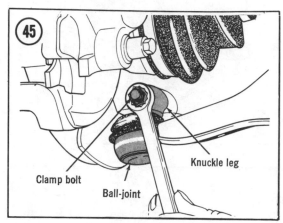

Knuckle leg
Clamp bolt
Ball-joint

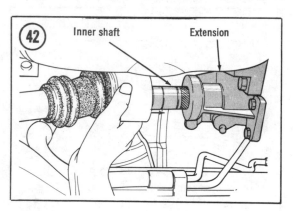

Inner shaft   Extension

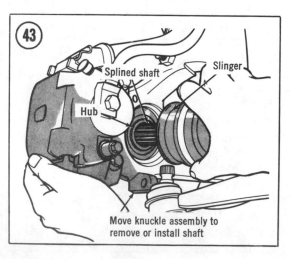

Splined shaft   Slinger
Hub
Move knuckle assembly to remove or install shaft

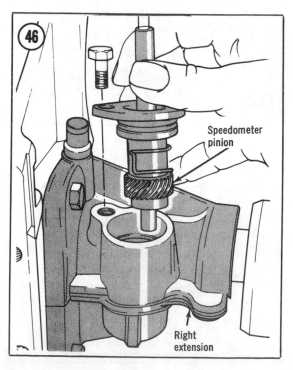

Speedometer pinion
Right extension

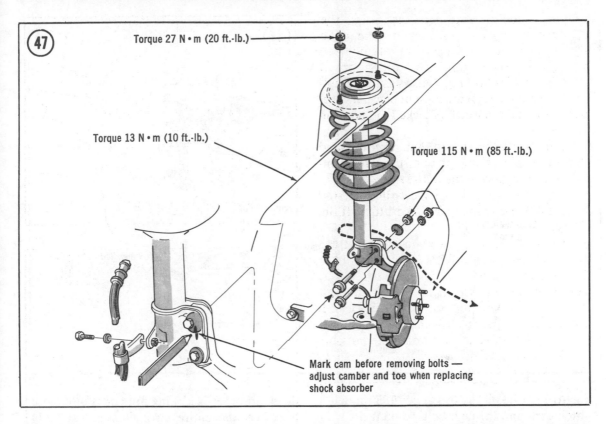

(47) Torque 27 N • m (20 ft.-lb.)

Torque 13 N • m (10 ft.-lb.)

Torque 115 N • m (85 ft.-lb.)

Mark cam before removing bolts —
adjust camber and toe when replacing
shock absorber

moval. Make sure to maintain a 9/32 in. (7 mm) clearance at the bracket edge as shown in **Figure 33**.

13A. For 1978 models, install a new hub nut and torque to 200 ft.-lb. (27.8 mkg) with the brakes applied. See **Figure 28**. Stake hub nut as shown in **Figure 29**.

> *CAUTION*
> *Always use a new hub nut, as use of an old one could lead to improper torque reading and resultant improper preloading. Use a staking tool with the dimensions given in **Figure 29**. Do not use a sharp chisel or a punch.*

13B. For 1979-on models, clean hub threads and install washer and new hub nut (**Figure 30**). With the brakes applied, torque hub nut to 180 ft.-lb. (24.5 mkg). See **Figure 28**. Place the nut lock over the hub nut, making sure to align the nut lock with hole in shaft threads. Install a new cotter pin and secure by bending arms of cotter pins as shown in **Figure 31**.

Constant Velocity Joints

If constant velocity joints require service or replacement, remove the drive shafts as pre-

viously described and take them to your dealer. Service of these joints requires special skills and tools.

SUSPENSION STRUTS

Removal/Installation

1. Loosen the front wheel lug nuts. Raise the front of the car and place it on jackstands. Remove the wheel/tire assembly.

2. If the strut is to be reinstalled, mark the cam eccentric bolt as shown in **Figure 47**. Remove the cam eccentric bolt, through bolt and brake hose-to-damper bracket retaining screw.

3. Remove the 2 nuts attaching the strut damper to the fender shield, then remove the strut from the car as shown by the dashed arrow in **Figure 47**.

4. Installation is the reverse of removal. Torque nuts holding strut damper to fender to 20 ft.-lb. (17 N•m) and brake hose-to-damper screw to 10 ft.-lb. (13 N•m). Index cam eccentric bolt to mark made in Step 2. On 1978-1982 models, tighten cam and through

11

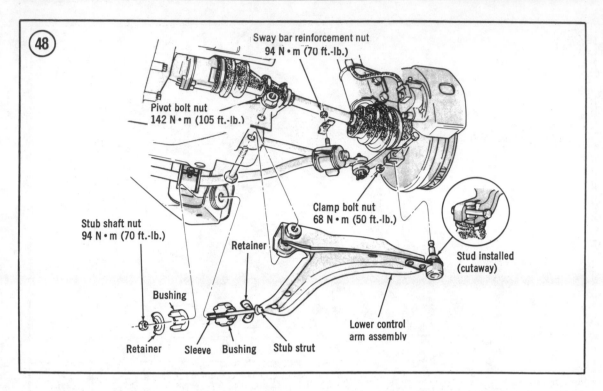

48

Sway bar reinforcement nut
94 N • m (70 ft.-lb.)

Pivot bolt nut
142 N • m (105 ft.-lb.)

Stub shaft nut
94 N • m (70 ft.-lb.)

Retainer

Clamp bolt nut
68 N • m (50 ft.-lb.)

Stud installed
(cutaway)

Bushing

Retainer   Sleeve   Bushing   Stub strut

Lower control
arm assembly

---

bolts to 85 ft.-lb. (115 N•m). On 1983 models, tighten cam and through bolts to 45 ft.-lb. (61 N•m), then tighten 1/4 additional turn. Install wheel and tighten lug nuts to 80 ft.-lb. (108 N•m).

Disassembly/Assembly

This procedure is impossible without a special spring compressor tool; it would be dangerous to improvise a tool. Remove the strut and take it to your dealer as disassembly is required to replace the coil spring, shock absorbers, or strut parts.

COIL SPRING REPLACEMENT

The coil spring is part of the suspension strut assembly. Since coil spring replacement requires disassembly of the suspension strut with a special tool, remove the strut assembly as described earlier and let a dealer replace the spring. Install the assembly following the same procedure.

SHOCK ABSORBER REPLACEMENT

The shock absorber is an integral part of the suspension strut damper assembly. If the

shock absorber is leaking fluid or is otherwise defective, the entire strut damper assembly must be replaced. Remove the strut assembly as described in this chapter and have a dealer install its spring on a new strut. Install the assembly following the same procedure.

LOWER BALL-JOINTS

Removal/Installation (Early 1978 Rivet Type Ball-joint)

Early 1978 production models were equipped with ball-joints that were riveted to the lower control arm. If the riveted type ball-joint requires replacement, the entire lower control arm and ball-joint assembly must be replaced.
1. Raise vehicle and remove pivot bolt, stub, strut nut, retainer and bushing, and ball-joint to steering knuckle clamp bolt. See **Figure 48**.
2. Separate the ball-joint stud from the steering knuckle with a pry bar.

CAUTION
Do not pull the steering knuckle away from the vehicle, as this can cause the inner constant velocity joint to separate.

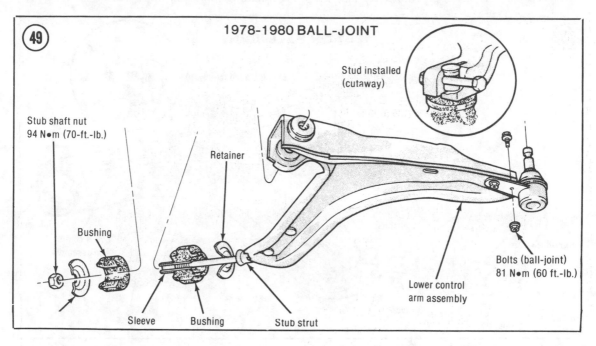

1978-1980 BALL-JOINT

Stud installed (cutaway)

Stub shaft nut
94 N•m (70-ft.-lb.)

Retainer

Bushing

Bolts (ball-joint)
81 N•m (60 ft.-lb.)

Lower control
arm assembly

Sleeve   Bushing   Stub strut

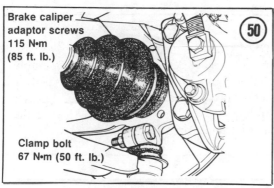

Brake caliper
adaptor screws
115 N•m
(85 ft. lb.)

Clamp bolt
67 N•m (50 ft. lb.)

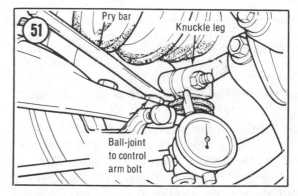

Pry bar   Knuckle leg

Ball-joint
to control
arm bolt

3. Remove the sway bar reinforcement nut and rotate the control arm over the sway bar. Remove the rear stub strut bushing, sleeve and retainer. Inspect control arm for distortion and bushings for deterioration.

4. Installation is the reverse of these steps. Tighten sway bar reinforcement nut to 70 ft.-lb. (9.7 mkg). Tighten ball-joint clamp bolt to 50 ft.-lb. (6.9 mkg). Install pivot bolt and nut and stub strut nut, then lower car and tighten pivot bolt to 105 ft.-lb. (14.6 mkg) and strut nut to 70 ft.-lb. (9.7 mkg).

Inspection
(1978-1980 Bolted Type Ball-joint)

Ball-joints on late model 1978 through 1980 cars are bolted to the lower control arm with the joint stud retained in the steering knuckle with a clamp bolt. See **Figure 49**.

1. Raise vehicle front end and secure with jackstands.

2. Make sure that the ball-joint clamp bolt is torqued to 50 ft.-lb. (6.7 mkg). See **Figure 50**.

3. Install a dial indicator to the lower control arm and place the dial indicator plunger tip against the steering knuckle leg as shown in **Figure 51**.

4. Place a pry bar between the steering knuckle leg and the ball-joint housing with the bar resting on top of the ball-joint to control arm bolt. See **Figure 51**.

5. Read the steering knuckle leg axial travel off the dial indicator by raising and lowering the

11

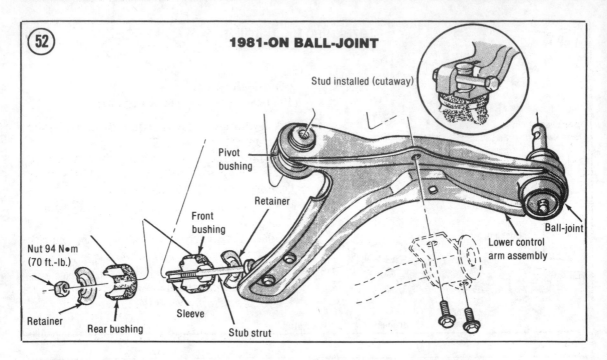

1981-ON BALL-JOINT

Stud installed (cutaway)

Pivot bushing

Retainer

Front bushing

Nut 94 N•m (70 ft.-lb.)

Retainer

Rear bushing

Sleeve

Stub strut

Ball-joint

Lower control arm assembly

steering knuckle with the pry bar. If an axial travel of 0.050 in. (1.2 mm) or more is obtained, the ball-joints should be replaced.

Removal/Installation (1978-1980 Bolted Type Ball-joint)

1. Remove the steering knuckle-to-ball-joint stud clamp bolt. Separate the ball-joint stud from the steering knuckle. See **Figure 50**.
2. Remove bolts securing the ball-joint housing to the lower control arm.
3. Position new ball-joint housing onto the control arm. Install new attaching bolts and tighten to 60 ft.-lb. (8.1 mkg).
4. Raise the lower control arm assembly and place the ball-joint into the steering knuckle. Secure with new clamp bolt and tighten to 50 ft.-lb. (6.7 mkg).

Inspection (1981-on Pressed Type Ball-joint)

The ball-joint housing is pressed into the lower control arm. The ball-joint stud is retained in the steering knuckle with a clamp bolt. See **Figure 52**.

1. Park the vehicle on a level road surface.
2. Grasp the grease fitting as shown in **Figure 53** and attempt to move the fitting.

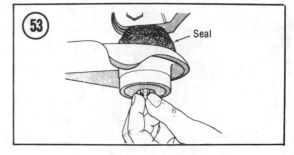

Seal

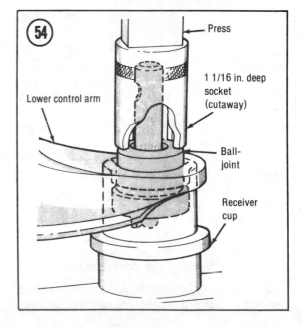

Press

Lower control arm

1 1/16 in. deep socket (cutaway)

Ball-joint

Receiver cup

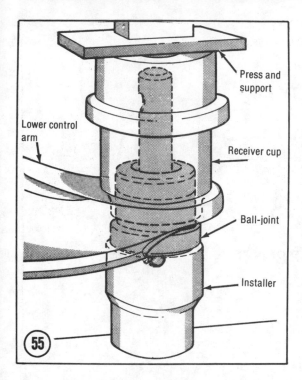

55

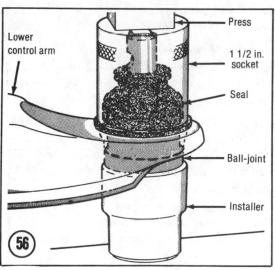

56

3. Ball-joint replacement is required if any movement is felt when performing Step 2.

Removal/Installation
(1981-on Pressed Type Ball-joint)

A hydraulic press is required for ball-joint replacement.

1. Remove the lower control arm as described under *Removal/Installation (Early 1978 Rivet Type Ball-joint)* in this section.

2. Pry off the upper ball-joint seal using a screwdriver.

3. Place the lower control arm in a press and support as shown in **Figure 54**. Then place a 1 1/16 in. deep socket over the ball-joint stud and against the upper joint housing and press the ball-joint assembly out of the lower control arm.

4. Position a new ball-joint into the control arm cavity. Place the assembly into a press and support as shown in **Figure 55**.

5. Press the ball-joint into the lower control arm until the ball-joint housing ledge stops against the control arm cavity down flange (**Figure 55**).

6. Press on a new ball-joint seal using a 1 1/2 in. socket. See **Figure 56**.

7. Install the lower control arm as described under *Removal/Installation (Early 1978 Rivet Type Ball-joint)* in this section.

STEERING KNUCKLES/ WHEEL BEARINGS

Removal and installation of the steering knuckles and wheel bearings require many special tools, including an arbor press. Steering knuckle and wheel bearing service should be referred to your dealer.

11

Table 1 FRONT SUSPENSION SPECIFICATIONS

Item	Acceptable	Preferred
Camber	-0.2° to plus 0.8°	+0.3°
Toe		
1978-1980	5/32 in. out to 1/8 in. in	1/16 in. out
1981-on	7/32 in. out to 1/8 in. in	1/16 in. out
Caster	Not adjustable	
Steering gear	Rack-and-pinion	
turns lock-to-lock	4.0	

CHAPTER TWELVE

REAR SUSPENSION

This chapter provides repair and replacement procedures for the rear suspension. Specifications (**Table 1**) are found at the end of the chapter. Except for wheel bearings, no maintenance or periodic adjustment is required.

> *CAUTION*
> *When a hoist is used to raise the vehicle, additional weight must be placed on the rear of the vehicle or the vehicle must be secured to the hoist before removing heavy rear suspension components. This is necessary to prevent tipping when the center of gravity changes.*

PASSENGER CAR REAR SUSPENSION

The passenger car rear suspension system is shown in **Figure 1**.

Shock Absorber Replacement

The rear shock absorbers are removed with the rear coil springs. To replace the shock absorbers, refer to the *Rear Coil Springs* section, below.

Rear Coil Springs
Removal/Installation

Refer to **Figure 1**.

1. Raise rear wheels clear of the ground.

2. Remove cover from upper shock absorber mount. See **Figure 2**.

3. Remove mounting nut, washer, and rubber disc shown in **Figure 2**.

4. Loosen and remove the lower shock absorber mounting bolt (**Figure 3**) and remove the coil spring assembly.

5. Installation is the reverse of these steps. Tighten upper mounting nut to 20 ft.-lb. (2.8 mkg). Tighten lower bolt to 40 ft.-lb. (5.6 mkg).

Rear Coil Springs
Disassembly/Assembly

Disassembly and assembly of the coil spring/shock absorber strut requires special tools and should be referred to your dealer.

> *WARNING*
> *Do not attempt to disassemble coil spring/shock absorber without using an approved spring compressor. The spring is under tension and could cause injury if released without restraint.*

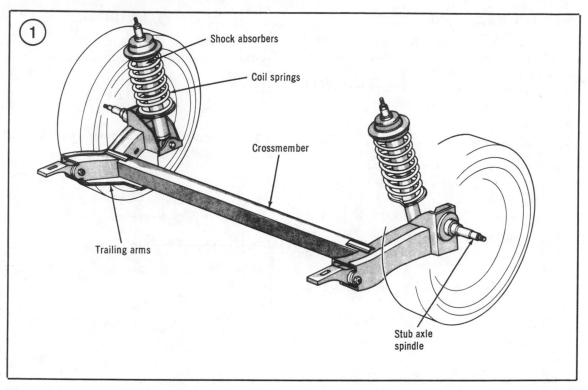

① Shock absorbers

Coil springs

Crossmember

Trailing arms

Stub axle
spindle

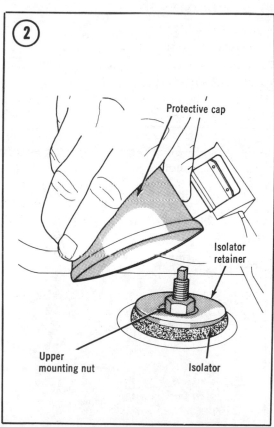

② Protective cap

Isolator
retainer

Upper
mounting nut

Isolator

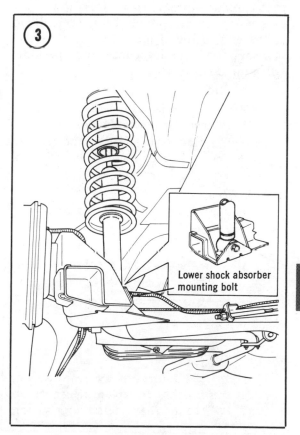

③ Lower shock absorber
mounting bolt

12

Stub Axle Replacement

Since both toe and camber must be adjusted when stub axles are replaced, all such work must be done on an alignment rack. Therefore, replacement work should be referred to your dealer or an alignment specialist.

Rear Axle
Removal/Installation

Refer to **Figure 1** for this procedure. See lifting CAUTION at beginning of this chapter, if hoist is used instead of jackstands.

1. Raise rear of vehicle on jackstands.

2. Remove both rear wheels.

3. Remove brake fittings and retaining clips. See **Figure 4**.

4. Remove parking brake cable adjusting connection nut. See **Figure 5**.

5. Release parking brake cables from brackets by slipping ball ends through connectors. Pull cable through bracket.

6. Remove cover from upper shock absorber mount.

7. Remove mounting nut, washer, and rubber disc shown in **Figure 2**.

8. Support rear axle with a garage jack.

9. Remove bolts securing shock absorbers and securing trailing arms to hanger bracket. See **Figure 6**.

10. Lower rear axle clear of body.

11. Installation is the reverse of removal. Tighten brake fittings to 10 ft.-lb. (13 N•m). Install fasteners finger-tight and lower vehicle to ground. Tighten fasteners to 40 ft.-lb. (56 N•m) with vehicle weight resting on suspension.

WHEEL BEARINGS

See *Rear Brake Drums*, Chapter Nine, for replacement and adjustment of the rear wheel bearings.

PICKUP TRUCK
REAR SUSPENSION

Pickup models use a tubular axle with leaf springs (**Figure 7**).

CAUTION
Do not install adjustable air shock absorbers or "helper" springs. These load-leveling devices will cause the rear

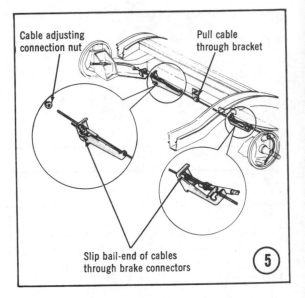

Cable adjusting connection nut

Pull cable through bracket

Slip bail-end of cables through brake connectors

5

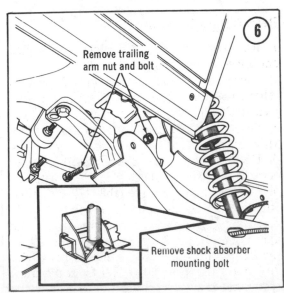

6

Remove trailing arm nut and bolt

Remove shock absorber mounting bolt

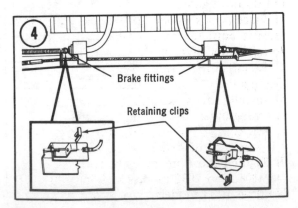

4

Brake fittings

Retaining clips

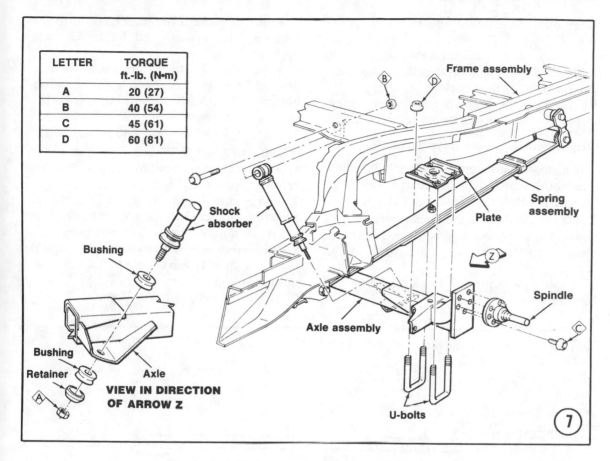

LETTER	TORQUE ft.-lb. (N•m)
A	20 (27)
B	40 (54)
C	45 (61)
D	60 (81)

Shock absorber

Bushing

Bushing

Retainer   Axle

VIEW IN DIRECTION OF ARROW Z

Frame assembly

Spring assembly

Plate

Spindle

Axle assembly

U-bolts

brake height sensing proportioning valve to misinterpret the load condition and their use may contribute to poor handling and/or erratic braking.

Rear Springs Removal

1. Raise the rear of the vehicle with a jack and place it on jackstands.

2. Raise the axle assembly with a jack to relieve its weight from the rear springs. Install jackstands to hold the axle in this position.

3. Disconnect the rear brake proportioning valve spring.

4. Disconnect the rear shock absorber lower ends at the axle bracket.

5. Loosen and remove the U-bolt nuts. Remove the U-bolts and spring plate.

6. Remove the jackstands from under the axle assembly and lower the axle enough with the jack to allow the rear springs to hang free.

7. Unbolt the front pivot bolt from the front spring hanger.

8. Remove the rear spring shackle nuts. Remove the shackles from the spring.

9. Remove the spring.

Rear Springs Installation

1. Install the shackle and bushings in the rear of the spring and spring hanger. Start the shackle bolt nuts but do not tighten.

2. Align the front of the spring with the hanger and install the pivot bolt. Start the nut but do not tighten.

3. Place a jack under the axle assembly and raise it until the axle is centered under the spring center bolt.

4. Install the spring plate with U-bolts. Tighten the U-bolt nuts to 60 ft.-lb. (81 N•m).

5. Install shock absorbers and start the attaching nuts.

6. Lower the vehicle to the floor to put the full weight of the truck on the wheels.

7. Tighten the front pivot bolt to 115 ft.-lb. (155 N•m) on 1982 models and 95 ft.-lb. (128 N•m) on 1983 models.

12

8. Tighten the shackle nuts to 35 ft.-lb. (47 N•m).

9. Tighten the shock absorber nuts to 20 ft.-lb. (27 N•m) on 1982 models and 40 ft.-lb. (54 N•m) on 1983 models.

10. Connect the height sensing valve spring. Adjust the valve as described in this chapter.

Height Sensing Valve Adjustment

If a new height sensing valve is installed, bleed both rear brakes. Refer to **Figure 8** for this procedure.

1. Raise the rear of the vehicle with a jack and place it on jackstands. Rear suspension must hang free and shock absorbers extend fully.

2. Loosen the adjusting bracket nuts (A and B, **Figure 8**).

3. Push the valve lever (C, **Figure 8**) to the rear until it bottoms and hold it in this position.

4. Rotate the adjustment bracket to the rear until all free play is removed from the spring, but do not stretch the spring. Hold the bracket in this position.

5. Release the valve lever and tighten nut B (**Figure 8**) enough to hold the bracket in place.

6. Mark the position of bracket nut B on the bracket support (E, **Figure 8**).

7. Loosen nut B and rotate the top of the adjustment bracket to the rear until nut B is 1/8 in. forward of the no free play position.

8. Without moving the bracket, tighten nut B to 250 in.-lb. (21 N•m). Tighten nut A to 250 in.-lb. (21 N•m).

9. Lower the vehicle to the floor.

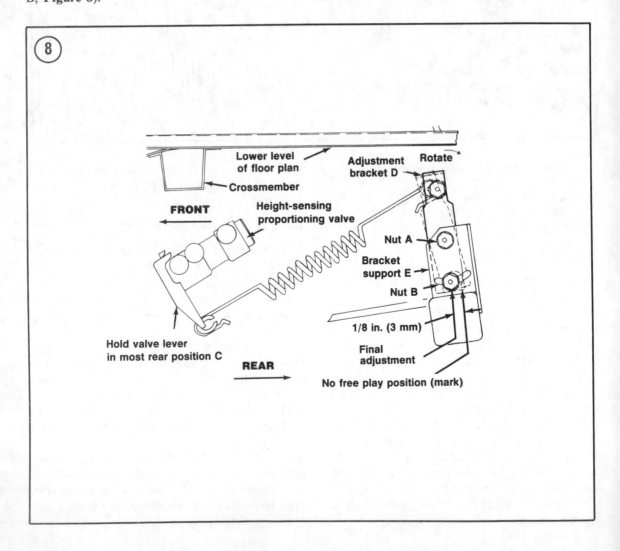

Table 1 REAR SUSPENSION SPECIFICATIONS

Type	Independent
Wheel alignment	
Camber	
1978-1981	-1.0°
1982-on	
Cars	-0.75°
Pickup	-0.6°
Toe	
Range	5/32 in. out to 11/31 in. in
Preferred	3/32 in. in

12

SUPPLEMENT

1984 AND LATER SERVICE INFORMATION

This supplement contains service and maintenance information for 1984 and later Plymouth Horizon/Turismo/Turismo 2.2 and Dodge Omni/Charger/Charger 2.2/Shelby Charger/ Rampage models. The information supplements the procedures in the main body (Chapters One through Twelve) of the book, referred to in this supplement as the "basic book."

The chapter headings and titles in this supplement correspond to those in the basic book. If a chapter is not included in the supplement, there are no changes affecting 1984 and later models.

If your vehicle is covered by this supplement, carefully read the supplement and then read the appropriate chapters in the basic book before beginning any work.

CHAPTER THREE

LUBRICATION, MAINTENANCE AND TUNE-UP

Lubrication, maintenance and tune-up procedures remain unchanged for 1984 and later models except as noted:

Engine Oil and Filter Change

Change the oil in turbocharged engines at 7,500 mile or 6 month intervals. Change the oil filter at alternate oil changes or 6 month intervals. If the vehicle is subjected to severe service conditions, change the oil and filter at 3,000 mile or 3 month intervals.

Chrysler Corporation recommends the use of SAE 5W-30 motor oil for 1986 2.2L engines instead of the previously recommended SAE 10W-30.

Air Cleaner Filter

Fuel-injected turbocharged engines use a remote air cleaner housing. Refer to **Figure 1** for this procedure.

1. Unclamp and disconnect the air cleaner hose at the throttle body adapter.
2. Release the 4 air cleaner housing clips holding the cover to the housing.

3. Lift cover with hose attached from air cleaner housing.
4. Remove the filter element from the air cleaner housing.
5. Install a new filter element in the housing with its screen facing up.
6. With clamp installed on throttle body hose, connect hose to throttle body adapter.
7. Install cover on air cleaner housing and snap clips into place.
8. Tighten throttle body hose clamp to 25 in.-lb. (3.6 N•m).

Fuel Filter

The disposable inline filter canister on fuel-injected turbocharged engines is bracket-mounted to the rear floor pan near the fuel tank. Refer to **Figure 2** for this procedure.

1. Relieve the fuel system pressure. See Chapter Six of this supplement.
2. Raise the rear of the vehicle with a jack and place it on jackstands.

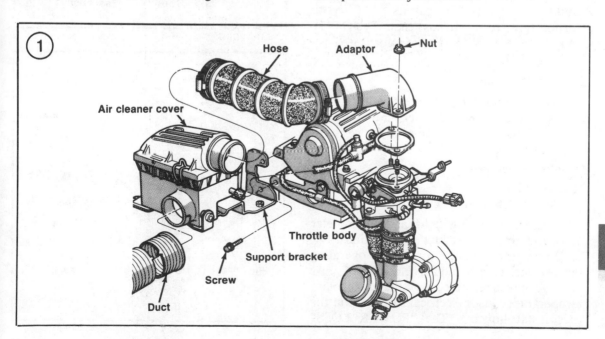

① Hose Adaptor Nut
Air cleaner cover
Throttle body
Support bracket
Screw
Duct

13

3. Loosen the inlet hose clamp at the filter and the outlet hose clamp at the rear fuel line.

4. Wrap the inlet hose with a clean shop cloth at the fitting to absorb any fuel and disconnect the hose. Repeat this step to disconnect the outlet hose. Discard the hose clamps.

5. Loosen the filter retaining screw and slide filter from bracket.

6. Install a new filter in the bracket until the stone shield shoulder touches the bracket, then tighten the retaining screw to 26 in.-lb. (3 N•m).

7. Fit new clamps on the inlet and outlet hoses, then connect the hoses to their respective filter fittings. See **Figure 3**. Tighten the clamps to 10 in.-lb. (1 N•m).

8. Remove the jackstands and lower the vehicle to the ground.

9. Start the engine and check for leaks.

Manual Transaxle Check

Change manual transaxle fluid at 15,000 mile intervals when vehicle is subjected to severe service conditions. Chrysler Corporation recommends the use of a quality SAE 5W-30 engine oil instead of automatic transmission fluid in 1987 transaxles.

Automatic Transmission Fluid

For vehicles which suffer from transaxle shudder during upshifts, Chrysler Corporation recommends that Type 7176 ATF (part No. 4318077) be substituted for DEXRON II.

Drive Belt Tension

A ribbed alternator and water pump drive belt is used on 1984 and later 1.6L and 2.2L engines. This eliminates the need for periodic belt tensioning. Belt deflection specifications remain unchanged.

Ignition Timing
(1985 Turbocharged Engine)

1. Connect a timing light and tachometer according to manufacturer's instructions.

2. Warm the engine to normal operating temperature (upper radiator hose hot).

3. Disconnect/reconnect the coolant temperature sensor electrical connector at the thermostat housing. The "POWER LOSS" warning lamp on the instrument panel should light and stay on.

4. Loosen the distributor hold-down clamp screw.

5. Refer to the VECI label for timing specifications. Turn the distributor housing until the timing marks align when illuminated by the timing light.

6. Tighten the distributor hold-down clamp screw when adjustment is correct. Recheck timing adjustment.

7. Shut the engine off. Disconnect/reconnect the positive battery quick-disconnect.

8. Start the engine. The "POWER LOSS" warning lamp should be off.

9. Shut the engine off, then turn the ignition switch ON/OFF/ON/OFF/ON to clear any fault codes from the system. Turn the switch OFF.

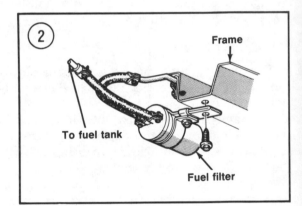

Frame
To fuel tank
Fuel filter

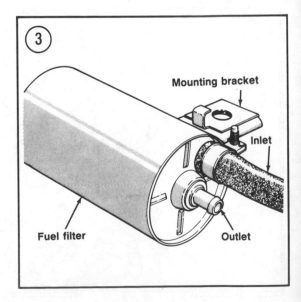

Mounting bracket
Inlet
Fuel filter
Outlet

CHAPTER FOUR

OVERHEAD CAM ENGINES

To extend the life of the camshaft lobes and rocker arms on 1984 and later 2.2L engines, a sintered metal insert is used on the top of each rocker arm where it contacts the camshaft. When replacing a rocker arm, make sure the new one bears the same part number as the one removed.

A high performance version of the 2.2L engine is standard on 1984 Shelby Charger, 1985 Charger 2.2/Turismo 2.2 and optional on some 1984 and later Charger/Turismo models. A fuel-injected turbocharged 2.2L engine is standard on 1985 Shelby Charger and optional on Omni GLH models. Service procedures that differ from those given in Chapter Four of the basic book are provided in this supplement. **Table 1** contains additional and revised specifications for the 1985 2.2L engine. It also includes specifications for the high performance and turbocharged engines that differ from those provided in the basic book. Be certain to relieve fuel system pressure as described in Chapter Six of this supplement before opening any fuel system connections.

CHAPTER FIVE

PUSHROD ENGINE

A new crankshaft front seal design is used on 1984 and later 1.6L engines. The seal is removed with tool part No. C-748 (**Figure 4**) and intalled with tool part No. C-4761.

Table 2 contains specifications for the 1985 1.6L engine that differ from those provided in the basic book.

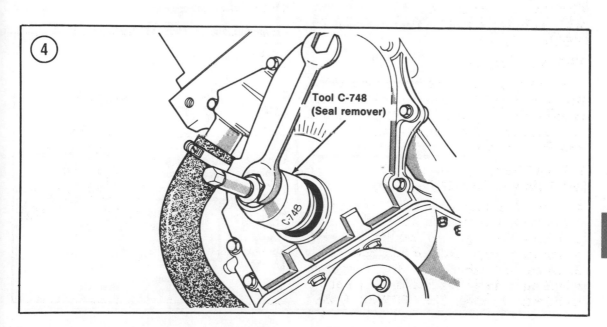

Tool C-748 (Seal remover)

13

CHAPTER SIX

FUEL, EXHAUST AND EMISSION CONTROL SYSTEMS

MULTI-POINT FUEL INJECTION

The turbocharged 2.2L engine is equipped with a multi-point fuel injection system. The fuel rail contains four electrically-operated injectors that meter fuel into the intake air stream under the direction of the logic module. The logic module receives electrical signals from various sensors, refers to its stored program memory and calculates the precise amount and timing of fuel required by the engine. Fuel delivery time of the injectors is modified by the logic module to accomodate special engine operating conditions such as cranking, cold starts, altitude and acceleration/deceleration.

A throttle body connected between the turbocharger and intake manifold provides the air intake system. A throttle position sensor (TPS) and automatic idle speed motor (AIS) are mounted on the throttle body housing. The TPS transmits a voltage signal to the logic module which varies according to the angle of throttle blade opening. The AIS controls the amount of air provided in the air-fuel mixture to maintain a pre-programmed idle speed according to directions from the logic module. **Figure 5** shows the components of the multi-point injection system including the sensors and output devices.

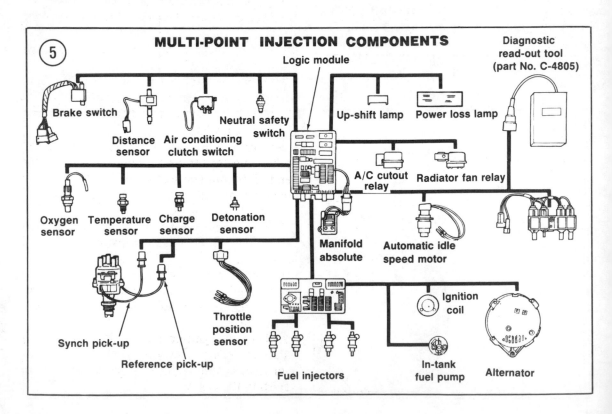

MULTI-POINT INJECTION COMPONENTS

Diagnostic read-out tool (part No. C-4805)

Logic module

Brake switch

Distance sensor

Air conditioning clutch switch

Neutral safety switch

Up-shift lamp

Power loss lamp

A/C cutout relay

Radiator fan relay

Oxygen sensor

Temperature sensor

Charge sensor

Detonation sensor

Manifold absolute

Automatic idle speed motor

Synch pick-up

Throttle position sensor

Reference pick-up

Fuel injectors

Ignition coil

In-tank fuel pump

Alternator

Non-electronic problems affecting system performance may be difficult to diagnose, since the logic module is programmed to compensate for certain problems such as low battery voltage, incorrect cam timing, vacuum leaks, etc.

System Operation

Filtered fuel is supplied to the fuel rail by two electric fuel pumps. A primary fuel pump delivering 55 psi is bracket-mounted to the frame outside the fuel tank; the secondary pump delivers 5 psi and is mounted in the fuel tank. When the ignition switch is turned ON, the automatic shut down (ASD) relay contained within the power module activates the in-tank pump to prime the injectors. If the power module does not receive a reference signal from the distributor, it then shuts down the fuel pump.

Fuel flow is controlled by varying the duration of injection (pulse width) according to signals from the logic module. Injectors are pulsed in pairs (1-2 and 3-4), with each pair pulsing once per crankshaft revolution. Excess fuel passes through a pressure regulator on the fuel rail (**Figure 6**) and is returned to the fuel tank.

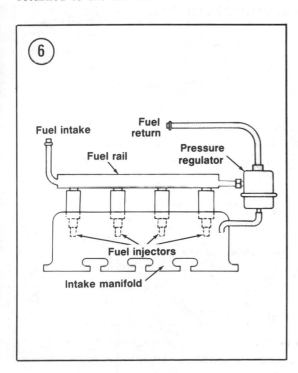

The logic module is pre-programmed to prevent damage from excessive engine speed or tampering with the turbo boost pressure. It will shut the fuel system off if engine speed exceeds 6,650 rpm or if boost pressure exceeds a specified value. When engine speed drops below 6,100 rpm or boost pressure drops below the specified value, the module turns the fuel system back on. If the wastegate malfunctions, the logic module limits engine speed to 2,000 rpm and switches operation to a "limp-in" mode, allowing the vehicle to be returned to a dealer for service.

Since the system is electronically controlled, no attempt should be made to adjust the idle speed or fuel mixture. Owner service should be limited to replacement only. If the fuel injection system is not working properly, take the vehicle to a dealer for diagnosis and adjustment.

System Pressure Relief

The fuel injection system is under a constant pressure of approximately 53 psi. Before opening any fuel connection on a fuel-injected engine, fuel pressure must be relieved to reduce the risk of fire and personal injury.

1. Loosen the fuel tank filler cap to relieve in-tank pressure.

2. Disconnect the wiring harness from the terminals of one injector (**Figure 7**).

3. Connect a jumper lead between one of the injector terminals and ground.

4. Connect one end of a jumper lead to the other injector terminal, then touch the other end of the jumper lead to the positive battery post for several seconds (not to exceed 10 seconds).

5. Remove the jumper leads, reinstall the fuel tank filler cap and perform the necessary fuel system service.

6. When fuel system service has been completed and all lines reconnected, reconnect the wiring harness to the injector terminals.

7. Turn the ignition switch ON, but do not start the engine. Inspect system connections for leaks and repair if necessary before starting the engine.

13

Fuel Rail Removal/Installation

1. Relieve fuel system pressure as described in this supplement.

2. Disconnect the wiring harness from the terminals of each injector (**Figure 7**).

3. Unclamp and disconnect the fuel inlet and return lines at the fuel rail. Plug the lines to prevent leakage.

4. Remove the 4 fuel rail-to-intake manifold bracket screws and 2 bracket-to-heat shield retainer clips.

5. Carefully lift the fuel rail with injectors from the intake manifold.

6. Cover the manifold injector openings to prevent contamination.

7. To separate injectors from the fuel rail, carefully slide the lock ring holding each injector to the rail, then remove the injector from the rail.

8. Installation is the reverse of removal. Tighten the bracket screws to 250 in.-lb. (28 N•m).

FUEL PUMP

Removal/Installation

Refer to **Figure 8**.

Primary pump

1. Relieve fuel system pressure as described in this supplement.

2. Raise the rear of the vehicle with a jack and place it on jackstands.

3. Disconnect the pump wiring.

4. Unclamp and disconnect the pump inlet and outlet hoses. Plug the hoses to prevent leakage.

5. Remove the nut and washer holding the pump to the frame bracket. Remove the pump.

6. Installation is the reverse of removal.

Secondary pump

Refer to **Figure 9** for this procedure.

1. Relieve fuel system pressure as described in this supplement.

2. Disconnect the negative battery cable.

3. Raise the vehicle with a jack and place it on jackstands.

4. Remove the screws holding the filler tube to the quarter panel.

5. Remove the draft tube rubber cap from

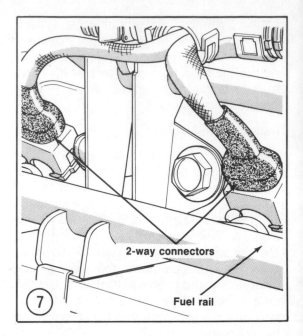

7 · 2-way connectors · Fuel rail

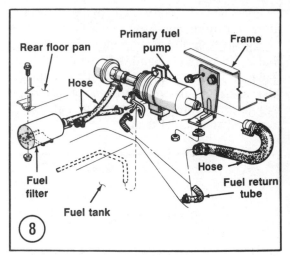

8 · Rear floor pan · Primary fuel pump · Frame · Hose · Hose · Fuel filter · Fuel return tube · Fuel tank

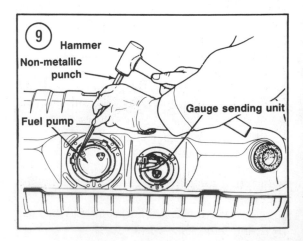

9 · Hammer · Non-metallic punch · Gauge sending unit · Fuel pump

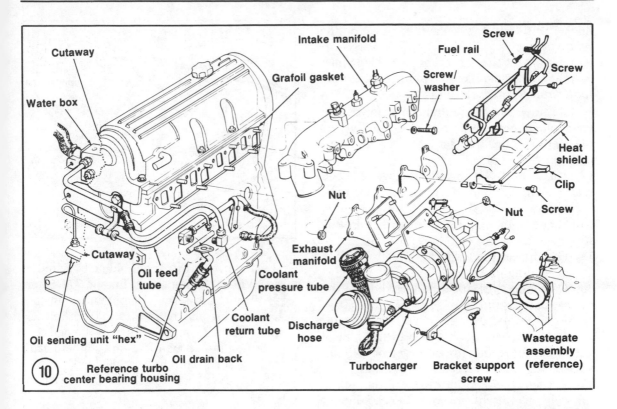

the fuel gauge sending unit. Disconnect the fuel supply hose at the sending unit and siphon the fuel through the supply line into a suitable container.

> *WARNING*
> *Never store gasoline in an open container, since it is an extreme fire hazard. Store gasoline in a sealed metal container away from heat, sparks and flame.*

6. Disconnect all electrical wiring connectors at the tank. Disconnect all fuel lines, covering each with a shop cloth as it is disconnected to absorb any leakage.

7. Place a jack and wooden block under the tank for support.

8. Loosen each strap nut enough to lower the tank slightly, then work the filler tube free of the tank.

9. Remove each strap nut assembly and lower the tank with the jack.

10. Carefully tap lock ring counterclockwise with a non-metallic punch and hammer. See **Figure 9**.

11. Remove the fuel pump and O-ring seal from the tank. Discard the seal.

12. Installation is the reverse of removal. Wipe O-ring seal area on tank clean and use a new seal. Do not overtighten lock ring or the seal may leak.

INTAKE/EXHAUST MANIFOLDS

Removal (Turbocharged Engine)

The intake and exhaust manifolds are removed as an assembly with the cylinder head and turbocharger. Refer to **Figure 10** for this procedure.

1. Relieve fuel system pressure as described in this supplement.

2. Disconnect the negative battery cable.

3. Drain the cooling system. See Chapter Seven of the basic book.

4. Raise the vehicle with a jack and place it on jackstands.

5. Disconnect the oxygen sensor electrical connector.

6. Disconnect the exhaust pipe at the exhaust manifold.

7. Remove the turbocharger support bracket at the engine block.

8. Loosen the oil drainback tube connector

13

hose clamps and move the tube down on the block fitting.

9. Disconnect the turbocharger coolant inlet tube at the engine block. Disconnect the inlet tube support bracket.

10. Remove the jackstands and lower the vehicle to the ground.

11. Remove the air cleaner box, hose and adaptor. See **Figure 1**.

12. Disconnect the throttle linkage, throttle body electrical connector and vacuum lines. See **Figure 11**.

13. Remove the fuel rail as described in this supplement.

14. Disconnect the turbocharger oil feed line at the sending unit tee.

15. Disconnect the upper radiator hose at the thermostat housing.

16. Remove the cylinder head. See Chapter Four of the basic book. Place cylinder head with manifolds and turbocharger on a clean workbench.

17. Loosen the end clamps on the upper turbocharger discharge hose. Do *not* loosen the center band.

18. Remove the throttle body retaining screws. Remove the throttle body from the intake manifold.

19. Disconnect the turbocharger coolant return tube at the water box and retaining bracket.

20. Remove the heat shield screws. Remove the heat shield.

21. Remove the nuts holding the turbocharger to the exhaust manifold. Remove the turbocharger.

22. Remove the intake manifold screws and washers. See **Figure 12**. Remove the intake manifold.

23. Remove the exhaust manifold nuts. See **Figure 12**. Remove the exhaust manifold.

24. Remove and discard the intake/exhaust manifold gasket. Clean gasket residue from manifolds and cylinder head.

Installation (Turbocharged Engine)

Refer to **Figure 10** for this procedure.

1. Install a new two-sided Grafoil intake/exhaust manifold gasket *without* gasket sealer.

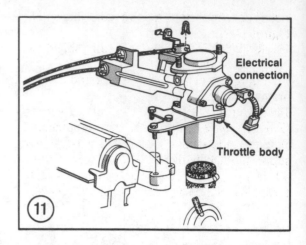

Electrical connection

Throttle body

2. Position exhaust manifold on cylinder head. Wipe head studs with Loctite 771-64 or equivalent anti-seize compound. Install retaining nuts and tighten to 200 in.-lb. (23 N•m) working from the center to the ends.

3. Position intake manifold on cylinder head. Install washers and screws. Tighten to 200 in.-lb. (23 N•m) working from the center to the ends.

4. Connect turbocharger outlet to intake manifold inlet tube. Fit turbocharger on exhaust manifold. Wipe manifold studs with Loctite 771-64 or equivalent anti-seize compound. Install retaining nuts and tighten to 40 ft.-lb. (54 N•m). Tighten connector tube clamps to 30 in.-lb. (3 N•m).

5. Fit coolant return tube to water box connector. Tighten tube nut to 30 in.-lb. (3 N•m) and install tube support bracket to cylinder head.

6. Install heat shield. Tighten screws to 105 in.-lb. (12 N•m).

7. Connect throttle body air horn to turbocharger inlet tube. Install and tighten attaching screws to 250 in.-lb. (28 N•m), then tighten tube clamp to 30 in.-lb. (3 N•m).

8. Install cylinder head to engine block. See Chapter Four of the basic book.

9. Connect turbocharger oil feed line to sending unit tee and tighten tube nuts to 125 in.-lb. (14 N•m).

10. Install air cleaner box, hose and adapter. See **Figure 1**. Tighten adapter nut to 55 in.-lb. (6 N•m) and air cleaner support bracket screw to 40 ft.-lb. (54 N•m).

11. Reconnect throttle cable, throttle body

electrical connector and vacuum lines. See **Figure 11**.

12. Reinstall fuel rail and air shield as described in this supplement.

13. Raise the vehicle with a jack and place it on jackstands.

14. Reverse Steps 1-10 of *Removal (Turbocharged Engine)* in this supplement. When installing turbocharger-to-block support bracket, tighten block screw first to 40 ft.-lb. (54 N•m) then tighten screw to turbocharger housing to 20 ft.-lb. (27 N•m).

TURBOCHARGER

Removal/Installation

Refer to **Figure 10** for this procedure.

1. Perform Steps 1-12 of *Intake/Exhaust Manifold Removal (Turbocharged Engine)* in this supplement.

2. Loosen the throttle body inlet hose clamps at the turbocharger. Remove the throttle body attaching screws. Remove the throttle body.

3. Loosen the end clamps on the upper turbocharger discharge hose. Do *not* loosen the center band.

4. Remove the fuel rail as described in this supplement.

5. Disconnect the oil feed line at the turbocharger housing.

6. Remove the heat shield screws. Remove the heat shield.

7. Disconnect the turbocharger coolant return tube at the turbocharger and water box. Remove the tube support bracket from the cylinder head.

8. Remove the nuts holding the turbocharger to the exhaust manifold. Lift the turbocharger off the exhaust manifold studs, swivel downward toward passenger side and remove it from the engine compartment.

9. Installation is the reverse of removal.

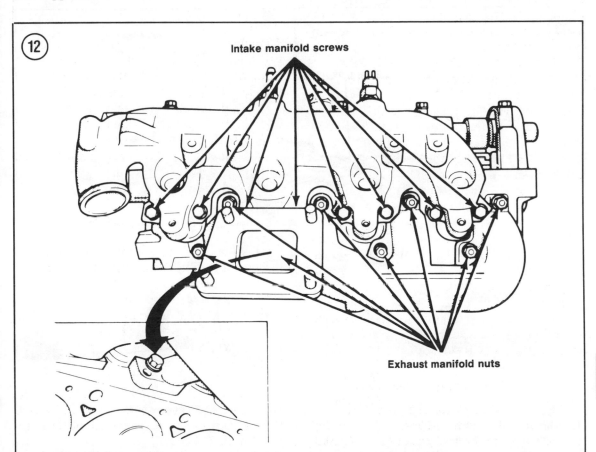

Intake manifold screws

Exhaust manifold nuts

13

CHAPTER SEVEN

COOLING AND HEATING SYSTEMS

To drain the coolant, it is recommended that the vacuum valve switch or plug in the water box housing be removed. This allows air to enter the cooling system and speed up the draining process.

RADIATOR

A crossflow radiator with aluminum tubes and injection-molded plastic end tanks is used with some 1984 and later 1.6L and 2.2L engines (**Figure 13**). Use caution when disconnecting or connecting hoses to prevent damage to the tank fittings. Excessive hose clamp torque can also damage the fittings.

Some vehicles equipped with an automatic transaxle may use an external oil-to-air cooler (**Figure 14**) instead of the internal oil cooler.

The radiator outlet fitting on 1986 models is changed from 1 1/2 in. to 1 1/4 in. and requires the use of a 1 1/4 in. hose and clamp. The "tee" connection in the lower radiator hose has been eliminated and the heater return line connects directly to the water pump.

Thermostat

The poppet valve on 1984 and later 2.2L thermostats has a rubber lip for better sealing when closed.

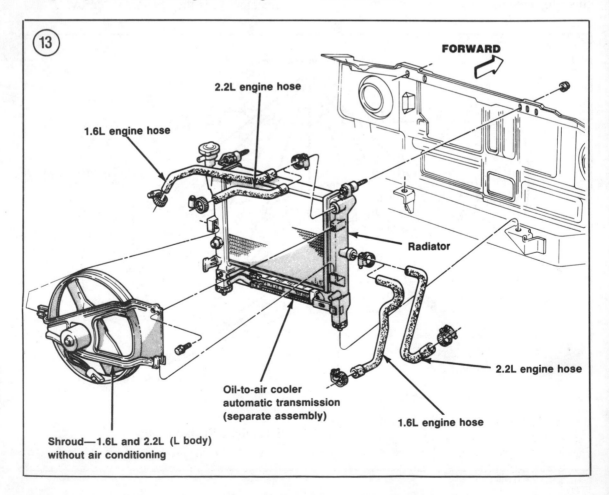

(13)

FORWARD

2.2L engine hose

1.6L engine hose

Radiator

Oil-to-air cooler automatic transmission (separate assembly)

2.2L engine hose

1.6L engine hose

Shroud—1.6L and 2.2L (L body) without air conditioning

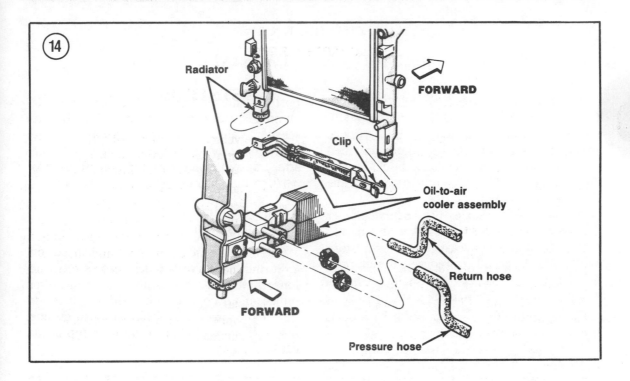

(14)

Radiator

FORWARD

Clip

Oil-to-air
cooler assembly

Return hose

FORWARD

Pressure hose

CHAPTER EIGHT

ELECTRICAL SYSTEMS

ALTERNATOR

The 1985 fuel-injected turbocharged 2.2L engine uses a new Chrysler 40/90 amp alternator. The voltage regulator is incorporated within the logic and power modules. Charging system troubleshooting requires the use of special test equipment and should be performed by a dealer.

FUSES/CIRCUIT BREAKER

Table 3 provides fuse functions for 1984 and later models.

MAGNETIC GAUGES

All 1984-on models with the optional gauge package instrument cluster use magnetic gauges for greater accuracy and reduced RFI interference. Magnetic gauges provide a reading with the ignition OFF, but the reading is not accurate.

IGNITION SYSTEM

A new "labyrinth" distributor is used on the 2.2L engine. The distributor is smaller with more insulation of the coil terminal from the rotor contact-spark plug terminals to increase voltage capacity. Service procedures remain unchanged, but components are not interchangeable with previous model distributors.

LIGHTING SYSTEM

See **Table 4** for interior and exterior bulb specifications.

Headlight Replacement

All 1984-on models use dual headlights. Replacement procedures remain unchanged.

13

CHAPTER NINE

CLUTCH AND TRANSAXLE

A close-ratio 5-speed manual transaxle (A-525) is optional with 1984-on 2.2L engines. Fluid capacity and service procedures are identical with those provided in Chapter Nine of the basic book for the A-465 5-speed. The A-525 differs only in the 2nd, 3rd and 4th gear ratios.

All manual transaxles use larger diameter 1-2 synchronizers of winged strut design and stop rings and a new cast iron 1-2 shift fork with wider fork pads to reduce shift effort.

Manual transaxles in Shelby Charger applications use high-strength steel gears.

Cable mounting brackets on 1986 models use a brace to eliminate flexing.

The 1987 transaxle uses a completely redesigned aluminum die-cast case. The transmission portion of the casting ends on the differential centerline, with a separate die-cast cover used to enclose the differential. This is designed to produce better sealing than the stamped cover previously used.

All 1987 manual transaxles use SAE 5W-30 engine oil instead of automatic transmission fluid.

Gear Shift Cable

Manual transaxle cable shift mechanism has been redesigned on 1984 and later models to reduce shift effort and provide more positive shifting action. The bell crank is eliminated from the lever assembly, with the selector cable connected directly to the operating lever. A change in the size of the adjusting pin holes requires the use of two 3/16×5 in. adjusting pins. See **Figure 15**.

Automatic Transaxle Cable Adjustment

Cable adjustment has been changed on 1986 transaxles, with bracket adjustment no longer required. To adjust the cable after replacement, connect both ends, then rotate the linkage in a full clockwise position and insert the locking clip provided on top of the cable.

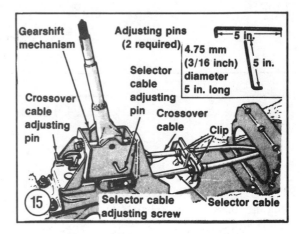

CHAPTER TEN

BRAKES

A dual proportioning valve with warning light switch replaces the pressure differential valve on 1984 and later models. Light brake pedal pressure sends full hydraulic pressure to the rear brakes. When heavy pressure is applied, the proportioning valve reduces the hydraulic pressure to the rear brakes to prevent a premature rear wheel lock-up and potential skid.

CHAPTER ELEVEN

FRONT SUSPENSION AND STEERING

The lug nut torque is increased to 95 ft.-lb. (130 N•m) on all 1984 and later models.

DRIVE SHAFTS

A dampening weight (**Figure 16**) is bolted on the left-hand drive shaft of 1984 and later models. When replacing the left-hand drive shaft, this weight should be removed from the old shaft and installed on the new one.

All turbocharged vehicles use an "equal length" drive shaft system; all others continue to use the "unequal length" system. See **Figure 17** for a comparison of the two systems. The "equal length" system differs in two ways: it has a rubber washer seal attached to the right inner CV joint not used with the "unequal length" system and a bearing/bracket assembly must be unbolted to remove the right drive shaft from the transaxle. In all other respects, both systems are serviced as described in Chapter Eleven of the basic book.

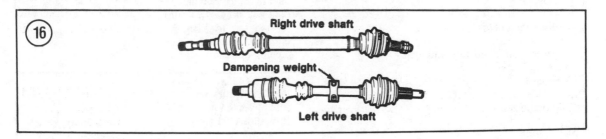

(16)

Right drive shaft

Dampening weight

Left drive shaft

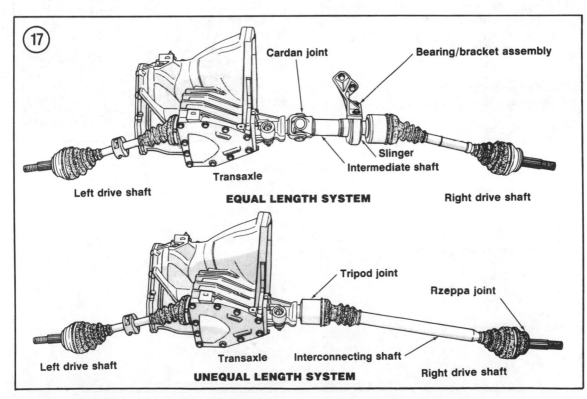

(17)

Cardan joint

Bearing/bracket assembly

Slinger

Intermediate shaft

Transaxle

Left drive shaft

EQUAL LENGTH SYSTEM

Right drive shaft

Tripod joint

Rzeppa joint

Transaxle

Interconnecting shaft

Left drive shaft

UNEQUAL LENGTH SYSTEM

Right drive shaft

13

Table 1 2.2L ENGINE SPECIFICATIONS

Valves	
Stem-to-guide clearance	
Intake	0.0009-0.0026 in.
	(0.022-0.065 mm)
Exhaust	0.0030-0.0047 in.
	(0.076-0.119 mm)
Valve Springs	
Free length	
Standard	2.39 in. (60.8 mm)
High performance/turbocharged	2.28 in. (57.9 mm)
Pressure	
Standard	
Open	144-156 lb. @ 1.22 in.
	(640-694 N @ 30.99 mm)
Closed	90-100 lb. @ 1.65 in.
	(440-445 N @ 41.91 mm)
High performance/turbocharged	
Open	168-182 lb. @ 1.22 in.
	(748-808 N @ 30.99 mm)
Closed	99-108 lb. @ 1.65 in.
	(442-482 N @ 41.91 mm)
Perpendicularity	
Standard	0.079 in. (2.0 mm)
High performance/turbocharged	0.06 in. (1.5 mm)
Piston Diameter	
Standard	3.443-3.445 in.
	(87.442-87.507 mm)
Turbocharged	3.4416-3.4441 in.
	(87.416-87.481 mm)
Piston Ring	
Side clearance	
No. 1 compression	0.0015-0.0031 in.
	(0.038-0.078 mm)
No. 2 compression	0.0015-0.0037 in.
	(0.038-0.093 mm)
End gap	
No. 1 compression	
Standard	0.011-0.021 in.
	(0.28-0.53 mm)
Turbocharged	0.010-0.020 in.
	(0.25-0.51 mm)
No. 2 compression	
Standard	0.011-0.021 in.
	(0.28-0.53 mm)
Turbocharged	0.009-0.018 in.
	(0.23-0.48 mm)
Oil ring	0.015-0.055 in.
	(0.38-1.40 mm)
Connecting rod bearing clearance	
Standard	0.0008-0.0034 in.
	(0.019-0.087 mm)
Turbocharged	0.0008-0.0031 in.
	(0.019-0.079 mm)
Crankshaft	
Main bearing journal diameter	
Standard	2.362-2.363 in.
	(59.987-60.013 mm)

(continued)

Table 1 2.2L ENGINE SPECIFICATIONS (continued)

Crankshaft (continued)	
Turbocharged	2.3622-2.3627 in.
	(60.000-60.013 mm)
Main bearing clearance	
Standard	0.0003-0.0031 in.
	(0.007-0.080 mm)
Turbocharged	0.0004-0.0023 in.
	(0.011-0.054 mm)
Bearing surface	
Out-of-round	0.0005 in. (0.013 mm)
Taper	0.0003 in. (0.008 mm)
Camshaft	
Journal diameter	1.375-1.376 in.
	(34.939-34.960 mm)
Lobe wear limit	0.010 in. (0.25 mm)

Table 2 1.6L ENGINE SPECIFICATIONS

Valves	
Stem-to-guide clearance	
Intake	0.0005-0.0018 in.
	(0.012-0.045 mm)
Exhaust	0.0013-0.0026 in.
	(0.032-0.035 mm)
Stem diameter	
Intake	0.3135-0.3141 in.
	(7.995-8.010 mm)
Exhaust	0.3127-0.3133 in.
	(7.975-7.990 mm)

Table 3 FUSES AND CIRCUIT BREAKERS (1984-ON)

Cavity	Fuse (amps)	Item
1	20	Hazard flasher
2	20	Back-up lamps
3	5	Speed control, heated rear window relay (except Rampage)
4	20[1]	Heater blower motor
5	Not used	
6	20	Stop, dome, glove box, console, ignition switch and cargo lamps, key-in buzzer, cigar lighter, ignition time delay relay and electronically tuned radio memory
7	20	Cluster (cavity 12), park, side marker, tail and license lamps, horn and horn relay, electronically tuned radio
8	20	Fog lamps
9	Not used	
10	20	Electric fuel pump (turbo model only)
11	5	Seat belt, brake and engine warning lamps; volt, fuel, oil and temperature gauges, seat belt buzzer, tachometer and choke
		(continued)

13

Table 3 FUSES AND CIRCUIT BREAKERS (1984-ON) (continued)

Cavity	Fuse (amps)	Item
12	4	Cluster A/C and heater, heated rear window, rear wash-wipe, liftgate release, ash tray, console, radio and console cigar lighter lamps
13	20	Windshield wiper
14	6	Rear wash-wipe (Omni, Horizon); liftgate circuit breaker release (Turismo, Charger, Shelby Charger)
15	5	Radio
16	20	Turn signal lamps; air conditioner clutch, slow idle solenoid, electronic spark advance

1. Air conditioned models use a 30 amp fuse.

Table 4 BULB CHART

Backup lamps	1156
Headlamps	
Omni, Horizon	H6054
All others	4656/4651
License plate lamp	168
Park and turn signal lamp	1157
Side marker lamps (front)	
Omni, Horizon	1157
All others	168
Side marker lamps (rear)	168
Tail and stop lamps	1157
Turn signal lamps	1157
A/C control illumination	161
Ash tray illumination	161
Brake indicator	194
Dome lamp	211-2
Engine indicator	194
Gear shift selector console	194
Glove box lamp	1891
Heated rear window illumination	161
Heated rear window indicator	LED
Heater control illumination	161
High beam indicator	194
Ignition switch lamp	1445
Instrument control illumination	194
Map lamp	562
Oil pressure/temperature indicator	194
Radio	74
Rear deck release switch illumination	161
Rear wipe switch illumination	161
Seat belt indicator	194
Speedometer illumination	161
Travel computer	37
Trunk lamp	912 or 212
Turn signal indicator	194
Vanity lamp	194
Volt indicator	194

INDEX

14

14

NOTES

NOTES

NOTES